Prince Hall Freemasonry in the Lone Star State

From Cuney to Curtis, 1875-2003

Robert L. Uzzel

EAKIN PRESS ✦ Fort Worth, Texas
www.EakinPress.com

Copyright © 2004
By Robert L. Uzzel
Published By Eakin Press
An Imprint of Wild Horse Media Group
P.O. Box 331779
Fort Worth, Texas 76163
1-817-344-7036
www.EakinPress.com
ALL RIGHTS RESERVED
1 2 3 4 5 6 7 8 9
ISBN-10: 1-57168-834-X
ISBN-13: 978-1-57168-834-7

Dedication

This book is dedicated to the memory of two men named "Tom"—Tom Wooten and Tom Routt—who were very special friends and who did much to encourage my Masonic endeavors.

Thomas Aaron Wooten (1945-1980) was a member of Waco Lodge No. 92, A.F.&A.M., and a Past Master of Whitney Lodge No. 355 in his hometown of Whitney, Texas. I first met him in Whitney in 1972 during my pastorate at the Whitney Missionary Baptist Church. He encouraged me in my advancement in the Blue Lodge and Scottish Rite and held my arm as I "crossed the hot sands" at Karem Shrine Temple in September 1973. Seven years later, following my suspension for non-payment of dues, he signed my petition for reinstatement, assuring me that he did not consider my interracial marriage a relevant issue. Tom died in a tragic automobile accident on December 17, 1980.

Thomas Henry Routt (1930-1991) served as Grand Master of the Prince Hall Grand Lodge of Texas from 1987 until his tragic death from colon cancer on January 3, 1991. One of his first actions as Grand Master was to create the office of Grand Historian and appoint me to it. Throughout his term, he did much to encourage my research and writing on Freemasonry. On January 8, 1991, I attended his funeral at Trinity United Methodist Church in Houston.

Two Toms—two outstanding Freemasons, one Caucasian and one Prince Hall. As far as I know, they never met while on this earth. I am confident, however, that they have met in the Celestial Lodge Above. The words of the 14° of the Scottish Rite are quite relevant here—*virtus junxit, mors non separabit* (virtue has joined, death will not separate).

Contents

Acknowledgments vii
Preface ix
Introduction xi
Norris Wright Cuney 1
Richard Allen 16
Leroy L. James 19
Abram Grant 21
Charles C. Dean 31
Rodolphus H. Bradley 34
Josiah Haynes Armstrong 35
John W. Madison 37
Wiley Lawson Kimbrough 40
John Wesley McKinney 44
Henderson D. Winn 52
John Adrian Kirk 64
William Coleman 71
Lucian L. Lockhart 84
John Theodore Maxey 96
Isadore Huddleston Clayborn 111
Reuben Glassell White 136
Thomas Henry Routt 152
Edwin Bernard Cash 165
Robert Edmund Connor, Jr. 179
Wilbert Marice Curtis 207
Epilogue 213
Endnotes 223
Bibliography 269

Acknowledgments

So many people helped to make the completion of this book a reality that it is hard to thank them all. At any rate, I intend to try.

I am grateful to Grand Master Wilbert Curtis for his support for this project and for his enthusiasm for Masonic research in general. I am also grateful to Grand Secretary Hubert Reece, Past Grand Secretaries C. A. Glaspie and John Pointer; and Administrative Assistant Angie Scoggins for the help they have provided during my numerous visits to the Grand Lodge office; and to Grand Recorder Edwin Moore for making available to me recent Grand Lodge *Proceedings*.

I am grateful to the late Past Grand Master Thomas H. Routt, who, in 1987, created the office of Grand Historian and appointed me to it. I am also grateful to Past Grand Master Edwin B. Cash; the late Past Grand Masters Reuben G. White and Robert E. Connor, Jr.; and Roberta Cathcart Clayborn, the widow of Past Grand Master I. H. Clayborn, for providing me with very informative interviews. Ritchie L. Routt, the widow of Thomas H. Routt, was very gracious in sending to me her husband's vita. I thank Isaac Cary, Sr., a very dedicated Texas Prince Hall Mason and outstanding photographer, for providing a number of the pictures used in this book.

A number of interviews were conducted with Prince Hall Masons during various sessions of the Grand Lodge in Fort Worth. Other interviews were conducted in Waco during the summer of 1992 in connection with a seminar in oral history at Baylor University under the direction of Dr. Thomas Charlton. While the focus of these interviews was Past Grand Master John A. Kirk and other leaders of Waco's black community, some interviewees also provided information on some of Kirk's successors in the Grand East. A complete list of interviewees is found in the bibliography. Past Grand Master Frank Boone, Grand Historian for the Prince Hall Grand Lodge of California, was very helpful in providing information about the California years of Past Grand Master W. L. Kimbrough.

I also must acknowledge the help provided by the staff of various libraries, including the Baylor University Moody Library, the Paul Quinn College Library, the Waco Public Library, and the Dallas Public Library. Especially helpful was the late Keith Arrington, Grand Librarian Emeritus for the Grand Lodge of Iowa, A.F.&A.M., whose outstanding library houses the proceedings of numerous Grand Lodges, both

Caucasian and Prince Hall. Bro. Arrington made numerous loans of materials by mail, without which the completion of this book would have been much more difficult.

I thank Bishop Othal H. Lakey, Merline Pitre, Ph.D., and G. H. Radford, Jr., D.D.S., for permission to use pictures from other books.

I am grateful to my family for tolerating the excessive demands on my time required by this research project. I thank my wife Debra for all of her love and support.

I thank our children, Ericha, Eric, JoAnna, and Elton; and our grandchildren, Richard, Dominique, Alicia, Kendra, Davion, Kayla, and Eric, for being who they are.

Finally, I extend praise and thanksgiving to my Lord and Savior Jesus Christ, the Lion of the Tribe of Judah in Whom is hid all of the treasures of wisdom and knowledge, according to Colossians 2:3, and Who daily gives me strength to meet the challenges of life. So mote it be!

Preface

The history of Freemasonry is a subject with which I have been fascinated for many years. I developed a deep love of all varieties of history as a child in elementary school. My first exposure to Freemasonry came in 1967 when, at the age of sixteen, I was initiated into the Order of DeMolay in my hometown of Waco, Texas. In 1970 I served as Master Councilor of Waco Chapter. In 1972, shortly after turning twenty-one, I petitioned for the degrees of Masonry and was accepted as a member of Waco Lodge No. 92, A.F.&A.M. I was initiated as an Entered Apprentice on August 21, 1972, passed to the degree of Fellowcraft on December 19, 1972, and raised to the sublime degree of Master Mason on March 20, 1973. I wasted no time in beginning my study of Masonic history and philosophy. In September 1973 I received the 32° in the Waco Scottish Rite Bodies. I soon became intrigued with Albert Pike's *Morals and Dogma*—an 861-page opus that many Masons own but very few have read. A copy of this book was given to me by a Mason I was visiting in Virginia (whose name I do not recall) during the summer of 1973. I eventually read it from cover to cover and, during the 1990s, devoted the third chapter of my doctoral dissertation to showing how Pike plagiarized many passages from the writings of the French Kabbalist Éliphas Lévi in writing this work.

When I first inquired about the admission of African Americans to Masonic lodges, I was told: "They have their own lodges." I later learned that white Masons viewed black Masons not as "separate but equal" but as "irregular and clandestine." I was appalled by such racism, seeing it as incompatible with Masonic teachings on the Fatherhood of God and the Brotherhood of Man. As a result, I began research on Freemasonry and other fraternal organizations, with special reference to the "color line." Eventually, I dropped out of Caucasian Masonry and, after experiencing Masonic racism firsthand when I tried unsuccessfully to reinstate, I became a Prince Hall Mason. I have been active in the Prince Hall fraternity since. The research and writing of this book has taken seventeen years and has been pursued amid many other commitments, including the completion of my doctoral dissertation in 1995. It has truly been a labor of love.

In his outstanding book on the history of Prince Hall Freemasonry in Louisiana, Joseph A. Walkes, Jr. wrote:

> The history of Prince Hall Freemasonry is in reality the history of the Black

Experience in America. In fact, if one wanted to explore Black history, one could do so equally as well, by pursuing the proceedings of the various Prince Hall Grand and individual Lodges. . . . The Black Church, Black educational institutions, the Black Press and, in later years, Black civil rights organizations may have been publicly perceived as the hegemony of Black America. This perception may have been misleading, for none of these Black institutions could match the quiet, determined, persistent role of leadership that came from the Masonic Lodges of Prince Hall Freemasonry; and often hidden from view and unknown by the public is the fact that the leaders of many of these institutions, were for the most part led by or sustained by Prince Hall Freemasons. For instance, the founding fathers of the AME Church and . . .the Black press was usually owned by members of the craft.[1]

The above statement applies as much to black history in Texas as it does in any other state. Masonic teachings of the Fatherhood of God and the Brotherhood of Man, when taken seriously, can have a tremendous influence on social, political, and economic policies. Thus, from the struggle to abolish slavery to the civil rights movement, Prince Hall Freemasons have always been in the forefront. No doubt, much of their inspiration has been derived from the lessons they learned in lodge. It is my prayer that people of all nationalities—Mason and non-Mason alike—will read this history and, as a result, be inspired with appreciation of a great fraternal order which has contributed so much to the African-American communities of Texas.

 x

Introduction

Prince Hall Freemasonry began on March 6, 1775, with the initiation of Prince Hall and fourteen other African Americans by Lodge No. 41, Irish Constitutions, which accompanied the 38th Regiment of Foot, British Army, posted at Castle William (now Fort Independence), Boston Arbour. Sgt. John Batt was the Master of this lodge. Hall became the first Master of the lodge composed of the black men who had been initiated by this military lodge. On March 2, 1784, he wrote to William Moody, Master of a lodge in London, England, that he had petitioned the American Grand Master John Rowe for a warrant but received "only a permit from Grand Master to march on Saint John's Day and bury our dead." Subsequently, he applied to the Grand Lodge of England for a warrant.

This warrant was issued on September 29, 1784, but did not arrive in Boston until April 29, 1787.[1]

In a deposition recorded in the Suffolk County, Massachusetts, Register of Deeds, made by Prince Hall in August 1807, just a few months before his death, he stated that he was a leather dresser by trade and that, in November 1762, he had been received into full communion with the Congregational Church which met on School Street in Boston. His Letter Books show that he was familiar with the works of the early Church Fathers, including Cyprian, Origen, and Tertullian. He appears to have been extremely well read and a great believer in education, often urging the city fathers in Boston and the Massachusetts legislators to provide schools for black children. He was an outspoken opponent of slavery and a spokesman for the Massachusetts black community.[2]

Prince Hall died on December 4, 1807. Newspapers in the Boston area reported his death and stated that he was seventy-two years old. He therefore must have been born about 1735. Newspapers do not mention his place of burial. According to tradition, he is interred at Copp's Hill Burying Ground, next to his first wife. A monument was erected there over a hundred years later. This monument is an important place of pilgrimage for Prince Hall Freemasons.[3]

African Lodge No. 459, along with a number of other American lodges, was dropped from the English roll in 1813, at the time the two rival Masonic organizations—the "Ancients" and the "Moderns"—settled their differences and formed the United Grand Lodge of England.[4]

Many state Grand Lodges, all composed primarily of African Americans, all tracing their lineage to African Lodge No. 459, and all for many years labeled "clandestine" by Caucasian Grand Lodges, were organized. During the mid-twentieth century, most of them incorporated "Prince Hall" into their official name. The dates of organization include the following: Pennsylvania, 1797; Massachusetts, 1827; New York, 1845; Maryland, 1845; District of Columbia, 1848; New Jersey, 1848; Ohio, 1849; Delaware, 1849; California, 1855; Indiana, 1856; Rhode Island, 1858; Louisiana, 1863; Michigan, 1865; Virginia, 1865; Kentucky, 1866; Missouri, 1866; Illinois, 1867; South Carolina, 1867; North Carolina, 1870; Florida, 1870; Georgia, 1870; Tennessee, 1870; Alabama, 1872; Mississippi, 1873; Arkansas, 1873; Texas, 1875; Kansas, 1875; Colorado, 1876; West Virginia, 1877; Iowa, 1881; Oklahoma, 1893; Minnesota, 1894; Washington, 1903; Nebraska, 1919; Arizona, 1920; New Mexico, 1921; Wisconsin, 1952; Oregon, 1960; Alaska, 1969; and Nevada, 1980.[5]

Between 1871 and 1873, under the leadership of Capt. William D. Matthews, Grand Master of the National Grand Lodge and a resident of Leavenworth, Kansas, the following lodges were established in Texas: San Antonio Lodge No. 22 in San Antonio, Mount Bonnell Lodge No. 23 in Austin, Magnolia Lodge No. 24 in Houston, Galveston Lodge No. 25 in Galveston, and Mount Lebanon Lodge No. 26 in Brenham.[6]

In June 1875 Deputy Grand Master Norris Wright Cuney and District Deputy Grand Master Richard Allen issued a call, requesting that each of these lodges send representatives to Saint John African Methodist Episcopal Church in Brenham on August 19, 1875, for the purpose of organizing the Most Worshipful Grand Lodge, Free and Accepted Ancient York Masons of the State of Texas (known today as the Most Worshipful Prince Hall Grand Lodge of Texas).[7] This organizing convention elected Norris Wright Cuney of Galveston as Grand Master, J. R. Taylor of Brenham as Grand Senior Warden, Edward Wilkinson of Austin as Grand Junior Warden, J. H. Morris of Galveston as Grand Secretary, J. P. Ball, Jr., of Brenham as Grand Recorder, Wilson Nichols of Galveston as Grand Treasurer, and John Lands of Galveston as Grand Tiler.[8] On January 19, 1876, these officers were installed in Houston by Grand Master Matthews.[9]

The newly organized Grand Lodge shortly granted charters to the following subordinate lodges: San Antonio Lodge No. 1 in San Antonio, Mount Bonnell Lodge No. 2 in Austin, Magnolia Lodge No. 3 in Houston, Amity Lodge No. 4 in Galveston, Widow Son Lodge No. 5 in Marshall, Mount Moriah Lodge No. 6 in Waco, Holloway Lodge No. 7 in Downsville, Roosevelt Lodge No. 8 in Kendleton, Paul Drayton Lodge No. 9 in Dallas, Pilgrim Lodge No. 10 in Denison, Western Star Lodge No. 11 in Victoria, Saint John Lodge No. 12 in Chapel Hill, Gulf Lodge No. 13 in Corpus Christi, Reed Lodge No. 14 in Luling, Jackson Lodge No. 15 in San Angelo, and Baldwin Lodge No. 16 in Fort Grant, Arizona.[10]

From 1875 to 1906, the Grand Lodge had no permanent meeting place, and annual communications were held in various Texas cities. At the 1876 session in Houston, Cuney was succeeded as Grand Master by Richard Allen of Houston.[11] At the 1877 session in the same city, Cuney was elected Grand Master but declined, stating that he

was unable to serve. Allen was then renominated and elected.[12] At the 1878 session there, L. L. James, another Houstonian, became the third Grand Master.[13] However, when the 1879 session again met in Houston, Cuney was returned to the Grand East.[14] He was reelected at the 1880 session in Galveston and presided for the last time in Austin in 1881.[15]

At the 1881 session, Rev. Abram Grant of San Antonio was elected Grand Master.[16] This future bishop of the AME Church presided in the Grand East in Waco in 1882, in Houston in 1883, in San Antonio in 1884, and in Dallas in 1885.[17]

At the 1885 session, Charles C. Dean of Houston was elected Grand Master. He presided in Victoria in 1886, in Denison in 1887, in Austin in 1888, and in Fort Worth in 1889. At the close of the latter session, he was reelected as Grand Master, while A. F. Jackson of Dallas was elected as Deputy Grand Master and R. H. Bradley of Dallas was elected as Grand Senior Warden.[18]

When the 1890 session of the Grand Lodge convened in Paris, it was Bradley rather than Dean or Jackson who presided as Grand Master.[19] The lack of proceedings or other records from this year makes it impossible to determine the reason for this change.

In 1890 Rev. J. H. Armstrong of Galveston was elected Grand Master. This future AME bishop presided over the sessions in Galveston in 1891 and in Austin in 1892. During the latter session in the capital of Texas, Austin native J. W. Madison was elected Grand Master. He presided over the sessions in Dallas in 1893 and in Waco in 1894. During the latter session, W. L. Kimbrough of Dallas was elected Grand Master. He presided over the sessions in Sherman in 1895 and in Austin in 1896.[20]

The 1896 Grand Lodge Communication marked the beginning of the longest term in the history of the Grand Lodge with the election of Grand Master J. W. McKinney of Sherman, a future bishop in the Colored (now Christian) Methodist Episcopal Church. McKinney presided in Gainesville in 1897, in Fort Worth in 1898, in Bryan in 1899, in Galveston in 1900, in Victoria in 1901, in Waco in 1902, in San Antonio in 1903, in Houston in 1904, in Dallas in 1905, and in Fort Worth in 1906. In the latter year, the Grand Lodge adopted a resolution that made Fort Worth the permanent headquarters and required that each Grand Communication be held in Fort Worth. McKinney presided at each annual session there between 1906 and 1916.[21] With the note on the Grand Lodge Temple paid in full and his responsibilities in the CME Church steadily increasing, McKinney decided that it was time for him to step down.[22]

McKinney was succeeded in the Grand East by H. D. Winn of Chapel Hill, who eventually relocated to Dallas and served from 1916 until his death in 1925.[23] Winn was succeeded by J. A. Kirk of Waco, who served from 1925 to 1930, when he decided to retire on account of declining health.[24] Kirk was succeeded by William Coleman of El Paso, who eventually relocated to Fort Worth and served from 1930 until his death in 1946.[25] He tied with I. H. Clayborn in serving sixteen years—the second longest term in the history of the Grand Lodge.

Coleman was succeeded by L. L. Lockhart of Houston, who served from 1946 until his death in 1955.[26] Lockhart was succeeded by J. T. Maxey of Galveston, who served from 1955 until his retirement in 1965.[27]

Maxey was succeeded by I. H. Clayborn of Dallas, who served as Grand Master from 1965 until his resignation in 1981 and as Grand Commander of the Scottish Rite, Southern Jurisdiction, from 1979 until his death in 1994.[28]

Clayborn was succeeded by Reuben G. White, who served from 1981 until his defeat by Thomas H. Routt in 1987.[29] Routt served from 1987 until his death in 1991.[30] Routt was succeeded by Edwin B. Cash, who served from 1991 until he was defeated in 1994 by Robert E. Connor, Jr., who served until his death in 2003. Connor's successor is Wilbert M. Curtis, the current Grand Master.

All Grand Lodge Communications between 1906 and 1998 were held in Fort Worth. In 1998 a resolution authorizing the holding of the annual sessions in various cities was adopted. As a result, the 1999, 2000, and 2003 sessions were held in Houston, while the 2001 session was held in Corpus Christi.

For the past 129 years, the Prince Hall Grand Lodge of Texas has done much to uplift humanity and has been a very positive influence in the African-American communities of the Lone Star State. Much about this great fraternity and the events that shaped its history—as well as the history of Texas and America—can be learned from the biographies of the twenty-one Grand Masters who have played such important roles. From Cuney to Curtis, the great Texas ship of Prince Hall Freemasonry continues to sail on!

Norris Wright Cuney

Norris Wright Cuney (1846-1898) was the first Grand Master of Prince Hall Masons in Texas. He was a high achiever in fraternal, business, labor, and political circles during the Reconstruction and post-Reconstruction periods of American history. The latter period was marked by the birth of the infamous "Jim Crow" laws aimed at turning back the clock on rights gained by African Americans during the former period. In her master's thesis on the life of Cuney, Virginia Neal Hinze observed that he was quite an extraordinary individual in view of the fact that he gained power in the South when most blacks were losing theirs and his life might be viewed as a transition between the Reconstruction and Jim Crow periods.[1]

Among historians, Cuney is best remembered as a politician—as the undisputed leader of the Texas Republican Party between 1883 and 1896.[2] It must be remembered that, during his lifetime, the overwhelming majority of black voters were Republicans, with black Democrats as rare at that time as black Republicans are today. However, he lived to see the beginning of the black disenchantment with the Republican Party arising from the development of a "lily-white" section within Texas Republicanism in opposition to his leadership. In response to these Republican racists, Cuney declared: "The colored man is a Republican of necessity and you can't make anything else of him. I think that no friend of the party will desire a division of his character."[3]

At that time, some "lily whites" were expressing a desire to push blacks into the Democratic Party.[4] Cuney could not see the logic of this. He was devoted to the Republican Party and experienced great anguish of spirit when he returned from the 1896 Republican National Convention feeling that the party to which he had contributed so much had betrayed him.[5]

Cuney was not only devoted to Republicanism; he was also devoted to the South. While, after the Civil War, many blacks chose to leave the South, seeking opportunities for a better life elsewhere, he would have none of this. On one occasion, he said: "I am of the South. It is my home. The home of my wife and babies. It is the home of my race. There lie our interest. I can elevate my people alone in the South. I am willing to dwell in their midst."[6]

Cuney was devoted not only to the South in general but also to his home state of Texas in particular. While involved in a political campaign in 1892, he asserted:

> Every hope we have is interwoven with Texas. Let us have peace and through industry and education and loyalty to our home make it what God and nature designed it—the grandest commonwealth of them all.[7]

No doubt it was Cuney's destiny to be the first head of African-American Freemasonry in the state of Texas, a state whose history has been permeated with Masonic influence.

Texas was a nation before it was a state, and the Grand Lodge of the Republic of Texas was organized in 1837—the year after Texas' independence from Mexico. The overwhelming majority of leaders of early Texas were Freemasons. No doubt Cuney was familiar with the influence of Caucasian Freemasonry in Texas and the important role played by Prince Hall Freemasonry in the North since the initiation of Prince Hall in 1775. Thus, it was only natural and right that he should choose to align himself with such an ancient and honorable fraternity. A study of his life reveals that Masonic principles had a tremendous influence on him, as expressed in his strong commitment to education, social justice, and fair play. He truly believed in seeking "more light" and in acting "on the square."

Norris Wright Cuney's ancestry was quite mixed, including African, European, and Native American. His white father, Col. Philip Minor Cuney, was the son of Richmond and Tabitha Wells Cuney.[8] The following compiled family history provides relevant background to an understanding of his life:

> The white Cuney ancestors came to North America from Wales in the late eighteenth century. According to family tradition, Philip's grandmother Louise left England with her young son Richmond Edmond after the imprisonment of her husband for an unknown political offense against the crown. The elder Cuney later died in prison. Louise Cuney first went to French Martinique, where she stayed for a short time, then to New Orleans, arriving sometime before 1780. In Louisiana the widow Cuney married Caesar Archinard, a recent immigrant from Switzerland.[9]

Colonel Cuney, who was born on March 15, 1807, moved to Texas in 1837.[10] Probably attracted to the cheap lands of East Texas, he settled along the Brazos River in Austin (now Waller) County, naming his plantation "Sunnyside," located about twelve miles southeast of Hempstead on the Jose Justo Lindo land grant bordering Iron Creek.[11] His first wife, Charlotte Scott, died in 1834. He married Eliza Ware in 1842. She bore him three children and died in 1849. Two years later, he married his third wife, Adeline Supurlock.[12]

Besides his three wives, there was another woman in the colonel's life. Like many white planters, he had a slave mistress. Her name was Adeline Stuart, and she bore him eight children, including his most famous offspring—Norris Wright Cuney. Adeline Stuart was the daughter of Hester Neale Stuart, a domestic slave of the Neale family who was born about 1800 of mixed ancestry. Unlike many of her fellow slaves, the older Ms. Stuart learned to read and write. Her daughter Adeline was born about 1825 in Virginia. She had Caucasoid features, straight black hair, and an olive complexion.[13] According to Hinze:

> She apparently became Cuney's mistress, probably in 1841, before he married his second wife in 1842. This protracted liaison, begun during her youth, Adeline was continued through her middle age and through two of Cuney's three marriages. Her influence on him was such that by 1860 he had manumitted her and their children and educated their three sons.[14]

After receiving her freedom, Adeline Stuart returned to Virginia and found her mother living in Alexandria. Thus they were reunited after forty years of separation.[15] Maud Cuney Hare, the daughter of Norris Wright Cuney, wrote:

> On May 12, 1846, my father was born at "Sunnyside," the plantation of the Brazos River owned by his father, Col. Philip Cuney. He was the fourth of eight children, all of whom, except two, were born at "Sunnyside." All of the children resembled the mother, except one of the daughters who was blonde like her father.[16]

In 1853 the Cuney family moved to Houston, where Norris Wright lived for six years. During this time, he became adept at playing the bass-violin as a result of lessons by "Henry the Fiddler." In 1859 his father freed him and arranged for his enrollment at Wyle Street School, a black institution in Pittsburgh, Pennsylvania, taught by George B. Vashon.[17] He left Pittsburgh in 1863, went to St. Louis, and thence to Cincinnati, spending much time working on steamboats on the Mississippi River. While working on the *Grey Eagle*, he was often in New Orleans, where he met Col. James Lewis and Lt. Gov. Pinckney B. S. Pinchback, who played important roles in Louisiana Reconstruction. Lifelong friendships were formed with these two outstanding African-American leaders.[18]

After the Civil War, Cuney settled in Galveston. In 1867 a yellow fever epidemic broke out. Volunteering his services as a nurse, Cuney ministered to numerous black and white victims of this dreadful disease. Eventually, he contracted the disease himself, but rapidly recovered.[19] Such willingness to make sacrifices for others became a prominent characteristic of his life.

Prior to his attendance at Wyle Street School, Cuney had never been to school or read any books. However, after he started reading, he became captivated by books.[20] After settling in Galveston, he began the process of self-education, studying literature and reading law.[21] He read widely, especially enjoying Hebrew, Greek, and Roman history. He liked the works of Byron and Shakespeare.[22]

Cuney was, throughout his career, a staunch advocate of black education. He believed that blacks should receive public education through general school funds and not derived solely from black taxpayers. On July 17, 1871, he was appointed one of the school directors for Galveston County.[23] During this period, the public schools of Galveston were segregated. An advertisement appeared for public school teaching jobs on December 17, 1881, which stated that "white and colored applicants will be examined in different rooms." Cuney joined other black citizens of Galveston in protesting this arrangement.[24] He complained that, while black Texans were taxed the same as other Texans, the only public institutions open to them were the penitentiary and the lunatic asylum. He called for the establishment of a school for deaf, dumb, and blind black youth.[25]

In 1878 Cuney supported the establishment of Prairie View Normal and Industrial Institute (now Prairie View A&M University) near his birthplace. He was, to the end of his life, a strong supporter of this school.[26] Even after its creation, however, he remained critical of using public lands to support nearby Texas A&M University as long as this state school barred blacks from attendance. He was quite helpful in finding scholarships and other financial assistance for students at Prairie View and at Paul Quinn College in Waco.[27] On June 5, 1895, he spoke at the Paul Quinn Commencement, telling faculty, staff, students, and others:

> Progressive national life means progressive industrial life. The one is dependent upon the success of the other. And that race which employs the energy and thrift is the one which quickly realizes the meaning of the term.
>
> As it is with other members of the human family, it must be with us. If we would succeed in life and place ourselves above a plane of continual helplessness, we must foster a spirit of industrial as well as intellectual life. In other words we must teach our boys and girls mechanical trades; encourage commercial undertakings and recognize manly and womanly capabilities. Thirty years of freedom have demonstrated that the colored man has a high degree of mechanical genius; that he can take his place, when properly trained, in the ranks of the skilled labor of the world, and there hold his own.[28]

Another black college which attracted his interest was Howard University in Washington, D.C. He visited the Howard campus in 1896. Contacts with friends in Congress that year resulted in the necessary appropriations to enable the school to continue. In appreciation of his "mastery of the arts of high living and noble thinking," he was given an honorary Master of Arts degree at Howard's 1896 commencement.[29]

On July 5, 1871, Cuney married sixteen-year-old Adelina Dowdie, the daughter and mulatto slave of a white planter father and mulatto slave mother from Woodville, Mississippi, who had migrated to Texas in 1864. A schoolteacher, she helped her husband in his work for better education in Texas.[30] She was an accomplished singer and pianist who sought to cater to her husband's musical tastes, which included old songs of Ireland, martial strains, and melodies from old Italian operas.[31] They had a very close and happy marriage for twenty-three years. Mrs. Cuney died of tuberculosis on October 1, 1895, at the age of thirty-nine.[32]

Lloyd Garrison Cuney, the son of Norris Wright and Adelina Dowdie Cuney, was named for Boston abolitionist William Lloyd Garrison. He was educated at Tillotson College in Austin and worked for many years as a clerk for the federal government in Washington, D.C. He was very active in the Congregationalist Church.[33]

Maud Cuney Hare, the daughter of Norris Wright and Adelina Dowdie Cuney, was born in Galveston on February 16, 1874. She was educated at the New England Conservatory and the Lowell Institute of Literature at Harvard University. She served as director of music at the Deaf, Dumb, and Blind Institute in Austin and at Prairie

View State College. In 1904 she married William P. Hare in Boston, where she established permanent residence. She had an outstanding career as a musician, director, and author. Her major works included *Norris Wright Cuney: A Tribune to the Black People* and *Negro Musicians and Their Music*. She died in Boston on February 14, 1936—two days before her sixty-second birthday. Her body was returned to Galveston, where she was buried next to her parents in Lakeview Cemetery.[34]

Cuney's daughter was his principal biographer. Her book provides an insight into holidays at the Cuney home:

> There was always a generous Santa Claus, but father gave his personal gifts on the first day of the year. The night before, we always had a family party enlivened by the visits of intimate friends. Father enjoyed reading aloud the poems of the old year, always closing with "Ring out the old, ring in the new." As midnight approached, we would guess the minute and all troop out doors to see the stars shining on the new–old world.
>
> "Open house" was held on New Year's Day, with the reception for the grownups.
>
> Christmas, with the children's party and the candlelighted tree, always brought us books galore. Our first introduction to New England was through a treasured Christmas book—*A Family Around Home*, by Edward Everett Hale and his sister.[35]

After the Civil War, Prince Hall Freemasonry spread to all the southern states, including Texas. Norris Wright Cuney, like many southern blacks seeking to better themselves, saw the great value of Freemasonry. He joined Galveston Lodge No. 25, under the jurisdiction of the National Grand Lodge.[36] On June 24, 1874, he was duly elected and installed as Right Worshipful Deputy Grand Master of this jurisdiction. One year later, he traveled to Boston, Massachusetts, to assist in the proceedings of the Prince Hall Centennial Celebration. At this meeting, a statement was issued in protest to the failure of white Masons to extend fraternal recognition to Prince Hall Masons. The brethren resolved to

> do all within our power to remove the hateful caste—to the end that equity of justice shall become the supreme and governing principle of the American people—to make smooth the ways of children and by education to lead them in those paths of knowledge in which shall be found the true happiness in this world and in that to come.[37]

Two months after the Boston meeting, Cuney, along with fourteen other Prince Hall Freemasons, met at Saint John African Methodist Episcopal Church in Brenham, Texas, to organize the Most Worshipful Grand Lodge, Free and Accepted Ancient York Masons of the State of Texas (known today as the Most Worshipful Prince Hall Grand Lodge of Texas).[38] With the organization of the new body, Galveston Lodge No. 25 became Amity Lodge No. 4.[39] This organizing convention elected Cuney as Most Worshipful Grand Master.[40] In his first Grand Master's address, he stated: "We have met for the purpose of installing the officers elected by the convocation that assembled in the City of Brenham, on the 19th of August last, and to interchange those friendly greetings which ought to cement all Masons so firmly and strongly together, that no earthly power could put them asunder."[41]

On January 19, 1876, Cuney and his officers were installed in Houston by Capt.

William D. Matthews, Grand Master of the National Grand Lodge and a resident of Leavenworth, Kansas.[42]

At the 1876 Grand Lodge session in Houston, Cuney was succeeded as Grand Master by Richard Allen of Houston.[43] At the 1877 session in the same city, Cuney was elected Grand Master but declined, stating that he was unable to serve. Allen was then renominated and elected.[44] At the 1878 session there, L. L. James, another Houstonian, became the third Grand Master.[45] However, when the 1879 session again met in Houston, Cuney was returned to the Grand East.[46] He was reelected at the 1880 session in Galveston.[47] His 1880 Grand Master's address included the following words:

> Let us keep in view, my brethren, the fact that we belong to an order whose influence for all that is good and pure in human nature has been felt throughout the world, no man has been felt throughout the world, no man could desire to engage on a cause more worthy of the best efforts than the one in which we are engaged. The common fatherhood of God and the universal brotherhood of man is one of the ingrain principles of our order.... We should be diligent in the requirement of useful knowledge, remembering that our future progress depends largely upon education, intelligence and morality, as these are the three recognized powers by all civilized races of men. We are making rapid strides towards the realization of the hopes of all colored Masons. I am proud to say that our legal existence is no longer questioned by an considerable number of intelligent men. What we want now to enable us to cope with our enemies is an intelligent devotion to the true principles and noble precepts laid down by the order . . . let us stop not at the first or second step, but go forward in search of more light, the Great Architect of the Universe . . . having faith in His commands of the moral law. . . . Our greatest need, my brethren, is the selection of our most worthy and intelligent members to occupy the East (remembering the old adage, like master like lodge), as the man selected as a teacher in a Masonic Lodge ought certainly be better enabled to impart useful knowledge and spread a ray of light to those meetings, I think, my brethren, if this rule was strictly adhered to in all of our lodges, we would soon find a marked improvement in them. I sincerely trust that you will endeavor to impress this upon the minds of the brethren of the subordinate lodges.[48]

At the 1881 session in Austin, Rev. Abram Grant (a future bishop of the African Methodist Episcopal Church) succeeded Cuney as Grand Master.[49] The following year, when the Grand Lodge convened in Waco, Past Grand Master Cuney served as Master of Ceremonies and as Chairman of the Committee on Foreign Correspondence. At election time, he was nominated to return to the office of Grand Master, but was defeated by Reverend Grant.[50]

Cuney was a member not only of the Masons but also of the Knights of Pythias and the Odd Fellows. In 1888 he wrote a letter to David Abner, Jr., Grand Master of the Grand United Order of Odd Fellows, regarding the need for funds for the legal defense of Charles M. Ferguson, another member of both the Odd Fellows and the Masons who was involved in litigation stemming from a racial incident in Fort Bend County, Texas. Cuney suggested an assessment of $5 per lodge.[51]

Early in his career Cuney was also a member of a political organization that was fraternal in nature and bore the strong influence of Freemasonry—the Union League. The latter organization was founded in 1862 to preserve the Union and became popular during Reconstruction for organizing blacks politically and welding them into a coherent voting force. The mulatto carpetbagger George T. Ruby and J. P. Newcomb, secretary of state under Governor Edmond Jackson Davis, served as state presidents for the Texas Union League. On July 18, 1871, the Galveston County Union League was established, with Cuney as president.[52]

Cuney was quite successful as a stevedore on the Galveston wharves. At one time, he employed 500 black longshoreman.[53]

As early as 1877 Cuney became established as a spokesman not only for his employees but for other black workers as well. That year a wildcat strike broke out among railroad workers who claimed they were not paid enough to support their families. Three hundred workers congregated in a marching group. Michael Burns, a white rabble rouser, harangued the crowd, threatening the railroad company with damage if the workers were not adequately paid. Cuney then spoke, warning the black strikers that they were being used as tools of white political opportunists and that violence would not help them. He warned them that 700 armed men from Houston could settle things in Galveston. He did not lose his temper or yield to the crowd's rage. The crowd dispersed peacefully, and some workers even received better wages afterward. Cuney's courage in the face of the mob won him friends among blacks and whites.[54]

In 1876 black longshoremen had organized the first black labor union in Galveston in the form of a benevolent association. The local white Trade Assembly at first rejected this union. As early as 1869 they expressed fear of black labor, forbidding any member, under the penalty of expulsion, to work with blacks; and employed white sailors as screwmen. Not until 1884 did the Trade Assembly vote to allow black representation.[55]

In 1883 Cuney obtained black scab workers from New Orleans and Galveston and procured them work by underbidding white longshoremen. On March 14, 1883, he bought $2,500 worth of tools and called together a group of black dock workers, which he organized into the Screwmen's Benevolent Association.[56] He submitted a letter to Col. William Moody, president of the Galveston Cotton Exchange, explaining reasons for the organization. He stated that there was a need for skilled labor to load cotton ships and that many blacks were qualified for this work. He said that black screwmen had formed a benevolent association just as had the white screwmen, who had a monopoly on the wharves. With his tools and men ready, Cuney informed the Exchange that he was prepared to contract for loading cotton on any vessel. He requested aid for his business and guaranteed complete satisfaction for his work. Moody replied that the Exchange welcomed additional labor on the wharves.[57]

Rivalry between black and white workers came to a climax on November 3, 1885, when white members of the Knights of Labor were put out of work by Cuney's men. The strike was finally settled following negotiations between Cuney, the Knights of Labor, and other parties.[58]

Cuney's longshoremen later organized Cotton Screwmen No. 2.[59]

As previously stated, Cuney was the undisputed leader of the Texas Republicans between 1883 and 1896. During this period, he controlled federal patronage in Texas during Republican presidential administrations.[60]

At the end of the Civil War, Cuney had met George T. Ruby, the aforementioned Union League president, who became his political mentor, introducing him to the "inner and higher" circles of the Republican Party and helping him to obtain his first political appointment as assistant to the sergeant-at-arms of the 12th Legislature in 1870.[61] He ran for mayor of Galveston in 1875, for state representative in 1876, and for state senator in 1882. He lost each of these elections.[62]

In August 1873 Cuney was appointed inspector of customs at Galveston by Governor Edmund Jackson Davis.[63] After Davis left office, G. B. Shields became collector of customs and expressed a desire to remove all of Davis' appointees. Cuney went to see Shields, hoping to save his job. Shields uttered a racial slur and ordered him out of his office. Following this dismissal, Cuney wrote to Davis who, in turn, wrote to former Secretary of State J. P. Newcomb on his behalf. The efforts of these two deposed Republicans were to no avail. After the new secretary of the treasury, John Sherman, took office on July 25, 1877, Cuney wrote to him, protesting that no black man in Texas had been appointed to any position of importance although four-fifths of the Texas Republican Party was black. But his dismissal remained in effect until Sherman left office in 1880. At that time, Cuney reapplied and, on May 31, 1881, was appointed chief inspector of customs. On January 20, 1882, he became special inspector. However, his election as alderman on the Galveston City Council on March 4, 1882, disqualified him from holding a federal position. Thus, he resigned and entered the stevedore business.[64]

During his service as alderman, Cuney served on the following committees: streets and alleys, market printing, harbors and wharves, cemetery, charter amendment, claims and accounts, and water supply.[65] In 1883-84, Cuney and the other black alderman, J. H. Washington, proposed allowing black children to attend a newly acquired school. Sadly, the white aldermen outvoted them and the new school was restricted to white children.[66] During his four years on the council, Cuney showed the whites that he could be as competent as an alderman as they could. During this time, he also made many business and political contacts that eventually helped him obtain the office of collector of customs in Galveston.[67]

In 1884 Cuney attended the Republican State Convention in Fort Worth, where he was selected as a delegate-at-large to the Republican National Convention in Chicago. There, he helped James G. Blaine obtain the Republican presidential nomination.[68] He was a member of a select committee chosen to travel to Augusta, Maine, where they notified Blaine of his nomination.[69] Blaine was defeated by Democrat Grover Cleveland. However, it is true that "Even though Blaine lost, Cuney's pluck and his steadfast support of Blaine won him friends in high places."[70]

Meanwhile, Cuney found it necessary to focus his attention closer to home. In 1888 young whites in Fort Bend County, Texas (where blacks outnumbered whites four to one and held many elective offices), formed the Young Men's Democratic Club. This organization—better known as "Jaybirds"—fielded a slate of candidates. Local Republicans—called "Woodpeckers"—attempted to hold on to power with an all-white slate. The Jaybirds sought to intimidate black voters but experienced a major setback when Democrat J. M. Shamblin refused to allow them on his plantation to intimidate his black workers. This refusal resulted in Shamblin's murder. On September 5, Jaybirds met at the Fort Bend County Courthouse and drew up a list of seven African Americans, ordering them to immediately leave the county. This list included County Clerk Charles M. Ferguson and teacher James D. Davis, both Prince Hall

Masons and friends of Cuney. When the Jaybirds failed to win at the polls, the county disintegrated into mob violence. Democratic Governor Sul Ross sent in the state militia, assigning his adjutant general to restore order. When the militia left, however, the Jaybirds were in complete control. The adjutant general reportedly stated that the next time he came back, he would "not come as an official but would come back to help kill every Negro in the county."[71] Cuney helped Ferguson sue in the U. S. Circuit Court under the Civil Rights Act of 1875. He wrote letters to Prince Hall lodges throughout the country, requesting "an assessment of five dollars per lodge" to finance the lawsuit. In a letter to Assistant Secretary of the Treasury George Tichenor, he proposed "to make a test case of this suit, as to whether a man can be driven from his home and his property, by the oligarchy which not only now rules the South, but proposes to rule the country—because he dares to differ with it on political issues." He charged that northerners were "asleep on this Southern question. . . . The South has ceased to be a democracy as far as the Negro is concerned." After a federal grand jury in Galveston indicted the sixty-two white perpetrators, the case was settled out of court.[72]

In 1888 Cuney again attended the Republican National Convention in Chicago as a delegate-at-large.[73] This convention nominated Benjamin Harrison for president. Harrison defeated incumbent Cleveland in the general election. Following the Harrison victory, Cuney declared:

> The Old Party is again in power and I hope it will do what it can to protect its friends in the enjoyment of their political rights in the South, and thereby make it impossible for the oligarchy which has so long ruled the South by murder and fraud, to continue to do so. We shall thereby be enabled to bring this government back to where it shall be ruled by the many and not the few.[74]

Cuney attended Harrison's inauguration and predicted that there would be no color line in the Harrison administration.[75] However, his prediction was too optimistic. It was in 1888—the year of Harrison's election—that white Republicans in Texas began to organize in opposition to him.[76] Cuney sarcastically called these dissidents the "lily whites."[77] Shortly after Harrison took office, the leading businessmen and politicians in Galveston (Democrats and Republicans alike) began a movement to secure for Cuney the appointment as collector of customs. At the same time, the Central Republican Club of Houston—a "lily white" organization—petitioned the president not to make this appointment.[78] Thus, Cuney's candidacy for this position became a national issue. As a result, Harrison delayed making a decision.[79] He discussed the matter with Postmaster General James S. Clarkson, a friend of Cuney. Harrison asked Clarkson: "If you were president, would you give the most important position in Texas and one of the most important in the whole South to a Negro?" Clarkson replied: "Yes, and be glad of the chance when so worthy and fit a man for the position, and a colored man endorsed as to fitness and reliability for the place by all the Democratic businessmen of the city, could be found." The president signed the appointment and sent it to the U. S. Senate for confirmation on July 20, 1889.[80] When the confirmation came before the Senate, Texas was represented by Senators John H. Reagan and Richard Coke. Reagan voted for the confirmation; Coke abstained. In January 1890 Cuney took office.⁸¹ His position has been described as "the most important post any African American would receive in the late-nineteenth-century South."⁸²

During his first year in the Customs House, Cuney visited many county fairs, delivering addresses on the tariff, industrial conditions, education, and race relations. About this time, a number of public schools were named for him.⁸³ He spoke out boldly against the proposed "Separate Coach Bill" pending before the 23rd Legislature. Unfortunately, in 1891 this bill was passed, becoming Texas' first "Jim Crow" law.⁸⁴

On September 11, 1891, Cuney attended a black convention in Galveston. This convention passed a resolution condemning the Separate Coach Law. Cuney was commended as a commissioner for the 1893 World's Fair to be held in Chicago.⁸⁵

By 1892, the Republican Party was no longer the party to which blacks could turn for refuge. At this time, Cuney was at the height of his influence but facing rigorous opposition from the "lily whites." That year, the Republicans did not nominate a candidate for governor of Texas. The Democrats split into the "Regular" and "Gold" factions. The Gold Democrats offered to form a coalition with Cuney, and he accepted.⁸⁶ In this election, the Regular faction nominated incumbent James S. Hogg, while the Gold faction nominated Judge George Clark.⁸⁷ Hogg sent his emissaries to the Republican State Convention, seeking black votes. Rumors of attempted bribery were widespread. On one occasion, Cuney kept silent and laughed when asked if the Hogg people had tried to bribe him. Hogg supporters circulated posters containing Hogg's proclamation offering rewards for the apprehension of lynchers in Cass, Lamar, and Rusk counties.⁸⁸ Cuney's role in this campaign has been described as follows:

> The Cuney-Clark Republicans campaigned diligently for their candidate. They organized Clark clubs among Negroes, made use of Negro leaders like Cuney, and tried to discredit the pro-Negro image Hogg had built up for himself. They distributed widely in East Texas a statement Hogg had made in 1890 campaign for Governor: "I'll be damned. It looks like the map of hell spread out before me when I look at these black devils."
>
> Cuney, who had been sick at Hot Springs, Arkansas, returned October 4, 1892, in order to carry out a month-long campaign for Clark. Wearing his normal campaign costume of flannel suit and shirt, with a sombrero on his head, he campaigned the length and breadth of Texas. He delivered his best speech in Seguin. After Clark had finished speaking, Cuney spoke in a cool deliberate manner without playing to racial prejudice. Some Negro supporters of Hogg interrupted him, but, unable to hold up under his witty retorts, they soon became his most attentive listeners. He criticized Hogg's antibusiness policy and castigated the Separate Coach Law . . . and laws prohibiting Negroes sitting on boards of examiners. Cuney also indicated that in South Texas Hogg had prejudiced the whites against Clark. Cuney denied vehemently that he had been paid to support Clark. The energetic campaign led many Republicans to expect a victory for Clark by a margin of 20,000 to 40,000 votes.⁸⁹

While Governor Hogg managed to avoid all overt racist attacks, all of his supporters did not. Senator Coke called for the defeat of the "Three C's"—"Clark, Cuney, and the Coons."⁹⁰ Hogg won the election. In his autobiography, Clark described what happened:

The election came on, and while I received 130,000 votes, Governor Hogg received a much larger one. I was defeated by 50,000 majority. Even the negroes who voted as a rule voted for Governor Hogg. I was told afterward that they had been promised a university at Prairie View, similar to the State University at Austin, by the whites.[91]

During the 1892 presidential election, Grover Cleveland defeated Benjamin Harrison and thus became the only president in American history to serve two non-consecutive terms. Following his 1893 inauguration, Cleveland received appeals from a number of Galveston businessmen, urging him to allow Cuney to maintain his position as collector of customs. Cleveland, however, rejected these pleas and removed Cuney from office.[92]

Another blow to Cuney's leadership occurred at the Republican State Convention in Dallas in 1894, when lily whites were successful in manipulating some of his enemies in the black community against him.[93] That year, the lily whites openly declared their support for segregation. Cuney declared that there is no common ground between true Republicans and the lily whites.[94]

No doubt, Cuney's failure to rally substantial black support for Clark in 1892, the loss of his federal appointment in 1893, problems with the lily whites in 1894, and the death of his wife in 1895 placed him under considerable stress. His disastrous experience at the 1896 Republican National Convention must have come as "icing on the cake." The year of 1896 has been described as a year of victory for William McKinley and a year of defeat for Norris Wright Cuney.[95]

At the 1896 Republican State Convention in Austin, Cuney supported William B. Allison for president, while another outstanding black Texan, William Madison ("Gooseneck Bill") McDonald, backed Thomas B. Reed. However, they cooperated against the forces behind William McKinley.[96]

When the Republican National Convention met in St. Louis in June 1896, Cuney's delegation was not seated, while the McKinley delegation led by Republican State Committee Chairman John T. Grant was seated. Grant, a protégé of Cuney, suffered from mental illness and was not effective in office. The entire convention was very humiliating for Cuney, and he went home feeling betrayed.[97] He was especially resentful of Grant, stating:

> That ex-inmate of a lunatic asylum is my creature. I warmed into life. He betrayed and stung me . . . I stood by him when he had not a friend. I gave him a chance to come to the front and held him up against the protests of my friends. And all the times plotting to undermine me.[98]

At a subsequent Republican State Convention in Fort Worth, Cuney attempted, with the help of McDonald, to make a comeback. His attempt was unsuccessful.[99] This marked his complete loss of power over the state organization. After this meeting, a newspaper reporter wrote that Cuney had told him that he "could stand the defeat, that he had stood it at Saint Louis and certainly could stand it in Fort Worth. He said he would take his medicine like a man and fight in the ranks as hard as any of them in the McKinley for president campaign. He meant what he said but I could see that the wound was paining him. It would require time to heal the wound."[100] By this time,

Cuney had been suffering from pulmonary tuberculosis for ten years. No doubt, the stress of this political defeat, combined with the stresses of the previous few years, weakened his resistance and aggravated his physical problems.[101] Nevertheless, he disregarded his doctors' orders and made several trips to campaign for McKinley.[102]

It appears that, at this time, a number of people were concerned about Cuney's health. This fact is thus indicated:

> The Negroes' place in the party still obsessed lily whites as late as 1897, for H. F. MacGregor wrote Newcomb in August that the course of the lily whites would depend on whether Cuney lived or died. MacGregor remarked that he thought Cuney was going to die, "but he doesn't seem to be in a hurry about it." The Negro would still be a part of Texas politics, he said, if Cuney didn't die, but with Cuney's death, the Negro as a controlling factor in the party would be gone.

As MacGregor wrote this letter, Cuney was dying in San Antonio, but he made his adversaries wait a while before the final act.[103]

The noted black historian Carter G. Woodson gave the following summary and evaluation of Cuney's political career:

> Cuney labored unrelentingly to advance the Negro in the enjoyment of his civic rights and never sought to profit personally by political victory thus achieved. He became the controlling spirit of the Republican party in Texas by 1884 in spite of some defeats and many cruel attacks, and his influence was not overcome until he had to succumb to the assault of the lily white element that played into Mark Hanna's hands when he brought up the southern delegations to nominate William McKinley in 1896. Norris Wright Cuney was not for sale regardless of the amounts made available for the rotten boroughs. He stood to the end for principle and saw his delegation unseated.[104]

Cuney's last days have been described as follows:

> His magnificent health gone, his spirit broken by his wife's death in 1895, his tuberculosis reactivated by cigar smoking and lack of rest, Cuney retired to San Antonio after the campaign of 1896. Maud had wanted her father to retire earlier, but he refused until a relapse following an attack of influenza forced him to do so. He was, however, still well enough early in 1897 to go to a patronage meeting in Houston, to attend a New Year's Eve Ball in Fort Worth, and to visit his son and daughter in Austin.
>
> Alone, except for an old faithful nurse and friends in San Antonio, Maud Cuney fought unceasingly and desperately for the life of her father. Occasionally, he was able to take drives in the cool mornings and evenings or to stroll in his garden and to walk the streets of San Antonio. Each day he read newspapers and corresponded with friends.
>
> The end came quickly on March 3, 1898. His mother, his brother Joseph, and his son Lloyd arrived from Galveston on the day of his death. Cuney, who was in full control of his mental powers until the end, had his aged mother led from the room just before his death. With his head cradled in Maud's arm, he whispered, "My work is ended." He kissed his daughter farewell and died.[105]

Cuney's body lay in state all day at Saint Paul Methodist Episcopal Church in San

Antonio and was then transported by special train to Galveston, escorted by the Excelsior Guards, a black militia regiment. Upon arrival in Galveston, his body lay in state at Reedy Chapel African Methodist Episcopal Church until it was transported to Harmony Hall (the local Masonic building) for the funeral on March 6.[106] Thousands of people, black and white, attended. The processional from Harmony Hall to Lakeview Cemetery was the largest processional in the history of Galveston. It included the following: mounted police, a Dixieland band, officiating ministers, Excelsior Guards of San Antonio, Cocke Rifles of Houston, Lincoln Guards of Galveston, Cotton Screwmen, Longshoreman's Aid Association, Knights of Pythias, Odd Fellows, Silver Trowell Lodge No. 47 of Houston, Magnolia Lodge No. 3 of Houston, South Gate Lodge No. 32 of Galveston, Amity Lodge No. 4 of Galveston, and Grand Lodge officers.[107]

According to Cuney's daughter:

> It was after one o'clock when the religious services began. Dr. L. H. Reynolds of New Orleans, assisted by Rev. M. R. Moody, pastor of Reedy Chapel, conducted the exercises, which were impressive to a degree.
>
> The Masonic service was conducted by Grand Master J. W. McKinney of Sherman, assisted by Deputy Grand Master Lawrence and past Grand Masters Allen and Armstrong. Mr. Wilford H. Smith of New York delivered an eulogy on behalf of the Masonic fraternity. Music was rendered by the Reedy Chapel quartette.[108]

In his eulogy, Dr. Reynolds said:

> He was courageous. N. W. Cuney was no trimmer. What he believed he held to with the tenacity of a great and vigorous mind, and then had the courage to proclaim when others fled or were discreetly silent. . . . He was a born leader of men. The ability to plan wisely and then to project those plans into the minds of others with such clearness and force as to secure approval, is no mean power. It is the basis upon which he rested the success of the world's great leaders. He was a resourceful man. No one ever knew when he was defeated. Often, when in the heat of battle, some one sounded retreat, when disaster seemed traced in letters of ominous blackness on the banner which floated over his scattered allies, he would emerge at the head of a new force and move on to victory. . . .
>
> Know ye not that a great man has fallen this day in Israel.[109]

On August 20, 1941, Grand Master William Coleman led the Prince Hall Masons of Texas in a gathering across from Saint John AME Church in Brenham to dedicate a monument to Cuney and the other brethren involved in the 1875 organizational meeting.[110] On June 21, 1964, Grand Master John Theodore Maxey led members of the craft in the dedication of the Wright Cuncy Monument beside their first Grand Master's grave at Lakeview Cemetery in Galveston.[111] In his dedicatory speech, Maxey said:

> It is good for men to pause at times and acknowledge the debt they owe to those who have gone before. By observing what men have done, we get inspiration for what we can do by reviewing the history and records of the past, we may better determine our course for the present and be able to foresee what its effect will be upon the future. . . .

In 1871-72 and 73, Masonry came to Texas: San Antonio Lodge No. 1, Mt. Bonnell at Austin, Magnolia at Houston, and Amity in Galveston. N. W. Cuney had been appointed by Capt. W. D. Matthews, the Grand Master of Kansas, as Deputy Grand Master. On August 19, 1875, the first and only grand lodge of colored Masons was organized.

Norris Wright Cuney was elected and installed as its Grand Master. Wright Cuney was a native Texan, born on the Sunnyside Plantation near the Brazos River on May 12, 1846. Cuney came to Galveston in 1867 and entered politics in the island city. He was employed as an Inspector of Port and, sometimes later in his career, he was appointed as collector of customs after serving his city, state, and nation efficiently and well. He became seriously ill and passed away near San Antonio, Texas, on March 3, 1898. When the news of his death reached Washington, a very prominent Congressman said: "I never knew a man in whose heart and breast there lived a more earnest and unfaltering love of country. In political conditions, he was a partisan, bitter sometimes, uncompromising always but, above all, he stood for justice. His friends were many, their cause was his. He never weakened, he never lowered his guard, and this was the glory of the life that passed away near San Antonio and was buried in this grave in Galveston." He was buried with Masonic honors by the Grand Lodge of Texas on March 6, 1898, from Reedy Chapel AME Church. . . . So, today is an historical day. We have met here to do that which should have been done many years ago. We are about to use our sense of dedication as we unveil this memorial to a great man, a Christian gentleman, a Mason, and a loyal American. . . .

While this Monument may list his name, it is only through humble, yet joyous citizenship sincerely performed that we can render true honor and respect for his soul. May those of us to whom he was bound by fraternal ties of kinship find in the great Ruler of the Universe true refuge and know that underneath are the Everlasting Arms. . . .[112]

Two days later, during the Grand Lodge Communication in Fort Worth, the following resolution, introduced by LaGrange Lodge No. 112, was adopted:

This monument to Honorable Norris Wright Cuney will remain to remind us and succeeding generations of the glory that once existed and the purpose of Masonry built by this great man and better fix in our minds the struggles which this Mason went to lay the foundation on which our present day Masonry is built.

As we and others look upon this monument, we will get a glimpse of the atmosphere under which Bro. Cuney labored and the bold demand made by him and so bravely fought for to give Freemasonry to American Negroes. It will also be a tourist attraction. This monument will fade not nor lose its meaning but will rather increase praise of Freemasonry. . . .

If N. W. Cuney could come back to life he would no doubt say: "Well done, I thank you all today."[113]

In September 1997 Grand Master Robert E. Connor, Jr., led the Prince Hall Masons of Texas to Galveston to celebrate the legacy of Norris Wright Cuney. During this commemoration, Grand Recorder A. D. Harris of Galveston spoke the following words of wisdom:

In the community of Sunny Side on the east bank of the Brazos River in Waller County, Norris Wright Cuney first said "Hello America" on the 12th day of May 1846. . . .

The Occasion is to chronicle his life and inform you of what history does not inform you. Midst the stigma of Southern prejudice, segregation, discrimination, ostracization, oppression, and suppression, Cuney had the audacity to wage war with the powers that be and challenge the system in trying to get better wages for the men who loaded and unloaded the ships that came into and went out of the port of Galveston.

He demanded a contract and organized what was then known as the Cotton Screwmen, but is now known as Longshoremen, extending from the Pacific to the Atlantic oceans, including the Gulf of Mexico.

His efforts met with stiff opposition and created animosity to the extent that his very life was threatened and probably would have been but for the loyal men who surrounded his home for three days and nights, armed with shot guns and rifles to ensure the safety of his home. Cuney was active in three distinct areas—labor, politics, and Masonry.

Secondly, the Occasion is to recall and praise him as a giant oak in the forest of the Republican Party, in which he held the office of sergeant at arms, as well as a member of several committees, including the powerful Nominating Committee....

He later became collector of customs and commissioner of water works, a position never before or since held by a black person in Galveston.

So admired and respected was he that, at his death, after the body had laid in state at Saint Paul Methodist Church, the officials of the Southern Pacific and Sante Fe railways furnished a special train, draped in mourning, to bring the body, family, friends, admirers, and supporters to Galveston.

Finally, the Occasion is to pay homage to the man that we can call our Masonic Grandfather. As first Grand Master of Texas, he worked hard assiduously in promoting Masonry in Texas.

Though he is gone, his spirit tells us that, when this Occasion is over, when this Occasion wound up Sunday, September 14, that Monday, September 15, will be a new day, a better day, a brighter day, a day of victory for the Prince Hall Grand Lodge....

That was the dream of Norris Wright Cuney. The Occasion is to keep that dream alive and perpetuate the legacy of the great man and humanitarian.[114]

In her 1965 thesis, Virginia Neal Hinze said of Cuney:

His position . . . in Texas history and in Negro thought has significance as a protester, as one who fought against the tide to keep democracy alive in a one-party state where racial prejudice was the norm. He moved one inch, only to be pushed back by the white majority. He, at least, made the effort; he burdened himself to smooth the way for future Negroes and whites. Men like Cuney are rare.[115]

Indeed they are! Norris Wright Cuney, businessman, politician, and Freemason, was a true son of Prince Hall. He met his fellowman on the level, acted throughout life by the plumb, and parted this life on the square. He was truly a great man!

Richard Allen

Richard Allen (1830-1909) was the second Grand Master of Prince Hall Masons in Texas.[1] A noted political and civic leader, Allen was born in slavery in Richmond, Virginia, on June 10, 1830. His master, J. J. Cain, brought him to Texas in 1837.[2]

Allen lived for a while in Brazoria County and then moved to Houston, the county seat of Harris County. He remained in Houston after he obtained his freedom.[3]

While a slave, Allen earned a reputation as a skilled carpenter. He is credited with designing and building the mansion of Houston Mayor Joseph R. Morris. After emancipation, he became a contractor and bridge builder. He had the distinction of building the first bridge ever constructed over Houston's Buffalo Bayou. He also worked as a commission agent and as a saloon keeper.[4]

Shortly after Emancipation, Allen married a woman named Nancy, who was born in Georgia in 1841.[5] The Allens were the parents of five children: Annie, Julia, Modestia, Venora, and Albert.[6]

Allen was quite active in politics. His political career began in 1867, when he went to work as a federal voter registrar. The following year, he served as supervisor of voter registration for the Fourteenth District of Texas and as traveling agent for the freedmen's bureau.[7] After one year with the latter organization, he became involved with the Republican Party and rose rapidly through its ranks. From 1869 to 1896, he was a delegate to every Republican State Convention. On five occasions he was also a delegate to the Republican National Convention.[8]

After assuming an active role in the Radical Republican meeting that nominated Edmund J. Davis for governor of Texas in 1869, Allen was elected state representative from the Fourteenth District, which included Harris and Montgomery counties. In this capacity, he advocated general measures for education, law enforcement, and civil rights.[9] He also introduced a bill providing for pensions to veterans of the Texas Revolution.[10]

Allen not only served in the state capitol at Austin but also held public offices in Houston, including customs collector of the port of Houston, city alderman, and city scavenger. Apparently, he was able to compensate for his lack of formal education by his native-born ability as an orator and his wit and humor, which he often used to sway audiences.[11]

Allen unsuccessfully sought the Republican nomination for United States Congress in 1870. The next year the Union League made him one of its vice presidents. He was reelected to the legislature in 1873, but the House seated his Democratic opponent, who had contested the election. In 1878 he was nominated for lieutenant governor. In the latter race, he was the first African American to seek statewide office in Texas. From 1882 to 1885, he served as quartermaster for the black regiment of the Texas Militia.[12]

As a politician, Allen occasionally was known to take controversial positions. In 1872 and again in 1879, he served as a delegate to the National Colored Men's Convention. He served as a vice president in 1873 and as chairman in 1879 of black state conventions that voiced concerns about civil rights, education, and economic issues. In 1879 he broke with most other Texas black leaders and endorsed the short-lived Exodus Movement, which sought to persuade blacks in Texas and other southern states to move to Kansas. In 1890, while serving as customs collector, he became involved in a labor dispute at the port of Houston. He defied white labor leaders but urged black workers to remain peaceful during the protests. In Houston he led Emancipation Day celebrations, promoted a park, and served on the board of directors of Gregory Institute, Houston's first black secondary school.[13]

Allen was a member of Antioch Baptist Church in Houston. He served that congregation for a number of years as Sunday school superintendent.[14] In July 1881 he was elected secretary of the American Baptist Missionary Association.[15] His grandson, Rev. R. T. Andrews (the son of Modestia), was once pastor of Saint John Baptist Church in Dallas and noted as one of the most outstanding and scholarly ministers of Texas and the Southwest.[16]

Allen was a member of Magnolia Lodge No. 3, Free and Accepted Masons, in Houston.[17] On August 19, 1875, while serving as District Deputy Grand Master for the National Grand Lodge, he traveled to Brenham, Texas, to participate in the organization of an independent Grand Lodge.[18] He served as president of this convention, which elected Norris Wright Cuney as the first Grand Master.[19] At the 1876 Grand Lodge Communication in Houston, Allen was elected as the second Grand Master.[20] At the 1877 session in the same city, Cuney was elected Grand Master but declined, stating that he was unable to serve. Allen was then nominated and elected.[21] At the 1879 session there, L. L. James succeeded Allen in the Grand East.[22]

On March 6, 1898, Past Grand Master Allen participated in the Masonic graveside services for Past Grand Master Cuney at Galveston's Lakeview Cemetery. He and AME Bishop Josiah Haynes Armstrong, another Past Grand Master, assisted Grand Master John Wesley McKinney in the last rites of the order.[23]

Allen died in Houston on May 16, 1909. At the 1909 Grand Lodge Communication in Fort Worth, Grand Master McKinney referred to him in his annual address as follows:

> Among the number of our deceased craftsmen referred to above is Past Grand Master Richard Allen, who was president of the convention in Brenham when our Grand Lodge was formed and Prince Hall Grand Lodge was notified.
>
> He volunteered his services to Masonry not for office, not for personal gain, but for the good of Masonry. He was a good executive and a pleasing speaker. He gave patient attention to every interest of the race, and more than once he spoke with clearness and vigor in its defense. My mind refuses an attempt to analyze the wonderful personality, or the barest outline of the brilliant career of this great man.
>
> He was with Masonry in the beginning and remained until his demise.[24]

Throughout his career, Allen made many enemies as well as many friends. However, Grand Master McKinney knew him well, and his words of tribute are testimony to Allen's importance to Prince Hall Freemasonry in the Lone Star State and to the esteem in which he was held by his brethren.

Leroy L. James

Leroy L. James (1850-?) was the third Grand Master of Prince Hall Masons in Texas. He followed in the footsteps of Norris Wright Cuney and Richard Allen. Sadly, however, little is known about his life. Efforts to obtain detailed biographical information—as is available on Cuney and Allen—have been futile.

Leroy L. James was born in 1850 in North Carolina. Both of his parents were native North Carolinians. His wife, whose name was Susan, was born in Texas in 1853.[1] James appears to have come to Houston in the mid-1870s. He is first listed in the Houston city directory in 1877. He worked as a mechanic and as a blacksmith's helper.

During the late 1870s, he boarded with a blacksmith named James Kyle.[2] In 1884 he was employed by the Houston and Texas Central Railroad. At that time, he boarded at the Houston Seminary, an African-American school. He is not listed in the 1886 directory. Unfortunately, the lack of death records from this period makes it difficult to determine if he died or moved away.[3]

James was a member of Magnolia Lodge No. 3 in Houston. He was present at the Grand Lodge's organizing convention in Brenham on August 19, 1875.[4] He attended subsequent Grand Lodge sessions and, in 1877, was elected as Grand Junior Warden. James served on the Committee on Dispensation and Charter, the Committee on Grievance, and the Committee on Finance during the 1878 Communication.[5]

At the end of the 1878 session, James was elected as Grand Master. He and his officers were then installed by Past Grand Master Richard Allen.[6] He presided over the 1879 Communication in the hall of Magnolia Lodge No. 3.[7] Unfortunately, his annual address was not preserved. At the close of this session, he nominated Past Grand Master Norris Wright Cuney to return to the Grand East. On the motion of F. C. H. Keeland, the rules were suspended and Cuney was elected by acclamation. On motion of Cuney, James was then elected Deputy Grand Master by acclamation.[8] James installed Cuney into office and Cuney, in turn, installed James and all other officers.[9]

James functioned as Deputy Grand Master during the 1880 Grand Communication in Galveston.[10] At the close of this session, he was not reelected but was succeeded in office by A. R. Norris.[11] He attended the 1881 Grand Communication in Austin, serving with Cuney on the Committee on Printing.[12] At the close of this session, Rev. Abram Grant was elected as Grand Master and A. R. Norris was reelected as Deputy Grand Master.[13] At the 1882 Grand Communication in Waco, recognition was given to Cuney, Allen, and James as the three Past Grand Masters in attendance.[14]

The *Proceedings* for the years 1883 to 1886 appear to have disappeared. The writer has found no references to Leroy L. James in the *Proceedings* for 1887 and subsequent years. As stated above, James is not listed in the 1886 Houston city directory. It is possible that he died or moved away about this time. However, the lack of death records for this period makes that determination difficult. We can only hope that future research will discover and bring to light the lost biographical information concerning our third Grand Master.

Abram Grant

Abram Grant (1848-1911) was the fourth Grand Master of Prince Hall Masons in Texas and the nineteenth bishop of the African Methodist Episcopal (AME) Church.

The office of Grand Master is the highest office in Freemasonry. Only a very small percentage of the millions of men who have been initiated into the Masonic order have obtained this exalted position. Likewise, the office of bishop is the highest office in Methodism. Only a small percentage of the millions of men and women who have held membership in the various Methodist denominations have obtained this position of great honor. The percentage of individuals to serve in both offices is even smaller. Rare indeed is the man who is able to gain the confidence of a majority in both the lodge and the church that he is elected to the highest office in each institution. However, in the history of Prince Hall Freemasonry in Texas, three outstanding individuals have accomplished such a great feat. Abram Grant was the first of these high achievers.[1]

Abram Grant was born in slavery in Lake City, Florida, on August 25, 1848. He was sold at auction at Columbus, Georgia. In 1869 he became a Christian and joined the AME Church. Shortly afterward, he was called into the Gospel ministry. The church ordained him a deacon in 1873 and an elder in 1876. He attended night school while working as a clerk in a grocery store in Jacksonville, Florida. While in Jacksonville, he served as inspector of customs and was appointed Duval County commissioner by Governor Sterns. In 1878 he transferred from Florida to Texas, where he was pastor of congregations in San Antonio, Austin, and Dallas. He also served as a presiding elder and as vice president of Paul Quinn College in Waco.[2]

Grant was a member of San Antonio Lodge No. 1, Free and Accepted Masons, in San Antonio, Texas.[3] He was a leader of Prince Hall Freemasonry in Texas from the time of the Grand Lodge's organization at Brenham in 1875. He attended the Sixth Annual Communication of the Grand Lodge which convened at Mount Bonnell Lodge No. 2 in Austin on June 7, 1881.[4] At the conclusion of this session, he was elected to the office of Most Worshipful Grand Master.[5]

Grant presided in the Grand East when the Seventh Annual Communication was held at Mount Moriah Lodge No. 6 in Waco on June 7, 1882.[6] At this meeting, he delivered his first Grand Master's address, which included the following words of wisdom:

> Assembled in these consecrated walls for the discharge of the important duties entrusted to our supervision, in the full enjoyment of peace, there is every reason for the expression of profound gratitude to the Almighty God, that, despite our frailties and shortcomings, His tender care has been ever manifest, and for humble aspiration that the present session and proceedings may be so conducted that not only shall they profit our venerable craft but also redound to the greater glory of our Heavenly Father, to whose name we ascribe all honor and praise. You have come here to declare your appreciation of the character and the objects of Freemasonry; to record your homage for its founders, and admiration of its splendid charities, and dedicate yourselves to the permanence and perpetuation of its principles. And we would leave here also for the generations which are soon to fill our places some proof that we endeavored to transmit the great inheritance unimpaired; that in our estimate of its principles, in our veneration of its charities, in our devotion to its morality, in our regard for whatever improves human happiness, we are not altogether unworthy of the high trust confided to us. Other places and other occasions you reserve for strife and disputation, and struggle for mastery and the sharp competitions of life. But here shall be peace and reconciliation. Within these walls, the knowledge and the morality, which are of no creed and no party, which are graceful and profitable for all alike, which are true and real to every mind and to every conscience, and in every brain and heart—these itself—these alone are inculcated here. Happy, especially, if we shall rouse ourselves to their utmost capacity—if we shall feel that we are summoned by a new notice and by an obligation unfelt before, to an unaccustomed effort to appropriate to our hearts and reason all the countless good which is hidden in the principles and teachings of Freemasonry.... I recommend the creation of a permanent committee on History of Freemasonry in Texas and its Jurisdiction. The works of this committee would be cumulative, suggesting of itself their line of investigation. The committee should be charged with the preparation of biographical notices of all elective officers in the life of the Grand Lodge, to be published annually with the proceedings.... M. W. Grand Master Samuel W. Clark of Ohio, has proposed the celebration of the one hundredth anniversary of Freemasonry among colored men on the completion of the century, September 1884.... I recommend that a committee be appointed whose duty it shall be to open correspondence with all the Grand Lodges in this country with reference to the proper observance of the one hundredth anniversary of the establishment of lodges of Freemasons among colored men on this continent.... "God be thanked for books," says Emerson. A higher culture, loftier attainments, alone fit us to meet the enlarging demand of the time and crisis, which swiftly approaches. Books are the voices of the distant and the dead and makes us heirs of the spiritual life of the past ages. Books are the true levelers. They give to all who will faithfully use them the society, the spiritual presence of the best and greatest of our race. I would therefore recommend that each member of our fraternity in this jurisdiction to be taxed ten cents annually, and said tax to be appropriated to purchasing a Library be placed as a cornerstone of our Masonic Temple—surer foundation can no man lay. Let us take pride in its growth until it shall educate the jurisdiction in the principle and practice of virtue, and make for us a reputation for intelligence world-wide. Appoint a custodian of said Library. Many friends stand ready to help with money and donations of

books. Let all the Grand and Past Masters and Secretaries be requested to deposit with said Librarian originals or copies of all letters sent or received pertaining to the history of the Grand Lodges, and all circulars, notices, etc. My brethren, I improve this opportunity to thank you most heartily for the honors which your partiality has for this year conferred upon me, and for the confidence implied by your actions. In the performance and my duties I have sought faithfully to administer the laws and practically the principle that those are governed best who are governed least.[7]

During this session, the Grand Lodge accepted the invitation of the president of Paul Quinn College to visit the campus.[8] The brethren agreed to establish their headquarters in Austin.[9] They accepted the invitation extended by Grant to lay the cornerstone for Metropolitan AME Church in Austin.[10] At the conclusion of this session, Grant was reelected as Grand Master, defeating Past Grand Master Norris Wright Cuney.[11] He continued to serve as Grand Master until 1885, when he was succeeded by Charles C. Dean of Houston. He was one of the founders of the Heroines of Jericho, a ladies' auxiliary to Prince Hall Freemasonry in Texas.[12]

By 1888, Grant had gained great fame not only as a Masonic leader but also as an outstanding pastor and evangelist. When the 1888 General Conference of the AME Church convened in Indianapolis, Indiana, he presented himself as a candidate for Bishop.[13] He was elected on the fourth ballot, receiving 138 votes.[14]

The 1888 General Conference assigned Grant to the Ninth Episcopal District, which included the states of Texas, Louisiana, and California. In 1890 he organized Delhi School in Louisiana and the following year was involved in the establishment of Payne Theological Seminary at Wilberforce, Ohio. The 1892 General Conference, which convened in Philadelphia, Pennsylvania, assigned him to the Sixth Episcopal District, which included Georgia and Alabama. On November 23, 1892, he organized the Central Alabama Conference at Demapolis. During his administration in Georgia, Morris Brown College in Atlanta completed its dormitory and inaugurated its first president.[15]

By the time of the 1896 General Conference in Wilmington, North Carolina, Bishop Grant was wielding great influence throughout the denomination. According to the recollections of another AME minister who was later elected bishop:

> At the time of our Wilmington meeting, the bloody Wilmington riot had not occurred. We received much tolerance on the part of the white citizens of Wilmington. The colored people had almost a monopoly of the skilled trades. They owned much property and for the most part seemed to stand for a high standard of domestic and social morality. The connection as a whole and not the Episcopal districts was the chief rallying point around which centered the church as a whole. Bishops B. W. Arnette, Abraham Grant, W. J. Gaines, and H. M. Turner, were the dominating figures in the leadership of the denomination.[16]

According to another eyewitness report:

> The address of Hon. D. L. Russell, the mayor's representative, evoked great enthusiasm. . . . Other addresses of welcome were delivered by Bishop Gaines, on behalf of the Second Episcopal District; J. W. Telfair, on behalf of the North Carolina Annual Conference; and E. J. Gregg, on behalf of Saint Stephen's African Methodist

Episcopal Church; A. H. Bonner (Presbyterian), on behalf of the city churches. Responses were made by Bishop Grant, on behalf of the bishops; O. P. Ross, on behalf of the ministers; and Counselor T. McCants Stewart, on behalf of the laity.... at the morning session of the ninth day, W. B. Derrick was elected on the first ballot. On the second ballot J. H. Armstrong and J. C. Embry were elected.[17]

No doubt Grant was pleased at the election of Armstrong, his brother-in-law and fellow- Past Grand Master. On the fourteenth day of this conference, Grant participated in Armstrong's consecration.[18] At the close of the conference, Grant was assigned to the First Episcopal District, which consisted of the Philadelphia, New York, New Jersey, New England, Nova Scotia, and Bermuda Annual Conferences; while Armstrong was assigned to the newly organized Tenth Episcopal District, which consisted of the Texas, West Texas, Northeast Texas, Central Texas, Louisiana, and North Louisiana Annual Conferences.[19] Grant must have left the General Conference feeling confident that Texas had been left in good hands.

When the 1900 General Conference convened in Columbus, Ohio, Grant was chosen to deliver the Quadrennial Sermon. His text was Genesis 28:19: "And he called the name of that place Bethel."[20] This sermon included the following words of inspiration:

> Thirty-six hundred years ago Jacob gave the name of that place Bethel. September 15, 1796, Richard Allen, on another continent that was never known to Jacob, received a charter from the old Keystone State of the nation, legalizing the name of another place, which Allen called Bethel. That was one hundred and four years ago, and now his followers, when they visit the historic city, Philadelphia, whether they are from America, the islands of the seas, or Africa, feel that they owe it to themselves to go and look at the place that Allen called Bethel; and then not rest until they reach the lower story and take a peep at the homes of him who named that place Bethel.
>
> Why should Jacob or why should Allen call the place Bethel? Because it signifies the House of God, for Jacob said, "This is none other but the house of God, and this is gate of heaven." It comprehends man's relations to two worlds, and this means his relation and duty to his fellow man in this one, and his responsibility to his God in both worlds. Let us fully appreciate the fact that threescore years and ten is but a short time and that only the physical man can reach his full growth and decay in that period. But when the mental and spiritual man is through with the physical body and is unclothed of earthly environment, he will find that he has only begun to grow. Have you thought of the number of houses of worship we have in the Connection bearing the name Bethel? Start with the New England Annual Conference, then to the metropolis of the nation, on to the city of monuments; rush to the capital of South Carolina, to the capital of Georgia, and of Arkansas, clear through until you reach California, then to Africa, and you will find monuments of loyalty to our Church and its founders in the churches named Bethel.
>
> The Bethel that Allen established is one of the branches of the Christian Church. At the close of Civil War we numbered about 50,000 members and, according to the reports from our statisticians, in 1895 our membership was 543,604. At the close of 1899 we had 663,906, an increase of 30,070. Now we have 204 presiding elders in our home work. In 1895 we had an enrollment of 4,365 ministers; in 1899 we had an enrollment of 5,245, an increase of ministers in four years of 880. In 1895 we had 9,749 local preachers, 6,356 exhorters, 215 local elders, and 649 local deacons. Our Annual

Conferences now number 64. Our increase since 1895 has been 2,506 members per month, 835 per day, or 34 per hour. This is food for the consideration of the pessimists in our Church who think every week that something serious is going to happen.

The sun sweeps through space with forty millions of burning worlds lashed to the chariot wheels, furnishing light and heat to all of them. The Church of God is passing through the world with all human inventions and institutions, all philosophy, reason, science, and art lashed to her wheels; and while all these agencies assay to apply mind to matter, it is the gospel of Jesus Christ that gives use and beauty to their application. Hence, whatever her discouragement, the Church cannot die, for "he called the name of that place Bethel."

For over one hundred and thirteen years our people under all circumstances and conditions have been coming to the agents of Bethel to receive counsel touching their welfare in the world, and to seek the best means of serving God acceptably; and when they were not in the swamps, in prison houses, in courts of justice, in the legislatures, in Congress, on land and sea; and we have met from time in our own councils to better inform ourselves. The age in which we live demands the very wisest consideration and counsel, and for this purpose we are now assembled at the capital of one of the greatest States in the Union. God grant that our deliberations and acts may have the approval of Him who holds in his hands the destiny of nations and people—of Him of whom it was said, which is wonderful in counsel."[21]

The 1900 General Conference assigned Grant to the Fourth Episcopal District, which consisted of Indiana, Illinois, Iowa, and Michigan.[22]

On April 16, 1904, the following letter was sent from the White House to the Fourth District headquarters in Indianapolis:

My dear Bishop Grant:
  I genuinely regret my inability to be present at the General Conference of the African Methodist Episcopal Church, which assembles in Chicago on May 2. I wish you well. Every decent citizen must feel a peculiar interest in every moment for the spiritual and material elevation of our colored citizens.
                    Sincerely yours,
                    Theodore Roosevelt[23]

Grant was the host bishop for the 1904 General Conference, which transferred him to the Fifth Episcopal District. At the time, the latter district consisted of Missouri, Kansas, Colorado, California, and Puget Sound. The 1908 General Conference in Norfolk, Virginia, reassigned him to the same district. This was the last such meeting he attended, for he died in Kansas City, Kansas, on January 22, 1911.[24] His body was returned to San Antonio for burial in the Masonic Cemetery at Commerce and New Braunfels.

When the Prince Hall Masons of Texas convened in Grand Lodge on July 11, 1911, John Wesley McKinney mentioned Bishop Grant in his Grand Master's Address. McKinney reported:

One hundred and five (105) of our own worthy craftsmen have fallen on sleep during the past year, many of whom were among our most loyal and faithful brethren. In this list who climbed the Mountain of Gladness and lovingly reached those immortal heights, is the name of Past Master, A. Grant, who . . . completed the labors in the earthly Quarries and joined the white robed procession to receive the wages which come as a reward of a well spent life of service. It was my privilege to know Past Grand Master Grant personally. He presided over this Grand Lodge before I was born. Probably few present have wrought with him in the Quarries—the majority of his compatriots having preceded him to that country from whose born no traveler returns. It behooves us who are active today to profoundly reverence the memory of those illustrious Masons who, in the face of adversity and surrounded by most unfavorable conditions, laid the foundation of our noble superstructure broad and deep and have handed down to us as a precious legacy an Institution replete with those virtues which enable us to enjoy to the fullest extent the civilization of all the great races of men. It is a source of inspiration to me to feel that from their lofty seats, the majestic shades of Cuney, Allen, Dean, Armstrong and Grant (peace be to their ashes) are looking down and smiling their benedictions upon me today.... I conducted the funeral ceremonies of Past Grand Master Grant, assisted by Past Grand Master J. W. Madison, and others.[25]

On the following day, S. J. Johnson, on behalf of the special Committee on Resolutions upon the Life of Past Grand Master Grant, read the following:

To the Most Worshipful Grand Master and Members of the Grand Lodge:
The swift messenger of death has invaded our ranks several times during this Masonic Year. On one of his invading tours he took from us one of the brightest stars in the Masonic constellation, one of the strongest men in the American nation, and one of the ablest churchmen in the African Methodist Church or any other church in Christendom, in the person of our beloved brother, Past Grand Master, Rt. Rev. Abraham Grant, Kansas City, Kansas.
In the death of our late Past Grand Master, his relatives sustained the loss of a mighty pillar, the Negroes one of its leaders and statesmen, the African Methodist Church its most beloved Bishop, the Masonic Fraternity, a tried friend, a Master Mason, who took hold of the helm in the darkest hours and helped to guide and develop it to the dawn of true Masonry in Texas.
The words of wisdom that fell from this Masonic giant, inspired and fired the hearts of the young men to such a degree that they rose in their feeble efforts and at last succeeded in placing Masonry on its present efficient and high plane in Texas; therefore, in memory of such noble manhood and eminent Christian character and in token of our respect for the glorious work he achieved in Texas among Masonry, Church and State, be it
Resolved, First, that in the death of this our beloved fellow craftsman, Past Grand Master Grant, the Jurisdiction sustains an irreparable loss and the fraternity at large a precious gem.
Resolved, Second, that we recommend his Masonic and Christian life to our Craftsmen for emulation, believing such will enable this Craft to meet the Grand Master of the Universe in peace and happiness.
Resolved, Third, that these Resolutions be spread upon the Minutes of the Most Worshipful Grand Lodge Free and Accepted Masons of Texas.

Respectfully submitted,
C. A. Harris, Chairman,
M. L. Calhoun,
D. S. Moten,

H. K. Knowles,
A. Jones,
W. M. Wallace,
J. A. Phoole,
John W. Madison,
F. B. Williams,
W. D. Cain,
A. W. Walker,
D. A. Shivers[26]

Following the unanimous adoption of this resolution, Grand Master McKinney arose and said:

Brethren, we have assembled to do honor to one of our former Grand Masters, Brother (Bishop) Abraham Grant, who was a great man. You all loved him. Your love for him was no greater than mine. He officiated at my marriage. It was my sad duty to officiate at his funeral. Born in obscurity, he was possessed of those inate (*sic*) qualities that made him great. Pardon me—I am not going to take up others' time. I have requested Rt. Worshipful W. H. Burnett, Grand Lecturer, to deliver an eulogy to this great man. I take great pleasure in presenting him to you.[27]

Burnett then delivered the following eulogy:

Most Worshipful Grand Master, Wardens, and Brethren:

Deep-sea philosophy and ethereal poetry may perform their astounding feats— the former by the power of reason, the latter by the power of imagination—and religion may yearn and cry most passionately for a happy reunion in the Great Beyond; but an honest history must weigh the facts and take cognizance of their significance in the great scheme of things without regard to our likes and dislikes. "Facts are brutal things" and, Banquo-like, "will not down!" That history should "take cognizance" of the relations of events is increasing demand. If it be largely true that the present has issued forth from the womb of an indefinite past, then it is rational indeed to say that prophecy must rest her feet on the sure ground of history. Idealism is the unsullied picture of some reality which its unpleasant features eliminated. It is realism speaking through prophecy; and a prophet is one who sees things as they are yet ensconced in the cradle of possibility.

The history of a grand canyon or a grand man cannot be complete without an adequate consideration of the forces and influences that were essential in the development. When in doubt or rank ignorance of the causes of favorable or unfavorable results, we glibly or gravely speak of "chance," "luck," or "fate."

These are just so many different expressions of our ignorance of the laws, governing the causes producing these given effects. A bubble bursts, a planet explodes, a fortunate throw of the dice from nature's hand giving us a Lincoln, a Fred Douglass or a Bishop Grant—all conform to some laws of development regarding of our conceits. Just how or why, we cannot fully answer. Yet the resultant facts are plain and significant. The value of a thing depends upon its relation to other things. Nature is so delicately poised upon the pedestal of law that the annihilation of one jot or tittle thereof would undoubtedly wreck the universe. Just what the fate of France, Germany, England and America would have been had not Napoleon, Bismarck, Gladstone and Washington, respectively, lived, we cannot conjecture.

The immediate and remote value of a man's life varies with his environment and the attitude of society to his teachings and labors. Ideas do not rule the world unless they become agents for their propagation. The diffusion of proper knowledge is the greatest enemy to superstition and the strongest ally to human liberty. Men become free thinkers (not "freethinkers"). For as a man thinketh so is he. Freedom of thought is the title-page of Masonry and bloody are the hands of him who seeks by any method whatsoever to snatch from another this God-given right.

"Liberty, fraternity and equality" are the watchwords of every true Mason and none but cowans dare deny. Then we gladly upon this memorial occasion pay tribute to whom tribute in justly due.

This afternoon, Most Worshipful Grand Master, lends a peculiar significance to the labors and contemplations of your six and one-half thousand craftsmen. When you laid upon the trestle-board the requirements of this hour, your burdened mind infused its spirit into the heart of every representative within this temple. You realized fully that a mighty prince had fallen in Israel. You realized most deeply the value of the labors of this great man. You realized that it was a duty for the Grand Master of Texas Masons to uncover this bowed head and lead unselfishly in giving the grand honors to the great spirit of Abram Grant as it marched through from the swamps of Florida, through the grand old State of Texas, through the nation, across the mystic Jordan triumphantly into the very sanctum sanctorum of the Great Architect of the Universe. The solemnity of this occasion and the unbounded praise freely and justly given to this Christian hero are eloquent with rich meditations and inspiring to the heart of any man who is willing to aid the distressed and defend the helpless.

Abraham Grant was born in Florida in 1848. The political condition of the country was anything but hopeful for the black man. It seemed more like a vast caldron seething with sectional hate.

It was a time when the oft-scourged Thos. Paine was really a greater man than thousands of the sacred cloth.

He had years before declared for the "rights of man" as a man, but many so-called ambassadors of God claimed that black men had the curse of shame upon them and were doomed to be servants of the dealers in human flesh. Strange to say that in a so-called Christian country too often the representatives of the lowly Nazarene follow their God-sanctioned rights—lashed, abused, shot and burned—these very men and their sympathizers, who used these representatives, I repeat, are standing like Peter of old, around the fire warming, denying their mission of Justice, mercy and truth, and thus endorsing crucifixion. Yes, Abram Grant was born in such a time, upon an ox-cart, while being transferred from one owner to another. He grew up under the severe conditions of slavery. When that period of youthhood arrived during which ambition begins to stir the soul to higher resolves, he would instinctively ask himself, "who made another man the custodian of my liberty." Yea, when the poetic vision of human equality, like Constantine's vision in the sky, loomed large before him, when out of the innermost sanctuary of his soul came forth the words of Burns, "A man's a man for a' that"! The hand of Providence removed the veil of bondage and the light of liberty flamed forth before his youthful eyes to guide him onward and upward to higher and holier ground. He was licensed to preach in 1873. He accepted what God did surely give him—the opportunity and power to preach a soul-stirring gospel to the souls of men. He did not know Greek, Hebrew and Latin but he knew more—men!

He came to Texas early in manhood, where the breadth of the rolling plains was a prototype of his broad judgment and sympathies; where the varied soil typified the fertility and resourcefulness of his great magnetic personality; where the lofty pines and stalwart oaks sang together of his future gigantic manhood both in body and soul. He was elected Grand Master of Masons in 1881. He served the jurisdiction with such satisfaction that he won the admiration of all who came under the sound of his gavel. He secured for Negro Masonry in Texas its legal status. He established in Texas the Grand Court of the Heroines of Jericho in 1886. His work in his church, his work in Masonry, his work among men whom he met and served elevated him to the bishopric of the AME Church in 1888. Such is but the barest outline of his work until his election as "Bishop" removed him from Texas to other fields which shared in his beneficience even as we did. He presided as bishop over one-half or more, of the whole AME Church in the USA.

He was possessed of a unique personality. His friends were in all the ranks of society—from the scavenger to the president of the United States. He was a race man preeminently. He was no compromiser, trickler, nor apologist. He once exclaimed with an unusual burst of eloquence that he had "rather be a free ass in the wilderness than a king chained in a palace." I have been reliably informed, Most Worshipful Grand Master, that he was a friend, an unyielding, unsubsidized friend to the Negro, even in the treacherous game of politics.

His influence in Texas did not rest merely with his church and lodge but at the request of a Texas governor he once rode a long distance on a special to quell a mob. He stood for a man in every phase of manhood. He believed in men! He loved men! He fought men! He defended men! He lived, suffered and died for men! He was a great man!

The life of P. Grand Master Grant was fruitful of the richest vintage that the vineyard of humanity has yet produced. He showed us the absolute necessity of leadership, of great men, of influential men. The natural animal jealousy in us makes us hostile to the progress of our associates—or especially those who have come from lower depths than we. But remember, Brethren, that man is greatest who accomplishes most with least means! That man who achieves greatness is alone really great.

Let us be willing to follow the lead of those who are more capable than we are ourselves—not blindly follow, but intelligently and unselfishly yield to weightier judgment than our own. We must learn to follow before we can make safe and sane leaders.

Abram Grant, born upon a moving ox-cart, was seemingly a child of destiny; for the inhuman shame of his birth became the glorification of his earthly triumph. Heredity must have surely held an antidote for his early poisoned environment. He rose, successfully, over every obstacle, leaving life's "low-vaulted past" in the rear for an ampler explanation of manhood and a grander view of God's ineffable glory just beyond the journey of the present day.

He was the full measure of generosity, and was charitable in his views, in his sympathies, in his judgment, and even wonderfully charitable in his purse. An old story is told of a strange bird once hatched among a brood of chicks. The stranger for a long time partook with seeming satisfaction of all the surroundings and requirements. He walked chicken; he talked chicken; he thought chicken—he was a strange chicken—that's all. One day as he was strutting proudly around the barnyard, he heard a strange cry from the upper vault. He was thrilled with the sound from above. He began to try his wings and to raise his head to a tone of unusual dignity. Another scream from above drove terror to the hearts of the fleeing chickens but brought an answer from this strange chicken-bird which proved to be an eagle. The call from above had awakened the dormant eagle—blood in his veins, it threw off the yoke of environment and yielded to the hereditary cloud-piercing crags of the mountain. It rose in majestic flight to join his blood mate in an ampler ether.

So with Past Grand Master Grant. He suffered early humiliations and privations but learned to adapt himself to his environment. But later in life, when the call of the blood bestirred every nerve cell in his imposing body, he left his dust-laden atmosphere of trivial things and rose majestically to higher and higher planes of thought and action. In his later years he used to sing, "Lord, plant my feet on higher ground."

Grand Master, Wardens and Brethren: This great man's task is done. He has served his time most commendably, and we do ourselves no injustice by paying his memory the full measure of human praise.

Then let us as noble craftsmen so live that it may be said of us that we did what we could. We cannot all be great—in the general meaning of the term; but we can be honest, sincere, friendly and charitable.

Let us believe in the immortality of deeds, the immortality that is now. Let us see victory in temporary defeat. Let us see glory, unsullied, triumphant glory in our temporary humiliations. The human rod cannot break a divine law. Law is inexorable! The divinity in man cannot be squelched by the proceedings of congress, parliament or legislatures.

Let us believe in ourselves! Believe that a black man is his own best friend or his own worst enemy. As Master Masons, our hope ends not with the grave.

> "For tho from out our bourne of time and place,
> The flood may bear me far,
> I hope to see my pilot face to face,
> When I have crossed the bar."[28]

Abram Grant left a great legacy in Prince Hall Freemasonry and in African Methodism. Both of these great institutions have been greatly enriched by his imprint. His name is enshrined throughout Texas and beyond. The Prince Hall lodge in Beaumont, Texas, is called Bishop Grant Lodge No. 72.[29] There are Grant AME Churches in Chicago, Illinois; Moberly, Missouri; Moultrie and Ellaville, Georgia; Los Angeles and Long Beach, California; Boston, Massachusetts; Amity, Louisiana; San Antonio, Austin, and Palestine, Texas; and Orlando, West Palm Beach, and Jacksonville, Florida. Grant Hall was erected at Paul Quinn College in Waco, Texas, and at Morris Brown College in Atlanta, Georgia, and there is a Grant Elementary School in San Antonio, Texas.[30]

As a pastor in the African Methodist Episcopal Church and as an active Prince Hall Freemason, the writer is proud to carry on the legacy of Abram Grant.

Charles C. Dean

Charles C. Dean (1844-?) was the fifth Grand Master of Prince Hall Masons in Texas. As was the case with Leroy L. James, efforts to obtain detailed biographical information have been futile. However, the writer has found more extant Masonic information, including some of the speeches Dean delivered from the Grand East.

Census records indicate that Dean was a mulatto born in Texas in 1844. His father was an Englishman and his mother a black woman from Louisiana. His wife, Hattie, was a native of Tennessee.[1] He lived at 129 Pease Street in Houston and worked as a carpenter. He first appeared in the Houston city directory in 1880 but was no longer listed in 1890. As was the case with Leroy L. James, the lack of death records for this period makes it difficult to determine if he died or moved away.[2]

Dean, like his predecessors Allen and James, was a member of Magnolia Lodge No. 3 in Houston. He was present during the 1878 Grand Communication in Houston, serving on the Committee on Finance and the Committee on Dispensation and Charter.[3]

During the 1879 session, he served on the Committee on Credentials.[4] When the Grand Lodge convened in Galveston in 1880, he served as Grand Sword Bearer and again served on both the Committee on Credentials and the Committee on Correspondence.[5]

His name does not appear in the 1881 *Proceedings*. More than likely, he did not attend the Austin session. However, when the 1882 session convened in Waco, he served as Grand Marshal and as a member of both the Committee on Dispensation and the Committee on the Grand Master's Address. At the close of this session, he was elected Deputy Grand Master.[6] He held this office for the next three years, working closely with Grand Master Abram Grant.

Dean succeeded Grant in the Grand East in 1885 and presided over the 1886 Grand Lodge Communication. On June 23, 1887, Dean delivered his second Grand Master's Address in the hall of Pilgrim Lodge No. 10 in Denison. He said:

Two years ago, when first called to the Grand East, the Grand Secretary reported 16 lodges in the state, with a membership of 324 Master Masons in good standing. We now have 41 lodges under the jurisdiction, an increase of 24 lodges in the last two years. We can now count 913 Master Masons in Texas, an increase in two years of 693 members. At this rate, we will soon be able to compare with the more prosperous jurisdictions surrounding us. . . . I have met with great encouragement from white friends of the order, who have done all in their power to help me in spreading the good work among our people.

Now, brothers, I thank you, doubly thank you, for the trust that I received at your hands for the second time. . . . Let our fraternal relations throughout the jurisdiction be more firmly cemented that the God of Peace and Love may delight to dwell with us in our sacred sanctuary, and that our hearts may become more familiar with the Godlike principles of Brotherly Love, Relief and Truth.[7]

On June 20, 1888, Dean delivered his third Grand Master's Address in the hall of Mount Bonnell Lodge No. 2 in Austin. He said:

Brothers . . . Rebellions, revolutions, and desolation of governments have shaken the earth to its foundations, while Masonry, like a stately ship, has sailed through the troubled waters. Masonry, like a stately ship, has sailed through the troubled waters of the past to a haven of security and rest. Giant-like it has come down the beaten pathway of departed ages with its science of symbols to beautify the civilization of every age and clime, nor has it come alone as a beneficiary of the more favored races of mankind.

All the good gifts of God were intended alike for all his creatures. Christ was no sectarian or clannish race worshipper, inasmuch as God said: "Go preach my Gospel to all the nations of the earth." Neither was Solomon inspired to build the temple for the glory of the Hebrews alone. Hiram Abif; Hiram, King of Tyre; and the marvelous skill of Tubal Cain added beauty to the famous structure. Stones were sent from distant quarries. Timbers were hewn in the forests of other lands and sent to Jerusalem.

Gold and precious stones came as donations from potentates of the earth, all to blend in the sacred edifice then being erected to the one God, the Architect and builder of the universe. Like the sun at high meridian, diffusing his rays over land and sea, has Masonry been diffused among mankind. Like the blending of the gifts of the nations into one common brotherhood, Masonry has since blended the great heart of nations into one common brotherhood. The Red Man breathes the mystic word, while Africa's dusky son reads and understands the hidden language of the science of symbols. We have but to bide our time. God lives; right and justice yet survives and perseverance on our part will yet result in establishing the Truth that Masonry is indeed universal, knowing no sect nor kin but the time-honored exponent of the common brotherhood of man and the fatherhood of God. . . .

In compliance with the order of the M. W. G. L. of Texas, I attended the Masonic convention held at Chicago, Illinois, August 23, 24, 25, 26. The convention was highly successful and consisted of Grand Masters and other Grand Lodge representatives of twenty-one jurisdictions. While in attendance, I had the pleasure of forming the acquaintance of such brilliant Masonic lights as M. W. Samuel W. Clark of Ohio, the famous author of *The Negro Mason in Equity*; the brilliant J. Hugo Johnson of Virginia, who produced a remarkable paper on "The True Status of Negro Masonry in America." P. G. M. J. C. Corbin, of Arkansas; and Bro. M. W. Clark, of the same state; and last, but not least, the brilliant, humorous and witty B. F. Watson, M. W. G. M. of

Kansas, whose wit shone like a thousand brilliant star points throughout the labors of the convention. No Masonic convention of the country has ever brought together such a complete body of representative Masons. . . .

Brothers, in conclusion, I desire to extend to you my heart-felt thanks for the honor conferred and the confidence implied by electing me, for a third term, to the grandest office known in Masonry. As hitherto, I have endeavored to do my duty to all the lodges under my control. The dignity of my office has never caused me to forget that official position should never carry the man so far above his fellows that he should ignore the sublime principle that places all men on a common level.[8]

On June 20, 1889, Dean delivered his fourth and final Grand Master's Address in the hall of Rescue Lodge No. 20 in Fort Worth. He said:

Through the dispensation of an ever indulgent Providence, we once more assemble within the consecrated walls of our sacred edifice, to legislate for the good of our time-honored institution.

May the Great Architect, who has promised to note the short-spanned existence of the tiny sparrow, also note and be with us in our deliberations on this occasion.

May we become impressed with a sense of our duty toward each other, and act according to our most ancient order.

Let us consider that "Masonry" has a spirit of grandeur in its composition; a magnetic power, chaining the hearts of its followers to its sublime principles. The sanction of the Almighty is mingled with its precepts like glittering particles of gold, and is scattered throughout its teachings as the innumerable worlds are dispersed throughout the azure canopy of Heaven. . . . An institution that had the approbation of the Almighty for its cornerstone and the wisdom of Solomon for its contrivance! The inspirational qualities of the institution are only felt and appreciated by those who have drunk from its founts of wisdom or have trodden its paths of antiquity. The echo of the tread of countless ages resounds throughout the cycles of time; and with each recurrent year, the sublimity of the order increases.[9]

At the close of the 1889 session, Dean was reelected as Grand Master, A. F. Jackson was elected as Deputy Grand Master, and R. H. Bradley was elected as Grand Senior Warden. Both Jackson and Bradley were from Dallas.[10] What happened in the Grand Lodge's line of officers during the following year is unclear, as no records have been found. When the 1890 Grand Communication was held in Paris, Texas, it was Bradley rather than Dean or Jackson who presided in the Grand East. Did Dean die during the 1889-90 Masonic year? This is certainly possible. He was not listed in the Houston city directory in 1890. Nevertheless, the absence of a death certificate makes this difficult to confirm. We can only hope that future research will discover and bring to light the lost biographical information on our fifth Grand Master.

Rodolphus H. Bradley

Rodolphus H. Bradley was the sixth Grand Master of Prince Hall Masons in Texas. He was the "mystery man" among Texas Grand Masters, as even less is known about his life than is known about Leroy L. James and Charles C. Dean.

A review of 1880 and 1900 U. S. Census records for Dallas showed no listing for Bradley.[1] He was listed in each of the editions of the Dallas city directory between 1885 and 1890. At the time, he was living at 919 Commerce, between Sycamore and Ervay. He was employed as the head waiter at the Grand-Windsor Hotel at the corner of Main and Austin. He was not listed in any later edition.

Bradley was a member of Paul Drayton Lodge No. 9 in Dallas. During the 1889 Grand Communication, he served on the Committee on Jurisprudence.[2] At the close of this session, Charles C. Dean was reelected as Grand Master, A. F. Jackson was elected as Deputy Grand Master, and Bradley was elected as Grand Senior Warden.[3] As stated in the previous chapter, what happened in the Grand Lodge's line of officers during the following year is unclear, as no records have been found. When the 1890 Grand Communication was held in Paris, Texas, it was Bradley rather than Dean or Jackson who presided in the Grand East.[4] Did Dean die during the 1889-90 Masonic year? This possibility exists, but we have found no proof. Since Jackson held the second highest office, one wonders why it was Bradley and not Jackson who presided in Paris.

Having found no records of the Paris meeting, we do not know what Bradley had to say in his Grand Master's Address. We do know that, at this session, Rev. Josiah Haynes Armstrong succeeded Bradley in the Grand East. We can only hope that future research will discover and bring to light the lost biographical information on our sixth Grand Master.

Josiah Haynes Armstrong

Josiah Haynes Armstrong (1842-1898) was the seventh Grand Master of Prince Hall Masons in Texas and the twenty-fourth bishop of the African Methodist Episcopal (AME) Church.

Armstrong was born in Lancaster County, Pennsylvania, on May 30, 1842. He joined the United States Army as a private in 1863 and soon was promoted to the rank of non-commissioned officer. After the Civil War, he established residence in Jacksonville, Florida. In 1868 he became a Christian and joined the AME Church. The same year, he was licensed to preach by Rev. C. L. Bradwell. In March 1869 he was admitted to the annual conference and ordained a deacon. The following year, he was ordained an elder. About this time, he taught school at Jasper, Florida.[1] He was elected to the Florida Legislature from Columbia County, serving in 1871-72 and again in 1875-76.[2] He was appointed as presiding elder of the Live Oak District in 1877. In the latter capacity, he had six charges under him. In 1878 he served as secretary of the Florida Conference.[3]

Armstrong transferred from Florida to Texas, where he established a close friendship with Rev. (later Bishop) Abram Grant.[4] Both men were Prince Hall Freemasons, and each rose rapidly in both lodge and church. Armstrong became a member of Amity Lodge No. 4 in Galveston. At this time, the Worshipful Master of Amity Lodge was Norris Wright Cuney, the first Grand Master of Texas.[5]

When the 1890 Grand Lodge session convened in Paris, Texas, Armstrong was elected as the state's seventh Grand Master. He served in this office for two years. In his July 12, 1892, Grand Master's Address, he said:

> We are permitted to assemble in the Seventeenth Annual Communication to review our labor for the past year. Let us return our heartfelt and sincere thanks to the Supreme Architect of the Universe, the All Wise Creator and Preserver of us all, for His manifold blessings in the past year. . . .

While our work is not perfect, it is progressing and holds a respectful place with other jurisdictions throughout the world. . . .

Owing to my absence from the jurisdiction during the principal part of April and June, and all the month of May, and the discouraging feature that I met with some part of the work during the winter, I have not visited the Southwest or the extreme Northeast, but I am convinced that as a general things the months of September, October, November, and December are the best of the year for our work. . . .

Brethren, after seventeen years of active service in the Craft, I have nothing to regret, and only hope that prosperity may attend the Craft in all generations while times marks the existence of men.

Please accept my thanks for all past honors conferred on me by the Craft of Texas.

And now I return to you this gavel, with the satisfaction of knowing that I have done all that was in my power for the good of the Craft in Texas. With you, brethren of Texas, I deposited my membership twelve years ago. I have concluded, while I am called away, my membership shall remain. . . .

May the God of heaven keep and preserve you all.[6]

Why was Grand Master Armstrong away from Texas so much in 1892? No doubt, the AME Church was requiring more and more of his time. When the 1892 General Conference convened in Philadelphia, he was elected financial secretary.[7] For him, this connecting office proved a stepping stone to the highest office in the church. At the 1896 General Conference in Wilmington, North Carolina, he was elected bishop on the second ballot.[8] Among the bishops involved in his consecration was his brother-in-law and fellow-Past Grand Master Abram Grant.[9] At the end of the conference, Armstrong was assigned to the Tenth Episcopal District, which included Texas and Louisiana.[10]

Armstrong's term as bishop lasted only one year and ten months. He died on March 22, 1898.[11] A few weeks before his death, he had assisted Grand Master John Wesley McKinney in conducting graveside services for Past Grand Master Norris Wright Cuney, who died on March 4, 1898. Both Cuney and Armstrong are buried in Galveston's Lakeview Cemetery. Armstrong's interment took place on March 27, 1898.[12]

AME Churches in New Castle, Delaware and Arlington, Texas, are named for this great servant of God. As a pastor in the African Methodist Episcopal Church and an active Prince Hall Freemason, the writer is proud to carry on the legacy of Josiah Haynes Armstrong.

John W. Madison

John W. Madison (1852-1929) was the eighth Grand Master of Prince Hall Masons in Texas. He was born in Austin, Texas, on August 15, 1852, the son of Emmanuel and Elizabeth Madison. Both of his parents were natives of Tennessee.[1] His mother was born in March 1822. She lived her last years with her son and his wife Letitia, who was born in April 1856. The Madison family lived at 805 East 11th Street in the capital city of the Lone Star State.[2]

Madison was an active member of Wesley Chapel Methodist Episcopal Church and served on the Board of Trustees of Samuel Huston College. For many years, he was employed as a mail carrier. In 1907 a friend gave the following description of him: "A leading citizen and a most excellent husband. Wherever the race is concerned, Mr. Madison can be called on. He is a great race man and by his quiet influence many are induced to follow the right path."[3]

Madison was a member of Mount Bonnell Lodge No. 2 in Austin. He served as Deputy Grand Master of Texas under Grand Master Josiah Haynes Armstrong. At the Seventeenth Annual Grand Lodge Communication, which was held in Austin in July 1892, Armstrong, who had been elected financial secretary of the AME Church, announced plans to retire from the Grand East.[4] On Wednesday, July 13, the annual election of officers was held. At this time, the craft voted to elevate Deputy Grand Master Madison to the highest office in Freemasonry.[5]

Madison presided at the 1893 Communication in Dallas and at the 1894 Communication in Waco. The latter session convened on July 10 in the hall of Mount Moriah Lodge No. 6. Following the ritualistic opening, the members of the Grand Lodge were escorted to city hall, where a very impressive program was conducted. This program included music by the choir of Saint Paul AME Church, a welcome by the Mayor of Waco, and an address by Prof. J. K. Williams, a member of Mount Moriah Lodge.[6] During the evening session, Madison delivered his Grand Master's Address. Some of the highlights of this historic message follow:

> The *true* Mason attends all meetings of his lodge, pays his monthly dues promptly, pays all death and other assessments without a murmur, contributes to the relief of worthy distressed Masons, their widows and orphans, acts on the square with all mankind. In fact, he does everything that an honest man ought to do.
>
> You will agree with me that never before in the history of Texas has times been so hard and work so scarce. But little work with poor pay. I have a letter from a brother in the piney regions stating that the men get but two days work in a week. This is only a specimen, and yet the greater number of the lodges have kept up, while some have gone down under the great pressure. . . .
>
> The Grand Lodge revenue is insufficient to meet the demands. No Grand Lodge or organization having a grand head is run on as cheap a scale as ours. Part of the time there is no money on hand. Especially is this the case immediately after the closing of the Grand Lodge, as it generally takes the last cent to pay expenses. For this deficiency I recommend that the taxes be increased to ten cents per quarter on every Master Mason in good standing. . . .
>
> I now recommend that it be made a law to take immediate effect. Money we must have. The business of the fraternity cannot be conducted without money. A corporation without financial backing cannot succeed. You must not expect your grand officers to transact business for you at their own expense. It is asking too much. Until you make provisions for this you will find yourselves lagging behind other institutions.
>
> Brother A. K. Weathersby, of Bloomfield Lodge at Forney, Texas, having been tried and expelled, appealed to me for redress. He stated his side of the case, and also stated how the trial was conducted. I wrote the Master of the Lodge to furnish me with a copy of the proceedings in the case that I might review them. This he, W. M. McDonald, Worshipful Master of Bloomfield Lodge, absolutely refused to do. Taking Weahersby's statement, I saw nothing but irregularity in the case. So I issued a stay of sentence until you could review the case. I have some startling statements in them. I will also lay before you Brother McDonald's ungentlemanly letters to me because I dared investigate the matter. I ask that this Grand Lodge, through the committee, either endorse or condemn his actions, and thus set a precedent. . . .
>
> Now let me return to you this gavel and say to you again that I thank you for past honors, and hope that my administration will go down in history as one void of discrimination, strife, misappropriation of Grand Lodge funds, but a clean, honest, straight-forward administration.[7]

Madison's concluding remarks indicate that he did not seek nor did he desire re-election.

At this session, Grand Junior Warden S. J. Sutton of San Antonio gave a report of his attendance at the Masonic Assembly that was held in Chicago in connection with the World's Columbian Exposition in August 1893. Sutton reported:

> There were representatives present from the grand jurisdictions of Arkansas, Louisiana, Florida, Mississippi, Texas, Ohio, Illinois, Maryland, Virginia, Missouri, New York, Delaware, Pennsylvania, Indiana, Tennessee, and Kentucky.
>
> Your representative is pleased to report that the assembly discussed fully the matter of death benefits in the several jurisdictions, with the almost unanimous conclusion that such benefits were beneficial in practice and Masonic in principle. The work in the various jurisdictions were exemplified by representatives of these jurisdictions. . . .

Especially strong condemnatory resolutions were passed against the men who, with evil intent, infested the various jurisdictions, advocating the unmasonic, obsolete and nefarious compact Masonry. The brethren from the South complained most of the depredations of these unscrupulous men. . . . .

The interchange of opinions and fraternal feelings cannot but be beneficial.[8] On July 12, 1894, the annual election of officers was held. Past Grand Junior Warden Wiley Lawson Kimbrough of Dallas was elected as the ninth Grand Master.[9] At 8:30 P.M., Past Grand Master Madison installed Grand Master Kimbrough and all elected and appointed officers. Following the installation, Madison, along with Grand Lecturer D. R. Stokes of Dallas, addressed the audience.[10]

Madison died at his home in Austin at 2:00 P.M. on Tuesday, March 19, 1929. His funeral was held at 3:00 P.M. on Friday, March 22, and he was buried in Austin's Oakwood Cemetery. He was survived by his wife and one daughter.[11]

Masonic graveside services were conducted for Past Grand Master Madison by Past Grand Master John Wesley McKinney of Sherman. At the 1929 Grand Lodge Communication, McKinney reported:

Brethren, it was an agreement between Brother Madison and me, made many years ago that if I should go first, he would officiate at my funeral and if he should be summoned to cross the bar before me, I agreed to conduct his funeral. In keeping with this agreement, upon learning of his death, I hastened to home to perform the sad rites at his funeral. The Grim Reaper Death has cut down one of the truly great characters of this jurisdiction. The government allowed him a pension for many years of service performed, but the Architect of the Universe will pay him a perpetual pension in the house not made with hands. He was my friend. He was yours. He loved man; he feared God. A life like his, like the light of a blighted star, will shine on.[12]

This session of the Grand Lodge authorized the payment of $50 to Past Grand Master McKinney and to Past Deputy Grand Master W. H. Mitchell of San Antonio to defray their expenses to and from the funeral of Past Grand Master Madison.[13]

John W. Madison contributed much to his church and community as well as to his beloved Prince Hall Freemasonry. The Madison family is highly esteemed in the history of Austin in general and of Austin's African-American community in particular. He appears to have provided excellent leadership during his two years of service as Grand Master. The Madison legacy should never be forgotten!

Wiley Lawson Kimbrough

Wiley Lawson Kimbrough (1852-1955) was the ninth Grand Master of Prince Hall Masons in Texas. He was born in Texas on May 10, 1852, the son of Richard and Susan Kimbrough.[1] He lived in Dallas during the last decade of the nineteenth century.

During this time, he was employed as a porter at a number of businesses. In 1890 he worked at Turf Exchange and Pool Room.[2] The following year he worked at Favorite Saloon.[3] From 1895 to 1899, he was employed by the Dallas Lodge of the Benevolent and Protective Order of Elks (BPOE). At this time, his address was 322 San Jacinto.[4]

Kimbrough was very active in Texas Prince Hall Freemasonry, both on the local and the state level. He served as Worshipful Master of Paul Drayton Lodge No. 9 in Dallas and as a Special District Deputy Grand Master.[5] He was elected Grand Junior Warden and was serving in that capacity at the time of the 1892 Communication in Austin.[6] However, he was not reelected to the latter office at the 1893 Communication in Dallas. Nevertheless, he was held in such high esteem by the craft that, at the 1894 Communication in Waco, he was elected Grand Master. The election took place on July 12.[7] At 8:30 P.M. that day, Grand Master Kimbrough and his officers were installed by his predecessor, Past Grand Master John W. Madison.[8]

Kimbrough presided over the 1895 Grand Lodge Communication in Sherman. At this session, his Grand Master's Address included the following words:

> I now bid you a fraternal and hearty welcome, to this our twentieth annual communication. Having around this sacred altar offered up prayers and adoration to Him who doeth all things well, let us turn our attention to the labors and duties which call us together today; keeping in view the three great tenets of Free Masonry— "Brotherly Love, Relief and Truth." . . .
>
> On the twenty-first of January I started out, making my annual visits to lodges; succeeded in visiting forty-one lodges, and traveling 6,282 miles in the interest of the

Order. It was not my object to do a great quantity of work in new fields; notwithstanding there were many calls for that character of service. Believing that the condition of old organizations demanded my time, I have gone forward in the most active labors among them. . . .

I have visited lodges that have never had a visit from a grand officer, or had never seen the Grand Master before my visit. Some of them have been visited by D.D.G.M.'s and Grand Lecturers; but I am sorry to report that only a few of these officers, in my opinion, have done their duties. . . . It is to be regretted by us that so much ignorance predominates in our lodges, as far as relates to our work. I find a very few secretaries that understand how to keep their accounts. In this case we need a uniform system of book-keeping. . . .

Judging from information received, our membership has increased greatly since we met last. I find that we have in our jurisdiction lodge property to the value of about $9,000, which is a creditable showing. Peace and harmony prevail among the craft with a very few exceptions. . . .

On the 21st of May I received an invitation to be present and to take part in the dedication of the Memorial Monument of Prince Hall, by the M.W.G. Lodge of Massachusetts, at Boston, on June 24. The meeting of this grand body today, prevented me from going.

On my official visit I took special care to visit many of the schools and colleges, where the opportunity permitted me. More education will aid in making better men and better masons. They will then better understand the art. . . .

I regret to you that by personal observation I find that less than three lodges in our jurisdiction understand the uniformity of our work. . . . I believe that if our lecturers would lay aside their manner of lecturing, which is speech-making, and open a school of instruction in these lodges, more good will be accomplished. . . .

According to your order I visited Bloomfield lodge for the purpose of investigating the case of Bro. A. K. Weathersby. On October 17 Bro. McDonald, the W.M., failed to assemble this lodge, giving us an excuse that he did not get my notice. I have no doubts about this, as the Master in a previous note to me, refused to assemble this lodge for me or for any other deputy for that purpose. I made another date with this lodge, on January 29, 1895, but received a card from the Master, stating that his lodge was not working, therefore it was not necessary for me to come. On January 24, 1895, I issued a decree of suspension, according to Article 38 of the Constitution of the Grand Lodge. The Lodge stands suspended, subject to your action. Our widows and orphans are suffering on account of lodges acting as this lodge has acted, and our Grand Lodge has been embarrassed financially. I have refused to reinstate this lodge because, according to law, it is the duty of this Grand Lodge to act in the case.[9]

While I was in Galveston on my visit, I found that Bro. E. Lawrence, D.D., and Bro. A. J. Johnson, G.S.W., had done a work that should claim a space in the history of this Grand Lodge, by convincing nine of W. D. Matthews' men that "Compactism" was no good. Bro. Lawrence healed six of them and I healed three while there, myself. When I was called to Denison, I administered the healing oath to one, making in all ten compact Masons captured during this year. . . .[10]

One very important question has presented itself to me; that is the question of ritualistic work. I have watched with a close eye the danger and exposure of the present ritualistic work used by this jurisdiction, that is the "Duncan ritual." It is true that some years ago we adopted this work, but we were not prepared at that time to do otherwise.

I have been searching diligently for the standard ritualistic work, and I am prepared to say that I have found it.

I have been for some time in correspondence with the firm that publishes this work, and have a letter from them with a copy of the standard work to submit to your committee. The work is *ecca orienta*. It is in the cipher. I have also the key to the work . . . since we met last I have seen men on the public streets with the "Duncan Ritual" in their hip-pockets, and to the gaze of the public. I do not know whether or not they were Masons, neither could I defy them, because these common books can be bought in any book store for the purchase price. . . .[11]

My work is before you subject to your action. I have served you faithfully in this important trust for one year. My labors have been very great; the workmen have not done their work as they should have done. They have formed their own designs by which to work, which have been very dissatisfactory. And now, dear Brethren, I have endeavored to be loyal to the trust reposed. I admonish you to overlook the faults that have been committed, considering that time heals all wounds, and that the shining goal is ahead of the faithful and enduring. Let us forget those things which are behind, and press forward to the mark of the high calling of Him who has for all these years of toil and labor upheld us by His great power, and enable us to demonstrate so clearly the wisdom and goodness of the great fraternity which is represented here today.

In His name, and with the view of exalting the time-honored principles which we hold dear and most sacred, let us go forth to duty and to labor until the long labors of life are over, and we are permitted to assemble in the halls of triumph where the King of all the earth shall let fall the great gavel of the ages eternal, and where the chants of angels swell the merry anthems of jubilee, and join us in the perpetual praise of Him whose virtues we extol, in our efforts to aid the widow and the fatherless, and to dry the tears of the orphan.[12]

At the conclusion of this session, Kimbrough was reelected as Grand Master and Rev. John Wesley McKinney of Sherman was elected as Deputy Grand Master. Kimbrough presided at the 1896 Communication in Austin. At the latter session, Deputy Grand Master McKinney was promoted to the Grand East. Thus began the longest term of any Grand Master in the history of Texas Prince Hall Freemasonry.[13]

During the early 1900s, Past Grand Master Kimbrough relocated from Texas to California, where he spent the rest of his life.[14] In 1920 he was living at 1526 Essex in Los Angeles with his wife Molly and his two stepdaughters, Flora and Bessie Freeman.[15] He was employed for many years as a bartender at the Los Angeles Elks Lodge.[16]

Kimbrough took an active part in Prince Hall Freemasonry in California, as he did in Texas. His name first appeared in the California *Proceedings* in 1910. By this time, he was a member of Saint John Lodge No. 5 in Los Angeles. On December 24, 1915, Grand Master T. A. Harris appointed him to a committee to secure additional paraphernalia for the Grand Lodge.[17] Kimbrough later served on a committee to select a site for a Masonic home. He also served on the Grand Lodge Jurisprudence Committee, which met during the Grand Communication held in Los Angeles June 5-8, 1916.[18]

Kimbrough died at Los Angeles County General Hospital, 1200 North State Street, at 1:30 P.M. on February 28, 1955. He was 102 years old. At the time, his address was 1408 East 99th Street in Los Angeles. His wife had preceded him in death.

His funeral was arranged by A. J. Roberts, Sons, and Company, and the burial was at Rosedale Cemetery.[19]

At the 1956 Texas Grand Lodge Communication, Grand Master John Theodore Maxey reported: "It is also with deepest regret that I report the death of W. L. Kimbrough, Past Grand Master of Texas . . . While in Texas, he was a member of Paul Drayton Lodge No. 9, Dallas, Texas. He lived and died in California."[20]

Although Kimbrough never served as Grand Master of California, he nevertheless played an important role in California Masonry. He was held in such high esteem by the California brethren that, in 1958, Wiley L. Kimbrough Lodge No. 91 in Santa Ana was named in his honor.[21]

Wiley Lawson Kimbrough, Grand Master of Texas and leader of California, lived a long and full life. He contributed much to Prince Hall Freemasonry in two states. Both Texas and California have been enriched as a result of his influence.

John Wesley McKinney

John Wesley McKinney (1864-1946) was the tenth Grand Master of Prince Hall Masons in Texas and the sixteenth Bishop of the Colored (now Christian) Methodist Episcopal (CME) Church. Born in Van Alstyne, Texas, on July 22, 1864, he was the eldest of four children born to Archie and Jane McKinney. The McKinney family had a reputation as high achievers. Grand Master/Bishop McKinney had two younger brothers. One of them was Rev. M. T. McKinney, a pastor and presiding elder in the CME Church, who died in 1942. The other was Dr. T. T. McKinney, a physician who practiced in Denver, Colorado, and became Supreme Medical Director for the Supreme Camp of the American Woodmen. Dr. McKinney died in August 1945.[1]

John Wesley McKinney was one of the first graduates of Prairie View State Normal School at Prairie View, Texas.[2] He studied law and was admitted to the bar. After moving to Sherman, Texas, he taught school and served for several years as assistant principal of Fred Douglass High School.[3] He began preaching in 1883 and served as a local preacher for several years before entering the itinerant ministry. He eventually served as a pastor and presiding elder.[4]

McKinney's first marriage was to Alice Warner of Waco, Texas. To this union, three children were born. All three preceded their father in death. His second marriage was to Ruby E. Cochran of Greenville, Texas. To this union, one child—William McKinney—was born. The latter individual taught school in Sherman for many years.[5]

After establishing residence in Sherman, McKinney became a member of Polar Star Lodge No. 33, Free and Accepted Masons. He served as Worshipful Master of this lodge.[6] In 1896 the Prince Hall Masons of Texas elected him as Grand Master, a position he held continuously until 1916, when, due to the pressures of church responsibilities, he asked that he be relieved of this position and a successor elected.[7] During McKinney's long term as Grand Master, he provided superb leadership and repeatedly demonstrated his concern for his fellowmen, inside and outside of Freemasonry, throughout Texas and beyond. On July 17, 1906, during the Grand

Lodge Communication in Fort Worth, his Grand Master's Address included the following words:

> No doubt that there have been many in our sister jurisdictions that have fallen asleep during the past year, but there was one whom we all should pause a moment to mourn her loss. Since we met in Dallas, the Angel of Death has visited the home of the beloved Most Worshipful E. V. Lampton, who had contributed so much to the greatness of her husband. No man can be great unless there is a great woman connected in some way with him. She was a devoted wife, and in every way worthy to be the wife of a great and good man, who helped to make his home a model Christian home. Let us pause a moment to sing
>
> > "We share our mutual woes,
> > Our mutual burdens bear,
> > And often for each other flows
> > The sympathizing tear."
>
> While sitting one day thinking of the fair city of San Francisco, Bret Harte expressed his thoughts in these lines:
>
> > "Serene, indifferent to fate,
> > She sits beside the Golden Gate."
>
> But the year 1906 has changed the expressions of all people, for the awful havoc of earthquake and fire in San Francisco will be recorded in all lands and climes as the most appalling calamity which has befallen this fair land of ours. Shook by the hand of God, the great city of the Pacific lay prostrate and bleeding at a billion veins. I haven't known the correct address of the Grand Master or I would have given them immediate assistance, but I recommend that we make appropriate donations to them now.[8]

At the same session, a telegram was received from Waco's Negro Business League, pledging $5,000 to the Grand Lodge's building fund. A ten-year plan for the building of a new Grand Lodge Temple was outlined.[9]

On August 20, 1907, during the Grand Lodge Communication, Dr. B. R. Bluitt, Grand Treasurer, presented to Grand Master McKinney a gavel made from wood grown on the farm of George Washington.[10] During his address, McKinney expressed a strong determination to ensure the success of the order despite an economic depression. He reported: "Early in the year I began visiting the Lodges, personally and by special appointed deputies. By this method I have been able to correct any errors that may have existed in the lodges and stimulated them to greater effort. . . . these lodges are situated in saw-mill districts, where the results of the panic are most keenly felt."[11]

On July 20, 1909, McKinney well described Freemasonry's beneficial influence upon mankind in the following manner:

> The world owes a debt of gratitude to masonry for the perfection of architecture and the arts which will be paid when the great Grand Master of the Universe shall wrap upon the table of Eternity with the gavel of time, calling us to meet him in the clouds. The first impulse to the systematic dissemination of learning was given to the world of Masonry. Masonry was a true and trusted guardian of literature and science during the dark ages, when the clouds of superstition obscured the vision of the remnant of the wise and prudent.[12]

In the same speech, this wise Grand Master answered those who find serious objections to Masonic secrecy:

> The disposition to discuss the work of the lodge room anywhere and at any time is increasing and some steps should be taken by this Grand Lodge to check the evil. Masonry is clothed in mystery. Life itself is a mystery. All the operations of nature are mysterious. Death and immortality are the greatest of mysteries. Doubtless, for a wise object, the Almighty has ordained it. Her secrets are but the keys to her treasures, and are offered to all on one condition only, that they be found worthy, of an unblemished character and a spotless reputation. Our lodge work must be our secrets. It is necessary for our self-preservation. It is to this mystery that Masonry owes its perpetuity and universality. Men are charmed by mystery; empires have risen and fallen, nations have passed away into comparative oblivion, yet Masonry still lives beautiful and vigorous. The wild winds of kingly despotism and the surges of popular fury may slash against her, but in vain, if the brethren observe the secrets of the lodge room.[13]

In his concluding remarks, McKinney declared:

> If our Masonic lodges are properly managed and the instruction is up to the right standard, it is compelled to elevate more than the handful of men whose names are on our rolls. A well-regulated lodge elevates all amenable to its influence, and by that we mean all those who in any remote kind of way come in touch with its members. If Masonry, Oddfellowship and other kindred lodges in this Southland are not making conditions better and making it more difficult for scoundrels, and making it easier for good, honest, upright men, then they are falling short of their purposes.[14]

On July 11, 1911, McKinney again extended words of sympathy when he said: "In the Grand East of Alabama, the mantle of mourning tells the sad news of the departure of our beloved Grand Master, H. C. Binford, and the truth comes to us that he will be seen on earth no more forever. He was a true and faithful Mason and under his wise leadership Masonry prospered in Alabama."[15] As usual, words of sympathy were followed by words of wisdom. Thus McKinney proclaimed:

> Masonry . . . makes demands of sacrifice. The initiate, upon his entrance soon discovers that masonry deals with matters of vastly more importance than petty self-interests or aggrandizement. He is taught that a real purpose of admitting him was that he might be encouraged in first recognizing God in all things. Secondly, humanity as God's family, and finally himself as a servant to both of them. He is taught another fact: that masonry, far from being a playground, is a preparatory field for the real labors of life, and that if he would remain loyal to her precepts, he, too, must work.
>
> In the subordinate lodges throughout our Grand Jurisdiction, the brethren conduct their affairs orderly, are held in high esteem as honest, right living men and are manly meeting the duties and responsibilities of life. In all communities where we have good lodges, the relations existing between the two races is more enlightened mind and cultured brain, when dominated by Masonic principles will solve every problem that confronts men and nations.[16]

At this session, McKinney stated that he was recommending that the remaining $6,480 due on the new Masonic Temple be paid during the year and that he would be inviting the Grand Masters of other jurisdictions of the world to visit Texas next year and join in a "mortgage burning."[17] He introduced Dr. J. M. Burgan, president of Paul Quinn College in Waco. Dr. Burgan spoke upon the ancient landmarks of Freemasonry.[18] The Grand Lodge approved the call for publication of a special Masonic edition of the *Dallas Express*. McKinney appointed Grand Recorder W. D. Cain of Waco to edit the issue.[19]

One of the major items of business at the 1912 Grand Lodge Communication was the establishment of the Fraternal Bank and Trust in Fort Worth under the leadership of Grand Secretary William Madison ("Gooseneck Bill") McDonald, who submitted a resolution that the Grand Lodge take $50,000 in capital stock, while 2,500 shares be reserved for the Grand United Order of Odd Fellows, 2,500 shares be reserved for the Grand Lodge of Knights of Pythias, and 2,500 shares be sold to individuals.[20] The Grand Lodge voted unanimously for the organization of this financial institution.[21] This session authorized the donation of the sum of $100 to a Houston Mason whose son had been convicted of murder and sentenced to death. The purpose of the donation was to aid in the legal appeals.[22]

On July 21, 1914—on the eve of World War I—McKinney declared in his Grand Master's Address: "As the State and Nation train men for the army to fight the battles against organized foes, so Masonry trains men to fight the battles of life against ignorance, waste and immorality. Soldiers take an oath to perform their duties in obedience to written law, but you have taken an oath to perform your duties in obedience to both written and unwritten laws of love and loyalty."[23] On the following day, the brethren celebrated their Grand Master's fiftieth birthday, recognizing that he had devoted over a third of his life "to the spreading of Masonry in the Lone Star State."[24] There can be no doubt that the Prince Hall Masons of Texas did their best to ensure that their beloved Grand Master had a very happy birthday! The following day, McKinney blessed his brethren with these words of wisdom:

> No Negro Mason should ever betray a public trust imposed on him by his fellowman, whether Masonic or non-Masonic. . . . the fact that a man is a Mason ought to be a guarantee of his integrity better than any bond or surety. . . .I would rather be a doorkeeper in the glorious temple than a ruler in a non-Masonic structure, and I was glad when they said unto me, "Let us go into the House of Hiram and Solomon," though it was as a humble entered apprentice.[25]

In December 1915 the note on the Grand Lodge Temple was paid in full. McKinney, whose responsibilities in the CME Church were steadily increasing, saw this as a sign that it was time to step down.[26] Thus, on July 18, 1916, he delivered his final Grand Master's Address, with the following "Farewell":

> Twenty years ago your humble servant was elected Grand Master of the Masons, at a session held in Austin. At that meeting the record will show that about thirty-five lodges were represented. There was no money in the treasury and nothing to start the work upon. The Grand Master, however, got on the job, and has been on it ever since. I need not tell you brethren, who were with me at Austin, what part I took in the great upbuilding of the order. You know every step of its onward movement.
>
> In taking my farewell of you going into private ranks, may I not carry with me your best wishes and your sympathies? While what has been done, has been done by

co-operation; for success could not have been accomplished: the temple paid for and 160 acres of land paid for and a judgment for your money. Whether I have as Grand Master endeavored to give the best in me unselfishly, you are witnesses. Now my brethren, in parting from you and in turning over into new hands this great and important work, may I not ask for those who come after me the same undivided support you have given me, to the end that a greater work may be done in the future than in the past; that we may grow in numbers and influence, until the radiance may illuminate to every part of the Masonic Fraternity. If I have done anything worthwhile, if you think my services for the past twenty years now ending, have been of any value to you, then my greatest reward will be in seeing the future growth and welfare of the order exceed that of the past and every member standing shoulder to shoulder for the one object "One for all and all for one."[27]

On the evening of Friday, July 21, 1916, Past Grand Master McKinney installed the newly elected Grand Lodge officers, including his successor, Grand Master Henderson D. Winn of Chapel Hill.[28]

In 1917, Past Grand Master McKinney was honored with a banquet in Sherman. This event was attended by a number of dignitaries, including Grand Master Winn.[29] During the same year, he received the honorary degree of Doctor of Law from Paul Quinn College in Waco.[30]

On July 17, 1917, Grand Master Winn delivered his first address to the Grand Lodge. In it, he gave credit to his eminent predecessor:

I feel very thankful for having been associated with our very excellent and worthy Past Grand Master in many storms of stress and strain and having drunk with him to the fullest extent the cup of sadness, sorrow, and wearisome afflictions that seemed to be leading to Calvary and the cross, with its crucifying terrors of backsliding, hatred, and opposition—still on the other hand, having quaffed with him the sparkling glass brimful of the wine of refreshment, though soothed by the oil of joy; yet strengthened by the corn of nourishment I am able to stand here at the opening of this Grand Lodge—a new era to the Masonic Grand Lodge of Texas both in Masonic life and Masonic history.[31]

From as early as 1890, two factions were emerging within the CME Church. By 1910, these two factions had formed two strong political camps vying for control of the church.[32] What proved to be the much stronger faction was led by Bishop R. S. Williams, who had become the political power of the denomination. The other faction was led by Bishop C. H. Phillips. In the months leading up to the 1910 General Conference, the two Bishops exchanged heated articles as political battle lines were drawn. In the course of his exchanges with Williams, Phillips said, "Once more I predict that the invincible forces which I am leading will prevail." Williams said during an annual conference in Alabama, "Stand by my administration in this fight and my administration will stand by you." Phillips' faction thus became known as the "Invincibles," and Williams' faction became known as the "Administratives."[33]

At the 1910 General Conference, the Administratives supported M. F. Jamison and G. W. Stewart for episcopal office while the Invincibles backed R. T. Brown and J. W. McKinney. When the conference convened at Trinity CME Church in Augusta, Georgia, the political maneuvering was most blatant and unprecedented. The

Administratives won a smashing victory, with the final vote as follows: Jamison, 136; Stewart, 127; Brown, 109; and McKinney, 39.[34] According to Bishop Othal Hawthorne Lakey, the denomination's leading historian: "Brown and McKinney, supported by the Invincibles, were sadly defeated though both of them would be elected twelve years later when the political climate was decidedly different."[35]

When the General Board of the CME Church met in Macon, Georgia, in May 1912, Joseph C. Martin, Secretary of Church Extension, resigned. The board selected John Wesley McKinney as his successor.[36] McKinney performed well in this position. His duties obviously required him to spend much of his time outside of Texas.

McKinney's absence from the Lone Star State was certainly a major factor in his decision to step down from the office of Grand Master in 1916. Another factor was the death of Bishop M. F. Jamison in 1918.[37] According to the aforementioned church historian: "The death of M. F. Jamison had left the 'West' without a bishop, and J. W. McKinney, who had, like J. C. Martin, been elected to a general office upon the resignation of an incumbent, was the best known personality from the West. He had served as Secretary of Church Extension for ten years and was well liked throughout the church."[38]

On July 20, 1921, the Grand Lodge gave official endorsement to the candidacy of Past Grand Master McKinney for the office of Bishop in the CME Church.[39]

When the 1922 CME General Conference convened in St. Louis, Missouri, election of Bishops took place on May 13, with the following results:

> A total of 238 votes were required for election. On the first ballot, R. T. Brown and J. C. Martin each received 253 votes, and J. A. Hamlett received 248. J. W. McKinney received 177 votes. J. H. Moore, 128, R. S. Stout, 106, and C. W. Holsey . . . 105, on that ballot. Brown, Martin, and Hamlett were elected. . . . When the conference reassembled to ballot for the fourth bishop, an unprecedented thing occurred: All the other persons who had received votes "tendered their resignation from the race for bishop in favor of Rev. J. W. McKinney." Accordingly, on motion by R. S. Stout the conference voted unanimously that J. W. McKinney be elected bishop—making the only time in the history of the church that a bishop has been elected by unanimous consent.[40]

On the evening of July 20, 1922, the Prince Hall Masons of Texas held a reception for McKinney to celebrate his election to high church office. Grand Master Winn introduced Bishop McKinney, who said:

> I realize that we're bound together by a cord that ties human hearts. I see your faces as the sons and daughters of true and tried men, who held my arms as I tried to plant seeds of Masonry in this grand and glorious Jurisdiction. Language is not sufficiently golden to express my deep appreciation for this expression. May God keep you until we meet on the golden sands of eternity."[41]

On the following day, McKinney thanked the craftsmen for the honor bestowed on him and spoke of his efforts to compile the history of Texas Masonry. Grand Master Winn honored his request and appointed W. D. Cain and J. H. Burnett to write biographies of the Past Grand Masters.[42]

Between 1922 and 1942, Bishop McKinney served his church with the same distinction that he had previously served his fraternity. He presided over annual conferences in Texas, Mississippi, Alabama, Georgia, and Oklahoma. He led a massive building drive which resulted in the construction of McKinney Hall on the campus of Mississippi Industrial College at Holly Springs, Mississippi. Under his administration, Texas College at Tyler, Texas, erected a great library.[43] He and Bishop Robert Turner Brown led in the establishment of the denomination in Trinidad, West Indies.[44] Because of declining health, he retired at the 1942 General Conference in Chicago, Illinois.[45]

Bishop McKinney spent the last four years of his life at his home at 505 East Pecan Street, Sherman, Texas. At the time he was suffering from Parkinson's disease. He died in Sherman on August 24, 1946, at the age of eighty-two. His funeral was held at Saint John CME Church in Sherman on September 4, 1946. Bishop H. P. Porter of Jackson, Tennessee, presiding prelate of the Third Episcopal District of the CME Church, delivered the eulogy. People came from various parts of Texas and the United States to pay their last respects to the eminent Bishop.[46] According to a reporter in attendance at the funeral:

> Rev. P. L. Gray was master of ceremonies at the funeral services here at St. John church. Bishop H. P. Porter led the processional. Rev. W. J. Johnson read the liturgy. Rev. C. E. Chapman, Kansas City, lined the familiar hymn, "Servant of God, Well Done." Rev. I. B. Brooks, Gainesville, gave invocation. "I Need Thee Every Hour" was feelingly sung by St. John's choir. Scripture lessons were read by Revs. J. M. Fountain and W. J. Johnson. The choir then sang "Don't You Hear the Bells Now Ringing?" Rev. Gray acknowledged condolences, florals and remembrances for the bereaved family. Rev. Bullock read the obituary, and remarks were then made by Revs. Bullock and Fountain. Bishop Porter gave the eulogy, using the words: "I waited patiently for the Lord; and He inclined me and heard my cry."
>
> Bishop Porter spoke of Bishop McKinney as "a man of great fortitude, and almost unmatchable patience; a man of prayer and of a forgiving spirit." He followed his leadership patiently and he was likewise patient in his own leadership. Of him it can be said that if he had any single trait which might be termed a "fault," it was that of having too much patience.
>
> Active pallbearers were: Revs. R. R. Northcutt, Denton, Texas; W. E. Patterson, McKinney, Texas; D. B. Davis, Denison, Texas; D. E. Coffee, Stephenville, Texas; J. W. Scott, Fort Worth, Texas; and I. B. Brooks, Gainesville, Texas.
>
> The body lay in state at the front of the altar in St. John church several hours before 1 P.M. Wednesday when the funeral was held. At the grave the ritual was read by Revs. C. E. Chapman and P. L. Gray.[47]

Burial was in West Hill Cemetery in Sherman under the direction of undertaker Paul H. Prince, 403 East Brockett Street, Sherman.[48]

John Wesley McKinney lived much and lived well during his eighty-two years. He contributed much to both Prince Hall Freemasonry and to the Colored (now Christian) Methodist Episcopal Church. His church changed its name ten years after his death. McKinney Hall at Holly Springs, Mississippi, and McKinney Chapel CME Church in Sherman, Texas, are named in his honor.

In this age of ecumenism, there is talk of a merger of various branches of Methodism. If and when that happens, members of the African Methodist Episcopal

Church will receive the legacy of John Wesley McKinney even as members of the Christian Methodist Episcopal Church will receive that of his two distinguished predecessors as Grand Master and Bishop—Abram Grant and Josiah Haynes Armstrong.

The contributions of these three spiritual giants to both lodge and church were great indeed!

Henderson D. Winn

Henderson D. Winn (1862-1925) was the eleventh Grand Master of Prince Hall Masons in Texas. His tenure of office included the time of World War I and the "years of normalcy."[1] He was born in Chapel Hill, Washington County, Texas, on December 27, 1862. The name of his father is unknown, but his mother's name was Jane Knoxson.[2] He started teaching in the public schools in Chapel Hill in 1885, eventually becoming a principal. He continued this employment until 1918, when he retired and moved to Dallas. It appears that the primary reason for this move was his responsibilities as Grand Master, an office to which he had been elected two years earlier. In Dallas he established residence at 2903 Flora Street. He lived there until his death in 1925.[3]

Winn married Roberta Hall in 1907. To this union, three daughters were born. Two of them eventually became teachers in the Dallas public schools.[4] Winn was an active member of the African Methodist Episcopal Church. In 1896 he was first chosen as a lay delegate to the AME General Conference. He was a lay delegate to every such conference between 1896 and 1924. He served as a member of the General Board of Education of the AME Church for four years. He also served as secretary of the Board of Trustees of Paul Quinn College in Waco.[5]

Winn held a number of offices in Masonry, including Deputy Grand Master. He was holding this office on July 18, 1916, when Grand Master John Wesley McKinney announced plans to step down after twenty years in the Grand East.[6] Later that day, elections were held. Grand Master McKinney nominated Deputy Grand Master Winn as his successor. He said: "I think you ought to consent for me to retire after twenty years' service as Grand Master, and let the mantle fall upon the shoulders of my deputy, who has so nobly stood by me. I now declare the election of officers for the ensuing year in order." McKinney expressed the opinion that approval of his work by the Grand Lodge could not be shown in a better way than to elect Winn as Grand Master by unanimous vote. S. J. Johnson was recognized and said: "I move that the part of the Constitution referring to the election of officers be suspended and that the Grand Secretary, Bro. Wm. M. McDonald, be instructed to cast an entire vote of the Grand Lodge for Bro. H. D. Winn, for the ensuing year." The motion was duly seconded by eight or ten brethren and was adopted by a unanimous vote. John Adrian Kirk was elected Deputy Grand Master, while S. J. Johnson was elected Grand Senior Warden and J. C. Redd elected Grand Junior Warden.[7]

At the 1916 Communication, William H. Burnett of Terrell was appointed reporter to daily newspapers. A donation was given to the Dixon Orphans Home.[8] The next day, the new Grand Lodge Temple was dedicated—free of debt! The speaker for this occasion was Bishop Joshua H. Jones of the AME Church. Winn introduced Bishop Jones in the following manner:

> It affords me no greater degree of pleasure in presenting to you the speaker of the hour, a distinguished churchman, scholar, and race-loving man—one who sat in the council of statesmen and who has ever been our friend at court. It has been my pleasure to serve with him on the Educational Board of his church and in other gatherings. I've always found him a safe, sane, and sound leader. He is at present presiding bishop of the Tenth Episcopal District of his Connection. I take great pleasure in presenting to you at this hour, Bishop Joshua H. Jones. Hear him.[9]

On the evening of Friday, July 21, 1916, Grand Master Winn and his officers were installed by Past Grand Master McKinney.[10]

During the 1917 Communication, Winn commented on World War I and black participation therein:

> While we assemble here today as craftsmen and brothers, cheerful and happy as children of one family, we are brought face to face with the greatest crisis the world has ever known, and what the end will be only God can tell. Europe with her glory and grandeur, once the pride of mother earth; now the streets of her mighty cities, the furrows of her productive fields, her rippling streams and leaping cascades run crimson with human blood, and upward of fourteen million men have given themselves for a cause they knew not. Far from the angelic song of more than nineteen hundred years ago, "Peace on earth and good will toward men." What meanest all this? The Divine would suggest, "Pride goeth before destruction, and a haughty head before a mighty fall." . . .
>
> The Negro's place in this conflict is the place of an American citizen. All we have is here, all we ever will have is here, all we ever hope to have is here—our lands, our homes, our families, our all are right here. And knowing as we do that the home is safe only as the country is safe, we ask in this as we have asked in all things else, simply a man's place and a man's chance. We ask for nothing more, we will be satisfied with nothing less. . . . It is the nation's call, and the Negro has heroically answered every such call from Boston Commons to Carrizal. "Though he slay me, yet will I trust him," is the unfaltering cry of the black man in the United States of America.[11]

Winn reported the death of Grand Chaplain Rev. R. Sloan and his burial at Brenham, Texas. Rev. R. L. Williams succeeded Sloan in this office.[12] At this session, the "Report on the State of the Country" included the following words:

Today a world war that was organized more than two years ago is still in progress. The nations that have taught religion and civilization for more than nineteen hundred years; the nations that are masters of art, science and philosophy; nations that lead in invention and discovery and the organization of governments; nations that fought under the shadow of the pyramids, that strove to wrest the sepulchre of Christ from the heathen—are now found in the deadly combat for the acquisition of power.

The imperial government of Germany by its acts of insolence and brutality toward the citizens of this country has forced us into this awful cataclysm—the tocsin has been sounded and the call to arms has been heard over the land. . . .

Brother Masons, the age is pregnant with results which shall redound to the future benefit of the Negro. God is not dead, and the government still exists.[13]

In his 1918 Grand Master's Address, Winn spoke of attendance of Masons throughout the state at the funeral of William Madison McDonald, Jr., the son of the Grand Secretary. The younger McDonald, who died while attending Howard University in Washington, D.C., was buried with Masonic honors on February 24, 1918.[14] In this address, he also declared that, since African Americans were fighting to "make the world safe for democracy," they should be entitled to more democracy at home. He said:

Expecting results. That when the war is over, and the Dove of Peace hovers over the nations of the earth, we are expecting to be free—free from segregation, free from ostracism, free from mob and mob violence—free, yes free full citizens.

Thousands of our men are now in the trenches, giving excellent account of themselves; thousands more will go; thousands more should go and fight for those things for which Masonry has contended, from the beginning—equal rights to all; special privileges to none.[15]

On July 18, 1918, the following resolution was submitted and adopted by the Grand Lodge:

WHEREAS many of the members of the Masonic Craft of this Jurisdiction of the State of Texas are now in the army and are still being drafted in the service of the country. Some are in the trenches of France and on the battlefield of Europe during (*sic*) their bit to help set up a world's democracy for mankind, destroying autocracy, their local and Grand Lodge dues should be exempted during their time in the service of the Government. Therefore be it

RESOLVED, That the local and Grand Lodge dues be exempted from financial obligation to the brothers in the army during the war and that a certificate be given to each one who has enlisted in the service of the country, stating that he is square and recommended to the favorable consideration of foreign jurisdiction of Masons wherever they may go by the Most Worshipful Grand Lodge of Free and Accepted Masons of Texas.

And that when the war shall close each of those alive and receiving certificate from the Most Worshipful Grand Lodge of Texas may return to their various lodges, exemption becoming null and void at the close of the war.[16]

Later that day, a resolution was adopted which called for the placing on the walls of the Grand Lodge Temple portraits of all Grand Masters and of Grand Secretary

McDonald, who was always "too busy to be Grand Master."[17] Also adopted was the Report on Education, which included a call for support for Prairie View State School.[18]

As news of the Armistice reached the Grand Lodge, the following report was adopted:

> WHEREAS, We have just received the glad intelligence of the valorous achievements and victory of American arms on the western front over the German autocracy; Be it
> RESOLVED, That a committee on nine (two of whom shall be the Most Worshipful Grand Master and Right Worshipful Grand Secretary); to draft a telegram to His Excellency, Hon. Woodrow Wilson, President, United States of America; and Hon. Newton D. Baker, Secretary of War; and a cablegram to General John J. Pershing, Commander of American expeditionary forces in France, expressing the hearty gratification of this Masonic Jurisdiction in the celebrated and historic event, and pledging our patriotism and loyal support in every way to the Government and the Army in the effort to establish freedom, justice, and liberty for all the people of all the earth.[19]

The following year, Grand Master Winn delivered his first postwar address, in which he declared: "We would rather that the bright side of life be turned to you, that you may see the beauties in labor, the grandeur and magnificence in perfect characters, the self-approbation to conscience for having finished a full year's work, rather than for you to behold 'Error wounded, writhing in pain, and dying among her worshipers.'"[20]

However, all of this address was not devoted to the "bright side of life," as he had the following tragedy to report: "On the night of Nov. 25, 1918, the 'Fire Fiend' visited my home in Chapel Hill, Texas, and in a very short time destroyed all of our accumulation of a lifetime. This news was sent out by the Grand Senior Warden to the lodges of the jurisdiction and many were they that responded to me with donations. I thanked them then—I again thank you."[21] Despite this negative experience, the Grand Master exhibited the following confidence: "The Negro has no idea of leaving America, that may be understood, once for always, having made our mark in society, church, state, and the battlefields. And today we have confidence that our causes are just, and the God of right is on our side to lead us to success. Discriminations, segregations, lynchings, and mob violence will come to an end, and they that do uphold them will soon have their part in that lake of fire."[22] He closed this address with the following beautiful poem:

> Toiling, sorrowing, rejoicing—
> Onward through life he goes,
> Each morning sees some task begun,
> Each evening finds it closed—
> Something attempted, something done,
> We earn a night's repose.[23]

At this session of the Grand Lodge, provisions were made for the entertainment of representatives and visitors at Fort Worth's Herman Park by the masters of Masonic entertainment—the Shriners.[24] Among the visitors introduced at this session was Rev. Prince K. Kaba Rega of Unford, Africa.[25] That year (1919) warrants were issued for a number of new lodges, including Eastside Lodge No. 88 in Waco.[26] The Grand Lodge adopted a number of resolutions, including two related to aid to the Grand Master in view of his losses from the fire.[27] The Committee on the State of the Country delivered their report, which was adopted by the Grand Lodge. This report included a tribute to organized labor:

> Our country is passing through a period of unprecedented prosperity. Our mills and factories are working overtime to supply the wants of a world trade that has been revived by passing of the late great war. The farmer is reaping and preparing to reap the greatest harvest in years. The average earners of this country, the great laborers of modern civilization are the highest paid and the best protected wage earners in the world. The American Federation of Labor, the greatest and most powerful labor organization in the world, under the leadership of that grand old man, Samuel Gompers, has battered down the door of racial discrimination in this great organization and extended the panoply of protection to all men regardless of race or color.[28]

Grand Secretary McDonald presented an address, entitled "Now What of the War?" He reflected on Masonic racism after World War I, stating:

> True, a few years ago, a Grand Lodge composed of white Americans here and yonder like the Most Worshipful Grand Lodge, State of Washington, showed signs of beginning to suspect that they may have been a bit hasty when they repudiated, rewrote, and revised the Ancient Landmarks, Constitutions, Monitors, and Rituals of Free Masonry and cut themselves off from all fraternal relations with us, that they may have acted without knowing all the facts of understanding the reasons and motives that prompted them. But for this or that reason, this dim sign of Masonic Fraternity was squelched and the Grand and lofty tenets of Free Masonry were stifled to death on American soil in the house of its so-called friends.[29]

He further observed:

> All colors of soldiers in France have been welcomed with open arms by English and French brethren, who have clasped them to their warm hearts with glad tears of joy. Side by side and shoulder to shoulder, they have fought in the trenches, panning out their mingled hearts blood in order that color-hate and prejudice may be washed from the earth and the world made safe for Masonic Fraternity. Should men, such as these, suffer any rule or regulation to keep them from uniting in the bonds of brotherhood at the altar of Free Masonry? Can the white Mason let the colored Mason die for the same principles, and yet refuse to take him by the hand?[30]

In his Grand Master's Address delivered during the first year of the new decade—the "Roaring Twenties"—Winn acknowledged the works of his many predecessors in the Grand East:

> Forty-five years have been counted in the journey of our existence as a Grand Lodge, each forming a "book" for the "records" of the year in which it was made, and each will serve to enlighten or guide the craftsman in his work.

The "first volume" contained three books, or years of administration, headed by the Hon. Norris Wright Cuney. This will be known always as the "formative period" of Masonry for the Free and Accepted Masons in Texas. The "second volume," containing two books, or years of administration, was the work of Grand Masters Allen and James. Then we were presented with the volume containing the works or administration of the Rt. Rev. Abram Grant, followed by Most Worshipful C. C. Dean, Josiah Armstrong, John W. Madison, W. L. Kimbrough, and the constructive, progressive and aggressive, Most Worshipful John W. McKinney. The volume of the last named, containing twenty books or years of administration.[31]

In the same address he presented the Masonic ideal: "Masonry should make visible improvement upon every one of us that believe in its teachings. Masonry must produce big-hearted, loyal, and high-minded men. But never let it be said that Masonry produces cheats, cowards, and traitors."[32]

Prominent at the 1920 Grand Lodge session was Rev. W. R. Carson, who was described as "the oldest Mason in Texas." Carson had the distinguished honor of having assisted in setting up the first lodges in Texas in March 1873, under Capt. William D. Matthews, Grand Master of the National Grand Lodge. His speech to the brethren was well received, and other elderly Masons in attendance confirmed the truth of his remarks.[33] Past Grand Master McKinney was appointed as Grand Lecturer due to the incapacity of William Coleman, who had suffered a back injury.[34] The Grand Lodge adopted a proposal that no one be permitted to serve as Worshipful Master without securing a certificate of ritualistic proficiency.[35] The Committee on Grievances issued its report, which included the following interesting case:

Austin Alexander vs. Mt. Moriah Lodge No. 234, P. A. Coleman, W. M. Henderson, Texas. Alexander was sent to the penitentiary (murder), and then pardoned. Before being pardoned he had been suspended from his lodge. He now wants to be re-instated. Since he is restored to citizenship by the state, it is up to the lodge to decide about re-instating him.[36]

In his 1921 Grand Master's Address, Winn spoke of Masons as "Pathfinders" and pointed out that Freemasonry, culture, and civilization are inseparably linked.[37] He stated that, wherever art flourishes, Masonry flourishes.[38] He spoke of Masonic opposition to intolerance, bigotry, and superstition. He expressed the following opinion regarding the causes of World War I: "Remember that spites and disagreements, born of hate, are not the common, universal, fellowship fraternity upon which true Masonry is based. These private piques and quarrels fermented the great world war that cost mothers, fathers, sons, daughters, wives, and husbands of every nationality much blood and tears through these accursed fires of hatred."[39] In spite of these realities, however, he reaffirmed his belief in the unity of the human race.[40] He commended various lodges for their celebration of Saint John's Day on June 24,[41] and he was very pleased to report a steady growth in Masonic membership in recent years.[42] Regarding the "State of the Country," he said:

We have tried to make ourselves believe that the condition of things tend to allow some improvements for the country in general and our people in particular, but, I am afraid to venture to make such a statement: The long cherished hope that a more friendly administration in the federal government would bring relief and give the oppressed people some assurance that a better time was coming; that they would return to "normalcy"; and that unjust actions of courts, discriminations before the bar of justice and race hatred would be ended; that mob violence would cease and that there would be no more lynchings of the weaker race. But alas! we are doomed to disappointment for the same "Order of Things" goes on continuously, and besides, a "New Evil" has been brought forward to terrorize our people and make our homes, families, and lives safe in the boasted "Land of the Free."[43]

He called for the erection of monuments to all Past Grand Masters.[44]

On July 21, 1921, Grand Master Winn, in response to a discussion of the secrecy of Masonic rituals, declared: "Any Worshipful Master in the jurisdiction using Duncan's Ritual in Masonic work hereafter, if known, will be suspended.[45] On the following day, the Committee on the State of the Country submitted the following report:

> We find that just as this country was beginning to emerge from the shadows of one of the most destructive wars that the world has ever known, just as labor and capital seemed to be riding along on the crest of the wave of prosperity and just as the commercial and industrial interests of this country seemed to be reaping the greatest harvest that the world has ever known, the dark clouds of reconstruction and deflation began to rise up in the eastern horizon and to spread its mantle of discontent throughout the length of this erstwhile prosperous country. Prices began to fall, mills and factories began to shut down, laborers were thrown out of employment by the millions. King Cotton, who had wielded a greater influence than the Kaiser of Germany, came down from his throne and lay rotting in the fields because he was not worth the cost of his picking.
>
> Today finds us in the grip of the world panic, but we are proud to say that the future looks brighter than the past. We believe that beyond this dark cloud we can see a silver lining. It appears to your committee that this is a time calling for the most careful, sincere, and prayerful thought on the part of the black man in this country.
>
> With that hydro-headed monster, race prejudice, continually sowing the seed of Jim Crowism, segregation, disenfranchisement, discrimination, and the depression and oppression of our people in a thousand other ways, it is absolutely necessary for us to lay aside our senseless prejudices toward each other and join our religious, educational, and commercial strength together and make one long, strong, and continuous pull for the uplift of the race.
>
> We believe that inter-racial committees should be appointed in every state, county, and community. These committees should be composed of broad-minded, liberal thinking men of both races, men who are willing to do right because it is right to do right.
>
> We find that, notwithstanding the many disadvantages under which our people are laboring, we are building up great religious organizations, educational institutions, fraternal societies and, in the last few years, we have invaded the domains of business and nearly every month we read where the Negroes are organizing big banks and other big industrial and commercial institutions whose capital stock ranges up in the hundreds of thousands of dollars. In our opinion, this indicates a great awakening among our people.[46]

In his 1922 Grand Master's Address, Winn spoke on the unavoidable subject of death, declaring: "We sometimes picture death as coming to destroy. Let us rather picture Christ as coming to save. . . . As we draw near to Death, a solemn gladness should fill our hearts, for death is God's great Morning, lighting up the sky. The night with its terrors, its darkness, its feverish dreams, the eternal passing away; and, when we awake, if we have lived as Masons, it will be into the Sunlight of God."[47] Winn noted the death of Grand Lecturer Joe M. McDonald. He predicted a bright future for Masonry,[48] but lamented the persistence of much social injustice, stating:

> We are made to think, seriously, of the conditions that confront us, and to answer to this Question, "Will the Judge of all the Earth, do right?" is the only consolation that we get for the many injustices the mobs, the impositions placed upon us by those that should be our protectors, the sins that are seen in high places, the discriminations of courts, the deaf ear that is turned to us by those that have power to defend us, and the disregard for the rights and the lives of our people make us long for the time to come when Justice and Truth will predominate the hearts of men and their dealings, we will be treated as other men.
>
> Again, I would admonish the Masonic Craftsmen to be good citizens, keep on the side of right, do good for the evil that is done unto us, looking ever for the day to come, when the God of right will measure out to every man his portion, according to his Works.[49]

On the subject of "Education," he made remarks inclusive of both the intellectual and the spiritual:

> We stand for Education. One of the fundamental pillars of FREE MASONRY is Education. The early promoters of Free Masonry held that education was one of the essentials. We must learn to subdue, learn to improve ourselves, learn to live acceptable, learn to prepare ourselves to fit into that Spiritual Building, that house that is not made with hands, but eternal in the heavens, learn what and when to serve, that the greatest good may be accomplished, and to learn our True relation and Duty to our fellowman. We believe in an education that will make us better than not only gives us knowledge of the things of earth, but will lead us to know that which is Spiritual.[50]

He prayed: "God hasten the day, when the influence of FREE MASONRY will be the controlling influence in every man, in every home, and in every state."[51]

In 1922 the Committee on the State of the Country submitted the following report:

> The condition of our country Politically, Socially, Educationally, Economically, is in an unsettled and uncertain state. . . . The old leadership, the old fundamental doctrines of political, civil, and religious equality are being affected. . . . Questions of race, labor, capital, taxation, finance, production, distribution, transportation, and consumption are being directed and controlled by a leadership that looks righteous. One authority says "where there is no vision the people perish."
>
> The demand for increased wages causes strikes in the basic industries of the country; the contribution of the poorly paid laborer to maintain high prices, increased cost of transportation and higher wages of the more highly paid laborer; the fluctuation in money values; the measure of wealth; the decrease in returns to the farmer for his

products against the increased profits and dividends to the large builders of the corporate interest of this country. All these alone are causing men to assemble in various kinds of organizations in the home or the street corners, to determine what ought, what must and will be done to bring us back to the primordial idea of the government of all the states, what will most benefit permanently and not what will temporarily please the people.[52]

The Committee expressed hope that the Dyer Anti-Lynch Law then before the United States Senate would pass.[53]

In his 1923 Grand Master's Address, Winn spoke of the death of the Grand Tiler, G. W. Leonard, whom he described as "a stalwart workman, a leader of lodges, and a designer worthy of emulation."[54] He commended various lodges for their success in erecting buildings and purchasing property. Regarding the "State of the Country," he said:

In this Twentieth Century age in which we live, when commercial activities take the leading part in the shaping of the destinies of Races, Nations, and Governments, we need not wonder if in the scuffle for supremacy the strong should oppress the weak, the rich should legislate against the poor, the wise and learned should spurn and ignore the outcast and ignorant; that labor should be arrayed against capital, or that the whites should be unfriendly to the man of color.[55]

In August 1922 the International Masonic Congress was held in Washington, D.C. Grand Master Winn desired to attend but was unable to do so because of poor health. William Coleman, who had recovered from his back injury and resumed his duties as Grand Lecturer, represented him at this meeting.[56] Coleman gave the following report to the Grand Lodge:

The Council met in the beautifully constructed and tastily arranged Scottish Rite Temple of the Southern Jurisdiction of the United States of America. The Conference was opened with an address of welcome, carefully and thoughtfully prepared by Grand Master Mitchell of the District of Columbia, a young man born in Navasota, Texas, and who is constructing under his plans a Masonic Temple in Washington at a cost of three hundred fifty thousand dollars ($350,000). . . . A committee was sent to memorialize the President of the United States, asking his consideration of the deplorable condition of our people in this country and that he use his influence toward their relief as far as could be done by governmental regulations. The committee was made up of Grand Masters.[57]

On July 15, 1924, Grand Master Winn delivered his final address before the Grand Lodge. Regarding the "State of the Country," he observed:

The organized life of Our Country is struggling in its Commercial, Educational, Spiritual, Fraternal, and Political Organism, to attain perfect Standards and Ideals of Liberty, Fraternity, and Equality.

The Commercial life of our group is advancing, but not as rapidly as our consuming power guarantees. Everywhere we note efforts on a small scale, by our people to secure a foothold of a creditable and profitable nature. In every way we should lend

our aid and encouragement to such attempts, and to see to it that as far as we Masons are concerned, that they do not fail, but become powerful, permanent fixtures in their several communities. Our schools and colleges are raising their standards, by which they are enticing a large number of our youths to take advantage of the preparation they furnish for useful lives.

We note with pleasure the increasing number of graduates from our high schools and colleges of all kinds—North and South. It is an omen of highest standards of activity, that will secure to our young people a share, as factors in the varied, intelligent operations of mankind.

The tendency toward better remunerative and permanent tenure borders the flowers of gratitude are blooming, exhaling the fragrance of rural schools that will secure longer terms, better classification, and the highest courses of learning, demand our careful consideration.

Questions affecting our Civic Life, and that demand righteous settlement at the ballot box, render it necessary for each of us to see to it, that we qualify ourselves in every way required by law, that we might cast an intelligent ballot, in every and all State or National contests, that are dependent upon the suffrage of all citizens.

Numerous propositions are being put before the citizens of our State and Nation for settlement this year; therefore, all men should formulate the habit of expressing their opinions at the ballot box, by voting in all Local, State, and National elections. Casting a ballot is one of the most important duties that a citizen can perform, and failure to practice this habit, by whatever way, might prove destruction to our Liberty, Happiness, and Independence.[58]

In conclusion, the ailing Grand Master said:

The pathway to happiness is paved with good deeds. Along its borders the flowers of gratitude are blooming, exhaling the fragrance of Love.

The most useful Life, the sweetest satisfaction, the serenest conscience, are the results of the joy of Service.

God has made no mistakes, and He has made happiness the reward of those who undertake to assist their fellows in the bearing of their burdens.

One of the most Sensible, Holy, and Wisest prayers that we can pray is this: "Grant us, Oh God, that we may make each day of use to someone."

The records will speak for us and submitting these concluding words, we are Conscious of the fact that others could have done better, yet we submit that all within us have been given to you.

"That man is great, and he alone,
Who serves a greatness not his own,
For neither praise nor pelf."[59]

At this session, Grand Senior Warden S. J. Johnson announced his departure from Texas as a result of assuming the duties of Secretary of Church Extension for the AME Church—an office to which he had been elected by the 1924 AME General Conference. He thanked the brethren for conferring on him honors which had helped him to obtain this high church office. He concluded by saying "I shall always regard Texas as my home, shall retain my membership in Beacon Light No. 50 and, when summoned to cross that bar, I want Texas Masons to take charge of my remains."[60] Bro. Birch, a blind Mason from Dallas, presented a Parker pen to Bro. Johnson, who said that his first use of the pen would be in writing his report on charity.[61] On July 17 Grand Master Winn presented Bishop McKinney, who gave a history of Masonry in Texas and suggested that proper steps be taken for fitting observance of the Grand Lodge's fiftieth anniversary in 1925.[62] Later that day, a committee was appointed to make plans for this jubilee celebration, with Winn as chairman.[63] It is sad that the Grand Master did not live long enough to participate in this historic event.

Winn had been ill during early 1924, but his condition improved enough that he was able to attend Grand Lodge. Shortly after the grand session, he suffered a relapse. He was admitted to a sanitarium at Battle Creek, Michigan. He spent over six weeks in that facility. On his return to Dallas, he seemed greatly improved. Soon, however, he again was stricken. Despite treatment by a number of specialists, he grew progressively worse. The end came at 5:00 P.M. on Saturday, February 28, 1925. He died at his home, with his wife and children present.[64] The cause of death was endocarditis.[65]

A special Communication of the Grand Lodge was held in the hall of Paul Drayton Lodge No. 9 in Dallas on Wednesday, March 4, 1925. Deputy Grand Master John Adrian Kirk was elected and installed as Winn's successor in the Grand East.[66] The newly elected Grand Master issued his first order:

> WHEREAS, Our Most Worshipful Henderson D. Winn, Grand Master, passed away Saturday, February 28, 1925, at 5:00 P.M., and
> WHEREAS, It is the desire and wishes of his beloved family, that he be given a Masonic burial: Now know ye that by power in me vested; an Occasional Grand Lodge is hereby called to meet in the Hall of Paul Drayton Lodge No. 9, at 10 o'clock Wednesday morning, March 4, 1925, for the purpose of taking charge of the body of our lamented Brother and bury it in accord with the Ancient Customs, Ceremonies, and Masonic usage of Free Masons and not otherwise.
> It is further ordered and decreed that all masters of Lodges holding allegiance to the Most Worshipful Grand Lodge of Texas, and its Jurisdiction drape their halls and official stations in mourning for a period of 30 days, in respect of our deceased Grand Master H. D. Winn.
> All Grand Lodge Officers and Master Masons who attend the Funeral of Grand Master H. D. Winn must be clothed in plain white aprons and gloves. No dress aprons can be worn. Herein take due and timely notice and govern yourselves accordingly.[67]

During the special session, H. C. Logan moved that the Grand Lodge assume the funeral expenses of the deceased Grand Master. The motion was duly seconded and passed. Grand Master Kirk then appointed the following brethren as pallbearers: W. S. Smith, D. L. Mackey, W. J. Perry, H. J. Mitchell, G. D. Smith, and B. J. Mashack.[68] Grand Marshal Candy Johnson led the assembled Masons in a procession from the home of Past Grand Master Winn. They carried his corpse in a funeral march down Flora Street to Ross, thence to Buford, thence to Leonard to Bethel AME Church, the site of the funeral. The eulogy was delivered by Past Grand Senior Warden S. J. Johnson.

Telegrams and letters of condolence were received from numerous individuals, including Grand Recorder W. D. Cain of Waco, CME Bishop John Wesley McKinney of Sherman, Past Grand Master John W. Madison of Austin, Grand Lecturer William Coleman of El Paso, and AME Bishop William Decker Johnson of Plains, Georgia.[69]

Messages of comfort were received from a number of organizations, both Masonic and non-Masonic.[70] Winn's funeral—which was conducted by People's Undertaking Company—was one of the largest funerals ever witnessed in Dallas. Masonic graveside services in Woodland Cemetery were conducted by Grand Master Kirk.[71]

On June 16, 1925, Kirk delivered his first Grand Master's Address, saying:

> Brethren, we come together this year under peculiar circumstances. For fifty years we have been laboring zealously for the advancement and the furtherance of the mystic tie of Free Masonry.... In these years we have never met before without the Grand head whom we had entrusted to oversee the work of this Jurisdiction for the year. As you know, on the evening of February 28, about five o'clock, our Grand Master was translated to the Supreme Grand Lodge above where he has greeted the Past Masters—Dean, Cuney, Grant, Armstrong, and others who have gone before. Hence it was left to us to carry on the work laid out by our Grand head, Prof. H. D. Winn.... Brethren, so it seems; it matters not how often we may see and greet each other, we may associate here for 25, 30, 40, or 50 years and yet when the summons comes it seems that we have just passed spoken one to another, then darkness and finally silence forever.
>
> Does it not seem so with those we have met here for years and especially with our Grand Master? ... Brethren too often are we reminded that death is certain, hence it behooves us to prepare for that eternal silence for it is said, that no sooner do we begin to live than we begin to die. Life is but a span; we are here to-day and to-morrow we are gone.
>
> As William Cullen Bryant says: "Let us live that when the summons comes we may wrap the drapery of our couch about us and lie down to pleasant dreams."[72]

Henderson D. Winn was a superb leader for Prince Hall Masons in Texas during World War I and the "years of normalcy." He did a good job training his very able successor—John Adrian Kirk—whose destiny was to lead the Grand Lodge into a new decade.

John Adrian Kirk

John Adrian Kirk (1860-1934) was the twelfth Grand Master of Prince Hall Masons in Texas. Of all the Texas Grand Masters, he was the only one who called Waco home.[1] Like others who occupied the Grand East, he contributed much to his community, his church, and humanity, in accordance with the principles he learned at the Masonic altar.

John Adrian Kirk was born on April 6, 1860, in Barnsville, Ohio. Later, his parents—Mr. and Mrs. Adrian Kirk—moved to Bellaire, Ohio. He graduated from Bellaire High School. He was the first black student at the latter institution. From Bellaire he went to Wilberforce University in Xenia, Ohio, graduating in 1886. His graduating class included Revs. Reverdy Cassius Ransom and John Hurst, both destined to become bishops in the AME Church.[2]

Kirk married Nettie A. Hamilton in 1889.[3] The first two years of their marriage were spent in Georgia, where he taught school. In 1891 they moved to Paris, Texas, where he served for two years as a principal of a local school.[4] In 1893 they moved to Waco, where he served as an instructor and administrator at Paul Quinn College for twelve years.[5]

Kirk became the second principal of Second District Negro School in 1905, following the death of the school's founder, A. J. Moore. He did much to develop this institution, hiring the pioneer faculty members, whose names have become well known in the history of Waco's African-American community. Such people included G. L. Wiley, Mrs. A. V. Jones, W. S. Willis, Mrs. M. D. Jackson, Mrs. Dinah Russel, Mrs. P. A. Talton, Mrs. Mary E. Moore, and Mrs. A. B. Thomas.[6]

When the frame schoolhouse over which Kirk presided was destroyed by fire, he led a community building drive. As a result, a new brick building was erected in 1923. At that time, Second District Negro School was renamed A. J. Moore High School in honor of its founder.[7]

Ometa White, a graduate of Moore High, recalled that Kirk tried to help students to believe in themselves—to instill a sense of self-confidence. She said he had a nice smile and a pleasing personality. She also remembered his having a good sense of humor.[8] Another former student, Henry Flowers, stated: "I don't think we could have had a better man down there."[9] Gladys Reed, who lived next door to Kirk for many years, recalled him as a kind person "who believed in doing right." She stated that he always "had a nice car" and "was nicely dressed."[10]

Kirk was an active member of Saint Paul AME Church in Waco. O. E. Wilhite, who worshiped at Saint Paul while a student at Paul Quinn College during the 1920s, recalled Kirk as a steward and an outstanding churchman.[11] John Q. Daniels, who joined Saint Paul in 1920, remembered Kirk as a Sunday school teacher and often saw him lift the Sunday offering. He stated: "He was a quiet man, highly dignified. He went about his affairs in more or less a dignified manner."[12] Eucolia Erby, a graduate of Moore High, remembered that Kirk was involved with the Red Cross and a number of other charitable organizations and led fund-raising efforts for such during an era before the establishment of the United Way. Recalling Kirk's involvement with the Knights of Pythias as well as the Masons, he stated that, in those days, everyone of any prominence in Waco's African-American community was either a Mason or a Pythian.[13]

Kirk served for a number of years as Worshipful Master of Mount Moriah Lodge No. 6 in Waco. He became very active in the Grand Lodge, arising to the office of Deputy Grand Master. He was promoted to the highest office in Freemasonry following the death of Grand Master Henderson D. Winn on February 28, 1925. At Winn's funeral on March 4, 1925, Kirk presided as Grand Master for the first time.[14]

At the 1925 Communication, a collection of $51.89 was taken and presented to a Bro. Leonard who had had the misfortune of being robbed of all of his cash on the previous night. Grand Master Kirk noted the fact that Bro. Leonard was the only member present who had attended the Grand Lodge's 1875 organizational meeting at Brenham.[15]

On June 18, 1925, the newly elected Grand Master received a telegram of congratulations from Grand Chancellor W. S. Willis on behalf of 25,000 members of the Knights of Pythias.[16] Commendations were given to Professor W. O. Bundy for completion of a biography of Grand Secretary William Madison "Gooseneck Bill" McDonald. Craftsmen were encouraged to purchase the book.[17] Joint memorial services were held for Past Grand Master Winn, with Masons, Eastern Stars, and Heroines of Jericho participating. The memorial address was delivered by Grand Secretary McDonald. At the conclusion of the meeting, Kirk was reelected as Grand Master.[18]

On June 15, 1926, Grand Master Kirk was presented with a gavel by L. R. Reed of Gonzales, Texas. This gavel was made from wood taken from a tree at Santanna Mound. In this presentation, Reed declared:

> Under this tree once stood the Hon. N. W. Cuney, the first Grand Master of Masons of Texas, when he was here in the interest of Hon. R. B. Hawley of Galveston, who were [sic] running for Congressman. Also under this tree once stood that famous Mexican General Santa-Anna; Also the late H. D. Winn stood under this tree and conversed with the members of Olive Leaf Lodge; and also the same place was visited by the Hon. Wm. M. McDonald, the man who [sic] the members of my lodge have the very highest regards for.[19]

In his 1926 Grand Master's Address, Kirk stated:

> Brethren, We come to you for the first time after having been your unanimous choice for the exalted position which I have the honor of holding.
>
> To be unanimously selected the head of a great Masonic jurisdiction such as ours is a position, the honor of which is worthy to be appreciated by any Potentate or King.
>
> In the twenty-five years in which I have been a constant attendant in this Grand Jurisdiction in which I have held many positions both appointive and elective, I have the first time to ask any brother to support me for any position for which I have been chosen. Hence the more sincerely do I appreciate and thank you for this great honor which I accept with timidity. . . . I believe firmly, my friends, that if we give the very best we have in us for any good cause, God will so arrange it that in some way the best will come back to us. Don't you remember the words of that inspired writer: "Be not deceived, God is not mocked, whatever you sow you will reap"? . . . We talk about our fraternal Societies but I tell you there is very little fraternalism practiced in any of our fraternal organizations. "Am I my brother's keeper?" rings down through the ages today as it did in the days when God said "Where is thy brother?" If we do not practice brotherly love then we are losing sight of one of the first principles of our profession. . . . Brethren, there is nothing selfish in Masonry, there is nothing in Masonry that does not in some way relate to the good of someone else. . . . The last tenet of our profession is that divine attribute which is eternal. And that is the reason Bryant says: "Truth crushed to earth shall rise again."[20]

On the following day, Kirk permitted W. O. Bundy the opportunity to speak about the book he had written.[21] That afternoon, Prof. N. A. Banks, acting president of Paul Quinn College, was introduced. Banks was Kirk's classmate in Ohio. He told of his work and stressed the importance of education.[22] Mrs. R. E. McKinney, the wife of Bishop John Wesley McKinney, brought greetings on behalf of the Heroines of Jericho.[23] These greetings were followed by a response from Grand Recorder W. D. Cain of Waco. Cain, who had a reputation as a humorist, said:

> I am sure the Grand Master does not desire to detract from this felicitous occasion by "raising Cain." We are really proud . . . beyond measure to have you with us. Before the speaker had said the words we noticed (admiringly) that this committee was all young and good-looking. That's another way of saying an article is "all wool and a yard wide." We do not object to you going into the right hand and left hand pockets of our pants. We only object to you "wearing the pants." . . . We love the Heroines of Jericho.[24]

In his 1927 Grand Master's Address, Kirk said:

> I feel that we ought to compliment ourselves as belonging to the greatest fraternal organization in the world. . . . I am sure, my friends, you have noticed that we have made very few lodges this year, not because men do not want to become masons, but this has been a very bad year financially.
>
> The year 1925 saw a great drought in some parts of the state and nothing was made; 1926 saw a great abundance of cotton but there was so much made until there was very little offered for it. In other words, the price was so small that farmers would not pay for picking it.

Added to this came the floods and the storms and our people were the sufferers. We have had some of the Halls of our lodges blown down; we have had some of our people deprived of their homes by destructive fires.

Only a few of our folks in the rurals can get insurance and, in almost every instance where these fires occurred, everything was a total loss.

In some of these towns where we have lodges, the brethren cannot buy property to put up a hall and, in other places, especially in some small towns, very few of our people can get work; they are told by the employers they are going to be forced to look more closely after our own folks and put our moneys together and give our people something to do that they may be able to support themselves.[25]

At the 1927 session of the Grand Lodge, note was made of the fact that the recent litigation involving the Grand Lodge and the Indemnity Bonding Company of Kansas City marked the first suit of record where a black institution was able to recover money from a bonding company on account of default by its officers.[26] The same session included the following tragic note:

Bro. (Bishop) J. W. McKinney said he had gone to Waco Palm Sunday to preach for the craftsmen. On arrival, he found death had entered the home of Bro. Cain, our Recorder, and claimed his youngest son, McDonald. He moved that the Masters of the Waco lodges on their return home, place a floral wreath upon the young man's grave. Motion seconded, put, and carried.[27]

Kirk delivered his fourth Grand Master's Address on June 26, 1928. In this speech, he stressed the need for qualified Worshipful Masters.[28] He pointed out that, at the time, there was little insurance available in the black community besides that provided by fraternal orders. In relation to this, he stated that Masonic relief dues were lower than the relief dues assessed by other organizations.[29] He chastised one Masonic lodge for renting their quarters from a Knights of Pythias lodge, urging them to purchase their own property.[30] Kirk called for more public display of the orders of York Rite Masonry.[31] In the following eloquent words, he asked "Who is a real brother?":

Brethren, this has been a year when God has called a goodly number of our brethren from labor to reward. Do occasions like this, my friends, bring to your mind days when you have met brethren in these halls, men whom you considered real friends, men who had been to you like real brothers, men who would not meet you, shake your hand, smile in your face and try to injure you behind your back. Brethren, that reminds us that every man who says he is a brother and who ought to be a real brother to you is not a brother. I tell you my friends it behooves us to live so brethren, with whom we have associated here, in the beautiful beyond. Think of it, we have lost a number of members who were with us this time last year but they have laid aside this mortal and put on immortality. Year after year we are impressed with the fact that life is fleeting. We are here today but tomorrow may never come. Again, it behooves us not to put off duty but labor while it is day.[32]

The Grand Lodge voted 935 to 345 to raise relief dues from $10 to $14 per year.[33]
On June 17, 1929, over 5,000 Masons, Heroines of Jericho, Eastern Stars, and

their friends assembled in the Masonic Mosque in Fort Worth to hear a report of thirty years of service by Grand Secretary McDonald.[34] At this meeting it was noted that when McDonald took office in 1899 there were 1,504 Prince Hall Masons in Texas; by 1929, the number had grown to 20,294.[35] No doubt McDonald's tireless efforts contributed much to this increase in membership.

In his fifth Grand Master's Address, Kirk made the following proposals which remain worthy of consideration today:

> Some Masters think simply to be elected Master of a lodge is the height of his ambition. He never has a meeting, he never studies the interest of his men nor the interest of his lodge. . . . I recommend that Masters of local lodges are instructed and commanded to hold one regular communication at least each lunar month in the year and failure to do so, he is by such failure automatically moved from office and the Senior Warden of said lodge will function as Master till the next regular election in said lodge. Difficulties because of illness or such inclemencies of weather that will prohibit such meeting may be an excusable cause for failure of holding meeting.[36]

The Grand Lodge donated to Paul Quinn College in Waco, Guadalupe College in Seguin, and Texas College in Tyler in the amount of $125 each.[37] June 20 was set aside as a day to honor the Grand Secretary.[38] The Committee on Education made the following report:

> Another step forward is indicated in the recent act of one of the northern educational societies in transferring one of its old landmark schools, Bishop College, from a longstanding white management to that of our group, with a Texas man as president, in the person of Prof. J. J. Rhoads. This is a score for both Texas as a state and the Negro as a factor in education.[39]

In 1930, due to declining health, Grand Master Kirk decided not to seek reelection. Thus he was succeeded in office by Deputy Grand Master William Coleman.[40]

By 1930, both Kirk and his wife were facing serious health problems. As a result, Catherine Jackson, the niece of Nettie Kirk, moved to Waco from Ohio in order to look after them. She reported that her uncle experienced a number of strokes following his retirement. However, she said, he remained fairly active between 1930 and 1933. During the last year of his life, she recalled, he was bedridden.[41] He died on September 29, 1934. His death certificate, which is filed at the City of Waco Bureau of Vital Statistics, lists the causes of his death as "Apoplexy" and "Bright's Disease." His funeral was held at Saint Paul AME Church. Masonic graveside services were conducted at Greenwood Cemetery.[42] He was survived by his wife, their niece, and a sister named Mrs. Ross, a resident of Philadelphia, Pennsylvania.[43]

A report of his funeral that appeared in a local African-American newspaper included the following words:

> Prof. J. A. Kirk, the last to become Past Grand Master of the Free and Accepted Masons of Texas, was laid to rest last Monday amid a simple, but impressive ceremony participated in by his own local lodge and other masons of the State.
> The funeral oration was delivered by Rev. J. A. Howard, Houston, former pastor

of Saint Paul AME Church, of which the deceased was a member. Short, but brimful of potent words, this sermon could scarcely tell the story of the life of the man whom death had but a short time held in its grasp.

The illness of Prof. Kirk had been of several years duration. Because of it he had been forced to offer his resignation as Grand Master of the Free and Accepted Masons of Texas, being succeeded by the present Grand Master, Prof. Wm. Coleman.

Among out of town Masons present at the funeral were Grand Master Coleman, Grand Secretary Wm. McDonald, Col. L. D. Lyons, and others.[44]

In his eulogy, Howard said of Kirk:

> He was a man of convictions. When he came to apprehend the realities of life illuminated by the realities of divine truth, it was in no negative mood, but with a vivid experience which made them his own. Faith was the substance standing under his personality. . . . . He was not a rover or a shifter, playing fast and loose with duty, but an earnest man, who having found truth, planted himself on it with a firmness invincible. . . . He could no more bear a sham than be a sham himself. He had no hiding place even for his faults. . . . He sympathized with human life in every stage and experience.
>
> The sorrows and struggles of others became his own. His consolations were swift to offer all his resources. Wherever you heard his name mentioned you seemed to hear the beat of a big heart. As one stands upon a steamer's deck and feels the engine and knows he is near force that helps him over the waves, so his friends were propelled by his power against adverse currents and over the crest of difficulties.[45]

The aforementioned newspaper published the following editorial at the time of Kirk's passing:

> One by one the individuals among us who have done constructive things toward race building in the first quarter of this century pass off the scene. The last among Wacoans to go was Prof. J. A. Kirk, a beloved character because of his kindly disposition and sympathetic nature.
>
> For years Prof. Kirk taught school. For many of these years he was principal of Moore High School. He left the school room to devote his time to Masonry among colored men of Texas. His health failed, many think, because of his too conscientious service—the woes of the people rested too heavily upon him and his years. He never recovered and a day or two ago amid friends and following a short impressive ceremony he was laid to rest. May we utter the oft repeated wish relative to the beloved dead—"Requiescat in pace."[46]

It has often been said that "behind (or beside) every great man, there is a woman." This was certainly true in the case of John Adrian Kirk. He and his wife, Nettie A. Kirk, were married for forty-five years. She not only gave him moral support in all of his endeavors but also had a remarkable career of her own. She was more than just "the Grand Master's wife" and deserves more than passing reference in this biographical sketch.

Nettie A. Kirk was born in Bellaire, Ohio, where she received her common school education. She attended Oberlin College but withdrew during her junior year due to health problems. She later attended Ohio Wesleyan College at Delaware, Ohio. She taught school in Greenville, Kentucky, and served as assistant principal of Cottonwood School near Paris, Texas. After moving to Waco, she became principal of the Normal Department at Paul Quinn College and held this position from 1893 to 1908.[47]

Mrs. Kirk was quite active in various fraternal orders, including the Order of the Eastern Star and the Heroines of Jericho. In 1908 she was initiated into Carnation Court No. 44, Order of Calanthe. In 1914 she was elected Grand Secretary-Treasurer of Endowment of the Grand Court, Texas Jurisdiction, of this ladies' auxiliary to the Knights of Pythias. In the latter capacity, she reportedly handled more money than any officer of any black state fraternal order in America. She held this office for many years and, in view of her reputation for efficiency, honesty, and thrift, she never had an opponent when she ran for reelection.[48] Mrs. Kirk maintained an office in her Waco home. This office was locked at all times. Auditors would come, lock themselves in the office, and audit the books of the Grand Court. Two secretaries came to the Kirk home and assisted her in performing her duties. This office contained a very tall safe. As a young girl, Catherine Jackson was not permitted to enter this office for any reason.[49]

Mrs. Kirk was an active member of Saint Paul AME Church, served on the Board of Joyce Stamps Day Nursery, was active in securing the Phyllis Wheatley Library for Waco, worked with the Young Women's Christian Association and the Community Chest, and was a member of Waco's Interracial Commission.[50]

Mrs. Kirk died at her home on April 6, 1941. Her funeral was held at Saint Paul AME Church.[51] The service included the following:

> Processional; music, Paul Quinn Choral Club; Resolution from the Knights of Pythias; Resolution from Grand Court Order of Calanthe; Music, St. Paul Junior Choir; Remarks by Bishop G. B. Young, presiding bishop of Texas, AME Church; Resolution, St. Paul AME Church; Obituary; Sermon, Rev. J. L. Alexander, pastor, St. Paul Church; "Nearer My God to Thee." Grand Court officers served as honorary pallbearers; Trustees of St. Paul were active pallbearers.
>
> The sermon was brief, with comforting words to those who mourned. Like a breath of spring, a renewed hope was born as Rev. Alexander pointed out the moments built by Mrs. Kirk by a serviceable life which she lived down through the years in movements fostered, in persons helped, and in friendships made.
>
> The entire services were under the auspices of the Grand Court Order of Calanthe, Jurisdiction of Texas and Carnation Court No. 44, Waco, of which Mrs. Kirk was a member, assisted by White Rose Court No. 33, and Pride of Waco Court No. 238, Waco. At the conclusion of the services, resolutions, telegrams and cards were filed with Mrs. P. E. Davis, Grand Worthy Counsellor, for publication. Interment was made in Greenwood Cemetery with Ellis Funeral Home in charge. Hundreds of persons accompanied Mrs. Kirk on her final journey.[52]

Following the death of this highly esteemed member, the Court of Calanthe established Nettie Kirk Court No. 472 in Waco.[53]

John and Nettie Kirk were truly a remarkable couple. While they had no children of their own, they served as parental figures and positive role models for several generations of young people in Waco. Their contributions to education, to community life, to the AME Church, and to fraternalism were great indeed. Waco is a better city and Texas is a better state as a result of the legacy of John and Nettie Kirk!

William Coleman

William Coleman (1876-1946) was the thirteenth Grand Master of Prince Hall Masons in Texas. His tenure of office included the time of the Great Depression during the 1930s and World War II during the 1940s. These were difficult times for all Americans, and African Americans especially were hit hard by these tragic events. Many organizations—black and white—were adversely affected and some were destroyed. In such "times that try men's souls," Coleman left a permanent imprint on Freemasonry in Texas. At the time of his death in 1946, a reporter observed:

> As the most worshipful grand master of the F and AM, he led in the completion of the mosque and establishment around the mosque of the playground which not only makes it a monument to Masonary (sic), but a beacon light of Negro enterprises for all to behold.
> Probably most significant of his leadership was the fact that the F & AM was one of the few men's fraternal societies in Texas, if not the only one, to come through the depression without any loss of property, or substantial decrease in its steady building impulse.[1]

William Coleman was born in Georgia on August 10, 1876, the son of Luke and Bertha Jackson Coleman. His father was a native of Georgia, while his mother was a native of Virginia.[2] He attended public schools in Georgia and received his higher education at Howard University in Washington, D.C. and Brown University in Providence, Rhode Island. He served as an instructor in Greek, Latin, and Modern Languages at Benedict College in Columbia, South Carolina.[3] It was perhaps while he was at Benedict that he met his wife Emma, a native of South Carolina, whom he married around 1901.[4] From all indications the couple had no children.

Coleman came to Texas as a young man and served for a while as assistant principal at a high school in Fort Worth. In 1908 he moved to El Paso, where he served nineteen years as principal of Douglass High and Grammar School. According to a history of his administration:

> He started his principalship in September of 1908. 260 bright faced youngsters greeted him the first year that he was here. This was the largest enrollment to date and was an increase of thirteen over the previous year. 136 of these were girls. . . . when Prof. Coleman was initiated into the new duties as principal, there were only four rooms in the building. One of the very first things that he did was to secure the money and the authority from the school board to construct an additional four rooms and a small scale experimental room for work in chemistry, physics, domestic science, domestic art, and manual training which was later added. The other subjects were new and unfamiliar to the students, especially the sciences.[5]

At Douglass, the Coleman administration was marked by many "firsts." On December 20, 1910, a midyear physical culture exercise and musical entertainment was sponsored by the school and held at Second Baptist Church. That same year, a joint fair was held with El Paso High School—the first interracial fair in the history of El Paso.[6] According to the same history:

> William Coleman was very sincere in his desire to see the school progress. This was evidenced by the fact that he spent much of his own money and time to further the work that the school board, students or teachers had started. His personality and willingness to work and contribute to things that concerned the school made him a very much loved and respected teacher. Through his influence and persistency, he gained for the school many things they would not have otherwise had.
>
> About this time, Mexican teams in the city were being formed and many evenings were spent playing these teams and other town teams in many baseball games. These teams were also organized by several Mexican schools and these also afforded opposition for the team from DOUGLASS SCHOOL. Volleyball as well as instrumental football was played by the students.[7]

The 1912 graduating class of ten students was the largest in the history of the school.[8] On May 28, 1914, a musical comedy called "The Captain of Plymouth," built around Henry Wadsworth Longfellow's poem "The Courtship of Miles Standish," was presented at the closing exercise of the school year at the Texas Grand Theatre, which at the time was El Paso's most fashionable theatre. The building was crowded to its capacity for this outstanding production.[9] Presentation of a play became an annual event. The play for 1918, entitled "The Nautical Knot," was performed before an interracial audience at the Crawford Theatre, with an orchestra providing the musical background. The class of 1918, in commemoration of the apparent ending of the First World War and the signing of the Armistice, placed an American flag draped about a staff on their graduation invitations. The class motto was "Liberty or Death."[10]

On July 14, 1919, the school entertained the Seventh Cavalry at Fort Bliss with an appreciative program at the Army YMCA. The building was overcrowded with soldiers who were so captivated by the program (which included a "Medley of Plantation Songs") that they requested a repetition of the performance in the near future.[11]

The Coleman administration was marked by occasional parties and socials in the school basement. These were always properly chaperoned by the teachers. One of the

72

students, Oliver Bendall, was quite adept at the piano and always furnished music for the dancing.[12]

Around 1920, Coleman was involved in an automobile accident in which he sustained a serious back injury. As a result, he was forced to wear a brace. However, this did not prevent the continuance of his school work.[13]

Douglass School's first football game was played on Armistice Day in 1920. Their principal opponent in the coming years was Beall School in El Paso. They also played against a number of Mexican-American teams in the city.[14]

About this time, a new school was built on a five-acre campus. Douglass and Woodlawn schools were merged, which greatly increased student enrollment. However, the following problems persisted:

> El Paso was still a western town in many respects. Its western atmosphere and distance from many Negro cities discouraged many Negroes from coming to El Paso, Texas. The scarcity of good and adequate employment also was one of the prime factors in keeping them away. This affected the growth of the school because it did not present the opportunity of adding more students. Although many people came here for their health, a possible equal number left the city for other places. One of the reasons that the school did not receive more things than it did from the school board was because of the small enrollment, as compared to that of other city schools.[15]

The new building included a small chemistry laboratory. Over time, a larger supply of chemicals was provided. Coleman served as the chemistry teacher for a number of years but was eventually forced to give up teaching in view of increased demands of his administrative post.[16]

The new building was the site of an increasing number of parties. The planning of such social events resulted in a conflict which seems to recur in every generation:

> There was still quite a bit of objection by the elder people and those who claimed that their religious beliefs were contrary to these practices, but in the end, they finally succumbed to the buoyant zestful spirit of the younger people.[17]

In the new building, there was an expansion in the school's curriculum. Three foreign languages—Spanish, French, and Latin—were alternately taught, while both English Literature and English History were stressed. Agriculture was also offered, and some other subjects were introduced.[18] The social side of school life was exemplified as follows:

> Dances in the auditorium of the school were held often. The students were allowed to use the auditorium for parties and on nearly all holidays, they had a big party at the school. Halloween, with all of its gayety and funmaking, was one of the most popular holidays of all. Sometimes, the auditorium was used as often as twice a month for class or school parties.
>
> May day was initiated into the school in 1924. This day was an annual holiday for the school, although students were required to be at school. . . . . These field day celebrations were unique and they immediately became popular with the patrons and students of the school. It gave the students an opportunity to show their skill in the various sports and provided their parents and friends with entertainment.[19]

In 1926 Coleman became very ill and thus was unable to perform his duties as principal. His wife was appointed to serve in his place for the rest of the 1926-27 school year. This was his last year as principal, for he resigned before the end of 1927.[20]

It is unclear whether Coleman's resignation was due more to his health or to increasing responsibilities to the Prince Hall Masons of Texas. A member of Sunset Lodge No. 76 in El Paso, he had held a number of Grand Lodge positions, including Grand Lecturer. On July 14, 1911, while serving as Chairman of the Committee on Banking, Coleman presented a report to the Grand Lodge, recommending the immediate organization and establishment of the Masonic Bank and Trust Company. The motion, which was introduced by Grand Secretary William Madison McDonald, gave plenary power to make such arrangements to Grand Master John Wesley McKinney and was carried unanimously by the Grand Lodge.[21] At the 1930 Communication, Grand Master John Adrian Kirk took great pride in reporting the bank's solid condition:

> The Grand Lodge Free and Accepted Masons of Texas and the Grand High Court Heroines of Jericho now control the Fraternal Bank and Trust Company. All of the profits and operating expenses belong to Texas Masons and the Grand Court Heroines of Jericho. It is our bank. . . . The Fraternal Bank and Trust Company has stood the test for 18 years and is as solid as the rocks of Gibraltar. . . . All colored people, and especially all Colored Grand Lodges, Mutual Benefit and Insurance Societies that wish a safe and an accommodating Depository for their checking accounts or their Reserve Funds are invited to put all such funds in the Fraternal Bank and Trust Company and we shall be glad to advance to the beneficiaries of their dead members such help in the way of loans on their claims as the claim will justify and the business system of the Order will warrant or permit.[22]

In 1930 William Coleman was serving as Deputy Grand Master, providing able assistance to Grand Master Kirk, another retired principal. At the 1930 Communication, Kirk was in declining health and chose not to seek reelection. Thus the Grand Lodge selected Coleman as Kirk's very able successor.[23]

Following his election as Grand Master, Coleman relocated from El Paso to Fort Worth—the long-time headquarters of the Grand Lodge. In the latter city, he remained for the rest of his life. His address was 1071 East Humbolt.[24] In 1931 he delivered his first Grand Master's Address, opening with words of homage to recently deceased Prince Hall Masons, including Caesar R. Blake, Chairman of the Committee on Foreign Correspondence of the Grand Lodge of North Carolina; and Jno. G. Lewis, Sr., Grand Master of the Grand Lodge of Louisiana.[25] In this address, he described Masonry as a progressive institution in the following manner:

> For the same purpose as we note in Bible text, the rule and guide of our faith and practice, it is given as a directive agency, helping us in knocking off the rough corners, laying aside the vices and superfluities of this life, that we may so prepare ourselves by righteous light that we may here enjoy a satisfactory modern existence as well as hereafter the felicities of that house not made with hands, eternal in the Heavens.[26]

Grand Master Coleman charged members of the craft to do all in their power to

retain present members and recruit new members.[27] He described fraternalism as "a safe remedy for intolerance, hate, and prejudice." He pointed out that Masonic secrecy and social services are inseparably linked,[28] and declared that Freemasonry seeks to obliterate all distinctions of race, color, and creed. Only ignorance and folly are responsible for an intolerant view of Freemasonry, he said.[29] He presented the message of spiritual rebirth as related to the Master Mason's degree:

> In keeping with the opinions of leading Masons, the essence of the great mystery of M. M.'s degree is spiritual and implies stewardship. It calls to our attention, re-birth, spiritual awakening, spiritual inspiration. As Jesus said to Nicodemus, "Ye must be born again." As one learned English Mason has said: "If there be any spiritual truth at all in the Greater Mysteries of Initiation, which have been recognized in all ages of human experience, surely they must lead to and beyond, THAT GREAT experience." Which I suggest is the true teaching of our third degree, which he calls spiritual re-birth, only the beginning of a new life wherein is the possibility of infinite progress.[30]

He pointed out a number of problems throughout the jurisdiction. For example, at Brackettville, a Worshipful Master and Secretary were found involved in activities which can best be described as "unsquare."[31] At Tenaha, four live Masons were reported dead and money was paid to false beneficiaries.[32] He placed the blame for the loss of members and money on careless and dishonest Secretaries.[33] On the positive side, he reported that "Masonic fever" ran high at a number of district meetings.[34] And he pointed out that the lack of ability on the part of some Masters to create interest in lodge to the degree that members enjoy their regular meetings was responsible for much nonattendance by members.[35] He declared: "Nearly all of the trouble of theft and other dishonesties I find this year arose from many small lodges who have no meetings except at election time. Sometimes I find they don't even have elections. This must and will stop."[36]

As previously stated, Coleman served as Grand Master during the hardships of the Great Depression. At the 1932 Communication, he spoke of how this period was affecting the lodges of Texas:

> The laboring man, the farmer, the business man, the financier, the speculator, the church, social and civic institutions have failed to secure the necessary funds to satisfy their claims and creditors. And I wish to inform the craft that we have not been the exception, for we too have suffered losses in numbers and finances. This then makes it necessary as never before since the inauguration and existence of our corporate existence for you representatives of the Grand Lodge to aid in the creation and hearty support of those plans that will enable us to regain losses in numbers and finances. Struggle harder to revive new life and interest in our Order, your Fraternal Society that possesses the essences in purpose, method, and management that will aid you to safely attain those conditions indispensable to successful maintenance of our needed institution.
>
> I am speaking to you in terms of experience, and not in quotations from any eminent Masonic authority who may not be qualified thru experience of such economic suffering such as has affected us these last two Masonic and calendar years to advise us. May I repeat, no government, corporation, or institution of whatever nature, has in the civilized world, since the time of Pharaoh, had to think and act as we have during this economic crash.[37]

He warned against dropping members from the lodge rolls unnecessarily, asking the following important questions: "How many men are OUT, that by a little effort on your part, you could have so advised them that they would have stayed in the lodge? How many are OUT, that by the exercise of the milk of human kindness would be in your lodge membership?"[38] He painted the following very sad picture:

> The financial conditions of individual Masons, I find in many places, because of lack of money, inability to secure any money, by borrowing, which many did, or by means of employment, to keep themselves square in our Order were pathetic. I have before me, as I speak to you, the vision of many Masons with tears in their eyes, begging that we do not suffer them to be dropped from the roll.
>
> Our membership consisting mostly of farmers and common laborers, have lost their Masonic financial standing because they could in no way raise the means to square themselves. Lodges have strained their financial standing, spent their money to save their needy craftsmen. Speaking for the Grand Lodge, we want you to know that our heartiest good will and brotherly love go out to you bee-hive Masons.[39]

Amid such dire reports, he also called for the following partial solution:

> It is our greatest hope, as a people co-operation. It is not un-Masonic for brothers to assist each other in securing employment wherever possible. Notify each Mason who wants employment of any opportunity to profitable service. In cities all lodges should have a central employment bureau where Masons can find work—places where persons needing employees may leave their requests for any kind of help. . . . We must not forget that the continued material existence of our institution depends upon the financial ability of our devotees to supply the necessary financial aid and they can not render this economic support, unless they are individually, economically able to do so. My statistics, not absolutely correct, point out to you the economic condition of our followers.[40]

He urged members to take advantage of available government services, including New Deal farm programs.[41]

Coleman took very seriously the problems of the Great Depression and their effects on lodge members. In 1936 he issued a dispensation authorizing reduction of initiation and reinstatement fees. The increase in membership which resulted confirmed the wisdom of this order.[42] He reported improvements made at the Grand Lodge Mosque and the use of cash rather than credit to finance such. Thus, he reported, the organization avoided going into debt.[43] As the leader of all Texas Prince Hall Masons, he declared that most excuses presented to him for neglect of duty were unacceptable. He said:

> The excuses for failure to hold regular stated meetings by certain Masters of some lodges are to me trivial and border upon the humorous. . . . if the lodges notified, or any others persist in such fatal neglects, failures, or refusals to hold stated meetings regularly, the Grand Master will be compelled to save Free Masonry from deleterious results in such communities by removing some irresponsible officers and replacing them with more zealous, reliable ones, or take such legal steps as will perpetuate Free Masonry creditably in such a community.[44]

Coleman mentioned the problem—not unknown today—of high death rates among older men accompanied by few initiations of younger men.[45] He pointed out the relation of Freemasonry to common human needs and declared that every community should support the Masonic Lodge, which is beneficial to the Church and other worthwhile institutions.[46] He described plans for collective, mutual assistance through the Bee Hive Investment Fund[47] and praised the common heritage of freedom exemplified by Prince Hall Freemasons.[48]

In his 1937 Grand Master's Address, Coleman observed that, via symbolic expression, allegorical presentation, ritualistic custom, and dramatic practice, Freemasonry points to the perfect social, intellectual, and spiritual standards of living.[49] In this address, he chastised lodges for their failures to measure up to high Masonic standards, declaring:

> Another trouble we are having with some lodges is their irregularity in holding lodge meetings. . . . Again some lodges do not hold elections. The officers are being continued by the hold over process. I am finding out that for varied reasons on the regular meeting night, it becomes impossible to hold an election. These are small lodges and they are not adding to their membership. In numerous cases, they are old men—members of long standing in the Order.
>
> I have threatened to take up their warrants, but because of their constitutional number and their losses through the depression, I haven't had the heart to act. . . .
>
> A lack of knowledge of the nature, the history, the aims, the principles, the teachings and the ritualistic practices of Free Masonry cause many loyal members of our fraternity to lose interest, become indifferent and drop out; the educated young men of our high school and higher institutions of learning become disgusted at the inability of some of the W.M.'s to perform their duties as constitutional officers intelligently. I have seen young men correct ignorant persons initiating them, in their enunciation, pronunciation, and interpretation of their ritualistic statements.[50]

He called upon lodge members to fight against an "increasingly deteriorating economic slavery" and charged all true Masons never to disregard the suffering of the unemployed and the starving.[51] He challenged the craft:

> Then let come what may on mountain top of Masonic ecstasy, or in the valleys of human despondency, amid the onflowing tides of bloody, national, or international revolution, or in the placid streams of internal or external change, we are safe under the aegis of the unchanging customs, traditions, teaching, principle, morals, dramas, laws, and landmarks of an undying spiritual entity Free Masonry.[52]

On June 24, 1937—at the time of the Grand Communication a ceremony was held for the unveiling of the McDonald Memorial, a gray marble stone erected on the north grounds entrance of the Masonic Mosque. This was built in memory of William Madison McDonald, Jr., the only child of the Grand Secretary, who had recently died at Howard University in Washington, D.C. The keynote speaker was Roscoe Conkling Simmons. He was introduced by the Grand Secretary's long-time friend, William H. Burnett of Terrell, Texas.[53] The Committee on the Grand Master's Address reported:

When the wheel of human activities no longer revolve; when the shuttle of patient toil is heard no more, when the fire of self-sacrifice of devotion no longer tries, as gold is tried by fire, the hearts that have been consecrated on the altar of our Masonic Charity for all mankind uplift and redemption; when the dim of sentiment, strife, and battle give place to songs of everlasting joys in this Masonic Mosque, and when we listen to the voice of God speaking to the Holy Angels, telling this group of human greatness to come up to the battlement of Glory and dip our wings in the sunlight of Christ's Eternal brightness and stand on the shores of this Mundane Creation, and echo our voices in Gabriel's golden trumpet, and call this earthly Grand Lodge to dwell in the Everlasting Grand Lodge to dwell in the world's burden bearers when we are summoned by the Recording Angel, may we as Christians, Masons answer, here am I Lord, a sinner saved by grace. Then all the world shall proclaim, Grand Master Coleman and the Grand Lodge of Texas' "GREAT MAN."[54]

As previously stated, in 1931 Grand Master Coleman paid tribute to the late Grand Master Jno. G. Lewis, Sr. of Louisiana. Ten years later, he paid tribute to the recently deceased Grand Master Scott A. Lewis, son and successor to the older Lewis.[55] In the same address, he discussed lodges visited during the past year. Among these was Plymouth Lodge in Marshall. He noted that one of the leading members of the latter body was Dr. J. J. Rhodes, president of Bishop College.[56] This address included a description of "Masonic Practices That Help." Regarding such practices, he said:

Certainly today the whole human race and our group especially find ourselves in a most complicated, distressing mass of difficulties. What are some unsolved problems of race relations existing today and affecting us that form a part of these difficulties and has our mystic art any contributions to make towards the solution of not only the local, the state, the national, but the world racial problem? . . . some would grant broad civic and social equality, but would deny a narrow and personal and social equality as inter-marriage, etc. . . . These are conditions confronting us that require sober, sensible consideration. We have an organization, Free Masonry, which in my mind include our whole existence.[57]

He expressed the firm conviction that Freemasonry has great potential to help improve race relations.[58] And he again urged the establishment of Masonic employment bureaus and agricultural cooperatives. Encouraging Master Masons to become involved in the Royal Arch, Knights Templar, Consistory, and Shrine, he also urged them to "turn out" with the ladies of the Order of the Eastern Star and Heroines of Jericho on Palm Sunday.[59]

Coleman invited all Masons and the general public to attend a celebration on August 20, 1941, at Brenham, Texas, which would be devoted to the erection of a monument as a memorial to the time, place, and leading personalities involved in the organization of the Grand Lodge in 1875.[60] He urged the provision of aid for sick Masons, and he presented the following statistics related to various lodge activities:

87 lodges lecture their craft monthly; 6 quarterly; 1 annually; 42 do not.

74 lodges have socials, regularly for the entertainment and pleasure of their craftsmen; 2 irregularly; 60 do not hold socials at all.

70 lodges observe Saint John's Festivals on June 24 each year; 52 observe Saint John's Festival on December 27; 4 do not observe either Festival.

92 lodges parade with the sisters of the Heroines of Jericho and the Eastern Stars on Palm Sunday; 1 partly and 43 do not take part with the sisters in their observance of Palm Sunday as day for their annual Religious Festival.[61]

Coleman concluded his 1941 Grand Master's Address with the following words:

As the late President Woodrow Wilson, speaking of the deceased soldiers, said in his address to the Veteran Soldiers of the blue and gray, at Gettysburg, at their reunion on July 4, 1913—"Their day is turned into evening. They look to us to perfect what they established. Their work is handed down to us. Our day is not over. It is upon us in full tide." He spoke of hosts of people, great and small, without class, or difference of kind, or race, or origin, that should be guided right by a safe vision.

In that spirit, let me say to you, fellow Masons, your day is NOT over. Your duty is not done. The true Masonic vision you have not yet caught. The real Masonic spirit you have not completely imbibed. The true Masonic methods you have not wholly learned and practiced. You have not actually experienced the sacrificial serving life that will force you to circumscribe and keep yourselves in due bounds in all your regulations with all mankind without regard to race, kind, or origin. This, the Free Masonry that will disclose to our human and spiritual view the vision that will impel us to respond to humanity's call. I charge you, my obligated brothers, to go forth under the canopy of heaven and keep in your fraternalistic and patriotic souls the great accomplishment of men who in a united brotherhood in this country achieved for the betterment of the free and enslaved men of this nation.[62]

In his 1942 Grand Master's Address, Coleman again took seriously problems faced by lodges and by individual Masons. He described a visit to a lodge at Midway, Madison County, Texas, noting that the majority of the farmers in the area were Prince Hall Masons.[63] He reported a white Mason delivering an address to a Prince Hall Masonic gathering at a church in Corpus Christi, and he revealed efforts of Masons in Corsicana to purchase interest in a building formerly shared with a defunct Odd Fellows Lodge.[64] His visit to a lodge at Eagle Lake was described as follows:

While here, we visited the public school. We saw here what we have seen in no other place in Texas. A Colored Public School, and Mexican School in separate buildings on separate but adjoining sites. The principals, teachers, and pupils are friendly and frequently communicate with each other.[65]

Coleman spoke of Masons renting sleeping rooms on the first floor of the lodge hall to men working in shipyards at Orange, Texas,[66] and he commended the work of Deputy Grand Master Lucian L. Lockhart in providing superb leadership in Houston.[67] He observed that, throughout Texas, Masonic work had been hindered by the call to arms of many young Texans.[68] He declared that ruinous world wars result in suffering, defeated, and dispirited people, and he called upon Freemasons to be compassionate and to work for peace.[69] Once again he urged support for Masonic employment bureaus and farmers cooperatives.[70] He gave the following report on the dedication of the Masonic Monument at Brenham:

On August 20, 1941, we held in Brenham, Texas a special Grand with which the exercise for the erection of the monument as a memorial to the honor of our first Grand Master, the Hon. N. W. Cuney, and the organization of the first Masonic Grand Lodge in Texas by our fore-runners in Free Masonry for our race in Texas.

Master Masons and friends from all parts of Texas were present. The monument was erected on a spot of ground bought by the Grand Lodge. It was paid for out of volunteering contributions by the members of our Grand Lodge at twenty-five cents each. Many did not give anything, not half of our membership contributed. The Hon. Wm. Madison McDonald was the orator of the day. He was introduced by the Grand Master Wm. Coleman. The ceremonies for laying the cornerstones with some modifications were used for erecting the monuments.

There was a shortage in amounts needed to defray the expense of erecting the monument. I want to appeal to those who did not contribute this twenty-five cents for this purpose to send it to the Grand Secretary in order that we might be able to clear the slate.[71]

The following year, Grand Master Coleman made further remarks on the idea of Masonic monuments when he declared: "Tablets of bronze and monuments of marble speak to us of the noteworthy deeds of those who have been instrumental in promoting the welfare or safeguarding the interest of mankind, but the most notable monument which can be erected to the memory of anyone is the kindly regard built in the minds and memories of men."[72] In his 1943 address, he explained a Grand Lodge policy which, from the writer's point of view, makes no sense at all:

> We have also emphasized, as decided, at our last Grand Annual Communication that men of the proper age and qualification and who have been inducted into the Naval and Military services of the United States, or any government engaged in the present war cannot be raised to the sublime degree of a Master Mason into any of our local lodges during the duration of the war. The reason for this was made clear to our representatives, but we also decided that such men who were raised to the sublime degree of a Master Mason for which they paid the regular local and Grand Lodge fee before the induction into such service would be kept on the roll until the close of the Masonic year in which they joined, but could not be permitted to pay annual, local, and Grand Lodge fees at the beginning of the Masonic year following the close of the year in which they were made Master Masons. After the duration of the war such Masons would be permitted, under proper Masonic qualifications, to re-enter the lodge from which they were dropped.... The said government had assumed complete supervision of all such inductees and made provision for the material and other care of these men and their children.[73]

In this same address, Coleman spoke of visits to lodges in various parts of Texas, including Magnolia Lodge No. 3 in Houston and Amity Lodge No. 4 in Galveston.[74] He noted the inability of the Houston lodges to make their usual numerical progress as a result of problems associated with the war. He also declared:

> Remember that the whole human race is now passing through the valley of the shadow of death which is our constant companion. This may be necessary to show us the folly of greed and lust of power in order to make us more valiant in our fight against the powers of darkness.
>
> Keep in mind that the war and turmoil in the world are like the behavior of a mass

of foolish children breaking their toys. When will they cease? Not until more men die to selfishness and are born again in faith, hope, and love.

Men and Masons were not meant to dwell in enmity with each other. Brotherly love is the solution of every problem. The fraternal feeling contributes to the universal brotherhood which is the foundation of Free Masonry and the ideal of the preservation of the safe, permanent human institution.[75]

In his 1944 Grand Master's Address, Coleman reported that, after a period of decline, lodge membership was again on the upswing.[76] He called for the recruitment of more young men in Masonry and commended the brethren in Fort Worth not only for their attraction of new blood into the craft but also for their proficiency in committing the ritual to memory.[77] Urging everyone to "Watch Houston," he commended the brethren there for their competitive spirit in seeing who could build up the biggest lodge.[78] Grand Master Coleman reported celebration of Palm Sunday in Houston and Easter in San Antonio.[79] He also described the Beaumont Masons meeting in the hall owned by Bishop Grant Lodge as an "unsurpassed Masonic hive of busy bees."[80] Coleman called for Masonic Stewardship and declared that Freemasonry is NOT the property of any one race,[81] and he made further remarks about the war, stating: "We should do all that we can to prevent our country, at least, from coming under the philosophy and spirit of Nazism, Fascism, or the religion of the Japanese."[82] Regarding plans for postwar employment, he stated:

> We are our brothers' keepers and cannot peacefully, happily, harmoniously live and prosper unless we do unto others as we should have them do unto us and cease to be respecter of persons. We should engage in profit paying concerns that will insure dividends and employment to many who will be thrown out of employment, in such places as Houston, San Antonio, Beaumont, Dallas, Fort Worth, Corsicana, and Waco. There are numerous opportunities for the establishment of grocery stores and other possible profitable business within their means that will give employment to many now insecurely gainfully employed. As stated by the President of the U. S., we within the government must look forward to increasing expenditures for the needy unemployed. It is clear to me that for one or two years after the war great hardships will be the lot of those who have saved no means and out of gainful employment caused partly by activities of labor organizations which prohibit freedom to work and independence of workmen. Many Masons who belong to labor organizations will be helped, but a larger number who are not connected with such societies will be wholly dependent and in numerous cases unemployed and denied employment.[83]

Coleman began his 1945 Grand Master's Address with a testimonial in memory of recently deceased Grand Senior Warden H. L. Price. He then expressed his opinion that World War II was disastrous but, nevertheless, necessary.[84] He gave tribute to "Our Sacred Dead" and authorized the Grand Chaplain to conduct a memorial service.[85] Coleman discussed the current controversy in various Grand Lodges regarding addition of the words "Prince Hall Affiliation" to the name, and he reported that the 1945 International Masonic Conferences had tried unsuccessfully to establish a Lodge of Research.[86] He called upon every Worshipful Master to dedicate himself to spiritual values.[87] In addition, he addressed the problem of Freemasonry's enemies, a reality then and now:

It is sad to think of the sublime divine principles that are the foundation of real Free Masonry that we have enemies in the order of different human groups, our own and others, and that we have among us those enemies who regularly and unceasingly strive to perpetuate disunity, foment hatred and prejudice between different classes and racial groups. They are busily engaged in producing confusion and feelings of uncertainty.[88]

Declaring that Masonry exists not for itself but for mankind, he called upon Masons to engage in war relief.[89] He encouraged all lodges to do their part in alleviating the problems of postwar unemployment and asserted that "Free Masonry is intended to improve men morally, socially, and spiritually. It is entirely practical and a good Mason is one who practices outside the lodge what he learns in it."[90]

O. E. Wilhite, a friend of the writer who died January 5, 1993, gave the following report of a visit by Coleman to his lodge in Rockdale:

We had a Worshipful Master who had taken the money we had raised. We had to pay 25 cents extra—every member—for the widows of Master Masons. And I found out that he was taking that money himself and wasn't distributing it to them. I had plenty of nerve. I was acting as Senior Warden and I reported it to Coleman and Coleman called both of us together and asked "Now, what did you do with the money?" He said "I had to use it for stamps and writing." He said "Now listen and let me tell you something—Don't you ever take another penny. If you do, I'm going to send you to the pen! Do you hear what I said?" Well, I'm the one who reported it! That made for a little confusion between me and the president—but I stopped him!"[91]

The late Rev. DeShong Smith of the Cumberland Presbyterian Church was raised to the sublime degree of Master Mason by Coleman in 1936 at the Connor Building on Second and Franklin in Waco. Smith only met him that one time, but he recalled that he was a very dignified man and a master of the ritual.[92] Charlie Wadley, Past Grand Marshal for the Prince Hall Grand Lodge of Texas and a long-time friend of the writer, met Coleman in the early 1940s. In response to the writer's question of "What kind of Grand Master was he?" Wadley replied: "He was a great one.... He was a man who loved to see things done just right. Take time and not rush." He recalled growth of membership during the Coleman administration.[93] The late A. D. Harris, who served for many years as Grand Recorder, first met Coleman in 1945 or 1946 at a district meeting at the Wright Cuney Center in Galveston. As a young Mason, he was "awed by the man." He recalled that Coleman gave an outstanding banquet speech.[94] T. W. Neal, who was raised to the sublime degree of Master Mason in 1923, remembered being impressed by Coleman's ritualistic skills and by the growth in membership under his leadership.[95]

Coleman attended an International Conference of Grand Masters in Hot Springs, Arkansas, January 21-27, 1946. Grand Master John Wesley Dobbs of Georgia was the presiding officer. However, after the first day, every Grand Master had the pleasure of presiding over a session. Coleman reported that this meeting was very enjoyable and marked great progress in bringing together Prince Hall Masons of various jurisdictions.[96]

Coleman's sixteen-year term in the Grand East came to an abrupt end when he died at Saint Joseph Hospital in Fort Worth on May 16, 1946. The primary cause of his death was acute nephritis, with arteriosclerosis as a contributory cause.[97] Funeral services were held on Monday May 16, at Fort Worth's Gilead Baptist Church, where he served as a deacon.[98] Services were conducted by Baker Funeral Home, 301 East Rosedale. Interment was in People's Burial Park.[99] O. E. Wilhite attended his funeral and remembered that he was buried with his Grand Master's hat and chair. He observed that this was the only time he had ever seen this done.[100]

At the 1946 Grand Lodge Communication, the Committee on the State of the Country reported:

> There is a broken link in the field of Fraternalism and Masonry throughout the length and breadth of the land. The Free and Accepted Masons of Texas are a great organization. The whole nation respects this organization as such. The names of "Free and Accepted Masons of Texas and Jurisdiction," Wm. Madison McDonald, and William Coleman have for years been linked together and considered as symbolical.
>
> But the other day, a giant oak in the woods of Masonry fell. So terrific was this fall that the repercussion echoes throughout the fraternal world. Our dearly beloved Grand Master, Wm. Coleman went home. He is not with us, but we, His bemoaning brethren are cognizant of his national stature and the loss of him to the fraternal world.[101]

The obituary in *The Dallas Express* described Coleman as "a conservative, steady leader who shunned flashy ventures."[102]

There can be no doubt that Grand Master William Coleman did an outstanding job of holding Prince Hall Masonry in Texas together and actually making progress during the difficult years of the Great Depression and World War II. It would now be the responsibility of L. L. Lockhart to steer the Masonic ship throughout the postwar years that were to follow.

Lucian L. Lockhart

Lucian L. Lockhart (1870-1955) was the fourteenth Grand Master of Prince Hall Masons in Texas. He took office in 1946, the year which marked the beginning of the postwar era, in view of the end of World War II in 1945. The United Nations was born in 1946. Harry S. Truman, Past Grand Master of Masons in Missouri, was serving as president of the United States. Truman had taken office the previous year as a result of the death of another Masonic president, Franklin Delano Roosevelt.[1] The conditions of 1946 have been thus described:

> Upon entering office, President Truman had promised to carry on the progressive policies of his predecessor. But that proved to be not entirely possibly even though the Democratic Party was to control both branches of Congress through 1946. The long tenure of the New Deal, the prosperity of business in the war years and afterwards, the impact of the war upon the political temper of the country, all worked to accelerate a definable drift toward the conservative position in Congress and the country alike. In particular, the southern wing of the Democratic Party, always restless under the New Deal, now often found itself voting as much against the administration as for it. . . . With the death of Roosevelt, the reform movement had lost its great leader, and the revolt of the conservative Democrats from Presidential direction became more marked with each passing year.[2]

As the United States of America lost a great leader with the death of Roosevelt on April 12, 1945, so Texas Prince Hall Freemasons lost a great leader with the passing of Grand Master William Coleman on May 16, 1946. However, the change in leadership was much smoother in Texas Masonry than in American politics. Lucian L. Lockhart had served for a number of years as Coleman's Deputy Grand Master and was more than equal to the task of providing the leadership needed for the occasion. It would be his responsibility to steer the Masonic ship throughout the postwar years that were to follow.

Lockhart was born on November 9, 1870, in Chapel Hill, Washington County, Texas.[3] He settled in Houston, where he worked as a letter carrier and as a public school teacher. He was an active member of Houston's Wesley Chapel African Methodist Episcopal Church. For many years he served as Worshipful Master of Magnolia Lodge No. 3, Free and Accepted Masons. He was promoted from Deputy Grand Master to Grand Master following the death of Coleman.[4]

Lockhart delivered his first Grand Master's Address on June 25, 1946, stating:

> BROTHERS:
>
> I have a hard time or rather, I have not been satisfied in trying to fill my own place on life's stage of action. Now it falls my duty to attempt to fill the place of an eminent scholar, a linguist, an honorable citizen, a Mason, and a Christian.
>
> Charity is the basis of our Grand Order. Lodges are held throughout our jurisdiction and charities are collected and sent to our Grand Lodge to be dispensed to those who have lost their loved ones. No exception is made to your civic or church affiliations. For in the sight of God we are equally His children and have the same parents and preserver. So we in like manner look on every Free Mason as our brother. No regard is paid to his birth, education, or political affiliation if he is a good man, an honest man, which is the noblest work of God. . . . our order . . . is calculated to unite mankind as one family. High, low, rich, and poor, one with another; to adore the name of God and observe His laws.
>
> Masonic brethren, during the conflict just ended, while being connected with various departments of the military and other departments, have visited many of our local lodges and enjoyed social brotherly contact in their association with Masonic brethren of our jurisdiction. There were many brothers who dropped out during the war, but since the demobilization are returning to the Masonic fold.
>
> We are receiving many new men since being demobilized from the army. . . .
>
> Let us remember that we are Christians and Masons, being ready to listen to him who craveth for assistance and from want never to withhold a liberal hand. So shall a heart felt satisfaction reward our labor and the produce of liberality must surely follow after. . . .
>
> Brothers throughout our jurisdiction, our lodge has had a great increase. Many of the lodges are specializing in getting young men in their lodges which is a fine move, for it is the young men who must keep the lights of the camp fire burning.[5]

After such an uplifting message, the new Grand Master then turned to a somber note:

> Brother Richard Guess, Past Master of Heights Lodge No. 280, Houston, was assassinated on Sunday night on the way from church to his home. Brother Guess was president of the Independent Union at the Hughes Tool Co. Brother Guess was reliable and trustworthy and charitable. Because Brother Guess held out in his union against these other unions, he was assassinated.
>
> We put out a call to the lodges in Houston and, on Sunday, they responded, putting up in escrow more than $1,200 together with $2,000 posted by the Hughes Tool Co., and $500 from the union of which he was president, making a total of $3,700 put up in escrow for the arrest and conviction of the assassin.[6]

Lockhart concluded his address with a number of recommendations. He called upon Worshipful Masters and District Deputies to learn their rituals, that they might be able to explain them to the craft. He urged the lodges to find a way to provide for "old men who through no fault of their own are unable to pay their relief dues." He also called for support of the National Association for the Advancement of Colored People (NAACP). Another important recommendation was directed at Masons involved in agriculture. He said: "You who are farmers consult your demonstration agents [regarding] the best methods of the care of your livestock, the best strain of laying hens, the best breed of hogs, and best cows for milk and butter."[7] It appears that Lockhart, in seeking to promote racial uplift through fraternalism, employed a holistic approach in dealing with spiritual, social, political, and economic problems.

The 1946 Grand Communication included an outstanding report on "State of the Country." This report, prepared by a committee chaired by Dr. J. W. Yancy II of Waco,[8] gave the following insightful picture of America in 1946:

> The forming of a United Nations Organization for the keeping of the peace has been perfected. America has been chosen as its permanent home. A branch of this great world organization has been designated as the Council on shaping policies for world humanity. Mrs. F. D. Roosevelt has been named as American representative to this organization. In the true Rooseveltian manner, Mrs. Roosevelt has stated that the American racial bias should be called to the attention of the United Nations Organizations.
>
> RECONVERSION is the watchword of the DAY. And many of the accompanying problems of this period are claiming the attention of the nation:
> 1. Housing is a major problem. Veterans must have homes to live in. But civilians cannot be forced out. So the government has put on a major housing project for returning soldiers.
> 2. The G. I. Bill of Rights is allowing each returning soldier to get a training in some phase of study. It also guarantees financial aid to those unable to find employment.
> 3. Rising prices and scarcity of material in the building industry and the shortage of food stuff are of great importance now. . . .
> 4. Strikes and labor disputes are rearing up in all fields of employment. Congress and President Truman are facing the severest period of the administration.
>
> The reconversion period has likewise brought to the front strained racial relationships. . . . we find heartening instances where minority races have won achievements and recognition and this gives us hope.
>
> On the dark side of the racial picture we hate to call attention to the KKK which is attempting to intimidate the Negro race. This is particularly true in California and Georgia.
>
> Through the forming of a coalition of a certain section of senators, the Fair Employment Practice Committee was abolished.
>
> We also note with regret that the Daughters of the American Revolution officially barred Miss Hazel Scott, the accomplished musician and wife of Congressman Adam Clayton Powell from appearing in concert at historic Constitution Hall in Washington, D. C., solely on the grounds that Miss Scott is a Negro.
>
> But . . . on the bright side of the racial picture . . .
> 1. The State of California has revoked the charter of the KKK in that State. And Georgia's Governor Arnall is throwing all of the weight of his office and state police force behind the prosecution of the KKK in Georgia.

2. Jackie Robinson, first and only Negro baseball star to sign a contract with a white major league, is chalking up a great success in sports.[9]
3. The statue of Booker T. Washington, the founder of Tuskegee Institute, has been placed in the Hall of Fame. This is the first time a Negro has been so honored.[10]
4. President Truman appointed Judge William Hastie the first Negro Governor of the Virgin Islands. This is indeed an historical epoch.
5. Dean O'Hara Lanier, former Dean of Houston College for Negroes, has been appointed Minister of Liberia.
6. And Mrs. Emma Clarissa Clement of Louisville, Kentucky, widow of the late Bishop Clement of the A.M.E.Z. Church, was chosen the "American Mother" of 1946. This is the first time that a Negro woman has been honored in such capacity.

To our way of thinking, much of the progress made by minority races recently has been credited to the impartial leadership and personal attitudes of our noble leader of State, President H. S. Truman.

President Truman, a 33° Mason, who was at one time the pianist and patron of the Order of the Eastern Star of Grandview Chapter in Missouri, and one who remembers and cherishes Masonic ties enough to pay a surprise visit at the meeting of Alexandria—Washington Lodge No. 22, on October 18, 1945, just to help confer the Master Mason's degree on the son of his friend, has faced minority problems squarely. And he has tried to give sincere thought to their solution.[11]

At the 1946 Communication, Lockhart was reelected as Grand Master. One major change in the line of officers was the promotion of Grand Lecturer John Theodore Maxey to Deputy Grand Master.[12] The Lockhart-Maxey team was destined to lead the Grand Lodge for the next nine years.[13]

Grand Master Lockhart presided over his second Grand Communication in 1947. At this session, Dr. Yancy again chaired the Committee on the State of the Country. Again, much valuable information about important events of the day can be gleaned from examining this report, which stated:

> Since we met in this body we have witnessed a change in control of one of our branches of national government—the legislative branch, which is Congress. Both houses have been won by the Republican victory at the polls. . . .[14]

> Mainly through the investigation of the Herman Sweatt case and the constant agitation of the same, a University for Negroes in Texas has been set up in Houston. One of the Regents, Mr. Cullen of Houston, has pledged his word that this institution will be equal to any in the country. The world is waiting to see the outcome of this new educational undertaking.[15]

> We cannot mention Negro Education at this point without bowing our heads in deep reverence and paying tribute to that matchless Negro Educator, the first President of Wiley College, that grand old school man of Texas and the Southwest—Dr. M. W. Dogan, who passed on to his reward last week, at the ripe age of 82.

> The long line of brave men who carved out the destiny of life in Texas and shaped the future of many is growing thin. They did their jobs well. Their rewards are awaiting them. Peace be to their ashes!

> Down in Georgia, the home of the KKK, a court decision gave a death blow to the Hooded Order. No more can the Grand Dragon and his clan sit in hooded secrecy

under the protection of the law and lay plans to terrorize Catholics, Jews, and Negroes.[16]

Possibly the most astounding mockery of American justice and human rights of which we boast so proudly came when the jurors of South Carolina turned loose all the twenty-seven self-acknowledged lynchers....

Masonry among the white brethren in Texas was rejuvenated this spring by the visit of a great Mason—President Harry S. Truman—Waco, March 6. President Truman came to receive an honorary degree from Baylor University. But the Masons greeted him in high honor. Special ceremonies were held for him at the Shrine Temple in Waco. The novices who were placed in a class to study for the spring initiation into the Shrine Temple were named "The Harry S. Truman Class." So eager were men to be identified with this special class that it became the largest class to be initiated in the history of the Waco Shrine Temple.[17]

The Committee on Foreign Correspondence, chaired by Deputy Grand Master Maxey, reported a number of developments in the Masonic world and stated: "In view of the discussions now going on among white Masons, and the recent decisions reported by a research committee of a white Grand Lodge, we feel that, as Free Masons, we must do our part to cooperate with those who favor us, and prove that we are worthy wearers of the Square."[18]

On Tuesday, June 24, 1947—the day of the Feast of Saint John the Baptist—a service was held in honor of Grand Master L. L. Lockhart and Grand Secretary Leon Maddox, both of whom had taken office the previous year. The Prince Hall Masons of Texas declared that they were determined "To pay respect to our beloved Grand Master and highly esteemed Grand Secretary, while they are yet alive."[19] At the conclusion of his Grand Master's Address, Lockhart called for the payment of the cost of a monument at the grave of his predecessor, Past Grand Master William Coleman.[20]

One of the highlights of the 1948 Grand Communication was the Report of the Committee on Banking, chaired by Bro. E. L. Gibson. According to his report, dated June 24, the Fraternal Bank and Trust Company had "served its apprenticeship and done remarkably well." Thus the committee recommended the widening of the scope of the bank. At the time, due to declining health, Past Grand Secretary McDonald was not present at the session. The Grand Lodge issued a Special Communication with prayers on his behalf during his illness and best wishes to him and his wife.[21] Greetings were received from Past Grand Master Wiley Lawson Kimbrough of Los Angeles, California.[22]

In his 1948 Grand Master's Address, Lockhart issued a strong plea for tolerance, declaring:

> Our Order . . . directs us to divest ourselves of confined and bigoted notions, and teaches us that humility is the soul of religion. We should never suffer any religious disputes in our lodge and, as Masons, for we as members of the Universal Church, are not narrowed to sect. Whilst as Christians, we worship God through Jesus Christ, we believe that in every nation, he that feareth God and worketh righteousness is accepted of God. All Masons, whether Christians or Jews, or whatever their profession, who violate not the rule of right written by the Almighty upon the table of the heart; who fear Him and worketh righteousness, acknowledged as Brethren and, though we take different roads, we are not to be angry with, or persecute each other on that ac-

count. We mean to travel to the same place; we know that the end of our journey is the same, and we hope to meet in paradisiacal lodge of the just men made perfect.

How lovely is an institution fraught with sentiments like these! How agreeable it must be to Him Who sits on the throne of everlasting mercy.[23]

Lockhart paid tribute to Past Grand Secretary McDonald and the late Past Grand Master Coleman, acknowledging their invaluable help in enabling him to rise through the ranks and obtain the highest office in Freemasonry.[24] The Committee on the Grand Master's Address, chaired by J. E. Anderson, had much praise for the Grand Master and expressed the opinion that his motives were well expressed by the following poem:

The Bridge Builder

An old man going along a lone highway,
Came at the evening cold and gray;
To a chasm, vast, deep and wide,
Through which was flowing a sullen tide;
The old man crossed in the twilight dim,
The sullen stream had no fear for him;
But he turned when safe on the other side
And built a bridge to span the tide.
"Old Man," said a fellow pilgrim traveler near,
"You are wasting your strength with building here;
Your journey will end with the ending day,
You never again will pass this way;
Why build this bridge at evening tide?"

The builder lifted his old proud gray head,
"Good Friend in the path I've come," he said;
"There followeth after me, today,
A youth, whose feet must pass this way;
This chasm which was a nought for me,
To this fair youth may a pitfall be;
He too must cross in the twilight dim,
Good Friend, I'm building this bridge for him."[25]

On June 30, 1949, in his Grand Master's Address, Lockhart stressed the fact that a Masonic lodge should be ruled by love and not by fear.

In the mechanism of Masonry, the graduated scale of rank in strictly and immutably observed, and subordination is perfect and complete; for its government is despotic. The Master in the East is absolute in his authority over the Brethren of his lodge. Yet this does not in the least militate against the doctrine of equality, which is inculcated both by precept and example in all the illustrations of Masonry. . . . In a word, a Masonic lodge is governed by **love**, not by **fear**. And if, in any instance, this officer should so far forget his Master's obligations as to exercise the despotic power with which the **bond of union** would be scattered to the winds of heaven—and the lodge, however numerous and respectable it might be, it would soon cease to exist.[26]

At the 1950 Grand Communication, as at many other sessions, Texas Masons were blessed by the presence of visiting Grand Masters. That year, Most Worshipful Jno. G. Lewis, Jr., of Louisiana and James C. Gilliam of Mississippi visited the Lone Star State.[27] On June 28 Grand Master Lewis called the Grand Lodge of Texas to order.[28]

In his 1950 Grand Master's Address, Lockhart reported that Texas Masonry had a normal death rate accompanied by a phenomenal intake of new members.[29] He reported visits to the Scottish Rite Supreme Council in Washington, D. C., to the "Cradle of Prince Hall Masonry" in Boston, and to the Conference of Grand Masters in Chicago.[30] He spoke on the social nature of man and how such nature harmonizes with the aims of Freemasonry. He concluded that Freemasonry "must ever be revered and cultivated by the just, the good, and the exalted mind, as the surest means of establishing peace, harmony, and good will amongst men."[31]

In 1950, as in previous years, Dr. Yancy chaired the Committee on the State of the Country. As in previous years, his committee issued a highly relevant report, observing:

> Dr. Ralph Bunche, a Negro who won international distinction as mediator of the dispute between the Arabs and Jews, has been mentioned several times as a possible choice for American Ambassador to Russia. . . .
>
> A Negro, Rev. P. E. Womack, of Austin, Texas, has announced his candidacy for the Lieutenant Governorship of Texas. . . .
>
> The Supreme Court recently has ruled that the University of Texas must accept the Negroes who applied for admission to the university. It also ruled that the segregation of Negroes at the University of Oklahoma must cease. The decision has shattered laws existing in some instances for more than sixty-five years. . . .
>
> Joe Louis had the ears of the world listening to hear him this spring make his historic announcement in the lobby of the College View Court-Hotel in Waco that he would retire permanently from the Boxing Ring. By way of digression, we must note here that our own Grand Master, L. L. Lockhart, was domiciled in the same room where Joe Louis slept at this hotel when Grand Master Lockhart was on one of his Masonic tours to Waco.[32]

The 1950 Communication was especially notable in view of the approval of the Report of the Committee on Jurisprudence, chaired by Deputy Grand Master Maxey. As a result of this approval, the organization's name was officially changed from "Most Worshipful Grand Lodge, Free and Accepted Masons, Texas and Jurisdictions Belonging, 'Prince Hall Affiliation'" to "Most Worshipful Prince Hall Grand Lodge, Free and Accepted Masons, Texas and Jurisdictions Belonging."[33]

On June 29, 1950, the Grand Lodge held a Silver Jubilee Celebration, expressing gratitude to God for seventy-five years of Prince Hall Masonry in Texas.[34]

The keynote speaker for this occasion was Rev. H. Oliver Scott, pastor of Mount Pleasant Baptist Church in Houston. His theme was "Give Me Men to Match This Mountain." He predicted that Freemasonry, like Christianity, would ultimately triumph over all of its foes.[35] Afterward, Deputy Grand Master Maxey spoke on the lives of the Past Grand Masters of Texas.[36]

On June 30, 1950, the Grand Lodge officers were installed and the Grand Lodge was officially closed.[37] However, within a week, the Prince Hall Masons of Texas received some sad news that brought many of them back to Fort Worth. At 11:35 P.M. on July 4, Past Grand Secretary McDonald died.[38] Although his death occurred after the close of the session, arrangements were made to have the following resolution included with the printed minutes for 1950:

RESOLUTION FROM THE GRAND LODGE IN LOVING MEMORY OF BROTHER WILLIAM M. MCDONALD

Brother McDonald first became a member of Pilgrim Lodge No. 10, located in Denison, Texas, in 1886, and he immediately interested himself in promoting the welfare of Masonry in general in the Jurisdiction of Texas.

In later years, he transferred his membership to Bloomfield Lodge No. 67, Forney, Texas. He formed an attachment for the membership of that lodge that caused him to keep his membership there throughout the remaining years of his life. He instilled many new ideas in Bloomfield Lodge and taught them to practice Masonry as it was originally practiced in the Landmarks.

He was a student of governmental affairs, as well as civic and religious affairs.

He was a philanthropist and a race builder. He made generous contributions to many churches and all worthwhile organizations. He sent many of his friends' children to colleges, such as Fisk, Howard, Southern, and other institutions of higher learning.

As a result of his generosity towards his friends and Masonic brothers, he was honored, revered, and cherished throughout the length and breadth of this nation.

He was elected Grand Secretary of the Most Worshipful Grand Lodge in 1899 at the Twenty-Fourth Annual Communication, and was re-elected Grand Secretary for forty-six consecutive years. During this period of years, he placed the Order of Free and Accepted Masons of Texas on a firm foundation. He was instrumental in acquiring much valuable property for the order, and a splendid cash reserve.

In 1946, he decided to retire from the office of Grand Secretary, knowing that his labor had been fruitful and that his work had been very well done. The Grand Lodge being fully aware of his vast financial interest and other personal business claiming the attention of our brother, very reluctantly accepted his resignation; AND, NOW, after more than two years of sickness and confinement, OUR BELOVED BROTHER has gone to rest from his labors, to his EVERLASTING REWARD.

We extend to the widow, relatives, and friends of our esteemed brother our most sincere sympathy in the loss that we all have sustained.

BE IT RESOLVED, that a copy of this resolution be printed in the minutes of 1950-51, and a copy be given to the family.[39]

At the 1951 Grand Communication, Texas Masons were again visited by Grand Master Lewis of Louisiana. Lewis spoke on the newly established Legal Defense Fund of the NAACP. As a result of this appeal, the Grand Lodge donated $1,000 to this fund.[40]

In his Grand Master's Address, Lockhart spoke of seventy-six years of progress, contrasting the five Texas lodges which existed in 1875 with the 509 lodges under warrant and eleven lodges under dispensation in 1951. He pointed out that no other jurisdiction in Prince Hall Freemasonry could claim as many lodges or as many assets (more than one-half million dollars) as Texas.[41] He spoke of "a rapid death of provincialism and the growth of the cosmopolitan spirit,"[42] and pointed out the important role which Masonry could play in world reconstruction in the years following World War II: "The feeling of fraternity is one of the noblest notes of our times.... Perhaps the greatest truth burned into our minds by the World War is that the good of the race as a whole does actually exist, and that no one race or land can reach its full potential by itself and enslaving the other parts of the world. In such a world, Freemasonry, the oldest and greatest fraternity known among men, must now do its work."[43]

With the outbreak of an undeclared war in Korea, Grand Master Lockhart was confronted with the prospect of Texas Prince Hall Masons becoming casualties of the conflict.[44] He therefore issued some guidelines for military Masons, recommending that the following words be added to the application for membership:

> I further agree that in the event I am accepted as a member, and I should die from any injury received, or disease contracted outside the "Home Area," as a result of war, or any act or hazard of war, or if I should die as the result of any injury received, while participating in aeronautic or aviation training, either before or after being returned to the "Home Area," the Grand Lodge liabilities shall be limited to the amount of relief premiums actually paid to the Order by me, and I agree that my beneficiaries will not assert any claim, or be entitled to any benefits other than as provided above.[45]

In his 1952 Grand Master's Address, Lockhart reported an intake of 3,000 new members since the 1951 Communication! He spoke on the importance of Masonic benevolence and stressed the obligations of Masons as citizens of the United States. In the latter capacity, he urged members to purchase government bonds.[46]

In his 1953 Grand Master's Address, Lockhart addressed the relationship of Masonry to religious creeds, stating: "The church with its creeds, links us of like religious opinions together; but Freemasonry ignores differences of denomination and its customs, and unites us under God into such an indestructible brotherhood that death alone should be able to sever."[47] He took note of the fact that, by 1953, urbanization and depersonalization had taken their toll and had resulted in economic and moral bankruptcy.[48] In this address, he declared that Freemasonry had great potential for being a powerful force for healing and reconstruction in such troubled times:

> I want to proclaim to you, there is a need of the re-establishment of neighborly bonds of friendship, fraternity, and fellowship which, as it is said, is "the soul of Freemasonry" ...
>
> We have an organization that can, at least among its own group, substitute strangers for friends, and surround each person with the spirit of comfort and security that will help the distressed, especially the distressed Brother, not as a pauper in the frozen feelings of public charity, but helpfully, as one friendly neighbor aids another. It is true, beneficent, strong society of friends.
>
> Other socially beneficent organizations are, in varied ways, struggling to promote the general welfare of those united with them. Such, for example, are the labor unions, divided into the AFLs and CIOs, the different cooperative societies of all forms: farming, wholesale and retail merchandising, producers and consumers, and agencies united for the purpose of securing for the personal use of their supporters more supplies for the common good for less money.
>
> Many Masons form a part of these different organizations because, as individuals, our existence is in some measure bound up on the industrial and economic life of our

districts and country. Nevertheless, as Masons, if we would be governed by the true aims of our Grand Old Order, we would labor or make men brotherly, women sisterly, oppose class division and caste-established differences.[49]

He described Freemasonry as "a universal oasis" and "an undying spiritual entity."[50] He reported that proceeds from Prince Hall Day Celebrations were being used to support the Grand Lodge Educational Program and the NAACP Legal Defense Fund. He denounced ignorance as the eternal enemy and reminded all not to forget that "color is not a barrier to intellect."[51]

During the 1953 election of officers, Deputy Grand Master J. T. Maxey unsuccessfully challenged Lockhart for the office of Grand Master.[52] Later, Grand Recorder J. H. McGowen unsuccessfully challenged Maxey for the office of Deputy Grand Master.[53]

At the 1954 Grand Communication, Texas Masons were again visited by Grand Master Gilliam of Mississippi, who praised Lockhart as one of the most outstanding Grand Masters in the United States.[54] In his Annual Report for District No. 2, District Deputy Grand Master James W. Bolden called the Texas Grand Master "a God-sent man."[55] In his Annual Report for District No. 7, District Deputy Grand Master J. H. McGowen observed that no trace of scandal had ever been associated with the name of Grand Master Lockhart.[56] Prof. George Edwards of Gonzales assisted the Grand Master in reading his reports and spoke on seventy-nine years of Texas Masonic history.[57]

In his 1954 Grand Master's Address, Lockhart had much to say about the interdependence of human beings. He stated: "We were not born for ourselves alone, nor merely to shape our course through life in the solitudes of tranquility, and to study that which should afford peace to the conscience at home, but men were made for society, and consequently, aid for each other no one among us, be he ever so rich, can subsist without assistance of his fellow-creatures."[58] At this session, the Committee on Education, chaired by Patrick Bolton, praised *Brown v. Board of Education*, the 1954 decision of the U.S. Supreme Court which declared racial segregation in the public schools unconstitutional.[59]

At the 1955 Grand Communication, Texas Masons were visited by Grand Masters P. G. Porter of Kansas and James C. Gilliam of Mississippi.[60] At the request of Grand Master Lockhart, Grand Master Porter presided over the opening of the session.[61] Grand Master Gilliam brought "greetings on behalf of the Prince Hall Masons of his great state, Mississippi."[62]

In his 1955 Grand Master's Address, Lockhart had much to say about charity and called for support of medical research.[63] Regarding the first anniversary of *Brown v. Board of Education*, he declared: "May 17, 1955, has been designated 'Freedom Day.' The Supreme Court of the United States issued this Edict—that segregation in public schools is unconstitutional. This proclamation has stirred the South, which is opposed to desegregation. We have the final decision of the Supreme Court and are waiting for the Edict to be put into effect."[64]

On June 29, 1955, Maxey again sought to unseat Lockhart from the Grand East. Again, Maxey's efforts were unsuccessful.[65] Maxey was destined to become Grand Master in 1955 but not during the Grand Communication. Probably neither candidate for the highest office in Texas Masonry knew that it would be Lockhart's last time to preside. A few months after the session closed, the Grand Master's earthly pilgrimage came to an end as his noble spirit entered the Celestial Lodge above.

Lockhart died on October 2, 1955, at Saint Elizabeth Hospital in Houston. The causes of his death included cerebral thrombosis and arteriosclerosis.[66] His funeral was held on October 4, 1955, at Wesley Chapel AME Church. His pastor, Rev. W. D. Williams, delivered the eulogy before some 1,000 mourners, at least half of whom were members of the Prince Hall Masonic family. In attendance were not only Texas Masons but also visiting brethren from Kansas, Arkansas, Louisiana, Mississippi, Georgia, and Washington, D.C. Reverend Williams told those in attendance: "He loved people. He was insanely honest. He was the depth, breadth, and height of a leader. . . . He blessed everything he touched because he had a heart of love." Many prominent members of the AME Church attended, including Rt. Rev. Joseph Gomez, the Presiding Bishop of Texas; Dr. George A. Singleton of Philadelphia, a 33° Prince Hall Mason and Editor of *The AME Church Review*; Dr. C. W. Abbington of Dallas, Editor of Religious Literature; and Rev. E. H. Branch of Kansas City.[67]

Masonic graveside services were conducted at Oak Forest Cemetery by Deputy Grand Master Maxey, assisted by Grand Senior Warden James H. Lockhart, Grand Secretary Maddox, Grand Recorder McGowen, and other prominent Masons.[68]

The Conference of Prince Hall Grand Masters convened in Boston, Massachusetts, on May 24, 1956. J. T. Maxey, the new Grand Master of Texas, spoke to this conference on "Our Fraternal Dead." In this speech he stated:

> My friends and brethren: I come to report that on October 2, 1955, we passed another toll-gate on life's highway and have paid the last mark of respect and affection, and final tribute of tears to a great and good man, L. L. Lockhart, the Grand Master of the Prince Hall Grand Lodge of the great state of Texas, who laid down the working tools of his earthly vocation, and we believed and desired to practice the doctrine that:
>
> "A rose to the living is more in filling love's infinite store,
> If graciously given before the hungering spirit has fled,
> A rose to the living is more than sumptuous wreaths to the dead."
>
> But, my brethren, as I stood by that beautiful tribute of perishing flowers, the mute and inanimate symbol glorified by the illustrious name of our beloved dead, I was reminded that, while abiding on time's side of eternity; he was sometime maligned, many times misunderstood, and often when roses were his due, he received thorns instead.
>
> However, he is now where neither praises nor blame will reach him, and I come today before this great fraternal conference to dwell with you in glad and fervent thanksgiving over the living memory of Grand Master L. L. Lockhart. For me, this is a proud and great privilege to try to express the deep appreciation of this great fraternal organization for its glorious friend, its syngamic associate, its generous servant, the incomparable Grand Master of Texas, and this is a sorrowful privilege to try to estimate through the limitations of language, the vibrant genius of this man, whose living presence has been so abruptly and tragically absorbed into the great mystery. Those of us who were witnesses of his great personality, his unflattering will, his vir-

ile intelligence, find even in our personal grief at his loss, a certain beauty in the fact that, while still wearing the purple of the fraternity, he passed in a bound to the other side.

It is not easy to express the value to Prince Hall masonry of such a man as L. L. Lockhart. Many of us here today and many that have gone before have given to Masonry our best love, our highest talents; but Lockhart gave his warm love, his sheer talents, his very life to the service of our Order. His was a fusion of mental ability and a force of individuality rare on earth.

He had the daring of youth, the vigor of mankind, the judgment of a genius, the wisdom of maturity. Joy and love in his service blended with intellectual strength made him a landmark of Masonry in Texas, and a human monument to our Order. His memory lives in our hearts and minds, a source of exaltation, of inspiration.

And so to us from falling hands he has thrown the torch, but ours to hold it high.[69]

In his 1956 Grand Master's Address, Maxey again praised his predecessor:

That the "Prince of Shadows" lives a shining mark was never more truly said than the sudden and untimely death of our beloved Grand Master, L. L. Lockhart. The news of his passing brought to us grief and a sense of loss, not only to our own jurisdiction, but to Prince Hall Masonry everywhere. So, in the presence of his bereaved family, his host of friends, and a large group of his Masonic brethren, he was laid to rest with the Most Worshipful Prince Hall Grand Lodge conducting the graveside services.[70]

From 1946 to 1955, Lockhart and Maxey were a team. Despite Maxey's two unsuccessful efforts to unseat Lockhart, it appears that the relationship between these two men was generally harmonious. No doubt Maxey learned a great deal from Lockhart, who did a very effective job leading Prince Hall Masonry in Texas during the postwar period. Thus Maxey was well qualified to take over the Masonic ship and steer into new waters during the Civil Rights era that was dawning.

John Theodore Maxey

John Theodore Maxey (1874-1973) was the fifteenth Grand Master of Prince Hall Masons in Texas. He took office in 1955— a year in which America was deep into the civil rights revolution. On May 17 of the previous year, in *Brown v. Board of Education*, the U. S. Supreme Court had declared that racial segregation in public schools and other facilities was a violation of the equal protection clause of the Fourteenth Amendment to the U. S. Constitution. In this decision, Chief Justice Earl Warren, Past Grand Master of Masons in California, wrote:

> We conclude that in the field of public education the doctrine of "separate but equal" has no place. Separate educational facilities are inherently unequal. Therefore, we hold that the plaintiffs and others similarly situated for whom the actions have been brought are, by reason of the segregation complained of, deprived of the equal protection of the laws guaranteed by the Fourteenth Amendment.[1]

In his 1955 Grand Master's Address, Lucian L. Lockhart called May 17 "Freedom Day."[2] A few months after delivering this address, Grand Master Lockhart was called from the Grand East to the Eternal East and Deputy Grand Master J. T. Maxey ascended to the highest office in Texas Masonry.

John Theodore Maxey was born on November 18, 1874, in Trinity, Texas, the son of Mr. and Mrs. John Joseph Maxey.[3] In Trinity, the elder Maxey was employed as a porter in a railroad depot. Later he was transferred to Round Rock, Texas. The Maxey family was living there when outlaw Sam Bass attempted to rob a bank and was killed by the Texas Rangers.[4] Eventually, young Maxey was sent to live in Houston with his grandmother, Mrs. Rachel Mitchell, who worked as a cook and housekeeper in Mrs. Bailey's Boarding House, a domicile for young white couples who worked in Houston offices. At the age of six, he was taken into the Bailey fold and studied with the governess of the Bailey children. He continued his education at a missionary school operated by two ladies from Boston and at a number of private schools before attending Gregory Institute, a high school in Houston's fourth ward. At the age of fourteen, he headed west to seek adventure. He and a friend saved money, bought some overalls, and caught a train to San Antonio. He found jobs in San Antonio, Austin, El Paso, Phoenix (where he worked for the Barnum and Bailey Circus), Los Angeles, San Francisco, St. Louis, Hutchinson, Denver, and Oklahoma City. He finally returned to Houston, after receiving word from his family that he was needed back home. At the time of the Spanish-American War, he worked as an extra porter on the Katy Flyer, with a division from Galveston to Smithville.[5]

In 1898 Maxey established residence in Galveston, where he remained for the rest of his long and productive life. Initially he went to work for J. H. Hill, general manager of the GH&H Railroad Company, as an office porter and messenger. During a 1966 interview, he recalled: "I was working the day the 1900 storm hit and remember it as if it were only yesterday."[6] He continued his work for the Galveston Island railroads, moving from GH&H to Santa Fe and acquiring more and more responsibility until he retired in 1949. During World War I, he worked for the federal government as a coach foreman to supply and service passenger equipment used in transporting American soldiers.[7] During this period, he served on the citizens committee called Four Minute Men, organized by the government to boost morale. This group was headed by Father Cirri, a well-known Catholic priest. For his work on this committee, Maxey received a certificate of merit from President Woodrow Wilson.[8]

In 1902 Maxey married Sallie A. Harris, a graduate of Galveston's Central High School. They built a home that year at 4316 Broadway. No children were born to this union. In 1952 they celebrated their fiftieth wedding anniversary. Sallie Maxey died later that year. In 1956 the eighty-two-year-old widower married Lucille E. Garrett of Galveston.[9] They continued to reside at 4316 Broadway. At the age of ninety-one, Maxey erected a twelve-foot-high fence around this house single-handedly. The building of the fence was followed by a "Texas-sized paint job."[10]

Maxey became interested in Masonry while living in Houston. He was involved in several lodges there and in Galveston. He devoted much more of his time to Masonry after his retirement from the railroad. The walls of his home office—which he constructed from an upstairs porch—were full of Masonic plaques and certificates of merit, including the Thurgood Marshall Award from the NAACP.[11] He was a member of Amity Lodge No. 4, a 33° Scottish Rite Mason, and a Noble of El Katif Temple No. 85, Ancient Egyptian Arabic Order of Nobles of the Mystic Shrine in Galveston.[12]

On June 27, 1956, Maxey delivered his first Grand Master's Address, expressing his one objective as the promotion of the welfare of the Prince Hall Grand Lodge of Texas.[13] In this address, he warned against frivolousness and carelessness,[14] but reported that the financial condition of the lodges was improving and the membership increasing.[15] Maxey also reported his attendance at the Conference of Prince Hall Grand Masters in Boston on May 21-24, 1956. At this conference, outstanding speeches were made by Grand Master Amos T. Hall of Oklahoma and NAACP Chief Legal Counsel Thurgood Marshall, whom he called "Mr. Civil Rights."[16] Maxey declared that Masonic education is as important to Masons as general education is to citizens.[17] At the conclusion of the 1956 Communication, Maxey was returned to the Grand East—as he was every year until 1965, when he announced his retirement.

On March 9, 1957, an Executive Directors' Stated Communication was called by the Grand Master. At this session, a number of resolutions passed. One of these approved the action of the Grand Lodge Trustee Board in purchasing property and erecting a building in the Lake Como area of Fort Worth, at a cost of $44,000. Another authorized sale of the Home for Aged Masons at 1404 Riverside Drive in Fort Worth for a sum of $125,000, less fee expense. At the time, this site was generating no income and had become a burden in taxes and upkeep.[18]

Much of the meeting of the Executive Directors was devoted to the crisis faced by Fort Worth's Fraternal Bank and Trust.[19] The seriousness of the crisis became apparent when the directors approved the deposit of $102,470 in the Continental National Bank rather than the Fraternal Bank and Trust. Maxey explained his difficulty in arranging a meeting with the Fraternal Bank's stockholders and directors. Eventually, Executive Vice-President I. P. Anderson appeared before the officers summoned by the Grand Master. In response to questions, Anderson reported that approximately $200,000 in bank loans were secured by real estate, that 6% was the normal rate of interest on loans, that loans were considered secured loans when there were one or two co-signers, and that there was $140,000 in liens against the bank held by Fort Worth National Bank.[20] When Maxey asked about the bank's ability to survive the sudden run of withdrawals that had hit in the past week, Anderson replied:

> Grand Master, the condition is very dangerous. As to the withdrawals during the past weekend, I cannot say how long it will last. This has happened at other times before, when rumors start circulating through the town, but we have always been able to withstand them. Frankly, I cannot say if it will be the same this time because I do not know how long it will last, or how heavy the withdrawals will be. However, we have had some of our heaviest depositors make withdrawals this week because of rumors leaked out of our last meeting with the Grand Lodge Trustee Board. . . . All banks experience the same kind of run in withdrawals at some time or other. It is just one of the things to expect in the banking business. But a substantial deposit by the Grand Lodge or Heroines of Jericho would tide the bank over this crisis and the customers would come back as they have always done.[21]

When asked if the bank had been borrowing money for the last thirty years, Anderson said: "No, the first year the bank borrowed was the first year that Bill McDonald took sick, and after that, it was three years ago?" In response to the question of "How much was borrowed in the past three years?" he said: "$100,000 the first year, $150,000 the next year, and $250,000 this year—all of which we have been able to pay back, except this year. The First National Bank understands our peculiar situation, in that we depend on the September and December deposits as a great means of operation and are willing to go along and play ball with us." These remarks were followed by a lengthy discussion of the bank's tendency to depend on these deposits for its operations, investments, and loans. It was suggested that the bank go into voluntary receivership rather than fail outright. Anderson responded that the only alternative to voluntary receivership would be large deposits by the Masons and Heroines. He recalled that Past Grand Master Lockhart had feared that the bank was shaky until he became the president and then said it was in good shape. He also observed that Lockhart had instructed his wife to sell all of his stock in the event of his death. He asked why Mrs. Lockhart could do so if the bank stock was not good. After Anderson was excused, the directors unanimously approved Maxey's suggestion that the initial payment received from the sale of the Home for Aged Masons, less fee expense, would be deposited in the Continental National Bank. The Grand Master announced that he would send notice to the Most Ancient Grand Matron of the Heroines of Jericho "informing her of action taken in trying to stem the tide as concerns the bank, and yet salvage something for the two heaviest depositors."[22]

On June 25, 1957, at the Grand Communication, Maxey informed the craft of the bank crisis during his Grand Master's Address:

> The news of the failure of the Fraternal Bank and Trust Company, which had been our depository for many years, was a shock to our membership and caused much distrust and some criticism by some of our members. So please permit me to say that it should be apparent to our membership that we are facing the most stupendous problems that directly affects of fraternal life is financial. As all of you know, this Grand Lodge was the owner of 700 shares in this bank, and being a private institution, we are held to be a partner and, therefore, all stockholders are held responsible to the depositors of the defunct bank. The causes that produced these conditions are manifold and complex, and their solution will be difficult and tedious. However, plans for its solution will be given to this Grand Lodge to accept or reject. . . . I requested that the bank be audited and was informed that the condition was such that it would not stand an audit. So . . . we thought it wise to arrange for another and safer depository. . . . After paying commitments and other bills, we deposited $55,223.54 in a checking account in the Continental National Bank. Having a very heavy death rate and also being required to redeem many checks that had been issued on the now defunct bank, we have exhausted our checking account and have been forced to draw on our savings so that we can continue to pay our first relief checks and operate the Grand Lodge. . . . On March 9, 1957, before the closing of the bank, I called a meeting of the directors to report my activities and findings and requested their approval.[23]

On the following day, Roger Hughes, chairman of the Trustee Board, gave the following report on the bank:

> Some three years ago, I was appointed to the building committee of this Grand Lodge. Some of the duties of this committee were to see after the affairs of anything pertaining to this Grand Lodge. We, as a committee, began to inquire about the Fraternal Bank and Trust Company. Bro. L. L. Lockhart, the Past Grand Master, would always stop us whenever we started to ask questions about the bank. He would say "I didn't put you on the committee to fool with the bank." So we were handicapped when we started on this subject. After the passing of Mr. Lockhart, Bro. Maxey took Bro. Lockhart's place, and the Building Committee became the trustees of the Grand Lodge. We began again to find out something about the bank, and with his full cooperation we began to go into different phases and inquiries. We found out that, in 1948 or '49, they borrowed $50,000 to pay the relief. In 1950, they borrowed $150,000 and, in 1956, they borrowed $250,000, all of this each year to pay off the relief checks in June. Knowing this all the time, we had gotten suspicious as to why they had to borrow money each year with the Masons and the Heroines having on deposit over $900,000 in a checking account. Mind you that, after the passing of Bro. Lockhart, we did not have a representative on the Board of Directors, nor on the

Board of Stockholders. We contacted Bro. I. P. Anderson about having had to own stock in the bank to be put on the board. I would like to call your attention to this. Every time we went in the bank as a committee to inquire about anything concerning the bank, we were told that we were not on any of these boards; consequently, we had no right to make certain inquiries. So we rocked along with this situation for some time. Finally, the trustees wrote Bro. Anderson a letter in October 1956 telling him that we demanded a representative on the Board of Directors to see after our interest. Not until then did we get them to accept Bro. Maxey on the Board of Directors. Then we found out that they owed the Fort Worth National Bank $200,000 and had a small balance in the bank. We had Bro. Anderson in the trustee meeting at his request and we found out from him then that we were sunk. The Grand Master then called a meeting of his Grand Lodge officers on March 9, 1957. He then told them what he had discovered and wanted their ideas and opinions as to what to do. They had Bro. Anderson to come before the committee and what we would call to lay the cards on the table. He told them just what he had run into, and left it in their hands as to what to do. What they did after that I do not know. As I outline this report, you can see how it looks up to now. During this time we were in the midst of selling the old folks home on Riverside Drive. We were soon to become in possession of over $50,000. Now here is the straw that broke the camel's back. They thought we would deposit this amount in their bank. Now, brethren, would you, after knowing the things I have told you up to this point, have put the money in this bank? I know you wouldn't. Well it was put in another bank, which I know was safe. We have used an attorney all along to advise us as to what to do. We knew all the time that even if they paid the Fort Worth National Bank that loan, they were not going to make them another loan.

So we began to do whatever was best to do, in order to have something to operate on in case of an emergency. During this meeting that was called by the Grand Master, one of the questions that was asked Bro. Anderson by me was, "How much money have the Grand Lodge and Heroines on deposit now?" The answer was $893,000. Then I asked if he could cash a check for $93,000? The answer was "no." Then I asked if he could cash a check for $40,000? The answer was "no." I only asked these questions for the benefit of the committee, for I knew he couldn't, but wanted them to know just what shape the bank was in. Can you imagine a bank with over one million dollars on deposit and couldn't cash a $40,000 check?[24]

The Report of the Chairman on the Bank was followed by a Special Committee Report, read by Chairman T. G. Givens. This included the findings of the auditing firm of Mendenhall and Carter, which outlined in detail the financial structure and reverses of the Fraternal Bank and Trust Company. The committee recommended "that the Grand Lodge empower the Grand Master and the Board of Trustees to proceed forthwith to borrow, or otherwise secure in any way they deem feasible and advisable, to the best results of the Grand Lodge, sufficient finance to acquire receivership of the Fraternal Bank and Trust Company and all of its assets."[25] The Grand Master spoke of legal action against certain customers and shareholders of the bank. In view of the Grand Lodge's grave financial situation which had resulted from the bank's closure, he called for temporarily reducing ready relief to $200.[26]

On June 28, 1957, the Report of the Committee on the Grand Master's Address was read by Chairman James F. Felton. This report indicates the great respect in which Maxey was held by Texas Masons. According to this report:

The detailed manner in which he outlined the unhealthy conditions existing in the Fraternal Bank and Trust Company prior to its closing, the present precarious position of the Grand Lodge as the result of its failure and the remedies suggested to preserve our position of eminence among fraternal institutions; the many visitations—both within and without the jurisdiction, the enormous administrative duties of his office and the almost endless demands on the time and energy of the Grand Master of a jurisdiction covering the area ours does and posing problems, many of which are unique with us, are a task which would faze a man of lesser strength, vision, and sagacity.

This Grand Lodge is most fortunate to have had his service last year and was most wise in virtually demanding that he continue his fine leadership at a time which is most critical in the history of our institution. We firmly believe that, with his expert generalship and hard work and the diligent support of every member of the jurisdiction of the Most Worshipful Prince Hall Grand Lodge F.&A.M. of Texas will remain the outstanding fraternal organization of Texas and the nation.[27]

Under Maxey's leadership, the Grand Lodge was able to weather the storm. One year later, when the craft reassembled in Fort Worth, a spirit of optimism was in the air. Deputy Grand Master J. H. McGowen quoted President Franklin D. Roosevelt, who said "All roads are open; all detours have been removed, and all signs read, FULL SPEED AHEAD!!!" McGowen declared: "As we work together toward our common goal, we have nothing to fear but fear itself!!!"[28] As during the previous year, Roger Hughes read his Report of the Chairman of Trustees, stating:

MEETING OF NOVEMBER 23, 1957: Reviewed action of $370,000 paid to receiver by permission of 153rd District Court to purchase assets of defunct Fraternal Bank and Trust Company. The $370,000 obtained as follows: $78,288.25 from Grand Lodge account, $62,500 note cashed for sale of Old Folks Home, $29,211.75 from sale of property in front of Mosque, $200,000 installment note made to Fort Worth National Bank, at 5% interest. As of May 31, 1958, a total of $90,000 plus interest had been paid on note leaving balance of $110,000 due Fort Worth National Bank. All non-shareholder depositors and creditors of defunct F. B. &T. Co. were paid back every cent. This was a great accomplishment. There is something about this situation that can never be written without mentioning the fact that it was a Masonic Lodge down in Texas that paid off every depositor after a bank that carried their name went broke. Accomplishments like this cannot be crushed for long. They have some way of coming up even if some people try hard not to give credit where credit is due. In the horrible and most unbelievable situation of the defunct F. B. & T. Co.—when it was in operation—loans seemed to have been made to every crook that came along and wanted some money, some with no security at all; most any good-looking woman could borrow with no security. . . . We have facts that have never been known before, we have real money—not book value or on paper—we as Masons should feel proud of what has been accomplished—we can look the world in the eye and know we have not let such men as Wright Cuney and others down. Again I say we are proud that we are Masons and there is no yellow streak down our backs. Again it has been demonstrated that right pays, and God continuously stays on right's side.[29]

In his 1958 Grand Master's Address, Maxey was candid about pressing problems but expressed a determination to keep things under control.

As we meet today our great country is passing through a period of unprecedented financial, political, and economical crisis, which has brought some distress and unemployment in many localities, and our Texas Masonry has not been entirely exempt from the unhappy effects of this universal catastrophe. While our records show some shrinkage, many new additions have strengthened us numerically and financially, and I take great pleasure in reporting that, despite the drawbacks to this Grand Lodge, we have made and are making marked progress in recovering from the tragedy caused by the failure of the Fraternal Bank and Trust Company. I will now present to you a condensed, but informative, report of our financial condition since the failure of the Fraternal Bank and Trust Company.

When this bank closed we lost every penny we had on deposit in the bank, which was $374,886.12. All stockholders not only lost their deposits, but were held responsible for all losses. So, to save our great fraternity from bankruptcy, we were forced to raise $370,000, which was the amount required to pay all non-stockholder depositors and other debts of the bank. As the other stockholders refused or failed to cooperate with us, we had to bear the financial burden alone. So, by mortgaging our assets, we borrowed $200,000 required. After all debts of the bank were paid, the receiver and his force was discharged and we became the sole owner of all notes, properties, and assets of the defunct bank.[30]

In the same address, Maxey reported his participation in a conference sponsored by the President's Minority Resources Committee at the Willard Hotel in Washington, D.C. on January 15, 1958. The purpose of this conference was to encourage mobilization of resources for the task of motivating minority youth to acquire training for an increasing number of skilled and technical jobs. He was delighted to see many other Prince Hall Grand Masters at this conference.[31] Maxey also reported his attendance at the Prince Hall Grand Masters Conference in Cleveland, Ohio, May 14-17, 1958. Presiding over this meeting was the conference president, Grand Master Amos T. Hall of Oklahoma. Highlights included inspirational addresses by Grand Master John Wesley Dobbs of Georgia, Jno. G. Lewis, Jr., of Louisiana, and Attorney Thurgood Marshall.[32] He reported the collection of $1,328.05 in the scholarship fund established for sons and daughters of Prince Hall Masons who desire a college education.[33] He concluded:

From my personal experience, I have learned one great truth: "One cannot get more out of anything than one puts into it." To attain great heights, we must climb and bear all the hardships of climbing. Just as one finds injustice and hardships in life, so one finds love, respect, and vivid interest. It is not life that matters, it is the courage you bring into it. If we meet the challenge of life with courage, then whether we succeed or fail, we shall have known the joy of trying.[34]

At the close of the 1958 Communication, Grand Master Maxey and Deputy Grand Master McGowen were unanimously reelected. Incumbent Grand Senior Warden J. H. Lockhart defeated O. W. L. Turner and Patrick Bolton. Incumbent Grand Junior Warden L. L. Davis defeated Dr. J. W. Yancy II. Grand Secretary Leon Maddox announced his retirement due to ill health. The Grand Lodge accepted his recommendation that Harold B. Baker be elected as his successor. Grand Treasurer A. H. Hollie, Grand Recorder A. D. Harris, and Grand Chaplain H. O. Scott were unanimously reelected. O. E. Nelson was elected Grand Tiler over Clinton Whitehead and Reuben G. White.[35]

In his 1959 Grand Master's Address, Maxey pointed out that eighty-four years of Prince Hall Freemasonry had meant much to black Texans:

> From its organization of five small lodges, with but few members, it has grown and prospered until today we have, in this jurisdiction, 560 subordinate lodges with a total membership of 29,867 loyal and faithful members. This membership includes many of the most prominent and leading citizens of this great state of Texas. . . . It is a pleasure to announce that despite misfortune and heavy financial losses, we are recovering at a rapid pace, and we hope in the very near future to pay our last note, and plan to place our great organization on a stronger financial base. . . . Since serving as Grand Master, I have had only one request for a fifty-year certificate. I think that our lodges that have members in the fifty-year bracket should present these old and deserving members a fitting recognition of their long and useful service as Master Masons.[36]

Maxey reported his attendance at the Prince Hall Grand Masters' Conference which was held May 13-15, 1959, in New York City. He had much praise for Attorney Thurgood Marshall, Grand Master Jordan of New York, and Grand Master Richard A. Henries of Liberia.[37] He called for support for the Scholarship Fund and the NAACP. He also recommended the adoption of "a modern, dignified, and symbolic graveside service that can be easily memorized by any intelligent Mason."[38]

It was obvious to anyone who knew Maxey that this outstanding Grand Master did not believe in wasting time and that he believed in giving credit where credit was due. The Committee on the Grand Master's Address, chaired by James F. Felton, took note of these facts in the following observation:

> While the speech was characterized by his customary brevity and was without unnecessary verbiage and ponder-phrases, the clarity of Bro. Maxey's ideas, the sincerity with which he attacked each problem and his almost unique masterful manner of delivery, make this easily the greatest and most momentous address ever delivered before this most worshipful body; great in that it showed that our Grand Master is keenly aware of the problems which are most pressing, and applies his energy to the solving of these rather than dissipating valuable time and energy on trivialities and extraneous diversions which might temporarily enhance his prestige but which would eventually work to the detriment to our honorable order and to himself—momentous in that some of the information given us was in the nature of a release from the anxiety which many may have felt about the eventual recovery of the Grand Lodge from the debacle of 1957, the failure of the Fraternal Bank and Trust Company. The disclosure that very shortly the major indebtedness in this connection will be liquidated was most welcome news. . . . In mentioning the lack of requests for fifty-year pins, the Grand Master reminded the Craft that it should honor those elder brethren who have borne the burden in the heat of the day.[39]

The year 1960 was the beginning of a new decade—one that would go down in history as an important decade of change for America and for the world. Texas Prince Hall Masons who had made the pilgrimage to Fort Worth for the 1960 Grand Lodge Communication recognized that a new day had begun. In his Grand Master's Address, Maxey reflected this spirit when he said:

> Now as we resume our labors, it should give us pleasure in our retrospect of the past years to know that, although we have suffered heavy financial losses in the past few years, and being faced with a very heavy death rate, yet, we are climbing to the heights; as we have paid our debts; made necessary repairs to our Mosque by applying a new roof, replacing fallen plaster, and repainting our lodge rooms; accumulated a reserve account for future protection, and after making the final payment to the 1956-57 beneficiaries, it will be a pleasure to announce that we can plant the flag of victory over the forces of evil on the four corners of our beautiful Masonic Mosque. . . .
>
> Masonic scholars tell us that Masonry is a living and not a dead philosophy. . . . We must remember that knowledge is gained by study and research and by the bright lights of today. We, as Prince Hall masons, must continue to dig into the quarries of history to search and find the truth and, above all, we should strive to learn just what Masonry is, so that we can remain young amidst aging toll of past years.[40]

In this address, Maxey spoke on the subject of leadership, stating: "The man who aspires to climb, who has the ambition to achieve something beyond the mediocre, must have within himself a veritable foundation of faith, an inexhaustible supply of courage, a willingness and readiness to go to the BAT with difficulties which look insurmountable." He quoted from an article in *Masonic Inspiration*, in which Charles Van Cott wrote: "Prince Hall is as legitimate as any white lodge. And God speed the day when there will be no white, black, or yellow Masons! Just a world of brotherhood of men of all races, colors, and creeds devoted to helping end the miseries of human life and bring about a better world for all of the sons of one eternal God!"[41]

The same spirit of optimism characterized the Report of the Deputy Grand Master, in which McGowen said:

> We Prince Hall Masons of Texas hold within our hands the possibilities of helping in the new birth of the day, and what great possibilities they are! At the same time, we possess the capabilities of standing idly by. It will be awful for the new day to dawn and we have no hand in it. . . .
>
> I cannot say how or when it began. Perhaps with Dr. Lonnie Smith, in pressing for the right to vote, perhaps with Herman Sweatt, as he was granted the privilege of entering the University of Texas. Perhaps with Dr. Martin Luther King, as he led his group in such a marvelous way in Montgomery, Alabama crises. The students and leaders in Little Rock had a hand in it. More recently, the "sit-ins" through the nation have been added to this list of efforts to usher in the New Day. The morning cannot be held back, the morning will come, and we must help make it come.[42]

Also significant was the 1960 Report of the Grand Lecturer, delivered by S. P. Smead, who urged Texas Masons: "Let us not engage in fault finding with our newly adopted Ritual, which was carefully selected by the best Masonic scholars among the Prince Hall Masons of America" and praised the pamphlets recently prepared for use in the Masonic Catechism.[43] Smead stressed the importance of quality instruction, insisting that "The lectures should be studied and accurately memorized by each candidate initiated. To accomplish this, he must be taught by a competent brother who not only has the knowledge, but has the ability to make necessary explanations of the difficult parts." He asked, "If the instructor be lacking in knowledge, how can the initiate learn?"[44]

At the 1961 Communication, Deputy Grand Master McGowen, in his Report of the Chairman of the Committee on Foreign Correspondence, stated: "I am glad to report to you that progress is being made and humanity is being helped, as Prince Hall Masonry goes marching on."[45] In his Deputy Grand Master's Annual Report, McGowen addressed a number of contemporary events in relation to civil rights:

> Some days ago, I noted with interest, an editorial report on a meeting of Southern State Attorney Generals in their Regional Conference. They were seriously disturbed because of current efforts on the part of some U. S. Congressmen to enact civil rights legislation, aimed at enforcing the Supreme Court's public school desegregation order of 1954.
>
> These elected public legal officials seem to envision only one possible replacement of the Southern way of life, and that is Communism. . . . It is exceedingly difficult to understand how individuals who are as conversant with the principles of the American Constitutional Law as these jurists are can equate the application of such legal measures as the Fourteenth Amendment to the U. S. Constitution with the principles of Communism.
>
> Thurgood Marshall and other prominent Negro leaders are asking in the courts of the land, if such an unjust system has any place in a Democratic State. Prince Hall Grand Lodges across these United States of America have contributed something like $175,000 to the Legal Research Fund of the N.A.A.C.P. to help in this great fight for "Freedom and Equality." College students of both races have employed the Mahatma Gandhi, of India, method of "Nonviolence" in combatting [sic] these unjust practices. The "Freedom Riders," a more recent "Nonviolence" group of protestors of the "Southern Way of Life" are riding into Alabama, South Carolina, Mississippi, and other Southern States. This is an integrated group of college students and Christian leaders. As they move in on "Old Jim Crow," they are being brutalized and imprisoned. . . .
>
> My fervent prayer is that the battle of right against wrong will continue, until the Brotherhood of Man and the Fatherhood of God is not only talked but is practiced.[46]

At this session, a letter from Richard L. Martin of the law firm of Alexander and Martin was read. This letter expressed much praise for the Prince Hall Grand Lodge of Texas "for the manner in which it has taken care of all of its obligations arising out of the near disaster caused by the insolvency of the Fraternal Bank and Trust Company."[47]

In his Grand Master's Address, Maxey reported his attendance at the Forty-first Conference of Prince Hall Grand Masters in Boston, Massachusetts, August 10-14, 1960. He was accompanied to this meeting by Grand Secretary Harold B. Baker. The conference was combined with the Decennial Celebration of Prince Hall Masonry. Various houses of Masonry were represented there. The Shriners and Daughters of Isis put on outstanding parades. The meeting climaxed with a visit to the tomb of Prince Hall in Copps Hill Burying Ground.[48] He also reported his attendance at the Forty-second Conference of Prince Hall Grand Masters at the Casa Italiana Hall in Seattle, Washington. At this meeting, he persuaded the other Grand Masters to bring their 1962 session to Houston. He reported that the Grand Banquet was held at the Chamber of Commerce Building and included talks by the mayor, governor, and Judge Thurgood Marshall.[49] In addressing the matter of Masonic education, he quoted

Dr. Joseph Fort Newton, who defined Masonry as "a philosophy of life, the depth, breadth, sanity, and nobility of which is not matched elsewhere, and not only a philosophy but a way of living, a method of building character, found nowhere else."

He stressed the importance of both Masonic history and ritual. He called upon Masons to "cast off the rags of triviality, flippancy, and self-indulgence." He recommended the observance of Prince Hall and Americanism Day on September 12 and called for the upkeep of the monument to the founding of the Texas Grand Lodge at Brenham.[50]

During the 1961-62 Masonic year, a number of prominent Texas Masons were called from labor to reward. On August 15, 1961, Grand Secretary Emeritus Leon Maddox died. D.C. Collins, Worshipful Master of Metropolitan Lodge No. 146 in Dallas, was appointed to succeed him on the Grand Lodge Trustee Board. At the meeting of the board on August 26, 1961, a resolution in memory of Bro. Maddox was approved.[51] Deputy Grand Master McGowen died at his home in Beaumont on December 29, 1961. Grand Master Maxey performed his Masonic graveside services near Beaumont. Grand Junior Warden L. L. Davis died on March 21, 1962. He was buried in McKinney. Graveside services were conducted by T. G. Givens, an educator from Paris who had succeeded Bro. McGowen as Deputy Grand Master. On May 15, 1962, T. W. Pratt, Grand Patron Emeritus of the Grand Chapter, Order of the Eastern Star, died in Dallas. He was buried four days later, with graveside services conducted by the Grand Chapter.[52]

At the aforementioned meeting of Grand Lodge Trustee Board, Grand Secretary Baker gave a report on the monument site in Brenham, stating that additional land had been added by the city, lights had been erected, and curbing had been placed around the entire site. He explained that the expense to the Grand Lodge was only the wholesale cost of the lights and curbing. The improvement of the monument site was under the supervision of B. T. Hogan, Worshipful Master of Star East Lodge No. 276 in Brenham and Associate Grand Patron for the Order of the Eastern Star.[53]

Although five years had passed since the failure of the Fraternal Bank and Trust Company, at the time of the 1962 Communication the bank issue was far from dead. At this session, a letter from attorney Richard L. Martin was read. The letter stated: "We will continue to work to try to recoup as much of the loss sustained by you as possible, through the collection of notes, judgments, etc., that are still outstanding. In all probability the collections have levelled [sic] off but should, for the next few years, remain a little less than the period from May 31, 1962, through May 31, 1963."[54]

In his 1962 Grand Master's Address, Maxey spoke about Masonic philosophy and showed great pride as he reported on the outstanding session of the Conference of Prince Hall Grand Masters hosted in Houston on April 19-21, 1962. This conference included a public meeting at Saint John's Baptist Church. A welcome was brought by the Honorable Louis Cutrer, mayor of Houston, who presented the key to the city to Oklahoma Grand Master Amos. T. Hall, the conference president. The closing address by Judge Thurgood Marshall was enthusiastically received. Maxey extended thanks to W. L. Hopkins, chairman of the conference committee; and to the sisters of the Order of the Eastern Star and Heroines of Jericho for their help in entertaining their distinguished guests.[55]

In his address, Maxey also discussed the cooperative system of Masonic relief, explaining the history and present status of such. He stressed the fact that Masonry is *not* an insurance organization. He explained that relief benefits are measured by the number of deaths in a Masonic year, in addition to the number of members on the rolls. He candidly admitted that "with our extremely heavy death rate in the last Masonic year, the legitimate beneficiaries may receive less than formerly, and will be governed by the number of financial members."[56] He addressed the perennial problem of lack of attendance at lodge meetings, stating: "I also find that many members only join the order for financial benefits and, therefore, do not attend lodge meetings, do not visit sick or decrepit brethren, do not attend Masonic funerals, but should HE get sick or disabled, he thinks that the lodge members should rush to his aid, and do for him the things that he has failed to do for them. This type of member has proven himself to be an 'Un-deserving Brother.'"[57] He also addressed the ever important matter of friendship, saying: "As we grow older, the thing that becomes more and more clear to us is the importance of friendship. I can conceive of no greater satisfaction than that of conducting myself that I may constantly add to my friends, and thereby obtain a fuller meaning of life. To live for the most there is in life must mean that we cannot live to ourselves alone. If we wish real success, we must work and build together."[58]

On June 26, 1962, Maxey was unanimously reelected as Grand Master. T. G. Givens was elected Deputy Grand Master, defeating three challengers. O. W. L. Turner, who had received the second highest number of votes, conceded the election to Givens. Isadore Huddleston Clayborn was elected Grand Senior Warden, defeating Reuben G. White and Elroy Combs.[59] Ernest Wisby defeated several other candidates for the office of Grand Junior Warden.[60]

On September 8, 1962, a meeting of the Grand Lodge Board of Trustees was held. At this meeting, Chairman Roger Hughes explained that the Grand Lodge's building was becoming obsolete and, looking to the future, there was for sale a building located at 2851 Evans Avenue which would serve the Grand Lodge well.[61] On December 14, 1962, the Grand Lodge received a communication from the officers and trustees of Tabernacle Lodge No. 1195 of the Grand Lodge of Texas, A.F.&A.M. (white), with an offer to sell their hall at this location. Grand Master Maxey called a meeting of the Grand Lodge trustees, who met with the officers and trustees of Tabernacle Lodge. After a thorough inspection, the Prince Hall Masons assembled decided to purchase the property. Maxey called a special meeting of the Grand Lodge Board of Directors of January 26, 1963, and convened a Special Grand Communication. On the latter date, a general inspection was made and the craft voted unanimously to purchase the building for $45,000. Of this amount, $13,500 came from note collections.[62] The Grand Lodge Board of Trustees met again on June 8, 1963. The board unanimously approved the motion of D. C. Collins that the Grand Lodge pay for Roger Hughes' elevation to the 33° and pay his expenses to the United Supreme Council session in New Orleans in October 1963.[63]

Among the highlights of Maxey's 1963 Grand Master's Address were the following words of wisdom:

> While the ancient operative builders erected temples, cathedrals, etc., all to the glory of the Grand Architect of the Universe, we as speculative Masons devote ourselves to

the task of building a citizenship of such character that will likewise glorify God, and today as Prince Hall Masons and loyal and patriotic Americans, we will continue to fight for our right to enjoy first class citizenship. . . . We as regular Masons are seeking the happiness of the human race and equal justice for all. We must not fail to do our sworn duty as Masons and eventually establish on earth, the belief in the Fatherhood of God and Brotherhood of Man. . . . We should always remember that the Brotherhood of Man depends upon the "manhood of the brother."[64]

At this session, Maxey was reelected Grand Master and I. H. Clayborn was elected Deputy Grand Master. The Grand Lodge Board of Trustees met on August 10, 1963, and discussed plans for moving the Grand Lodge office from 405 East Ninth Street to 2851 Evans Avenue. At this meeting, plans were outlined to solicit contributions from each member to erect a monument to the first Grand Master of Texas, Norris Wright Cuney. On January 14, 1964, the board members traveled to Brenham to inspect the monument there and then to Galveston to inspect Cuney's gravesite at Lakeview Cemetery. All members agreed to purchase the Wright Cuney Monument from Ott Monument Works at 40th and Broadway streets in Galveston for $1,010. Sunday, June 21, 1964, was set for the unveiling and dedication. On June 6, 1964, a final meeting for the 1963-64 Masonic year was held. Assignments were made for the Wright Cuney Monument service at the Grand Communication. Roger Hughes was appointed as chairman of the special bus to carry Grand Lodge officers and members to the service in Galveston.[65]

After arriving in Galveston on the scheduled Sunday, Texas Prince Hall Masons assembled in Reedy Chapel AME Church. They proceeded to open an occasional lodge, form a motorcade, and gather at the cemetery, where Grand Lodge officers performed the dedication ceremonies. There was a short address by the mayor of Galveston and remarks by Past Masters and other speakers. The highlight of the program was a speech by Maxey in honor of Cuney.[66]

On June 23, 1964, Maxey delivered his Grand Master's Address. He spoke of much progress and development in Texas Prince Hall Masonry during the past eighty-nine years and of the challenge to Prince Hall Masons to face the struggle for first-class American citizenship. He reported that the Grand Lodge was in a prosperous and flourishing condition, with relatively few suspensions for nonpayment of dues, greater interest in the lodges shown on the part of more members, and the erection of new lodge halls and the renovation of others.[67] He gave reports on his participation at the United Supreme Council on October 20-22, 1963, in New Orleans; the Grand Masters Conference in Denver on May 14-16, 1964; and the unveiling of the Wright Cuney Monument in Galveston on June 21, 1964.[68]

When the Prince Hall Masons of Texas assembled in Fort Worth for the 1965 Grand Communication, there was a feeling in the air that a new day was dawning—both for America and for Texas Masonry. Deputy Grand Master I. H. Clayborn, in his Report of the Chairman of the Committee on Foreign Correspondence, revealed that he had truly caught the *zeitgeist* of the 1960s.[69] In his Report of the Committee on Public Relations, Dr. Yancy reported that, on June 25, 1965, Grand Master Maxey, along with other Prince Hall Grand Masters, was scheduled to meet with a group of white Grand Masters in New York City. Maxey was unable to attend due to the fact that his own Grand Lodge was meeting at the same time.[70] Yancy recommended that "the existing Masonic Scholarship be changed and named: J. T. Maxey Memorial Prince Hall Scholarship."[71]

On June 23, 1995, Maxey delivered his final Grand Master's Address. As usual, he reported his participation in District Meetings, the United Supreme Council, and the Conference of Prince Hall Grand Masters. He discussed the nature of Masonic charity, calling on the craft to address the serious problem of unemployment.[72] Sadly, he had the responsibility of reporting a major tragedy to the craft. After the close of the 1964 Communication, Grand Secretary Harold B. Baker became ill and was confined in a hospital in Fort Worth. He was dismissed from the hospital and, after returning home, he experienced a severe mental disturbance. As a result, on August 21, 1964, he assaulted and cut his wife and stabbed his daughter to death. He was arrested and charged with murder. However, he was found insane and was sent to Rusk State Hospital. Maxey called upon the brethren to extend sympathy to his family and prayer for his recovery.[73] He appointed Bobby G. Webber as acting Grand Secretary and urged the Grand Lodge to unanimously elect him to this office.[74] In his address, the retiring Grand Master gave an account of ten years of stewardship:

> The great debts that we inherited when I came into the office as Grand Master in 1955 have been paid in full. We have erected a Masonic Temple and business building in Lake Como, we have purchased a modern Masonic office and lodge hall on Evans Avenue and Glen Garden Drive, bought and paid for extra property across the street from our office, and we have a cash reserve in our several depositories that is paying interest, and these funds can be used should we decide at some future period to erect a modern Masonic Temple to house the Masons, Heroines of Jericho, and the Order of the Eastern Star. The spreading of honesty, truth, efficiency, and righteousness has been carefully practiced, and we are recognized and appreciated for our good citizenship and well doing, which is revered by all true Prince Hall Masons. . . .
>
> Now, my good friends and fellow craftsmen, my labors as your Grand Master are about to come to an end, as I surrender the gavel of authority to my successor, it is my hope and prayer that this Grand Jurisdiction of Prince Hall Free and Accepted Masonry will continue to grow and prosper and that it will become a Landmark not only in the great state of Texas, but for the entire Prince Hall Free and Accepted Masons throughout the world.
>
> So I deem it an honor and a personal pleasure to receive the distinguished honor of being the only living Past Grand Master of the Most Worshipful Prince Hall Grand Lodge of Texas.[75]

During the 1965 Grand Lodge elections, Deputy Grand Master Clayborn was unanimously elected as Grand Master. Grand Senior Warden Reuben G. White was elected as Deputy Grand Master after T. G. Givens declined nomination. Grand Recorder A. D. Harris was nominated for Grand Senior Warden but declined, stating that he felt he could render better service as Grand Recorder. D. C. Collins was elected as Grand Senior Warden, W. L. Hopkins as Grand Junior Warden, Bobby G. Webber as Grand Secretary, A. H. Hollie as Grand Treasurer, A. D. Harris as Grand Recorder, J. H. Lockhart as Grand Lecturer, and E. H. Branch as Grand Chaplain.[76]

On June 25, 1965, an Audit Report was read. According to this report, during the 1964-65 Masonic year, $10,894.18 was received from the trust fund set up for liquidation of the assets from the defunct Fraternal Bank and Trust Company.[77] The latter institution had failed early in Maxey's administration. He had provided wise leadership in enabling the Grand Lodge to survive the loss of the bank. It appears that, by the end of his term of office, the bank issue was still present, but was no more a matter of great concern.

After the 1965 Communication, the ninety-year-old Past Grand Master returned to Galveston, where he spent his last eight years in retirement. However, as long as his health permitted, he continued to travel to Fort Worth to attend his beloved Grand Lodge, even serving as Chairman of the Committee on Foreign Correspondence (C.C.F.C.). In 1966, Grand Master Clayborn observed:

> As we meet this year we are certainly in the midst of something new, for we have in our number for the first time in years, a living Past Grand Master who on his own volition chose to be retired. The Honorable J. T. Maxey, whose report as C.C.F.C. you heard on yesterday, and under whose guidance we trod along the highway of Masonry unafraid of those hedges and shadows and darkness, because we knew that at the helm of our ship was a captain who had been tried and found to be in possession of the real fundamentals of a Grand Master.[78]

It appears that Maxey's brilliant mind and persevering spirit were active until the end. He died at 11:30 A.M. on Monday, February 12, 1973, at Saint Mary's Hospital in Galveston. On the night of Wednesday, February 14, a wake was held at Fields Funeral Home. Funeral services were held on Thursday, February 15, at Reedy Chapel AME Church, where he was a long-time member. The eulogy was delivered by Rev. S. L. Green. Burial was in Galveston Memorial Cemetery. Active pallbearers were members of the local Prince Hall lodges. Honorary pallbearers were all members of the Prince Hall Grand Lodge of Texas.[79]

During his 1973 Grand Master's Address, I. H. Clayborn paid tribute to his mentor:

> This time last year when I stood, one of the great men and Masons was in our midst, and today, he rests in the arms of our great "God." It is very appropriate at this time that we pay tribute to the late Bro. J. T. Maxey. You see there may be a few of you who aren't aware of the truth and fact that, if John Theodore Maxey had not had the right people to work with and the know how to lead men, we just might not be here today. Most of you know that he was a master of men and the arts and sciences of this body, known as Masonry. He did not have to back off from any man in regard to Masons and their duties to man.
>
> We pay homage and tribute to the Grand Old Man of Prince Hall Masons of the World, not just Texas, but to a man who was a man, to a brother who to me was brotherly, to a Past Grand Master who was a Grand Master who knew the trestle board of the School of Hard Knocks as well as the University of Getting a Job Done. Therefore, my brothers, I say to you as J. T. Maxey would say if he were here, "Mount up, and go aboard the ship, heist her masts, and let the ship of the Prince Hall Masons of Texas sail on, sail on, and on."[80]

Truly the ship of the Prince Hall Masons of Texas continues to sail on and on. The sailing is not always smooth, but the waters would be much stormier today but for the excellent leadership provided during an important decade of history by John Theodore Maxey.

Isadore Huddleston Clayborn

Isadore Huddleston Clayborn (1913-1994) was the sixteenth Grand Master of Prince Hall Masons in Texas and Sovereign Grand Commander of the Scottish Rite of Freemasonry, South Jurisdiction (Prince Hall Affiliation). This great man—who was the first Prince Hall Grand Master with whom the writer was personally acquainted—was born on July 21, 1913, in the community of Harrison Switch, near Waco, McLennan County, Texas. He grew up in McKinney, Collin County, Texas.[1] Clayborn became a Christian in 1929, at the age of sixteen,[2] and later moved to Dallas, Texas, where he was an ardent member of Good Street Baptist Church for over fifty years. He served his church as a deacon, trustee, Sunday school superintendent, and choir member. He taught the Bible class for the junior deacons, their wives, and associates and served as secretary of the Finance Committee and advisor to the Junior Deacon Board. On numerous occasions his church recognized him for outstanding service.[3]

Clayborn graduated from Frederick Douglass High School in McKinney. After studying at Jarvis Christian College in Hawkins, Texas, and at the University of Houston, he received the honorary Doctor of Laws degree from Arkansas Baptist College and the honorary Doctor of Humanities degree from Bishop College in Dallas.[4]

In 1936 he met Roberta Cathcart in Dallas. They were married on January 17, 1941. They lived in Chicago for a time, working in private homes.[5] Clayborn was inducted into the United States Army in 1942 and served in both the European and Pacific theaters during World War II. In 1945 he received an honorable discharge with the rank of master sergeant. He experienced a wide range of employment in the Dallas-Fort Worth Metroplex, including nineteen years as a maintenance supervisor for Eastman Kodak Corporation and twenty years as president and chief executive officer of Pioneer Management Company.[6]

Clayborn was also a member of the board of management of the Moorland Branch YMCA, the board of directors of Guaranty Bank, the United Way campaign committee, the capital improvement committee of the Oak Cliff Chamber of Commerce, the American Airlines Admiral Club, the Dallas Urban League, the Dallas Black Chamber of Commerce, the Dallas County Democratic Party, and the City of Dallas Planning and Zoning Committee. He served as a member of the Blue Ribbon Task Force '82 for the Dallas County Commissioners Court in evaluating the Criminal Justice Department.[7]

Clayborn was raised to the sublime degree of Master Mason in 1950. He served as Worshipful Master of Paul Drayton Lodge No. 9 in Dallas. Under his leadership, this lodge grew into one of the largest Prince Hall lodges in Texas. He received all of the degrees of the York Rite, serving for more than five years as Grand Recorder for the Lone Star Grand Commandery of Knights Templar. He received the 32° of the Scottish Rite in Dale Consistory No. 31 in Dallas and served as Commander-in-Chief of that body. Eventually he received the 33° from the United Supreme Council, Ancient and Accepted Scottish Rite, Southern Jurisdiction. From 1961 to 1965, he served as Deputy for Scottish Rite Masons in Texas. He also served the Supreme Council as Grand Marshal and as Grand Master of Ceremonies, and he served as Lieutenant Grand Commander from 1973 to 1979 and Sovereign Grand Commander from 1979 to 1994. A member of Zakat Temple No. 164, Ancient Egyptian Arabic Order of Nobles of the Mystic Shrine in Dallas, he was designated in this order as an Honorary Past Imperial Potentate and served as chairman of the Fraternal Relations Committee.[8]

Clayborn held a number of offices in the Prince Hall Grand Lodge of Texas. He served as Grand Senior Warden from 1962 to 1963 and as Deputy Grand Master from 1963 to 1965.[9] While holding the latter office, he gave the following speech to the Grand Lodge:

> As we sit, stand, or tramp around before the mystery boxes called TV sets to watch, hear, and wonder about the upward thrust of those mighty missals of space made by man and wait on reports from 108 to 180 miles up, it brings me to an abrupt stop—to say thanks be to "GOD" for life and the knowledge of the fact that we are living in that period of the Holy Bible that speaks of this era—when men would mount up on wings as birds and fly to the outer extremities of GOD's creation. So be it that we that our "GOD" for this privilege we now enjoy.
>
> Due to the circumstances over which we had no control, the work of the Grand Master and this speaker, as of last August 1964, became much greater in scope than before. I had to visit more to the Grand Lodge office and look and listen for every summons from the Grand Master. However, amidst all trials and tribulations, it's my feeling that "GOD" never places more upon our shoulders than we can bear if we only trust Him. In conformity with the Constitution, I joined the Grand Master, the Grand Treasurer, and the Assistant Grand Secretary in completing the work of the Committee on Grand Lodge Relief and Charity. . . . I am reminded of the sainted soul of our time, Martin Luther King, as he stood before national network TV and radio to make this statement: "I have a dream that, one day on the red hills of Georgia, the sons of former slaves and the sons of former slave owners will be able to sit down together at the table of brotherhood.
>
> "I have a dream that even in the state of Mississippi, the state that's sweltering with the heat of oppression, sweltering with the heat of injustice, will be transformed into an oasis of peace and love. I have a dream that one day my four little children and

yours will be able to 'live' in a nation where they will be judged not by the color of their skin but by the content of their character.

"We have a hope. This is our hope. This is the faith that I go back to the South with, that from the mountain of oppression we will be able to hue a stone of 'hope.'"

As your Deputy Grand Master, I have a dream that, as I go across our jurisdiction, I will find peace and harmony.

"I have a dream" that one day we will be able to sit down with the other at the table of Masonic brotherhood.

"This is my hope" that we will not only remain the greatest Masonic family on earth, but that the Great Architect of the Universe will smile His blessings on us to the extent that we will be welcome above when we move from this scene.[10]

On June 23, 1965, after Grand Master J. T. Maxey announced his retirement, Deputy Grand Master Clayborn was unanimously elected to succeed his mentor in the Grand East.[11] During his sixteen-year tenure as Grand Master, more than $80,000 in Masonic scholarships would be awarded to deserving students, while decent housing would be supplied to many low-income residents of various Prince Hall apartment complexes.[12]

In 1966, Grand Master Clayborn presided over his first Grand Communication. On June 27, Grand Master Amos T. Hall of Oklahoma addressed the craft. Hall called for recognition of Prince Hall Freemasons by their white brethren and announced plans for the Conference of Prince Hall Grand Masters to contact the United Grand Lodge of England to ask "Why has she forsaken her black children?"[13] On June 28, Grand Master James Gilliam of Mississippi spoke on voter registration and praised President Lyndon Baines Johnson for his numerous black appointments.[14]

Clayborn expressed appreciation to the Grand Lodge for purchasing and maintaining for him an automobile for use in his extensive Masonic travel.[15] He reported joining D. C. Collins, the Deputy of the Scottish Rite for Texas, in setting to work Key West Consistory No. 307 in Wichita Falls on December 5, 1965.[16] He also reported a visit to the Stringer Grand Lodge of Mississippi on December 7, 1966, and participation in the Prince Hall Grand Masters Conference in Kansas City, Missouri, on May 5, 1966.[17] At the 1966 session of the Supreme Council in Louisville, Kentucky, he said, Grand Master Hall referred to him as the "Baby Grand Master."[18] He complained about one of the pressing problems of 1966: "Our York Rite bodies aren't moving as they should and it's because some of our leaders locally are telling the craftsman when he gets the first three degrees, that's all he needs. I beg to differ, for there is more to the apple than meets the eye. You take it from there."[19] The new Grand Master then proceeded to invoke the noble legacy of Prince Hall Freemasonry in the Lone Star State:

Our late Grand Master L. L. Lockhart challenges us from the grave with better than 32,000 members, and Past Grand Master Maxey stands today, challenging us with the wizardry of leadership in the realms of finance, "What Will Our Answer Be?"

I say this . . . give me men who like to be challenged, and I will take those men and meet the challenge. Give me some men who dare a charge and I will take those men and keep the charge. . . .

Each setting of the sun prepares us for another tomorrow, each rising of the sun presents a tomorrow to us and prepares for us a new experience which we have not encountered before, and challenges each of us, asking can you or will you make a definite contribution to life's building that one can be proud of the fact that he had lived in this fast moving age that we are now in?

Will we as Prince Hall Masons live and build in such a way that our children and our children's children will be Prince Hall Masons because their parents were of that lineage? . . .

Yesteryear, Norris Wright Cuney and the Brothers laid the original foundation for us, and each succeeding generation thereafter has played a key part in foundation building for our time, and unless we build on it for the generation of tomorrow, then we will have failed our forerunners and those who must follow after us.[20]

At this session, Grand Master Clayborn, Deputy Grand Master Reuben G. White, and Grand Senior Warden D. C. Collins were reelected unanimously. Grand Junior Warden W. L. Hopkins was reelected after challenger Benjamin Smalls conceded defeat.[21] The election was followed by the Report of the Committee on State of the Country, which addressed the civil rights movement and the Vietnam War as the two most important issues facing America. The latter conflict was described as "bringing untold deaths, misery, and deep anxiety."[22] The committee also praised Popes John XXIII and Paul VI for their promotion of Christian unity at the Second Vatican Council.[23]

On June 30, 1966, the Report on Public Relations was presented by a committee chaired by Dr. J. W. Yancy II. This report included a discussion of an impressive visit of Grand Master Clayborn to West Texas, where he was described as a "Big Negro." Yancy reported that Paul Drayton Lodge No. 9 in Dallas really "put on a show when it leveled the cornerstone for Smith Chapel AME Church there." He also described some of the activities of white Masons in Texas, including scholarships, the Knights Templar Eye Foundation, and plans for the erection of the Lee Lockwood Scottish Rite Library and Museum in Waco.[24] He concluded: "It has been a pleasure to work under Grand Master Clayborn. In the same manner of cooperation which has been given former Grand Masters, we have strived so to do. Yet we know that each Grand Master is obligated to build stronger than the last. To this task we assert ourselves. Much money out of my pocket, long hours of work, and hard days of study have gone into the work of this year. Yet, it is a pleasure if it is appreciated and valued by Masons."[25]

On June 28, 1967, the second day of the Ninety-second Grand Lodge Communication began with the Report of the Committee on the Grand Secretary's and Grand Treasurer's Report. This committee had much praise for the Grand Secretary:

We wish to thank the Honorable Past Grand Master, Bro. J. T. Maxey, for discovering and employing our Grand Secretary, Bro. Bobby G. Webber. Just one year ago, Bro. Webber worked out and recommended a plan to this Grand Lodge that has put it on solid ground. In the years before, we were operating in the red every year, but now we are in the black and, despite the heavy deaths that we have had this Masonic year, we are still in the black, and we are able to pay the beneficiaries of our deceased brothers a reasonable amount of relief. The work of Bro. Webber stands out. He has proved himself to be a good man and Mason, as well as a good businessman.[26]

Later that day, Clayborn delivered his second Grand Master's Address, in which he promoted both the Scottish and York Rites and reminded everyone that "God is not dead." He reported the scheduling of the opening of the first low rent housing complex of the Supreme Council in Dallas in late September 1967 as well as plans for the establishment of similar complexes in Fort Worth and Port Arthur.[27] He also reported a number of important visitations. Such included a trip to Athens to inspect some land on July 31, 1966; speaking for Prince Hall Day in Beaumont on September 11, 1966; speaking for Mosier Valley Lodge No. 103 in Euless on October 2, 1966; laying the cornerstone for the temple of Paul Drayton Lodge No. 9 in Dallas on November 27, 1966; setting up a regional meeting for Grand Matrons in Houston on January 28, 1967; dedicating a temple for Paul Drayton Lodge No. 9 in Dallas; addressing the Supreme Council, Northern Jurisdiction, in Milwaukee, Wisconsin, on May 7-8, 1967; and involvement in the Grand Masters Conference in Detroit, Michigan, on May 11-13, 1967.[28]

On the following day, warrants were issued to lodges in Mineral City, Johnsfield, and Kaufman, which had been operating under dispensation.[29] That afternoon, the Committee on Registration reported the attendance of 525 delegates and a number of distinguished visitors, including Hon. Jno. G. Lewis, Jr., Grand Master of Louisiana; Illustrious Albert Lee Powell, Sr., and William A. Guthrie of Oklahoma; and Charles Bynum, National Director of the March of Dimes in New York City.[30]

The mood of America in 1967 was well expressed by the Committee on the State of the Country, which observed: "With war clouds everywhere, every power out to get more territory and power. Little nations rising up against each other, taxation, inflation, poverty, any and every consumable force cutting profits to the bone. The Civil Rights movement forcing its course to every mile of the way. This is our charge . . . what shall we do about them? This is our challenge."[31] The Committee on the Grand Master's Address recommended that the Grand Lodge send Grand Master Clayborn to Liberia "to participate in this African nation's centennial celebration."[32] The Committee on Resolutions commended President Lyndon Baines Johnson for "his fair mindedness and the prosecution of his civil policies as regards Our People."[33] Grand Recorder A. D. Harris presented the following recommendations regarding Masons in the military to the Committee on Jurisprudence:

> WHEREAS: The Most Worshipful Prince Hall Grand Lodge of Texas is a fraternal and charitable organization, and is not an insurance company, and WHEREAS: the present "War Clause" on all application blanks of the Grand Lodge carries the implication of being an insurance company, and WHEREAS: members of the Texas Grand Lodge are penalized by this "War Clause," plus it prevents otherwise eligible young men from becoming members because they are of draft age, or are already members of the Armed Forces:
>
> And WHEREAS: The young men in service who are making the Supreme Sacrifice that we may enjoy an abundant life, are there not always by choice, but by draft; furthermore, it is the feeling that any member of the Prince Hall Grand Lodge of Texas who serve their country with valor, honor, pride, and sacrifice, they or their beneficiaries should be, and are entitled to all benefits as if they were not in service.
>
> THEREFORE, it is recommended: That the "War Clause" on all application blanks of the M.W.P.H.G.L. of Texas, F.&A.M. be declared null and void, as of the close of

this grand session; furthermore, that it be stamped void on the present application blanks, so that they may be used up before others are printed.[34]

This report was adopted.[35]

At the conclusion of the session, Grand Master Clayborn and his officers were installed by Past Grand Master Maxey. The Grand Lodge approved Clayborn's proposal that Maxey be honored with life membership and exemption from both local and Grand Lodge dues.[36]

Sunday, June 23, 1968, was a day of many "firsts" for Prince Hall Freemasonry in the Lone Star State:

> Again, history has been made by the Most Worshipful Prince Hall Grand Lodge of Texas under its present administration! For the first time, the Grand Lodge celebrated St. John's Day as a body; for the first time since 1906 the Memorial Services were held outside the confines of the Masonic Mosque. Master Masons, Eastern Stars, and Heroines of Jericho from the four corners of Texas, from the plains of Amarillo and mountains of El Paso to the piney woods of Longview and Kilgore; from the rocky dales of Wichita Falls and Quanah to Corpus Christi and Brownsville on the Gulf of Mexico they came to share fraternal greetings and brotherhood together.
>
> The St. John's Day observance was in the Allen Chapel Methodist Church at 3:30 P.M. The sermon was delivered by Rev. A. C. Johnson, with whom the Holy Spirit dwelt throughout the sermon. The Spirit was so high and every one was so well benefitted [sic] spiritually, that Grand Master Clayborn decided to hold the services at the same church next year.
>
> Memorial Services for deceased Master Masons, Heroines of Jericho and Eastern Stars were held in the Mt. Olive Baptist Church, with the Grand Chaplain, Rev. E. H. Branch, delivering the eulogy. The text was found in 1 Samuel 14:17 and Hebrews 11:13. He chose for a subject, "Call the Roll and See Who is Absent."[37]

On June 25, 1968, Clayborn delivered his third Grand Master's Address. He pointed out that 1968 was the year of the HemisFair in San Antonio and that, at the time, many Prince Hall Masons were still not accustomed to staying in hotels. He reported his attendance at the Supreme Council in Washington, D.C., in October 1967 and at the Grand Masters Conference in Oklahoma City in May 1968. He also reported much progress in efforts to provide quality housing for low-income persons. Such progress was seen in the ground-breaking ceremony for Prince Hall Villa in Silsbee and the initial closing on Prince Hall Garden in Fort Worth and Prince Hall Plaza in Navasota.[38]

In 1968 Clayborn was able to conserve time and resources by replacing numerous district meetings with eight regional meetings. According to the Committee on the Grand Master's Address, these meetings added strength to the jurisdiction.[39]

The American scene in 1968 was well described by the Committee on the State of the Country: "College students blow their minds with illegal LSD and claim sensational insights as a reward. . . . Most Americans are not only fearful of violence, but are sick of lawlessness in all forms. Lawlessness is a key issue in the 1968 election campaign."[40]

At the conclusion of this session, Past Grand Master Maxey again installed Grand Master Clayborn who, in turn, installed his officers.[41]

On June 24, 1969, Clayborn delivered his fourth Grand Master's Address, in which he discussed the state of the jurisdiction:

> Our membership stands at the top spot in Prince Hall Masonry, but there is room to enlarge this, for the harvest is plenteous, but we need good Masonic workers to glean it. All we need do is every member go and get a man and assist him to become a member. I know it will work. All you need do is try it.... I have been directly responsible for new or reinstated members in no less than four (4) lodges in Dallas and one in Houston... The State of the Texas Jurisdiction is great and let's keep it this way.[42]

The Grand Master then informed the craft about the necessity of payment of property taxes in view of unsuccessful litigation. He explained that the courts had ruled: "Because we contribute to families only because of death, that we are not a charity organization" and, thus, not entitled to tax exemption.[43] He reported plans for participation in the 1970 Prince Hall Pilgrimage to Boston, Massachusetts. He also reported closure of the purchase of Prince Hall Terrace in Houston with 172 units and Prince Hall Chambre in Dallas with 192 units, adding that "there are seven different complexes in Texas that are sponsored by you and will eventually be owned by you exclusively." He urged the practice of nonviolence in the continuing struggle for civil rights, stating that "There have been major breakthroughs and the evidence is in favor of man outliving his tribulations of race and nation, language and creed, and moving toward a community based on the worth of each individual."[44]

Later that day, Grand Master Clayborn, Deputy Grand Master White, Grand Senior Warden Collins, and Grand Junior Warden Hopkins were reelected. With the retirement of Bobby G. Webber, Volney B. Phillips was elected Grand Secretary.[45]

On June 23, 1970, Clayborn delivered his fifth Grand Master's Address. He reported his involvement in the meeting of the Supreme Council in October 1969. This session was held in Oklahoma City, and "Texans were all over that big town." Eighty-two Scottish Rite Masons received the 33°. This number included twenty-three Texans. Clayborn served as class advisor and Robert Davis, Jr. of Dallas was elected as class president.[46] Clayborn then gave the following plans for the Grand Masters Conference:

> This meeting was reset to meet in Boston, Massachusetts August 13-14 in order to allow us Grand Masters to be present for the trek to the grave of our Father in Masonry, honorable Most Worshipful Prince Hall, on Saturday, the 15th. A tour of Freedom's Trail will be had, thus allowing all who wish to attend or go and on Sunday, the 16th, we go to the grave site as Master Masons, which means we will have on pure white aprons and white gloves as we march up to Copps Hill. After this, the Imperial Council will take over for the full week, 17th-21st....[47]

Clayborn further stated that, at the 1969 session of the Imperial Council of the Mystic Shrine in Baltimore, Maryland, he spoke on behalf of the Grand Masters and the Imperial Potentate "let it be known that, for the first time to his knowledge, a Grand Master from the Lone Star State was in attendance as a Noble."[48] He also reported a summit of leaders of various branches of Prince Hall Freemasonry in Chicago in February 1970 "to try to find out what was wrong with Prince Hall masonry." All those involved departed with the firm conviction that "we can and will make smooth ones out of the rough." He noted further progress in the area of housing, stating that there were Prince Hall apartment complexes in Dallas, Fort Worth, Houston, Silsbee, Crockett, and Navasota. He predicted that the Grand Lodge would own a ten-million-dollar housing enterprise by the year 2010.[49]

Clayborn's address was followed by remarks by Grand Masters S. J. Bennett of Alabama and X. L. Neal of Georgia.[50] Later that day, Clayborn and his principal officers were reelected. He then introduced a number of ministers, including his pastor, Rev. C. A. W. Clark of Good Street Baptist Church in Dallas.[51]

On the following day, the Committee on the State of the Country took a good look at America in 1970 and reported:

> Our continued national involvement in the Vietnamese-Cambodian conflict is still absorbing much of our national financial, mental, and spiritual energy. It is taking our attention and care from many needed problems at home such as water and air pollution, the traffic of narcotics and other crimes, school integration, education, unemployment, inflation, malnutrition, and many more problems which are sectional in nature.
>
> The solution to many of these problems must originate from bodies such as this grand body here assembled. . . .
>
> As Christians and as Masons, we can get much inspiration from the Master of all teachers when he said in John 10:10: "I am come that they might have life, and that they might have it more abundantly."[52]

On June 22, 1971, Clayborn delivered his sixth Grand Master's Address. He reported the 1970 Supreme Council session in Washington, D.C., where he served for the last time as a class director and for the first time as Grand Master of Ceremonies.[53] He also reported a number of uplifting experiences in Boston, where both the Imperial Council of the Mystic Shrine and the Conference of Prince Hall Grand Masters convened. Members of these two outstanding Masonic bodies made the pilgrimage to the grave of Prince Hall in Copps Hill Burying Ground. He noted that, for the first time in history, a Caucasian Grand Master was in attendance.[54] He spoke fondly of his November 1970 visit to Liberia, where "we planted a seed of brotherliness across the sea and the Liberian brothers think that you are somebody."[55] He spoke of the completion of extensive repairs on the Masonic Mosque and gave God all the credit for providing the needed funds. He charged: "We need now, to re-write our ways and know that tomorrow will be a better day because we passed this way." In response to the eternal question of "What time is it," he declared: "It is time to work the valleys."[56]

At the 1971 session, Clayborn made a number of important recommendations to the craft, urging each and every local lodge "not to forget the aged Mason who becomes inept and unable to cope with some demands and assessments and, in place of kicking him out, lend to him an understanding and helping hand."[57] He urged the Grand Lodge to make a donation to the Scottish Rite Hospital for Crippled Children in Dallas. The Grand Lodge approved this recommendation, and Lee Flanagan of Abif Lodge No. 61 came forward with the first $100 contribution to the cause.[58] Clayborn also recommended members "to plan the work and work the plan" for the upcoming Grand Lodge Centennial scheduled for 1975."⁵⁹

As usual, the Committee on the State of the Country gave a very insightful report for 1971. This committee, chaired by A. M. Johnson of Teague, reported:

> The Vietnam War is still with us, but there is a national trend to bringing all of our soldiers back home as quickly as possible. It is also believed that much of our expenditures spent in Vietnam could and should be spent on our domestic needs. . . . Sen. Hughes of Iowa stated before a Congressional Committee (June 1971) that there is an estimated number of 250,000 soldiers in Vietnam using heroin. . . .
>
> America has for a long time boasted of being a Christian nation. Christianity has had a great impact upon our national life. . . . Now we find in more increasing numbers of Negroes turning toward the Islamic faith. What is the reason for this change? When you compare the doctrines of Christianity with the Mohammedan religion—that Christ taught non-violence while Mohammed taught that if it took blood-shedding to reach one's objective, then the shedding of blood and death were justified. We firmly believe that violence on such a large scale will be self-defeating for Negroes.[60]
>
> The decisions of several Supreme Courts in the past years, namely the decision of 1954 that "separate but equal" doctrine was unconstitutional and the 1971 decision which stated that busing was constitutional, if necessary, to have balanced mixing of the races, will change all America in many ways of human relationships. . . .
>
> Our church life will be affected the same as our school life because the same pupils who go to school will be some of the same who go to church. They will carry some of the same thoughts to church that they received at school.[61]
>
> Many of our young Negroes have discovered that ruthless slave masters used the teachings of Christ, "turn the other cheek," as a means of subjugating their slaves. This knowledge does not provide just cause for one to turn his back on Christianity and toward a religion that condones retaliation, e. g., the Islamic Faith.[62]

The Ninety-sixth Annual Grand Communication included the reading of a proclamation of Mayor R. M. Stovall of Fort Worth, proclaiming June 21-24, 1971, as Prince Hall Grand Lodge Days.[63]

During Clayborn's 1971 visit to Liberia, President William V. S. Tubman (a Prince Hall Freemason) designated him as an Honorary Citizen of the Republic.[64]

In May 1972 Clayborn attended the Prince Hall Grand Masters Conference in St. Paul, Minnesota. At this meeting, the white Grand Master of Minnesota brought greetings.[65] At this session, Grand Master Clayborn joined Grand Master Lewis of Louisiana in eulogizing the recently deceased Grand Master Amos T. Hall of Oklahoma.[66] In his 1972 Grand Master's Address, Clayborn reported serving as Master of Ceremonies at the 1971 meeting of the Supreme Council in Atlanta, Georgia. He stated that, at this meeting, the 33° was conferred upon "the largest class ever assembled" and this class included his pastor, Rev. C. A. W. Clark. The banquet speaker, he said, was Atlanta's Vice-Mayor, Maynard Jackson, a Prince Hall Freemason who spoke "with all the fervor" of his grandfather, the late Georgia Grand Master Dr. John Wesley Dobbs. He spoke of plans for the 1972 session in Monrovia, Liberia. He compared the role of a Grand Master to that of a Gospel preacher, stating that holders of both positions are stewards who must give account to God. He then, like a good preacher, proceeded to "feed the flock."[68]

On June 27, 1972, Grand Master Clayborn and Deputy Grand Master White were reelected unanimously. Grand Senior Warden D. C. Collins defeated challengers Bobby Webber, Jimmy Hardeman, and O. W. L. Turner for reelection. All other officers were reelected.[69] Later that day, in his report, Grand Junior Warden W. L. Hopkins declared: "We must come to the realization that there is no Black Power, there is no White Power, there is no Brown Power, and there is no Red Power, but 'all men are equal' and created by the same 'Almighty God' and that this earth was created for man . . . and everyone has the rights to share it 'equal.'"[70] On the following day, the Committee on the State of the Country submitted their report, in which they declared that segregation, whether done by blacks or whites, was in no one's interests. They urged the craft to "keep the deeds to that old farm we still own and make it a profitable investment."[71]

At the 1973 Communication, the Grand Master's Address was preceded by a memorial period conducted by Rev. B. L. McCormick, pastor of Saint Paul AME Church in Dallas.[72] Clayborn then began his address with a memorial tribute to Past Grand Master J. T. Maxey, who had died in Galveston on February 12, 1973.[73] He reported a superb meeting of the Supreme Council in Monrovia, Liberia. During this visit to the African nation, President William R. Tolbert (also a Prince Hall Freemason) bestowed upon him the Grand Band and dubbed him Panamon Chief.[74] He discussed a subsequent meeting in Memphis, Tennessee, where he was elected Lieutenant Grand Commander.[75] He gave the following report of the 1973 Grand Masters Conference:

> This year in New Haven, Conn., Grand Master Bolden and Past Grand Master Leroy Fitch left no stone unturned. We saw in our entertainment, brotherhood in action, Masonic Hospital in operation, where Prince Hall Masons contribute to it and are patients in the hospital and live in the Masonic Home. We were spoken to by a Past Grand Master of the white Grand Lodge at lunch which was sponsored by the white Grand Lodge, and at the banquet, the present Grand Master and his wife were at the head table, also members of the Grand Cabinet and their wives, ladies. We saw and heard brotherhood in action and Dr. Leon Sullivan of Philadelphia, Penn. was our speaker.[76]

Clayborn declared that, contrary to the U. S. government, the Prince Hall Grand Lodge of Texas had no Watergate or credibility gap.[77] He recommended that Good Street Baptist Lodge, which met at Good Street Baptist Church in Dallas and had been operating under dispensation, be warranted with the number 182. He stated that "Worshipful Master Edwin B. Cash and the brothers that are there now and those who will follow surely will make some of the people I know wish that they had said 'Why not a church lodge?'"[78]

On June 26, 1973, Grand Master Clayborn and Deputy Grand Master White were reelected. James Patrick tried unsuccessfully to unseat both Grand Senior Warden D. C. Collins and Grand Junior Warden W. L. Hopkins.[79] Following the election, on the recommendation of the Grand Master, the craft donated a free will offering in the amount of $325.55 to the Scottish Rite Hospital for Crippled Children in Dallas.[80] In his report, the Grand Senior Warden declared: "And are we yet alive to see each other's faces, praise and glory to Jesus give for His redeeming grace. In the midst of high waters and floods, tornadoes, earthquakes, and the Watergate, God has brought us thus far on our way."[81] In his report, the Grand Junior Warden spoke about an increasing number of blacks recently elected to public office and urged support for black colleges.[82]

In his 1974 Grand Master's Address, Clayborn stated:

> This has been a very good year with us in many ways. There have been many demands made upon the office of the Grand Master and "God" sustained the Grand Master at every hand.... He gave strength and the desire to keep trying to lead, while with the rest of the world we talked, we heard "Watergate" but I thank "God" that you Prince Hall Masons of Texas do not have to worry about cover ups, for it is all in your hands in the form of the important report and for our "Watergate" go to the Holy Bible, in the 8th chapter of Nehemiah and do as the people did in that day, ask for the reading of the word so that they may be strengthened.[83]

As usual, Clayborn gave honor to the beloved dead. One of those mentioned was Samuel Cathcart of Terrell, one of the first District Deputies appointed by Grand Master William Coleman.[84] He gave reports of successful sessions of the Grand Masters Conference in Indianapolis, Indiana, and of the Imperial Council of the Mystic Shrine in Detroit, Michigan.[85] He praised the contributions of such outstanding black Freemasons as Prince Hall, Bishop Richard Allen of the AME Church, and U. S. Supreme Court Justice Thurgood Marshall.[86] He recommended that the Grand Lodge sponsor Grand Recorder A. D. Harris for the 33° in 1975.[87]

The Grand Lodge voted to give $50 per month for life to Roger Hughes, who was losing his eyesight. The craft also voted to donate $302 to the Scottish Rite Hospital for Crippled Children and rendered aid to T. D. Givens, who was the victim of a brutal attack and robbery at the Continental Bus Station.[88]

In its 1974 report the Committee on the State of the Country quoted Congresswoman Barbara Jordan regarding Watergate: "The events of the past several years have revealed to us a very shocking pattern of disregard for constitutional principles. It is apparent that the powerful tools of government (spying and espionage against private citizens in pursuit of their lawful activities) have become or have not kept within the legitimate bounds of self-restraint and self-discipline."[89] The committee reported that history was made in San Antonio when Dr. J. Garfield Owens, a black minister, was appointed to the pastorate of the prestigious white Jefferson United Methodist Church.[90] They declared, "Prince Hall Masons can be of much assistance by helping young people in the community to select a meaningful vocation."[91] In his report, the Grand Junior Warden spoke of an energy crisis and a Masonic crisis, expressing regret that so few young men were showing interest in Masonry.[92]

The year 1975 marked the centennial of Prince Hall Freemasonry in the Lone Star State and the bicentennial of Prince Hall Freemasonry in the United States. In celebration of these two historic events, Grand Master Clayborn issued the following proclamation:

> WHEREAS, Prince Hall and fourteen other Negro freemen were made Master Masons on March 6, 1775, thus establishing the foundation of Freemasonry among men of color two hundred years ago, approximately one year and four months before the Declaration of Independence whose bicentennial will be celebrated in 1976;

WHEREAS, Prince Hall was a man of God, a devout Christian, and a dedicated minister with a fixed belief in the fatherhood of God and the brotherhood of man;

WHEREAS, Prince Hall was an American patriot, having shared the dreams of the great nation which America could become, he volunteered to serve in the Continental Army and fought in the Revolutionary War, believing that the abuses suffered by all people of that day could only be extirpated by the sword;

WHEREAS, Prince Hall was a pioneer in public education who memorialized the legislature of Massachusetts to establish a school for Negro children in his own home;

WHEREAS, Prince Hall established the Order of Freemasonry for and among men of color, and these Prince Hall Masons through the ages have not only immortalized his name, but have made and continue to make immeasurable contributions to the creation and preservation of America and its national purpose;

WHEREAS, Prince Hall devoted his entire life making America a better place for all to live by keeping alive the spark of liberty and freedom in the breast and minds of all oppressed people;

NOW, THEREFORE BE IT DECREED that I, I. H. Clayborn, Most Worshipful Grand Master of the Prince Hall Masons of the State of Texas and Jurisdiction, do hereby proclaim the Year of Our Lord 1975, and the Year of Light 5975, as the centennial year of Prince Hall Masonry throughout the State of Texas and its Jurisdiction;

BE IT FURTHER OBSERVED, that all Prince Hall Masons of Texas and Jurisdiction rededicate themselves to: the full celebration of our centennial year, continuing the struggle for justice, equality, and human dignity for which Prince Hall lived and died; and secondly, manifesting the noble objectives of Freemasonry by strengthening our lodges numerically and financially, and finally, letting the lessons which Freemasonry teaches reflect themselves in our lives and living.

Given under my hand this 1st day of May A.D. 1975; A.L. 5975.

I. H. Clayborn
Most Worshipful Grand Master[93]

The Centennial Souvenir Journal contained a letter from the president of the United States:

The one hundredth anniversary of the Most Worshipful Prince Hall Free and Accepted Masons of Texas records a tradition of splendid humanitarian service. I am pleased on this occasion to send my best wishes to the members of your fine organization.

As a fellow Mason, I particularly appreciate the pride you must all feel on this occasion, while reflecting on the many contributions you have made to the well-being of your communities and their citizens.

I wish you every future success.

Gerald R. Ford[94]

The journal also contained letters from U. S. Senator Lloyd M. Bentsen, Texas Governor Dolph Briscoe, Fort Worth Mayor R. M. Stovall, Congresswoman Barbara Jordan, State Representative Eddie Bernice Johnson, Congressman Dale Milford, and Fort Worth Chamber of Commerce President H. C. Clemons.[95]

Clayborn issued the following Centennial Letter, addressed "TO ALL FREEMASONS AND APPENDANT BODIES, WHEREVER DISPERSED AROUND THE GLOBE":

I GREET YOU, AS Most Worshipful Grand Master of the Most Worshipful Prince Hall Grand Lodge of Texas and its Jurisdiction;

WHEREAS, on August 9, 1875, on a triangular plot in Brenham, Texas, a call was made, and five (5) lodges appeared under the gavel of Most Worshipful Brother W. D. Matthews of the National Compact, to set in motion the organization of the Most Worshipful Grand Lodge of Texas, A.F.&A.M., and

WHEREAS, THE FIVE (5) small lodges grew and continue to grow, and in 1925, this Grand Lodge changed its name to the Most Worshipful Prince Hall Grand Lodge and its Jurisdiction, F.&A.M., Inc., I welcome you to "GOD'S" chosen land, that part of the United States where He loved it so much, until He visited the Garden of Eden and flung her luscious fruits all over the rich Rio Grande Valley; Likewise, "GOD" visited the Sahara Desert and brought portions of hot sand to the westernmost part of our state and to the Amazon, Nile, even the Jordan River, and snaked these through Texas, and the long, big Colorado River, you can cross eleven (11) times between Austin and Bay City, Texas.

"GOD" loved Texas so much He brought portions of the ocean waters, one calm and one turbulent, and dropped them in places like Gaza—Little Elm, Tawakoni, and the Livingston Reservoir, so we could be reminded of the greatness of "GOD," our Father. He gave Texas sun, the same that shines just as hot as if you were from the Equator, and snow and ice, as if it were from the North Pole. Join in with us and enjoy the celebration of our century, for truly our "GOD" is showing forth His handiwork.

We know how wonderful it is to live in unity; likewise, we know that a plumbline has been placed among His people, and we will remember and revere our Creator each and every day. Therefore, let us hear the conclusion of the whole matter and fear "GOD" and keep His commandments.

Thanks for joining in and making this celebration one that will not soon be forgotten. Welcome to all that we have, and may the blessings of "GOD" be upon each participant.

                    Fraternally,
                    I. H. Clayborn
                    Most Worshipful Grand Master[96]

The 1975 Communication was visited by Grand Master Curtis Rhyne of Ohio, X. L. Neal of Georgia, H. M. Thompson of Mississippi, and Jno. G. Lewis, Jr., of Louisiana.[97] In his 1975 Grand Master's Address, Clayborn spoke of the significance of the year 1975: "This is a mark in history that comes only once in modern man's life. This is a mark in history that the Father of Freemasonry among men of Ebon Hue will be happy to lean over the balcony of the Heavenly Lodge and say 'wonderful.' You see, 100 years in Texas and 200 years in the USA, and still they wear my name . . . 'PRINCE HALL.'"[98] Clayborn reported his receipt of the Gold Medal Achievement Award at the 1974 Supreme Council session in New Orleans.[99] He also reported his attendance at the 1974 session of the Imperial Council of the Mystic Shrine in Philadelphia. He expressed great pleasure at the election of Dr. Laddie L. Melton of Beaumont, Texas, to the office of Deputy Imperial Potentate, and he reported his presentation of a paper entitled "Executive Role of the Grand Master" at the 1975 Grand Masters Conference in Portland, Oregon.[100] In his concluding remarks, he addressed the political situation of 1975, declaring:

We viewed the economy of our beloved country rise and fall, we saw a man installed as President of our nation, who had not been elected, one leave that high office in disgrace, and a second man nominated and installed in less than a year as Vice President, that we, the people, did not elect. . . .

As we declare and celebrate our Bi-Centennial Year, I know that each of you feel PROUD to be a part of the greatest organization under the canopy of heaven. After "God's" church, that has to be the Most Worshipful Prince Hall Masonic Organization.[101]

At this session, the Grand Lodge donated $400 to the Scottish Rite Hospital for Crippled Children and the same amount to the NAACP Legal Research Fund.[102]

In their 1975 report, the Committee on the State of the Country had much to say about the evils of conservatism, pointing out how conservatives manufacture such slogans as "Law and Order," "Safe Streets," "Welfare State," "Overpopulation," "Women's Liberation," and others "to keep Americans divided in order to conquer."[103] Regarding "Foreign Affairs," the committee observed:

> This is another area in which the conservative groups have tried to take the old path which led up to the Vietnam Conflict. Here brothers fought brothers and finally the losers, over 100,000 of them, had to be brought to this country to protect them. This is a case in which the separation of people is a very costly venture.
>
> The challenge to Prince Hall Masons is one in which a good, intelligent, and powerful man (P.H.) should follow the teachings of what Isaiah said in chapter 1. Take the initiative, get up, move out, and vigorously help to do those things that will be of benefit to his family, church, and nation.[104]

Grand Secretary Phillips gave the report for the Ways and Means Committee, urging the establishment of a Masonic Credit Union "while many of us still brood over the liquidation of the Fraternal Bank and Trust Company almost two decades ago."[105]

In his 1976 Grand Master's Address, Clayborn reported that the recent meeting of the Supreme Council at the Adolphus Hotel in Dallas was "the greatest session of the Council ever held" with the largest class of new 33° Masons and "1,178 souls" at the banquet.[106] He spoke of his attendance at the 1975 Imperial Council of the Mystic Shrine and stated that he was looking forward to the 1976 imperial session in Los Angeles when Dr. Laddie L. Melton would be elected Imperial Potentate.[107] He also reported a very cordial meeting with San Antonio's Robert B. O'Connor, the white Grand Master of Masons in Texas.[108]

The Committee on the State of the Country, again chaired by A. M. Johnson, went into great detail to describe conditions in America and in the world during 1976, the bicentennial year of the United States. The following was included in this committee's report:

> Violence is being committed in many parts of the world. A religious war is continuing in Ireland between Catholic and Protestant factions. The murder of Ambassador Francis E. Meloy, Jr. and Economic Counselor Robert Warning in Lebanon and the wholesale killing of Black Africans in South Africa are good examples of where passion controls nations instead of reason and regard for human life or for others.
>
> Because the people in the United States have adhered to the principles and teachings of the Holy Bible, she has incurred the hostility of many Arabic states that have

begun in recent years their quest for Arabian nationalism. Christians in the United States are not against the Ishmaelian descendants as they reverence the genealogy of the descendants of Abraham down through the birth of Jesus Christ.[109]

In 1977 the Grand Lodge welcomed a number of distinguished visitors, including H. M. Thompson, Grand Master of Mississippi; Edgar Bridges, Deputy Grand Master of Mississippi; Joseph Henderson, Grand Secretary of Mississippi; William L. Hunter, Grand Representative of Colorado; and Beaumont dentist Laddie L. Melton, Imperial Potentate of the Shrine.[110] In his Grand Master's Address, Clayborn expressed great joy over Melton's election and said: "Let the roads, the skyways, and trains, if there be any, to Miami Beach be filled with Texas to be there when Brother Melton carries the scepter of authority as top officer and makes a great session even greater."[111] He reported an enjoyable meeting of his Supreme Council in Washington, D.C. And also reported visiting the Supreme Council, Northern Jurisdiction, in Philadelphia. At the latter session, he said, Russell S. Gideon of Seattle was elected Sovereign Grand Commander and Booker T. Alexander of Detroit was elected Lieutenant Grand Commander.[112]

On June 27, 1977, Grand Master Clayborn and Deputy Grand Master White were reelected. Edwin B. Cash was elected Grand Senior Warden and Jesse Baines was elected Grand Junior Warden.[113]

In their 1977 report the Committee on the State of the Country had much praise for President Jimmy Carter. They highlighted his commitment to human rights and his appointment of Andrew Young, a Prince Hall Mason, as ambassador to the United Nations.[114] They had much good to say about the book *Roots* by Alex Haley (another Prince Hall Mason) and the television miniseries based on this outstanding work, recognizing that it was quite a "shot in the arm" for both black history and genealogy.[115]

On June 26, 1978, a public opening ceremony was held at Mount Olive Baptist Church in Fort Worth. This ceremony included a welcome address by Mayor Hugh Parmer of Fort Worth and Judge Thomas H. Routt of Houston. The speaker for this occasion was Grand Master H. M. Thompson of Mississippi.[116] On the following day, in his Grand Master's Address, Clayborn spoke of the predicament of 1978:

> We have watched and viewed the longest coal strike in history. The farmers marched on Washington and camped at many shipping points right here in Texas and yet we do not have the answer.
> Our energy situation gets worse each day and yet there is no answer. I ask . . . is there no balm in America and the world? "Is there no word from the Lord?"
> I say that we, the proudest of proud nations, must come home America and hear the words of the Lord. I feel that all of our beautiful homeland need to pay heed to the prophet Jeremiah, for his prophecy on that day and time fits us on this day and time.[117]

Clayborn reported speaking at the 1977 Centennial Session of the Prince Hall Grand Lodge of West Virginia. He also reported enjoying the 1977 Imperial Council meeting in Miami Beach. He said that the Prince Hall Grand Lodge of Texas was "proud to be the Mama" of Imperial Potentate L. L. Melton.[118] He further reported good meetings of the Southern Supreme Council in Kansas City, Missouri; of the

Northern Supreme Council in Chicago; and of the Grand Masters Conference in Seattle.[119]

The issue of school integration was well addressed on June 27, 1978, by the Committee on the State of the Country, which stated:

> Many of our larger cities throughout the United States of America, including some cities in Texas, have not presented approved plans to the United States Supreme Court, plans of which are satisfactory or constitutional. On June 16, 1978, Benjamin Hooks (Director of the NAACP) stated on the Phil Donahue Show that private schools (grades 1 through 12) should not be given financial support from the federal government. It is a fact that many of the private schools have loopholes in their administration that give them a chance to continue segregation and that such perpetuation is unconstitutional.[120]

The committee linked school segregation with fraternal segregation, citing the chapter "They Faced Segregation in their Brotherhood" in Dr. Charles H. Wesley's book *Prince Hall: Life and Legacy*.[121]

On the following day, the Committee on Ways and Means reported the organization of Masonic Credit Unions, with A. M. Johnson serving as director for the Southeastern Region and Harold Butler serving as director for the North Central Region.[122]

In his 1979 Grand Master's Address, Clayborn urged the craft to read Dr. Wesley's book as well as Joseph A. Walkes, Jr.'s *Black Square and Compass: 200 Years of Prince Hall Freemasonry*.[123] He reported a good session of the Supreme Council in Los Angeles in 1978—the council's last session under the leadership of Sovereign Grand Commander Jno. G. Lewis, Jr. He sadly reported the death of Bro. Lewis on April 1, 1979, and stated: "As Elijah dropped his mantel into the hands of Elisha, so did Dr. Lewis leave his earthly leadership into hands that he trusted."[124] The hands to which Clayborn referred were his own![125] He reported that, at the 1979 Grand Masters Conference, "proper respect and homage" was paid to Lewis by Grand Masters Charles Williams and Earl Bradford.[126] Among the new lodges recommended for charter was Jno. G. Lewis Lodge No. 622 in Copperas Cove.[127] He also spoke of his attendance at the Imperial Council in Kansas City, where Noble L. L. Melton passed the gavel to the new Imperial Potentate, Noble Eugene Dickerson, Jr.[128] In regard to "foreign relations," he told of the reception of Ephraim S. Alphonse Lodge No. 621 in the Republic of Panama into Prince Hall Freemasonry.[129] The Grand Lodge approved the provision of aid in transporting a member of this lodge, Roberto Duwane, who had been severely burned in an acetylene explosion, to Brooke Army Medical Center and Burns Institute in San Antonio.[130]

The 1978-79 Masonic year was marked by the deaths of Grand Chaplain Rev. E. H. Branch and Grand Lecturer J. D. Palely, both of Houston.[131] The Committee on Necrology paid homage to both of these outstanding Masons, along with Grand Master Lewis.[132]

In their 1979 report, the Committee on the State of the Country covered a number of developments, including the tragic mass suicide by members of People's Temple in Guyana, South America; and the hopes for peace resulting from the SALT II agreement of U. S. President Jimmy Carter and Soviet President Leonid Brezhnev.[133]

On June 24, 1980, the Grand Lodge welcomed as distinguished visitors Grand Master H. M. Thompson of Mississippi and Paul Best, Executive Secretary of the Phylaxis Society, from Des Moines, Iowa.[134] Later that day, Clayborn delivered his Grand Master's Address, in which he sought to summarize fifteen years of service in the Grand East:

> "Fifteen years," some up, some down, some very fruitful, some not so productive, but through it all, we walked in the pathways of duty and by the grace of "God," Texas has not relinquished one foot of her reputation in the world.
>
> One decade and one half has passed since I promised with my hand on the Bible and with my eyes glued into the greatest pair of Germanic eyes ever seen and promised you and John Theodore Maxey, before the Prince Hall family, but more especially before "God," **that I would** (not try) to the best of my ability serve this vantaged office as a good steward should. Well, I think that the past fifteen years of Freemasonry (PHA) has been in one way, second to none.
>
> I hope you will allow me to back track, or as we say now . . . recapitulate. 1966 got my feet wet with my first full year as the man to be blamed, but we found the path that had "Togetherness." . . .
>
> Let's move up . . . 1967—68—& 69, saw the Most Worshipful Prince Hall Grand Lodge of Texas venture into a field of people care and you said "yes" to low income type housing. You will find encouched in our 1968 minutes . . . that this was a great move on our part. . . . 1968—The Regions—the story is no myth, they are real and my people have shown that we can change, so each year our regional meetings have moved up to a higher plateau.
>
> 1970—Brought us the great Chicago summit meeting on February 7-8, where 42 of the 43 Most Worshipful Grand Masters were present . . . a Committee of Evaluations were appointed with our Grand Master as a member of that committee to decipher the hieroglyphics of esoteric thinking by the two Sovereign Grand Commanders, consultants with the 42 Grand Masters present.
>
> Hence, our 18-year-olds and we got our share, also made the pilgrimage to Boston with us in August to attend the Grand Masters Conference.
>
> From 1970-1975, we made other strides of success and prepared for our centennial celebration and until **this** day I say, when tomorrow comes, there has been none greater. . . .
>
> The first ten came and went and now we were used to each other. Some of our stalwarts exchanged the place of meetings and went home to be with the Lord, so they now meet around the altar where John saw the 4 beasts and the 4 and 20 elders all round the throne of "God," where the new heaven and new earth protruded and a pure river ran from the throne of "God" and the Lamb, oh! How I love Jesus, oh yes I do.
>
> We had to join that host this past year . . . 680 . . . and they don't live here any more. You see, they are somewhere around the throne of "God." I must apologize if I am a bit long today, but do you know what it is to serve 15 years and yet be able to praise "God" and not be afraid to lay down at night? . . . Some may have distrusted my ability to lead you but thank "God" who told Moses to say . . . "**I AM**" sent him. Well the same **I AM** still gives direction and holds our hand if we let him. . . . Just be assured that your Grand Master, I. H. Clayborn, has a greater Grand Master and invites Him into his living room and parlor each and every day.[135]

Clayborn reported a successful October 1979 session of the Supreme Council, Southern Jurisdiction, in Washington, D.C. This was his first time to preside as Grand

Commander. He also reported enjoying the May 1980 session of the Supreme Council, Northern Jurisdiction, in Philadelphia. He observed: "Our fraters up north have found some southern style." He also reported an outstanding meeting of the Imperial Council of the Mystic Shrine in New York. This convention, he said, included a parade "right down Broadway." He was saddened to report the deaths of a number of prominent Prince Hall Freemasons, including Bishop Howard Z. Plummer, Imperial Lecturer for the Shrine; and President William R. Tolbert, Jr., of Liberia.[136] He then made the following concluding remarks:

> Fifteen year... and some of you have not heard the voice of the Lord asking Prince Hall Masons.. "What seeth thou?" Nor have we answered "a plumbline," so that the Lord could say to us that **He will** place a plumbline amongst us and will not again pass us by....
>
> Fifteen years of teaching, pleading, and asking that we remember now our Creator in the days of our youth. I have not stopped there. I know that you remember that grinders ceasing, window being darkened, pitchers being broken at the fountain and the wheel broken at the cistern. Oh my Brothers, if we could just step forth and reaffirm to ourselves and to Freemasonry before "God" that, from this day forward, we will walk with "God" with our eye on the mark of the high calling so that when our summons comes, be it fifteen, more or less years, but whenever, we will hear the welcome voice saying... "Enter into the joy of Him who loves you..."
>
> FIFTEEN YEARS
> I THANK YOU[137]

Following this speech, Clayborn was elected to a sixteenth year in the Grand East. Deputy Grand Master White, Grand Senior Warden Cash, and Grand Junior Warden Baines were also reelected.[138]

On the following day, the Committee on Registration and Visitors, chaired by Harold Butler of Tyler, gave its report, calling for aid to aged and disabled Masons and for support for the Phylaxis Society.[139] A. M. Johnson, for the last time, served as Chairman of the Committee on the State of the Country. Regarding religion, he wrote:

> As Masons we have been taught that the Holy Bible and the Koran are the proper sources of light to be recognized by our Order.
>
> Therefore, a comparative study of the Koran to get a clearer picture of the spiritual light of many, since that helps us to understand the culture and discipline of those who use the Koran as we who use our Bibles.
>
> The sacrifice of the many lives of the Jim Jones Church in Guyana, South America, is a good example to people who do not fully understand the part of an Abundant life which a religion should bring to a good believer.[140]

This report called for social as well as political equality for all people and described the Iranian Hostage Crisis as "a good example of unsolved problems which have existed for many years."[141]

The Committee on the Grand Master's Address, chaired by Deputy Grand Master White, commended the Grand Master for fifteen years of outstanding leadership and recommended that "this Grand Lodge give Grand Master Clayborn a standing ovation that he will long remember and cherish in the years to come."[142]

On June 23, 1981, Clayborn delivered his final Grand Master's Address. He reported that Pioneer Management Company (of which he was the president) was now in charge of the Grand Lodge's housing projects. Pioneer, he said, was a good example of "what is known in HUD as a top flite [sic] management company." He discussed the 1980 session of the Supreme Council, Southern Jurisdiction, in Orlando, Florida, in which "the Floridians had it all together for our coming," and he announced plans for the 1981 session in Mississippi, "another of the Lord's favorite states." He reported attendance at the centennial celebration of the Supreme Council, Northern Jurisdiction, in Philadelphia, Pennsylvania[143] and at the Imperial Council of the Mystic Shrine in Cleveland, Ohio. At the latter meeting, Clayborn said, Noble Harry E. Smith of Toledo, Ohio, "the great man of intellect and height," was elected Imperial Potentate.[144] He also described the meeting of the Grand Masters' Conference in Nassau, Bahamas, under the leadership of Grand Master Samuel T. Daniels of Maryland.[145] He concluded his speech with the following words:

> Now, because of you, we have climbed the mountains and we walked through the valleys, but praise "God" our loads have not been too heavy, nor has the road been too rough, for with "God" we girded up our loins, we put on the proper breastplate, we wore the shoes of righteousness, we put on brotherliness and went marching, marching up to Zion together; and when we get there, my hope is and will be, that Hiram, Hiram, Solomon, Tubal-Cain, Jeptha, David, and so many others that I can't name them, will be at the gate to say . . . "Hail brothers from Texas, all is ready," but that will not fully satisfy me, for I will want to see and hear Jesus my Lord, my Master, Warden, and Tiler, then I can be in joy for everybody will be happy over there.[146]

This, Clayborn's sixteenth Grand Master's Address, was hailed as "the crowning piece of all."[147]

When the time for the election of officers came, Clayborn announced that, for the first time in sixteen years, he would exercise his prerogative as Grand Master and preside over the election of officers. Many were then surprised and stunned when he declared: "The first officer to be elected is the Most Worshipful Grand Master and I nominate Reuben G. White." The craft followed Clayborn's direction and elevated White to the Grand East. Grand Senior Warden Edwin B. Cash was then promoted to Deputy Grand Master. Thomas H. Routt was elected Grand Senior Warden. Jesse L. Baines was reelected Grand Junior Warden. These officers were then installed by Past Grand Master Clayborn.[148]

A number of outstanding reports were presented in 1981. Grand Junior Warden Baines spoke of the perils of Reaganism and the challenges faced by African Americans in the 1980s.[149] The Scholarship Committee paid tribute to the memories of Bros. W. F. Bledsoe, Jr., and A. M. Johnson.[150] The Committee on the State of the Country, chaired by O. E. Wilhite of Rockdale,[151] gave the following assessment of integration in 1981:

> The overall blending of all people within the confines of equalization through integration has wrought well, yet in this present day of 1981 we are still experiencing many difficulties. . . .

Our present administration—"The Reagan Regime"—is considering proposals that Congress make major changes in sections of the Voting Rights Act of 1965 scheduled to expire next year. . . .

Another phase is the rise of the KKK since the Reagan regime, with their paramilitary camps in the Houston area and not far from Fort Worth in North Texas.

The resurgence of the Ku Klux Klan has moved with un-interrrupted measures to increase membership and its activities in approximately twenty (20) more states, including Texas.[152]

The year 1981 marked the first time since the death of J. T. Maxey in 1973 that the Prince Hall Grand Lodge of Texas had a living Past Grand Master. For the next thirteen years, Past Grand Master Clayborn remained quite visible in the Grand Lodge, attending state and regional meetings and serving as a wise counselor to Grand Masters Reuben G. White, Thomas H. Routt, and Edwin B. Cash. Each of these Grand Masters appointed him as Chairman of the Committee on Foreign Correspondence (C.C.F.C.). In the latter role, he gave an outstanding report at each Communication. His retirement from the Grand East, of course, allowed him to concentrate his energies on his position as Sovereign Grand Commander of the Scottish Rite, Southern Jurisdiction. He presided over each session of the Supreme Council from 1979 to 1993, and he was given a seat of honor at each session of the Supreme Council, Northern Jurisdiction; and of the Imperial Council of the Mystic Shrine. Each year, *Ebony* magazine listed him among "100 Most Influential Black Americans."

On October 8-11, 1983, Clayborn presided over the Ninety-seventh Session of the Supreme Council in Little Rock, Arkansas. This session included an address by Arkansas Governor Bill Clinton.[153] Sovereign Grand Commander Clayborn welcomed Sovereign Grand Commander Russell S. Gideon of the Northern Jurisdiction and Imperial Potentate Roswell A. Taylor of the Shrine to the meeting. He presented special awards to two 33° Masons: his pastor, Rev. C. A. W. Clark; and Rev. T. J. Jemison, president of the National Baptist Convention, USA, Inc.[154] In his allocution, Clayborn said:

Little Rock, Arkansas—The Honorable Jno. G. Lewis' elevation and coronation 1926 Little Rock, Arkansas; the open shelter for Mrs. Daisy Bates; the confrontation at Central High for the first nine black students. How sweet it is for us to be here not only in this fine facility, but we are here with the blessings of "God" and the City Fathers . . .

The cancer of the President's Cabinet is still a great concern of mine, in the oval office, and in the White House. When we left Washington last year, unemployment was at a height that undefinable, and today it's not much better. We still have 11 million or more Americans without jobs, and a vast number of those are young black people. There are many hungry folk in America, and we are still sinking good money into Central America, and the cancer eats on, and we sit idly be. And are we, or are we not making plans, and do we see us working? The plans for cleaning the White House and the government departments of our national cancer? Will we sit by and trim our lamps the last week in October 1984? Oh my Brothers, now is the time to strike the anvil, "not tomorrow: or "next year," "THE TIME IS NOW." . . . When we can do that I see our national cobalt machine saying we have overcome the wiles on nontogetherness and now! Now! We are free at last, and we shall be free of the cancer of crabitis, and enjoy the true elixir of togetherness.[155]

Thus, I. H. Clayborn, a staunch Democrat, blasted the policies of Republican President Ronald Reagan, as he often did during the "Reagan Era" of 1981-89.

Clayborn had been one of the early supporters of the Phylaxis Society, the Prince Hall Masonic research society established in 1973 by Joseph A. Walkes, Jr., and patterned after the predominately white Philalethes Society. Clayborn was made an honorary Fellow of the Phylaxis Society and was awarded the Jno. G. Lewis, Jr. Medal of Excellence for his many contributions to Prince Hall Freemasonry.[156] He, along with his Texas representative Hubert L. Reece and Grand Master Reuben G. White, invited the Phylaxis Society to convene in Dallas in March 1985. Bro. Walkes, the society's president, accepted this invitation.[157] At the Friday luncheon, Walkes was the speaker. At the Saturday luncheon, Clayborn was the speaker. As usual, he was quite inspiring. He had much praise for the work of the Prince Hall Masonic fraternity and other worthwhile institutions. As usual, he had much criticism for President Reagan, who was advocating a larger defense budget while vetoing a bill aimed at helping farmers. Clayborn correctly observed: "You can't eat bullets."[158] At the Saturday night banquet, Imperial Potentate Carl Wilson of the Shrine was the speaker. Wilson was named "Master Mason of the Year" by the society.[159] The convention, as a whole, went well. However, serious problems existed in view of a conflict between Past Grand Master Clayborn and Grand Master White. According to Walkes, this conflict "cast a cloud over the entire jurisdiction."[160]

The Supreme Council, Southern Jurisdiction, again convened in Washington, D.C. on October 17, 1988. In his allocution, Clayborn described Prince Hall housing complexes in Texas and Alabama as being "in real good operating form." He reported leading a southern delegation to a recent meeting of the Supreme Council, Northern Jurisdiction, where Sovereign Grand Commander Booker T. Alexander and the northern fraters "saw fit to it that we were comfortable and we enjoyed a great session." In his remarks about the Imperial Council of the Mystic Shrine, he brought in the 1988 presidential race between Democrat Michael Dukakis and Republican George Bush:

> We were treated with a feast for the heart and mind on Sunday. Illustrious (Dr.) Benjamin Hooks fed the people and all was well and on Monday morning Noble Jesse Jackson desired to be in and witness the actual opening of the temple. Imperial Potentate [Earl] Gray allowed him to be in, but no signs were given because his federal body guards would not leave him to our protection. I said to one of the guards that Brother Jackson was more safe with us than with them. . . .
>
> I did not expect Dukakis to pick Brother Jackson [for Vice President]. My belief was and is that, had he picked Brother Jackson, all of the Reagan Democrats and many other "rednecks" would have flooded the polls for Bush, and on the 16th of August Bush says "Give me Quayle." So now it is time to go into the bush and hunt "quail" . . . go to the polls and vote.[161]

Clayborn had been a strong supporter of Freemasonry on the African continent since his 1970 visit to Liberia. On March 10, 1989, he caught a plane to this West African nation, accompanied by Grand Masters Earl Bradford of Louisiana, Edgar Bridges of Mississippi, and Melvin Smotherson of Missouri. Two days later, they were greeted at the airport by Grand Master J. L. Brumskine and a host of Prince Hall Masons and members of the Order of the Eastern Star.[162] He described the events in

Liberia in his allocution to the Supreme Council in New Orleans on October 9, 1989.[163]

At the 1990 meeting of the Supreme Council in Houston, Clayborn said that he had to say something "with a little hope that I might stir up some of our southern blood." He asked, "Are we being led or hoodwinked?" in regard to the policies of politicians such as Richard Nixon, Ronald Reagan, and George Bush. He expressed hopes that "Our young men would be on their way home from Saudi Arabia, Iraq, and parts of the Middle East by the time I gave this report" and observed that "I am brought to wonder if anyone cares about the slaughter of mankind."[164]

In October 1991 the Supreme Council returned to the nation's capital, where Clayborn, in his allocution, presented a lengthy itinerary of Masonic travels, giving the impression that, at the age of seventy-eight, he was showing no signs of slowing down. He reported:

> I travelled to Jacksonville, FL soon after our 104th Annual Session in heavenly Houston and attended the high spirited Council of Deliberation, and presented them their new active member, Dr. George Washington . . . Most Worshipful Grand Master of Florida. . . .
>
> The first weekend in December found me and a host of others in Jackson, MS, as guest of the Most Worshipful Stringer Grand Lodge and Most Worshipful Grand Master Bridges; Feb. 8-10, with Ill. Zeno Lamarr in Las Vegas (Council of Deliberation for AZ and NV), Feb. 21-25 with Deputy Robert W. Brown (Gold Medallist) and his Council of Deliberation; March 1-3 Lake Charles, LA with Deputy J. B. Henderson and the fine people that you call CAJUN.
>
> The Sovereign Grand Commander's visitations: Mar. 8-10, GA with Deputy Willis Brown and the great people of GA on Jekel Island. Apr. 5-6, Dallas, TX Apr. 26-28, Little Rock, AR with Deputy Joel Day and MWGM Howard L. Woods and the great people of AR. I fell backwards off the rostrum and bumped my head. May 6-10, New Orleans, LA, Prince Hall Grand Masters Conference. Our general host, the Hon. Earle L. Bradford, made the visit great. I worked with the C.C.F.C.'s, a fine group of men. May 17-21, we travelled to Minneapolis, MN to be with Dr. Booker T. Alexander and our fraters of the Northern United Supreme Council. . . . June 22, Texas Shrine Day; June 23, Prayer Breakfast, Scholarship Essay, St. John and Memorial Services, Texas MW Grand Lodge to the close at high noon Thursday June 27. July 6-8, The 82nd Annual N.A.A.C.P. Convention in Houston, TX; July 21 my birthday found me in Montgomery, AL, attending the Grand Lodge of Al with MWGM S. J. Bennett, a man of renown in control of 31,000 members and $12 million. July 31, I was called in attendance of a special called national board meeting in Washington, DC of the N.A.A.C.P. In that meeting, the board voted not to support the nomination of Judge Clarence Thomas for the Supreme Court. That same afternoon, the AFL-CIO announced no support! Aug. 15, we departed for Los Angeles to attend the Imperial Council of Prince Hall Shriners. Upon our arrival in LA, we found everything in total order and, thus, began the work for 1991. We met with and discussed the 1992 meeting for which much work had been put in on behalf of Dallas, TX Metroplex. Deputy Robert W. Brown saw to our comfort and Ill. Hubert L. Reece drove my car that the Transportation Department supplies for my use. Then, it was out to the lovely home of our Grand Chancellor, Ill. Frank G. Allen, where a feast was prepared for all. . . . There was food for kings, had there been some in attendance. Bravo, Ill. Grand Chancellor, and thank you![165]

In early 1992, Clayborn recognized that the time might be right for a change in American leadership. Thus he wrote:

> My brothers, 1991 passed this life and is now history, and 1992 came in and introduced itself and times are no better than they were in 1991 but 1992 and the President of the United States of America promises that things will get better. . . .
>
> Now, I ask that we forget not that this is an election year and we need to get abreast with issues and promises and vote our true convictions when the elections come around.
>
> We owe it to ourselves and our community to be up-to-date citizens and VOTE, VOTE, VOTE.[166]

Past Grand Master and Grand Commander Clayborn, at the age of seventy-nine, did not want to slow down. However, it soon became apparent that health problems left him no choice. In June 1992 he was forced to miss the Annual Grand Lodge Communication. At the time, he was having serious problems with his kidneys which required him to undergo hemodialysis. He sent a letter to the Grand Lodge, requesting the prayers of all of the brethren and expressing hope that he might soon be able to "kiss the kidney machine goodbye." He also submitted his final report as Chairman of the Committee on Foreign Correspondence (C.C.F.C.), requesting to be relieved of the duties of this office.[167] The writer was in attendance at this Communication and, along with many others, signed a gigantic get well card to be sent to our beloved elder statesman. In October, Clayborn was able to preside over the 1992 Supreme Council session in Memphis, Tennessee.

The 1993 Communication turned out to be the last session of his beloved Grand Lodge that Past Grand Master Clayborn would attend. On the afternoon of June 23, he collapsed on the platform. An ambulance was summoned and, in the meantime, Grand Medical Director, Dr. Ulysses W. Watkins, Jr., tended to him. Clayborn was rushed to the hospital, where he spent a few days and was discharged.

On July 21, 1993, Grand Commander Clayborn celebrated his eightieth birthday. Three months later, in St. Louis, Missouri, he presided over his last session of his beloved Supreme Council. In his final allocution, he said:

> Last October we had a very good session of the Supreme Council. . . . When we left Memphis, we carried good thoughts and prayers that the people of America felt the way a lot of us felt. And then came November, and our friend was duly elected to the President of the United States of America. Then the shattering of tradition—a black man headed the President's transition team. . . . Now look at the cabinet of the President and see black after black after black (4) and more than one Chicano. I noticed that meetings were called to order and to work. I wrote Mr. Clinton and told him that I had observed him on TV with Bible in hand, going to church and I felt that a God-fearing man owed it to himself and God to begin his meetings with a prayer. Yes, I received a reply from him, declaring that both he and the Vice President would cater to my desire. I have seen it in action. Praise the Lord. . . . I declare that the state of our nation is much better than any of the past 12 Republican years. Amen and Praise the Lord. . . .
>
> The hands of death did not leave us alone because there is a good Democrat in the White House. The rider of the black horse came into the ranks of our Sovereign

Grand Inspectors General and moved from this transition scene Thurgood Marshall, George Washington, Joshua Clark, Marcus Neustadter, Joseph Telfair, Willie Worley, and James A. Mingo, a total of seven (7) Sovereign Grand Inspectors General. I cannot recall if we have had a number like that in all my Scottish Rite life. It tells me that we need to cling to the cross with this thought in mind, that in the Cross of Christ I glory and, if we do, all of our problems can be solved and we can sing "Praise the Lord."

The Supreme Council of Italy and Germany communicates to me in their own language and you know that I love it. I'm not Italian or German, but I do enjoy every bit of it. Praise the Lord. And you need to know that there is a pamphlet published by the Supreme Council 33° (white) Northern Jurisdiction which is led by Dr. Francis H. Paul, with both Prince Hall United Supreme Councils therein also. Our Illustrious Deputy of the District of Columbia, Brother Aubrey E. Ballard, is on hand-shaking terms and lunching with the Grand Chancellor, and the Sovereign Grand Commander wants to be included in the number and no one has mentioned the statue of Albert Pike. *The Supreme Council will not be involved in moving the Albert Pike statue.* Our fraternal relations are in good shape. Praise the Lord now.[168]

The earthly sojourn of Past Grand Master I. H. Clayborn came to an end on Monday, April 4, 1994. He was survived by his wife of fifty-three years, Roberta Cathcart Clayborn; a son, Gregory Lynn Clayborn; a granddaughter, Kasheeda Clayborn (all of Dallas); a brother and sister-in-law, Dr. and Mrs. David A. Williams of Austin; and a host of nieces, nephews, cousins, and other relatives and friends. Masonic memorial services were conducted by Dale Consistory No. 31 of the Scottish Rite and Zakat Temple No. 164 of the Mystic Shrine on Friday, April 8, at Good Street Baptist Church in Dallas. Funeral services, under the direction of Black and Clark Funeral Home, were held the following day at Good Street. The program included resolutions by Good Street Baptist Church, Paul Drayton Lodge No. 9, the United Supreme Council, the Prince Hall Grand Lodge of Texas, State Representative Dr. Jesse Jones, State Senator Royce West, and Dr. Benjamin Hooks of the NAACP. The eulogy was delivered by Grand Chaplain Dr. C.A.W. Clark, Clayborn's long-time pastor.[169] Burial was in Lincoln Memorial Cemetery, with Masonic graveside services conducted by Grand Master Edwin B. Cash and his officers.

The resolution from the Grand Lodge, which was signed by Grand Master Edwin B. Cash and Grand Secretary C. A. Glaspie, summarized Clayborn's service to the various houses of Prince Hall Freemasonry and stated:

> BE IT FURTHER RESOLVED, that the entire Masonic Family of Texas and its Jurisdictions will thank GOD for such a man as Brother Clayborn. As we cherish the memories of this great life, we shall forever strive to show to the world the lessons learned. And while there is remorse, we can rejoice in the fact that our departed friend and brother was well prepared for his journey—a journey to that land to share the rich blessings of the Grand Master of the Universe.
>
> BE IT FURTHER RESOLVED, that we extend to this family our deepest sympathy. This is merely a chapter completed, a page turned, a rest well earned. May you find peace and comfort in the knowledge that your loved one has completed but one chapter in the book of eternal life. GOD bless you, GOD keep you is our prayer.[170]

The resolution of the Supreme Council, signed by Lieutenant Grand Commander S. J. Bennett and Grand Secretary General Matthew Ellis, Jr., also highlighted his lengthy Masonic career and declared:

> No man among us stood so tall, with firm, yet humble grace,
> None could rise to the dais, and get such silence in the place;
> None emphasized as much, God's place within our midst,
> None of us could master the language, with such piety and wit.
>
> No man among us was as proud of the great Order that he led,
> None of us could claim misunderstanding, in anything he said;
> None acknowledged family more, than I. H., who was proud,
> He boldly boasted love for his family, and he did it in a crowd.
> No one knew more than I. H. That some day the bell would toll,
> And no one knew better than he, the preparation of his soul.
> But what a joy to know for sure, that he served this Order well,
> Joy must have filled his heart, when God rang the final bell.[171]

The resolution of the Imperial Council of the Mystic Shrine, signed by Imperial Potentate Arthur T. Shack and Imperial Recorder Marion Cheatham, included the following words:

> Whereas the Grim Reaper—"Death"—that solemn visitor, has invaded our ranks and taken from this life NOBLE ISADORE H. CLAYBORN, one of our most beloved Nobles....
>
> We pray the rich blessings of Allah upon those left, who sustained this irreparable loss.
>
> Be it ... Resolved, That as the body of our brother returns to Mother Earth, from whence it came, that the radiance of the Star of the East, and the Splendor of the Crescent guide his soul to the City of Mecca, that Holy City, and there let the Angels dwell and have compassion upon him, that he may slumber on in eternal rest and quiet.
>
> "Sweetly May He Rest!" Alhamdu Lelai.[172]

Resolutions were also received from the Prince Hall Grand Lodge of Colorado, Wyoming, and Utah, signed by Grand Master Claude W. Gray, Sr. and Grand Secretary Robert N. Andrews; and from the Prince Hall Grand Lodge of Michigan, signed by Grand Master Leon J. Austin and C.C.F.C. Clanton N. Dawson.[173]

On June 28, 1995, Texas Grand Master Robert E. Connor, Jr., recommended that a number of lodges which had been operating under dispensation be chartered and numbered. The Grand Lodge approved this recommendation. Among these lodges was I. H. Clayborn Lodge No. 641 in Beeville, Bee County, Texas.[174]

To summarize the life, death, and legacy of Isadore Huddleston Clayborn is no easy task. The author counts it a privilege to have known him and worked with him in various houses of Prince Hall Freemasonry. His long and productive life should be an inspiration to many who, like him, strive for excellence in all walks of life. As a Christian and a Mason, Bro. Clayborn, in obedience to Philippians 3:14, truly pressed toward the mark of the high calling of God in Christ Jesus!

Reuben Glassell White

Reuben Glassell White (1917-2002) was the seventeenth Grand Master of Prince Hall Masons in Texas. Born on September 25, 1917, in Shreveport, Louisiana, he came to Texas at the age of thirteen, settling in Galveston County. After maintaining residence in La Marque from 1934 to 1988, he moved to Texas City in 1988.[1]

White spent eleven years in the U. S. Army and sixteen years in the U. S. Air Force. He retired from the military in 1965 and began working for American Oil Company as a laborer and heavy equipment operator, retiring in 1984. He was a member of Rising Star Baptist Church in Texas City for over fifty years.[2]

White began his Masonic career in April 1947, when he was raised to the sublime degree of Master Mason in La Marque Lodge No. 373. He served as Worshipful Master of this lodge for thirty-five years. He was a member of Winn Consistory No. 243, Ancient and Accepted Scottish Rite; and El Katif Temple No. 85, Ancient Egyptian Arabic Order Nobles of the Mystic Shrine. Both of these bodies are located in Galveston. He served for forty years as Worthy Patron of Silver Circle Chapter No. 101, Order of the Eastern Star.[3]

White was long active in the Prince Hall Grand Lodge of Texas, serving on various committees and presenting numerous resolutions. He served as Grand Tiler from 1958 to 1961, Grand Senior Warden from 1961 to 1964, Deputy Grand Master from 1965 to 1981, and Grand Master from 1981 to 1987.[4] He was elected Deputy Grand Master at the time of the retirement of John Theodore Maxey and the elevation of Isadore Huddleston Clayborn to the highest office in Freemasonry. Clayborn and White were destined to direct the affairs of the Grand Lodge for a total of twenty-two years.

On June 28, 1966, Deputy Grand Master White gave his first report to the Grand Lodge, stating, "Though it has been but a short twelve (12) months since we gathered for the same purpose; nevertheless, it has been a period in which we have witnessed the changing of events racing against time, for we are now engaged in a civil, nonviolent upheaval coupled with a far flung conflict stretching into the rice paddies of Vietnam." He reported that, on August 1, 1965, he had represented Grand Master Clayborn at the funeral of Past Grand Junior Warden Ernest Wisby of Texas City. Bro. Wisby, he said, had served as a Grand Lodge officer for thirty years.[5]

On June 28, 1967, White gave his second report, chronicling his attendance at numerous Masonic functions and declaring: "Our labor has at all times been for the progress of the Most Worshipful Prince Hall Grand Lodge in particular, and to instill the principles of integrity, sincerity, honesty, and pride of achievement for our race in general."[6]

On June 26, 1968, White gave his third report, describing his involvement in a number of Masonic activities, including the meeting of the United Supreme Council, Ancient and Accepted Scottish Rite, Southern Jurisdiction. The latter session was held October 7-10, 1967, at the Shoreham Hotel in Washington, D.C. There, White and eighty-five others received the 33°.[7]

On June 25, 1969, White gave his fourth report, describing his attendance at a number of Masonic functions, including the North Central Regional Meeting at Bishop College in Dallas on October 5, 1968.[8] He gave the following description of the nature of fraternal leadership:

> The brotherhood of man is never a foe to man, but is always in harmony with all men. As we embark upon our duties for the ensuing year, let each of us live that day by day our influence upon others cannot be measured; that every word, every gesture, every expression may be watched by another who is looking up to us for guidance.
>
> May we pause and ponder the following in our minds: When someone looks to us for leadership, do we lead him in the right direction or is ours the kind of leadership that pulls him down rather than lifts him up?[9]

The year 1970 marked a new decade, a decade in which Grand Master Clayborn and Deputy Grand Master White resolved to continue providing outstanding leadership to the Prince Hall Masons of Texas. On June 24, 1970, White delivered his fifth report, calling for stalwart men who would be "solid, dedicated, dependable, and committed soldiers" in the cause of Freemasonry. He described such as "Men of aim and purpose in life, so subjugated to *Christ*, so subdued and controlled by the *Holy Ghost*, so conquered by *God* that all else is counted as refuse, that we may know *Christ* and the power of *His* resurrection and be an instrument in the hand of God Almighty for any service, any time and in any land under any circumstances." He then asked the all-important question: *"Will you pay the price to be that kind of man?"*[10]

On June 23, 1971, White gave his sixth report, which included the following words of inspiration:

> Although these are the most unusual days we have ever seen, or may ever see again, we can be happy indeed if we strive to be peace makers and remain in fellowship with Christ. Just a few years ago, we witnessed World War II; today we are facing another crisis and struggle which could result in a world revolution. Every country on the globe is in some manner involved.

Armies and navies of nations are scattered over all the earth and seas. Soldiers, cadets, sailors, marines, Army and Navy officers may be seen on every land. War is crushing the earth under its heel of iron. For these calamities, there is a reason. The reason is that we have left our first love and have ceased to seek diligently after the *ways of peace.*

Our time is now up, but it is at hand. We must, in this new Masonic year, search for the enduring Mountain of Peace which will give us the deeper inner quietness of heart and the staunch assurance that God is still the Father of Mankind. . . .

We as followers of Christ have a mission: to pray for Peace, to believe in Peace, and to practice Peace. Just now the world is in confusion but, if we trust fully in the Author of Peace, hearken to his commands and do them, then Peace shall lap the shores of the earth like a mighty river, and righteousness shall cover the land.[11]

He then, as during the previous year, asked: *"Will you pay the price to be that kind of man?"*[12]

White delivered his seventh report on June 28, 1972, describing his involvement in a number of Masonic and non-Masonic activities, including a campaign dinner in La Marque on April 15, 1972, for Texas gubernatorial candidate Frances "Sissy" Farenthold.[13]

On June 27, 1972, White delivered his eighth report, in which he declared:

The world is not a playground; it is a schoolroom. Life is not a holiday, but an education, and the one great lesson for us all is how better we can love. I have talked about the elements of love, but these are only elements. Love itself can never be defined. To secure it, we must brace our wills. We try to copy those who have it, we watch, and we pray. But these things alone will not bring love into our nature. Love is an effect. Only as we fulfill the right condition, can we have the effect.[14]

Among the activities reported were attendance at the 1972 session of the Supreme Council in Monrovia, Liberia, and the Eastern Regional Meeting in Kaufman, Texas.[15]

On June 25, 1974, White gave his ninth report, entitling it "A Man for the Job." He stated:

One of the truths we cannot evade today is the need for workers in God's Vineyard.

The world is suffering for the need for men to do the job for God. In Matthew 9:37, Jesus stated that the harvest was plenteous but the laborers were few. He stated further, "Pray therefore, the Lord of the harvest, that He will send forth laborers into His harvest" (vs. 38). . . .

When we consider the community, we are again reminded of its needs and problems. The housing problem, the street problem, and other things are all of great concern. What about the men who run our Government? What and where is their chief concern? The recent Watergate scandal and other related events cry with a loud voice, shouting to a bewildered public, that their concern is personal gain and glory through blackmail and fraud.

As Christians, we are citizens of two communities; an earthly community and a heavenly community. We are concerned about everything that affects either one. While our primary concern is for our heavenly community, we are living in this earthly community and we must not hesitate to show our concern in selecting the right man for the job.[16]

Thus he urged Texas Prince Hall Freemasons—who are obligated to always act upon the square—to do what is right despite all of the wrongdoing which was manifested in Richard Nixon's Watergate scandal!

The Bi-Centennial Year of Prince Hall Freemasonry and the Centennial Year of the Prince Hall Grand Lodge of Texas were observed in 1975. Deputy Grand Master White played a prominent role in the Texas festivities. In his tenth report, delivered on June 24, 1975, he declared: "Realizing our need each for the other in our respective areas of endeavors, we journeyed the year in the faith of Nehemiah 4:6: 'So built we the wall; and all the wall was joined together unto the half thereof, for the people had a mind to work!' All of us could not play the role of 'the star' but each of us tried to play a good supporting role to make our year a successful one."[17]

On June 22, 1976, White delivered his eleventh report. As usual, he spoke of attendance at a number of Masonic activities, including the Southeastern Regional Meeting in Teague, Texas.[18] He gave the following charge to the craft for the Bi-Centennial Year of the United States:

> As men and Masons, we must become more and more involved in the good things and necessary things about us that touches a part of our daily lives whether it be social, political, economical, or educational. Help somebody today, tomorrow, and every day that you can.
>
> You may have come through many trials and various experiences and have reached your goal, you may have been successful in your particular field; there may not be any more worlds for you to conquer, remember, there is someone that you can help to reach the same heights by lending them a helping hand. They may be young and inexperienced. They need you.[19]

White delivered his twelfth report on June 28, 1977, describing attendance at a number of Masonic and non-Masonic events, including the National Federal Credit Union meeting in Mexico City and the Conference of Prince Hall Grand Masters in Washington, D.C. At the latter meeting, one of the speakers was Dr. Benjamin Hooks, then commissioner for the Federal Communications Commission. White described Hooks as "at his best."[20] At the Washington conference, he attended a workshop for C.C.F.C.s.[21]

On June 17, 1978, White delivered his thirteenth report, which included the sad news of the deaths of a number of prominent Prince Hall Freemasons, including Grand Master James E. Greene of Liberia, Past Grand Masters Arvell W. Denton of Oregon, Louis Fair, Jr., of New York, Clement F. Isaacs of Massachusetts, and Joseph W. Givens of Pennsylvania.[22]

White's fourteenth report, delivered on June 27, 1979, included a reference to his attendance at the funerals of Grand Chaplain Rev. E. H. Branch and Grand Lecturer J. D. Paley. In this speech, he also said: "I wish to express my sincere thanks to you, my brothers, who saw fit to elect me as your Deputy Grand Master for another year of service."[23]

A new decade that began in 1980 found the Clayborn-White team still in charge of the Prince Hall Grand Lodge of Texas. On June 25, 1980, Deputy Grand Master White delivered his fifteenth report, in which he spoke of his attendance at the Conference of Prince Hall Grand Masters in Boston in May 1980. Such included the awesome experiences of viewing the charter of African Lodge No. 459, which is kept in a Boston bank vault and viewed once every ten years; and visiting the grave of Prince Hall in Copps Hill Burying Ground. He declared: *"Prince Hall Masonry is still on the march! And since we are in this Prince Hall Army, let us shoulder our arms, carry the fight to the enemy of Masonry, fly the Prince Hall Banner high, continue to love your brother, support his every good endeavor, ever remembering that he is but human and may grow weary on the way. That is the time to remember the Fourth Point of the 'Five Points of Fellowship.' Extend a strong right arm and hold him up."*[24] He also brought sad news of the deaths of the following C.C.F.C.s: Cecil W. Bond of Pennsylvania, James L. Wasson of Oregon, Past Senior Warden Joseph D. Young of West Virginia, Past Grand Masters I. A. Robinson, Sr., of West Virginia, Harry A. Brewer of California, Lawrence A. Millben of Canada, and Frederick T. Hicks of Maryland.[25]

On June 24, 1981, Deputy Grand Master White gave his sixteenth and final report. He described a very enjoyable session of the Conference of Prince Hall Grand Masters in Nassau, the Bahamas. He also reported sad events surrounding the revolution in Liberia, which temporarily shut down Prince Hall Masonic activities in the West African nation. He stated: "Today, my heart is sad . . . yes, sad to no end when I realize and think of the tragedy that befell our brothers in Monrovia, Liberia. . . . We can only say . . . *God's Will has been done and so mote it be.*"[26] At this Communication, Grand Master Clayborn announced that, rather than seeking reelection, he desired that Reuben G. White succeed him. The craft followed Clayborn's direction and elevated White to the Grand East. The new Grand Master and the other officers were installed by Past Grand Master Clayborn.[27]

In the September 1981 issue of *Texas Prince Hall Masonic Quarterly*, the newly elected Grand Master wrote:

> For the first time as Titular Head of our great Most Worshipful Prince Hall Grand Lodge of Texas and Jurisdiction, I write from your office this letter which is open, so all who are concerned may read and be informed.
>
> First, it is my prayer and hope that, upon returning home, each of you found your loved ones hale and hearty and enjoying all the rich blessings of the Great Grand Master of the Universe . . . "GOD." . . .
>
> In the humblest manner I could say it, let me thank you for the confidence shown by you and your representatives unanimously electing me to serve this wonderful position.
>
> Secondly, may I plead with and to you, to be knowledgeable of the fact and truth that we cannot afford to stand still and rest on our laurels. For sixteen (16) years, all of us have, like true soldiers, joined in to follow the lead of our Grand Master, who now is our Past Grand Master and who has not quit working yet. . . .
>
> May the Lord of Heaven bless and keep each of you, but keep this in mind, we *must* grow if we are to survive.[28]

In his last communication for 1981, he wrote to the craft, charging them to take Masonry seriously and to strive to leave behind a brand of Masonry better than what they received.[29]

Early in the new year, White described the Prince Hall Grand Lodge of Texas as a giant oak in the fraternal forest and Masonic activities as the soil, rain, sunshine, and fertilizer on which the roots of the Masonic tree feed. He called upon all craftsmen to do their part to make a healthy, sturdy, fruit-bearing tree.[30]

During each of the 1981-82 regional meetings, Grand Master White delivered a speech entitled "Where Do We Go From Here?," which included the following interesting illustration:

> There is the story of an old woman immediately after slavery who had the knowledge of curing many ills, by collecting various roots, herbs, and leaves. She cured everything from colds to whooping cough; insomnia to pneumonia, and from measles to mumps. She never shared the secret of the ingredients with anyone, not even her immediate family.
>
> When she died, her secret died with her and the community suffered and many died from lack of her knowledge.
>
> Don't be like the old woman, don't kill your community; don't kill your lodge; don't kill Prince Hall Masonry! Bestir yourselves and keep Prince Hall Masonry; walk and talk Prince Hall Masonry. . . .
>
> Blend your strength in a united front to break down barriers, open new horizons, and march, yes . . . MARCH. March on to victory. . . . Climb the ladder to the top rung, climb the tree to the farthermost branch and pluck the fruit, the sweet fruit of success.[31]

On June 22, 1982, White delivered his first Grand Master's Address, beginning with the question of "Watchman, what of the night?" as a way of addressing the condition of the Grand Lodge. He happily declared that the condition of the beloved body was stable in every respect, with the numerical growth exceeding the losses through death. He reported that the Prince Hall housing complexes were thriving and self-sustaining, that no request for charity had gone unheeded, and that fourteen young people had been aided by the J. T. Maxey Scholarship Program.[32] White told of highly positive experiences at the meetings of the Supreme Council in Jackson, Mississippi, and of the Conference of Grand Masters in Richmond, Virginia.[33] He gave the following charge to the craft:

> As Masons, we should be builders. Probably there are builders sitting in this assembly . . . carpenters, plumbers, cabinet makers, brick layers, and general contractors. There may be cattlemen and farmers who can be classified as builders, for they feed the nation and contribute to the economy and well being of their community. You are builders.
>
> But I cannot and will not ignore the fact that we can and should be builders in another sense. We owe it to ourselves, this Grand Lodge, our communities and especially to our young people to lay the foundation and build a better society in which to live.[34]

Later that day, I. H. Clayborn presided over the election of officers for the first time in his new capacity of Past Grand Master. A. R. Jernigan moved that all elected officers succeed themselves. This was seconded by O. W. L. Turner, T. M. Morgan, and Lee Majors. The motion was adopted unanimously.[35]

On June 24, 1982, Grand Master White recommended that each brother be assessed $1.50 payable in May and $1.50 payable in September, for refinishing the floors of the mosque. It was moved by C. A. Glaspie and seconded by a host of brothers to accept and adopt this recommendation. The motion passed by an overwhelming majority.³⁶ Later that day, Past Grand Master Clayborn installed Grand Master White, who proceeded to install his elected and appointed officers.³⁷

In the December 1982 issue of *Texas Prince Hall Masonic Quarterly*, White sent a Christmas greeting to the craft, full of praise for the person of Jesus Christ, His virgin birth, His humiliation, His earthly ministry, and His sinless life.³⁸ He concluded this greeting with the following beautiful "Evening Prayer":

> The woods and fields are silent now,
> The birds have gone to rest;
> Of all the times of day I love
> The quiet evening best.
> For twilight stillness is, I think,
> Like one soft wordless prayer
> When tiny creatures give themselves
> Into the Father's tender care.³⁹

Early the following year, White wrote a very inspiring column entitled "Self-Encouragement," in which he declared:

> Today we encounter many things in life which discourage us. Our problems sometimes discourage us, and certainly hardships and sickness discourage us. Something most nearly is always present to make us less hopeful or enthusiastic; Therefore, today, I would like to discuss briefly the thought of self-encouragement. In I Samuel 30:6, we find David in a situation which certainly had him distressed, disturbed, and discouraged; but the latter part of the verse states: "But David encouraged himself in the Lord his God." Of all the benefactors that we meet in this world, there are few who render so great a service as the "courage bringer." There is no finer art than that of putting heart into people—people who have become despairful. There is no more splendid service than any of us can possibly render than that of relighting the candle of hope and expectancy in the darkened lives of those about us.⁴⁰

In June 1983 Grand Master White presided over his second Grand Communication. This session included a report of the receipt of $1,525.45 in oil royalties to apply against judgment and interest related to the Fraternal Bank and Trust, which had operated in Fort Worth for forty-five years before declaring bankruptcy in 1957. On June 28 he delivered his second Grand Master's Address, in which he declared:

> The United States of America is presently under a Republican administration. Don't fight the Republicans as such; fight what they stand for. . . . fight their asinine social programs. . . . fight their foreign "give away policies" while their poor and elderly suffer at home. . . . fight to the very death their bank interest withholding program that makes the poor get poorer. Raise your collective voices, write your Congressman, express your opinions, and let the world know that you are **Men and Masons**.
> Don't try to prove it to each other, but to the community in which you live. The Holy Bible, Book Divine, says that you don't light a candle and put it in a bushel, but on a candlestick so that it gives light unto all the house.⁴¹

White reported joining Past Grand Master Clayborn in laying a cornerstone for Good Street Baptist Church in Dallas and talked about the dispensing of a great deal of Masonic charity and the participation of twenty-two high school graduates in the J. T. Maxey Scholarship Program. He expressed great pleasure at the appearance of the floors of the mosque as a result of the refinishing which had been completed during the 1982-83 Masonic year. Later that day, he and his officers were reelected.[42]

On the following day, the Committee on the State of the Country, chaired by John Bullock, reported that, according to the U. S. Commission on Civil Rights, President Ronald Reagan had made numerous efforts to reduce federal civil rights enforcement in education. The committee also reported that former Mississippi Governor Ross Barnett, a die-hard segregationist, had accepted an invitation to ride in a parade honoring slain civil rights activist Medgar Evers. It appears that Charles Evers, brother of Medgar, invited Barnett to participate in order to show how far Mississippi has progressed in the twenty years since his brother's murder.[43] The same report hailed the election of Harold Washington as Chicago's first black mayor.[44] The committee concluded by rededicating themselves to the fight for economic advancement of blacks.[45] On June 30 Past Grand Master Clayborn installed Grand Master White, who proceeded to install his elected and appointed officers.[46]

Reuben G. White was still presiding in the Grand East in 1984, the year made famous in 1948 by British novelist George Orwell in "a stark, scarifying portrait of a future totalitarian society ruled by the ubiquitous, yet unseen, 'Big Brother.'"[47] Early in 1984, White wrote to the craft, stating that he was stunned by the fact that, during the previous Masonic year, more than 300 lodges added no new members to their rolls. In seeking an answer to the serious problem of lack of growth, he rejected the possibilities that young men are not interested in Masonry or that they have no money to spend on initiation fees.[48] He concluded:

> I cannot but believe that the harvest is ripe, but the laborers are few. There are men out there who are desirous of becoming Masons but don't know the proper steps to take or who to contact. It is incumbent upon each Master Mason to sell Prince Hall Masonry to their friends, neighbors, co-workers, and associates. Make yourself a committee of one to enroll just one new member this year.
>
> I am of the opinion that many of you are not putting forth any effort at all to gather some of the harvest that is waiting to be plucked.... Some Worshipful Masters don't want new young men, learned young men, and coming generations.[49]

Shortly before the 1984 Communication, White published his address, entitled "It Is Later Than You Think," delivered at the various regional meetings during the 1983-84 Masonic year. This address included the following remarks:

> The world situation tells all of us that society is changing and, with one country taking over another country, the world map is changing. I ask, as many others no doubt have asked, *"What is wrong?"* When innocent airlines are being shot from the skies, when 269 innocent people are sent to a watery grave in less than three minutes; when no formal apology is extended to the countries or relatives; when for the first time in the thirty-year history of the space program, a black man is hurled into space; when for the first time a black woman is crowned Miss America, ... changes are being made and *"It is later than you think!"*

Don't sit back on your laurels and say like that certain Biblical character, "Soul, take your rest."[50]

At the 1984 Communication, another statement regarding the liquidation of assets of the defunct Fraternal Bank and Trust Company was presented. According to this report, the amount of oil royalties received during the Masonic year was nearly three times the amount received during the previous year. Nevertheless, it was also reported that the income from such royalties was not enough to pay the interest. The statement concluded that the Grand Lodge had probably recouped its original investment of $370,000 despite expenses related to collections, legal fees, and taxes; and that the unpaid judgments represented a strong potential source of revenue which should not be overlooked.[51]

One of the distinguished visitors to the 1984 Grand Communication was Joseph A. Walkes, Jr., founder and president of the Phylaxis Society. Walkes attended this session in an effort to generate interest in the Phylaxis Society Convention to be held in Dallas in March 1985.[52]

White delivered his third Grand Master's Address on June 26, 1984, expressing sorrow over the deaths of a number of brethren, including Grand Marshal Sam Kelley of Texas and Grand Master H. M. Thompson of Mississippi. He reported that all of the Texas regional meetings had been well organized and that much constructive work was done at the Grand Masters Conference in Wilmington, Delaware. He stressed the crucial importance of bringing new members into Masonry and insisted "We can achieve." In conclusion, he asked "Where will we go from here?" and reminded the craft that "The challenge is yours." Later that day, he and his principal officers were reelected.[53]

On June 27, 1984, the Committee on the State of the Country, again headed by John Bullock, gave its report, decrying a number of setbacks in civil rights and affirmative action legislation and praising Rev. Jesse Jackson for his leadership of the Rainbow Coalition and his candidacy for president of the United States. The committee concluded with a quotation from Amos 3:3: "Can two walk together, except they be agreed?"[54] On the following day, Past Grand Master Clayborn installed Grand Master White who, in turn, installed his elected and appointed officers.[55]

White published an article in September 1984, in connection with the annual celebration of Prince Hall and Americanism Day.[56] Unfortunately, this article contained numerous historical errors, as it was based largely on the now discredited Grimshaw myths which have circulated in Prince Hall Masonry since 1903.[57] White's last article for 1984, in the writer's opinion, was much better. The latter dealt with Operative and Speculative Masonry and stressed the idea of Freemasons as builders of brotherhood. The Grand Master concluded that "*True* brotherhood is for the salvation of the race from its misery and pain" and asked, "Do you know of any *greater task*?"[58]

In his first article for 1985, White addressed the matter of "Our Behaviour," stating:

> Discipline, not only within the organization but within ourselves, is an absolute necessity. Undisciplined emotions are as unregulated explosions, causing destruction and ruin by their senseless waste of energy. Any deviation from the accepted rules and customs of Masonry should be met with unyielding resistance.
>
> Our behaviour while attending lodge is of great concern to every well-thinking Mason. Expression of opinions is a fundamental right; however, this was not meant to be construed as an outlet for the release of destructive and undue criticism.[59]

In March 1985 the Phylaxis Society held its annual convention in Dallas. The convention, as a whole, went well. However, serious problems existed in view of a conflict between Past Grand Master Clayborn and Grand Master White. In his history of the Phylaxis Society, President Walkes reported that this conflict "cast a cloud over the entire jurisdiction."[60] After this meeting, White gave Walkes a ride to Houston, where Walkes attended a meeting of Blacks in Criminal Justice.[61]

At the various regional meetings during the 1984-85 Masonic year, White spoke on the question "Am I My Brother's Keeper?" He began this address with a quotation from Genesis 4:9, where Cain asked this question when the Lord called him to account after he had slain his brother Abel. The Grand Master cited a number of outstanding black Americans—including Frederick Douglass, Booker T. Washington, W.E.B. DuBois, A. Philip Randolph, Clarence Mitchell, Walter White, Roy Wilkins, Benjamin Hooks, Martin Luther King, Jr., and Paul Robeson—all of whom accepted the responsibility of being "my brother's keeper."[62]

At the 1985 Communication, a report on the Prince Hall-sponsored apartment complexes was submitted. These complexes were purchased during the administration of I. H. Clayborn and are insured by the Federal Housing Administration. According to this report, the projected value of these at the end of twenty-five years, when they were scheduled to be paid off, would appear to be $2,300,000. The committee noted that "If the Grand Lodge decides to get out of the housing business at any time, it could have good equities built up over and above the existing loan balances."[63] There were comments regarding the liquidation of the assets of the Fraternal Bank and Trust Company, including the notation that, during the 1984-85 Masonic year, the oil royalties from production in Cooke County was $2,401.21, but property taxes totaled $682.99. Thus the net total was $1,718.22.[64]

On June 25, 1985, White delivered his fourth Grand Master's Address, in which he stated:

> My brothers, the Masonic year of 1985-86 has arrived, as the Masonic year of 1984-85 has passed and left in its wake many memories, many defeats, many victories, many joys, and many sorrows. But whatever our state, we can not but thank God that it is well with us as it is, for we are still in the land of the living. . . .
>
> Things have not always been as successful as I had hoped, for a couple of projects of importance have not as yet been culminated in the manner hoped for. However, this has not dulled my enthusiasm nor blunted my optimism. I am committed to "Fight On." . . .
>
> Be proud of your lineage, heritage, from whence you came, and of your Masonic roots. Then stand four square and proclaim to the world who you are, for I say to you today that . . .we ought, we can, we must, and we shall fight on and on and on and on. . .[65]

White reported attending the Grand Masters Conference in Oakland, California, and making a number of visits to Tucson, Arizona, in view of legal problems.[66]

Later that day, White was reelected as Grand Master, defeating his challenger, Grand Senior Warden Thomas H. Routt. Edwin B. Cash was reelected as Deputy Grand Master. Routt was then reelected to his office. Grand Junior Warden Jesse L. Baines, Grand Secretary-Treasurer Volney B. Phillips, Grand Chaplain C. A. W. Clark,

Grand Recorder A. D. Harris, and Grand Tiler B. T. Jackson were reelected. O.W.L. Turner was elected Grand Lecturer, succeeding Sherman Wilson.[67]

On June 26, 1985, the Committee on the State of the Country, chaired by Bullock, gave its report. Highlights of this report included the continued Fundamentalist control of the Southern Baptist Convention and the recent condemnation of Freemasonry by the British Methodists. The committee urged the craft: "Let us pray and stand tall as Masons in a world of adversaries."[68] Later that day, the Grand Lodge adopted a number of recommendations of the Grand Master, including the granting of charters for J. D. Maxey Lodge No. 630 and Impulse Lodge No. 631; and an assessment on each lodge in the amount of $26.80 for each reinstated member. One brother asked how to get a crippled child admitted to the Scottish Rite Hospital for Crippled Children in Dallas. Past Grand Master Clayborn stated that the Worshipful Master should complete an application form, deleting the "A" from "A.F.&A.M.," adding "Prince Hall Affiliation," and mailing it in. He expressed confidence that this procedure would insure a child's admission.[69] On June 27, 1985, Past Grand Master Clayborn again installed Grand Master White, who, in turn, installed his elected and appointed officers.[70]

In early 1986 White acknowledged that we encounter many things in life which bring discouragement and insisted that one of the greatest benefactors in the world is the "courage bringer." He called for self-encouragement and reminded the craft that, when we encounter hatred, misunderstanding, or unpopularity, we always find encouragement in the Lord our God.[71]

The year 1986 was important in the history of Prince Hall Freemasonry in the Lone Star State. That year, Grand Master White and his board of directors were able to sell the old Masonic Mosque on East Belknap in Fort Worth for $2,000,000 and complete the building of the present Masonic Mosque at 3433 South Martin Luther King Freeway and Highway 287. The cornerstone was laid on the evening of Monday, June 23, 1986. White regarded this as his greatest achievement as Grand Master.[72]

At the 1986 Grand Communication, distinguished visitors included Grand Masters Edgar Bridges of Mississippi, Earle Bradford of Louisiana, McCowan of Colorado; Past Grand Master Logan of Pennsylvania; Secretary General James Mingo of the United Supreme Council, Scottish Rite, Southern Jurisdiction. At the opening session on June 24, 1986, a free will offering in the amount of $625.85 was raised for the Scottish Rite Hospital for Crippled Children.[73] White's fifth Grand Master's Address was entitled "Let's Climb the Mountains." White told the craft:

> Amid the turmoil of the past since we met here one year ago, the catastrophic events world wide, nationally, and even within the borders of our state, the topsy-turvy conditions that greet us on every hand, spiritually, economically, and politically; indecisions, right decisions, and wrong decisions spawned in the minds of world leaders....
>
> For we too could have been numbered among those who have been touched by calamity to one degree or another and even the cold finger of death. Consider those citizens of Chernobyl in Russia, those who were left homeless and destitute.
>
> As the aftermath of the great mudslide in India, and tragedy witnessed by millions of television viewers in this country when the space craft Challenger disintegrated before their eyes only three minutes after lift off.
>
> But, thanks to the indomitable will and dedication of man, time and progress have

failed to stand still and the blessed survivors have started again to . . . Climb The Mountain . . .

Climbing our mountains require us to use the tools of brotherhood, unity, local programs, and recruitment. . . .

On yesterday, we made history. Today, we are adding to that history. It had not been my fondest hope and dream that we would be assembled in the new Mosque today. When the devastating storm struck Fort Worth last month, we had the assurance from the builders that the meeting place would be ready. When the damage was surveyed and the estimate time was determined for its occupancy, at first I was disheartened and grieved at heart. But one night a voice that seemed to come from every direction at the same time, spoke to me and said . . . "Question not the handiwork of God." . . . Since that time, I have not fretted, worried, or questioned, only become more determined.

Brothers, if we accept God and His providence, we can become strengthened to better . . . Climb The Mountain.

A little better than three score years ago, Grand Master McKinney and Grand Secretary McDonald conceived the idea of a permanent meeting place for Prince Hall Masons in Texas. This was a mountain in their lives. But, linking hands with the brothers across the state, they began to climb that mountain. They climbed until they reached the top. Most of us here have camped on that top for many years.

But the vicissitudes and ravages of time and nature began to take its toll and the top of the mountain began to crack and change and crevices appeared.

So on last year, you spoke out and said "Let us climb another mountain. Being obedient to your command, we set out to do just that. And I say to you today that: any time you can trade, exchange, swap, or bargain three point four acres of land and a sixty-four-year-old building for seven point five acres of land and a new modern two-story building, you are doing some good horse trading. . . .

I don't just ask you, I beg you, exhort you to join hands, lock arms, and form a solid chain among Prince Hall Masons from the Gulf of Mexico on the south; to the Red River on the north; from the Pine Woods on the east to the Rugged Mountains on the west; and as a mighty army with a single purpose . . .

Let's Climb The Mountain Together.[74]

Some of the brethren present noted that Grand Master White "was at his best," with the address "delivered with force and clarity." Following this outstanding speech, White was again reelected, withstanding a second challenge from Grand Senior Warden Thomas H. Routt. The other officers, including Routt, were then reelected.[75]

On the following day, Bullock and his Committee on the State of the Country described America as "in a constant up and down motion." They highlighted a number of events, some positive and some negative. They observed that twelve noted space physicists and astronomers signed a pledge not to work on President Reagan's Strategic Defense Initiative, better known as "Star Wars," because of their conviction that this project was technically dubious and politically unwise. They proudly reported that Bracy Lovelady, a 1980 recipient of a J. T. Maxey Scholarship, had completed his college education and established a new lodge, under dispensation, in Houston. They praised Grand Master White's performance in leveling the cornerstone for the new Masonic Mosque on the previous evening, declaring that "the new building will be a legacy to the Prince Hall Masonic Family in Texas." In conclusion, they reminded all of the Texas Masons present that "We are into our Sesquicentennial

Celebration, so let us be proud Texans and Americans. *In God We Trust.*"[76] On the following day, Past Grand Master Clayborn installed Grand Master White, and he then installed all other officers and closed the 111th Grand Communication.[77]

In his last article for 1986, White commented on the great achievement of this very historic year:

> Building the new Masonic Mosque has indeed been the most interesting of my Masonic experiences. I have enjoyed the exposure to new and challenging demands. Certainly, because of the richness of Masonry, its deep meaning, and lofty ideals, I am convinced that Masonry is worth the time and energy one expends in its pursuit.
> *I always enjoy a little chit-chat with the Master Masons of this Grand Old Order.*[78]

On June 23, 1987, White delivered his fifth and final Grand Master's Address. This speech reflected less enthusiasm and optimism when compared to those of previous years. It seems that, during the twelve months since the close of the last Communication, there had been much controversy related to the handling of the money raised from the sale of the older property. White responded:

> My brothers, we have come face to face with all such things this Masonic year. Rumors and lies have run rampant this year. I met with debilitating rumors on every hand; insipid lies as far away as South Carolina. But putting all faith in the omnipotent Father, I found them all innocuous and shed them as a duck sheds water from his back.
> Former President Harry Truman once said . . . "If you can't stand the heat, get out of the kitchen." Facing these innuendoes, suspicions, rumors, and lies everywhere I go becomes heart-rending and discouraging, but, in spite of . . . in spite of, I am still trying to prepare a fraternal meal for the Prince Hall Grand Lodge of Texas.
> Therefore, I gave up worrying about rumors; I stopped worrying God for an answer; maybe he will give me the answer through some of you. If so, someone please tell me when did the Grand Master borrow $164,000 from one of our brothers in order to operate the Grand Lodge????
> When did that brother change the locks to the doors of this Mosque building??? When and why did this brother bar the Grand Master out of this building??? If none of you can answer, I will start worrying God again.
> There is one last question one man should be able to answer. "Dr. I. H. Clayborn." . . . Dr. Clayborn . . . when did this Grand Master suspend you?????????
> My brothers, can't you see the deceit; can't you see the trickery; can't you see the seed of suspicion, the seed of doubt, and the seed of division . . . ???? Some of you have heard these rumors, but I say to you today . . . don't fall into the trap of "divide and conquer," for this is simply that intent . . . to get us fighting among ourselves. Don't believe everything you hear.[79]

The 1987 Report of the Committee on the Grand Master's Address, chaired by Deputy Grand Master Edwin B. Cash, was not a typical committee report but contained the following significant observations:

> The Grand Master's Address was one of an attempt to rectify a situation that developed, or is developing, from rumors that are false and unfounded. These are the type of rumors that tend to weaken our Masonic foundation and create trouble for our craft.

Let's examine the steps involved in the growth of this address; first, the Grand Master's analysis of the previous Republican Administration as to scandals is good. He states that, in spite of what happened, we did bounce back. He stresses the point that perseverance is the key to successfully mounting obstacles.

Rumors and untruths are the focus of the latter part of his address. Some of these were of the very, very personal type and would cause any person to react. Personal attacks have no place in our fraternal order. It is said that some of us have journeyed here full of rumors and varied suspicions. Some of us believe that Grand Lodge officers have absconded with large sums of money. It is hard to understand where these rumors start. Some of us can not find anything positive to say about the Grand Old Order, our Mosque, or the Grand Master.

We emphasize strongly that we all are created by our Heavenly Father to practice truth and brotherhood. We should stay clear of hypocrisy and deceit. He is determined to accomplish goals in spite of certain opposition.

It is the Lord who goes before us. He will be with us. He will not fail us nor forsake us.

In summary, we must address the future and direct plans to arrive at some recognizable goal. There should be an outright campaign to boost our membership. The future of our order or any institution is based on what is prepared in the present.[80]

The 1987 Report of the Committee on the State of the Country was presented by John Bullock. This report included references to the world summit conference on Acquired Immune Deficiency Syndrome (AIDS), the scandal involving the Board of Regents of Southern Methodist University headed by Texas Governor William P. Clements, the bank fraud epidemic, and closure of Texas Safeway stores, the presidential candidacy of Ku Klux Klan leader David Duke, and the sexual scandals involving televangelist Jim Bakker and Dallas United Methodist pastor Walker Railey.[81]

On the following day, the election of officers was held. Prior to the election, Grand Secretary-Treasurer Volney B. Phillips asked Grand Recorder A. D. Harris to read the following letter which he had written:

> I have tried to serve in this office with my best wisdom, knowledge, and know-how for the last (20) years. I have enjoyed the work and I have enjoyed you. I appreciate your cooperation in helping me to do these (20) years.
>
> However, from the weakness of my body, at this point causes me to take under consideration, how necessary it is for the person who serves as Grand Secretary to recognize when his time is up. The holder of this office needs to be a man of strength, courage, and intelligence.
>
> Therefore, I'm passing the office to whom you may choose as your next Grand Secretary or Grand Secretary-Treasurer. I shall be happy to share my experiences, if desired.
>
> Please remember me in your prayers. May many good things come to all of you and your families. Therefore, please do not place my name in nomination.[82]

For the third year in a row, Routt challenged White to the highest office in Masonry. This time, however, Routt's efforts were crowned with success. Edwin B. Cash was reelected as Deputy Grand Master. Hubert Reece was elected as Grand Senior Warden, Robert E. Connor, Jr., as Grand Junior Warden, C. A. Glaspie as

Grand Secretary, Kerven Carter as Grand Treasurer, B. T. Jackson as Grand Tiler, Lawrence Anderson as Grand Lecturer, C. A. W. Clark as Grand Chaplain, and A. D. Harris as Grand Recorder.[83] On the following day, the newly elected officers were installed by Past Grand Master Clayborn. For the first time since 1946, the Grand Lodge had two living Past Grand Masters.[84]

During the 1988 Communication, Grand Master Routt appointed a Trial Commission, chaired by Past Grand Master I. H. Clayborn and consisting of Grand Legal Advisor E. Brice Cunningham, Deputy Grand Master Edwin B. Cash, Grand Secretary C. A. Glaspie, Grand Recorder A. D. Harris, Grand Junior Warden Robert E. Connor, Jr., Grand Senior Warden Hubert Reece, and Grand Treasurer Kerven Carter. The purpose of this commission was to consider charges of Unmasonic Conduct against Past Grand Master Reuben G. White, as filed by Charles Fleming, Worshipful Master of Cowan Lodge No. 421, and Quintus Moss, Worshipful Master of Hi 12 Lodge No. 559. Members of the Trial Commission advised White of his rights. They then interrogated and heard testimony from both White and the two Worshipful Masters and reviewed the legal documents and other evidence presented. White pleaded not guilty of the charges of taking or stealing money from the plaintiff lodges. The Trial Commission found him not guilty. White pleaded guilty to the charge of Unmasonic Conduct in his opening a checking account in the name of the Most Worshipful Prince Hall Grand Lodge of Texas, with names of individuals listed as officers on the account who were not actually officers. White was found guilty of this charge. However, in view of his acquittal on the charge of stealing money from the two lodges, the Trial Commission became deadlocked regarding whether suspension for a definite period of time or reprimand was the appropriate punishment. On June 29, 1988, the Grand Lodge adopted the report and voted on punishment. Four members of the craft voted for indefinite suspension, twelve voted for definite suspension, but the overwhelming majority voted for reprimand. Thus, Past Grand Master White was ordered to stand before the altar, where he received a stirring reprimand from Grand Master Routt.[85]

After his 1987 defeat, Past Grand Master Reuben G. White remained active in the Prince Hall Grand Lodge of Texas, serving as advisor to Grand Masters Thomas H. Routt, Edwin B. Cash, and Robert E. Connor, Jr. On January 8, 1991, he and Past Grand Master I. H. Clayborn led a delegation of Texas Prince Hall Masons to Houston for the funeral of Grand Master Routt. Following participation in Masonic graveside services, White was involved in the formation of an occasional lodge which elected and installed Edwin B. Cash as Grand Master.[86] White succeeded Clayborn as C.C.F.C in 1992.[87] The death of Bro. Clayborn on April 4, 1994, resulted in White's becoming not only Senior Past Grand Master but the only Past Grand Master.[88] However, this situation did not last long. In June 1994 Robert E. Connor, Jr., was elected Grand Master, defeating Cash, and Texas again had two Past Grand Masters.

The long and productive life of Past Grand Master Reuben Glassell White came to an end on the Feast Day of Saint John the Evangelist—December 27, 2002. His funeral was held on Saturday, January 4, 2003, at Rising Star Baptist Church in Texas City. Rev. W. W. Jackson, pastor of Mount Paran Baptist Church in Texas City, officiated. Members of LaMarque Lodge No. 373 served as active pallbearers. The Prince Hall Grand Lodge of Texas, Winn Consistory, and the brothers of Rising Star Baptist

Church were designated as honorary pallbearers. Masonic burial services were conducted by Past Grand Master Edwin B. Cash. Interment took place on Monday January 6, 2003, at Houston National Cemetery in Houston, Texas.[89]

Grand Master Wilbert M. Curtis, while serving as Deputy Grand Master, wrote about his illustrious predecessor:

> Past Grand Master White was the Grand Master when I came into the Masonic Order. I was a Fellowcraft when he leveled the cornerstone of our lodge hall building, St. James Lodge #71 in Temple, Texas. All I could do was watch from a distance. Later, when he leveled the cornerstone for New Light Lodge #242 of Killeen, Texas, I was able to participate.
>
> As I think of Past Grand Master White, I think of how he supported the Grand Lodge for many years. I am reminded of how after he passed the gavel to his successor that he continued to attend the Grand Lodge and support every way he could. He did no unwaveringly until he went to that lodge of perfection on high.
>
> The work that Past Grand Master White did for the Grand Lodge reminds me of the work that King David did in preparation to building a permanent place for the Israelites to worship God. Freemasons know of it as King Solomon's Temple.
>
> In I Chronicles, Chapters 28 and 29, there is an accounting of how David made preparations for the building of the Temple. David wanted the Temple to be built to the glory of God. He knew that he would not be allowed to build it himself because of the blood that he had on his hands. God told him that his son Solomon would build the Temple. That did not stop David from making preparations for the building of the Temple. . . .
>
> Just as David did, Past Grand Master White assisted his successors every way that he could. He gave more than lip service. He did not try to set stumbling blocks in the way of progress. He provided wise counsel and assistance. He challenged the craft to move forward and, most importantly, never leave God out of our works.[90]

Thus ended over half a century of dedicated service to Texas Prince Hall Freemasonry.

Thomas Henry Routt

Thomas Henry Routt (1930-1991) was the eighteenth Grand Master of the Prince Hall Masons in Texas. He was born on March 5, 1930, in the Bakers Hill community, near Navasota, Grimes County, Texas. After serving in the United States Air Force, he moved to Houston, where he spent most of his life. On December 22, 1954, he married Ritchie L. Wilson. To this union, two children—Lora Dean and Thomas, Jr.— were born.[1] At the time of their father's death on January 3, 1991, Lora was employed as a management analyst in the City of Houston's Department of Finance and Administration and Thomas, Jr., was a graduate student at the University of North Texas in Denton.[2]

Routt attended public schools in Bon Weir, Brazos County, Texas, and graduated with honors from George Washington Carver High School in Navasota in 1945. He attended Prairie View A&M University in Prairie View, Texas, from June 1945 through August 1947 and Texas Southern University in Houston from September 1950 through January 1952. He received a Doctor of Jurisprudence degree from Texas Southern's Thurgood Marshall School of Law in 1961. Always concerned about keeping up with new developments in the judicial field, he graduated from the Academy of Judicial Education of the University of Alabama in 1970, from Texas College for the Judiciary in Austin in 1974, and from National College for the Judiciary (now National Judicial College) in Reno, Nevada, in 1975. He took a number of graduate courses and seminars from the latter institution between 1975 and 1985. His law school designated him as Outstanding Alumnus in 1984.[3]

Routt was licensed to practice law by the State of Texas in 1961 and was later authorized to practice in all four Federal District Courts of Texas, as well as the U. S. Court of Appeals for the Fifth Circuit. In 1967 he was authorized to practice before the U.S. Supreme Court. He was involved in private practice in Houston from December 1961 through June 1965 and employed as sole practitioner, staff attorney, and assistant chief of the Enforcement Division in the Office of the Attorney General of Texas in Austin from July 1965 through July 1966. He then returned to Houston, where he served as managing attorney for the Houston Legal Foundation from August 1966 through August 1968 and as judge of the Municipal Court from September 1968 through December 1972. He then returned to Austin as assistant attorney general, holding that position from January through August 1973. He was then named judge of the Harris County Criminal Court at Law No. 6—the first African American appointed to such a position on a full-time basis—and served until May 1977. The following month, he was appointed by Texas Governor Dolph Briscoe as judge of the 208th District Court of Texas, thus becoming the second African American appointed to a criminal district court in Harris County. He was elected to this position in 1978 and reelected in 1982, 1986, and 1990. On January 1, 1991, his old friend State District Judge Carl Walker, Jr., came to his home and swore him in for his fourth term. At the time, Routt was suffering from colon cancer and was too weak to walk. As a result, the swearing-in took place in his bedroom, surrounded by family and friends. Routt died two days later.[4]

One of Routt's most controversial actions as a judge was the granting of shock probation in 1980 to former state District Judge Garth Bates, releasing him from prison after he had served four months of an eight-year sentence for bribery. This type of punishment is intended to shock a first offender into lawful behavior by subjecting him to a brief prison term. Routt argued that Bates, convicted of agreeing to accept a $59,000 bribe to guarantee probation for a defendant, had lost his pride, prestige, and office; and no purpose would be served by keeping him in prison with people he had sentenced. In 1983 Routt stirred up further controversy by granting shock probation to Ed Jay Riklin after he had served four months of his four-year sentence for acting as the go-between in the Bates bribery case. Also controversial were the generous fees he awarded to attorneys he appointed to represent indigent defendants in his court.[5]

Routt was a member of the State Bar of Texas, the American Bar Association, the American Judicature Society, the American Judges Association, the Houston Lawyers Association, the American Correctional Association, and the Phi Alpha Delta Law Fraternity. In 1984 he received the Achievement Award of the National Bar Association.[6]

Always interested in community affairs, Routt served on the boards of directors of a number of charitable, educational, and medical organizations. Such included the South Central Branch of the Young Men's Christian Association, the Houston Urban League, the Texas Southern University Ex-Students Association, the Texas Southern University Law Foundation, Riverside General Hospital, Wesley Community Center, Greater Houston Chapter of the American Red Cross, Greater Houston Council of Camp Fire Girls, Methodist Hospital of Houston, Saint Elizabeth Hospital Foundation, Houston Business and Professional Men's Club, Houston Council on Human Relations, Texas Gulf Coast United Way, Martin Luther King, Jr. Community Center, and Goodwill Industries of Houston.[7]

Routt was a member of Trinity United Methodist Church in Houston. In this congregation he served on the finance committee, as chairman of the administrative board, and as charge lay leader. He also served the United Methodist denomination at the district and conference levels.[8]

Routt was a member of Sigma Pi Phi Fraternity (Nu Boule) and Omega Psi Phi

Fraternity, Inc. In 1969 the latter organization named him Citizen of the Year. He received the Community Service Award from the Delta Sigma Theta Sorority in 1970, the Distinguished Service Award from Frontiers International in 1973, and the Outstanding Volunteer Award from the American Red Cross in 1977.[9]

Routt's name appears in *The Martindale-Hubble Legal Directory*; *The Dictionary of International Biographies*; *The National Roster of Black Elected Officials*; *Black Texans of Distinction*; *Who's Who Among Black Americans, 1975-76*; *Personalities of the South, 1977*; *The American, 1977-1979*; *Notable Americans of 1976- 1977*; *Who's Who in the South and Southwest, 1978*; *Who's Who of Houston*, 1980; *Directory of Distinguished Americans, 1981*; *Who's Who in American Law*; *Personalities of America*; *International Who's Who of Contemporary Achievement*; and *International Who's Who in Crime Prevention*.[10]

Freemasonry played a major role in the life of Thomas Henry Routt, beginning in 1951, when he was raised to the sublime degree of a Master Mason in Oyoma Lodge No. 222 in Navasota. He later became a member of Ever Ready Lodge No. 506 in Rosenberg, Fort Bend County, Texas. He served as this lodge's Senior Warden from 1975 to 1978 and as Worshipful Master from 1978 to 1982. He served as Special Deputy for District No. 16 from 1978 to 1982 and as District Deputy Grand Master from 1982 to 1984.[11]

Routt was an active York Rite Mason. In Sunrise Chapter No. 77, Royal Arch Masons, he served as King in 1981 and High Priest from 1982 to 1984. In Sanderson Commandery No. 2, Knights Templar, he served as Generalissimo in 1981 and Eminent Commander from 1982 to 1983. On the state level, he served the Most Eminent Prince Hall Grand Chapter of Holy Royal Arch Masons as Grand Lecturer in 1980; and the Lone Star Grand Commandery as Grand Lecturer in 1981, Grand Captain General from 1982 to 1984, and Deputy Eminent Grand Commander from 1984 to 1986.[12]

Routt was also an active Scottish Rite Mason. In 1975 he received the 32° in Goodwill Consistory No. 238. The following year, he received the 33° from the United Supreme Council of the Ancient and Accepted Scottish Rite, Southern Jurisdiction. He served the Council of Deliberation of the State of Texas and Second Lieutenant Commander from 1978 to 1980; as First Lieutenant Commander from 1980 to 1986; and as President for the Southern Area from 1982 to 1987. He served the Commanders of the Rite for the Valley of Rosenberg and the Orient of Texas as both Vice-President and President.[13]

Routt was created as a Noble of the Mystic Shrine in Doric Temple No. 76 in Houston in 1975. He served his temple as First Ceremonial Master in 1975, as Assistant Rabban in 1976, as Illustrious Potentate in 1977 and 1978, as Chairman of the Council of Past Potentates in 1979, as Imperial Deputy of the Oasis in 1980, and Director of Group Supervision in 1981. He served the Desert Conference as Chairman of the By-Law Committee in 1977, Chairman of the Budget, Finance, and Audit Committee in 1978 and 1979, and Chairman of the Audit Committee from 1980 to 1987.[14]

Routt had a great interest in Masonic research. In 1979 he joined the Phylaxis Society, a society for Prince Hall Freemasons who seek more light and who have light to impart.[15] He attended a number of annual sessions of this research organization.

Routt was present at the One Hundred and Sixth Annual Grand Communication of the Most Worshipful Prince Hall Grand Lodge of Texas on June 24, 1981. At this Communication, Grand Master Isadore Huddleston Clayborn announced plans to retire from the office he had held for sixteen years and nominated Deputy Grand Master Reuben G. White as his successor. The craft followed Clayborn's direction and elected White. Grand Senior Warden Edwin B. Cash was then promoted to Deputy Grand Master; Routt was elected Grand Senior Warden, and Jesse L. Baines was reelected Grand Junior Warden. These officers were installed by Past Grand Master Clayborn.[16] Routt was reelected as Grand Senior Warden in 1982, 1983, and 1984. He was nominated for the office of Grand Master in 1985 and again in 1986. Each time, however, he was defeated by Reuben G. White. Following each defeat, he was renominated and reelected as Grand Senior Warden.

On March 5, 1986, Routt delivered the opening speech at the 13th Annual Session of the Phylaxis Society in Albuquerque, New Mexico. In this inspiring message, he declared:

> Any member of a Masonic organization, just partially informed or observant, has to recognize the fact that Freemasonry is on the decline and is not doing the job for which it was designed. This includes my state, in spite of the fact that, during the last Masonic year, our Grand Lodge posted a small increase in membership in our subordinate lodges—the first in over a dozen years.
>
> This is generally true across the board in all houses and in all jurisdictions, Prince Hall and Caucasian. . . .
>
> Prince Hall Freemasonry is under heavy attack from many angles.
>
> On the one side, there are members of organizations whose own regularity is questionable, who fabricate information in order to deny our regularity, without regard to the universality of Freemasonry. Racism, unfortunately, overrrides their consideration for their Masonic oaths. Objective research and interpretation upholds our regularity and raises questions concerning theirs.
>
> On another side, men of color hold themselves out as Masons on the strength of nothing more than a state-issued charter and enlist some good uninformed or misinformed men and women. Still others are operating in our midst, based on nothing but audacity, and obviously intended only to turn a fast buck.
>
> On still another side, universal Freemasonry is under attack as an institution and our Charter Mother Grand Lodge finds itself fighting to keep its members from being declared ineligible for certain employment in the government, based totally on Masonic membership; there is again being raised papal objections to Catholic membership; and even here in the U. S. A., discussions and attacks are taking place, both by organized bodies and singularly, on radio nation-wide, and from the pulpit. We have been called many things and connected with many other organizations, none to our credit. What we don't understand, we fight and destroy. Unfortunately, our weaknesses are highlighted.
>
> I personally, however, think that our most serious problem is not from without but from within. Our Masonic ignorance is abysmal and inexcusable. . . .
>
> When we have educated our craft to the real meaning of Freemasonry, our task will have largely been accomplished. When men understand Freemasonry and its teachings, rather than simply rotely learning to recite the lectures, these men will understand what brotherhood means. And maybe, just maybe, by osmosis or otherwise, our Caucasian counterparts will better understand their oaths. A brother living the tenets

of Freemasonry is a walking showcase. A lodge of brothers living brotherhood and dispensing charity is a force unassailable. A brother, well-prepared in the history and ritualism of Prince Hall Freemasonry, will be our strongest bulwark to stem the "Bogus Mason" tide. He is a walking advertisement of the peace that comes from completeness through patience. That man does not have to beg friends and acquaintances to join his lodge. They beg him.

One of the most effective ways to draw good men is for the lodge brothers to dress Masonically (as prescribed in their jurisdiction) and worship at a brother's church . . . just the brothers seated together and worshipping together has its effect.

Each of the Prince Hall Grand Lodges dispense thousands of dollars to charities outside our membership, through Christmas assistance boxes, scholarships and donations to worthy causes without any or very little publicity. Many of our local bodies do not report their activities to the Grand bodies; and no compilation is made of all jurisdictions. Is it any wonder that the public questions our value and has some difficulty justifying our existence? . . .

A story is told of a company on the battlefield during World War I. The standard bearer kept having to be told not to advance the banner too far ahead of the company. Finally, the commander told him to bring the standard back. The soldier yelled back to the commander "bring the company up to the standard." And that demand resulted in victory in that skirmish and battle. . . .

Prince Hall, 211 years ago, started advancing the standard, being motivated by love for his fellowman and thirst for equality. Can we do less than dedicating our lives to holding high that glorious torch for all the world to see?

I suggest that we cannot.[17]

During the 1986 Albuquerque meeting, the writer talked with Judge Routt about his campaign for Grand Master. The judge agreed that, if and when he was elected, he would create a new office entitled "Grand Historian" and appoint the writer to it.

In 1987, for the third year in a row, Routt challenged White to the highest office in Masonry. This time, however, Routt's efforts were crowned with success.[18] On the following day, the newly elected officers were installed by Past Grand Master Clayborn.[19]

The writer was not able to attend the 1987 Grand Communication. However, shortly after receiving word of Routt's election, he telephoned him to extend his congratulations and to repeat the request made in Albuquerque in March 1986. Routt agreed and, this time, had the authority to issue such an appointment. On August 3, 1987, he sent to the writer a letter which stated: "I have created the office of Grand Historian and am appointing you for the rest of this administrative year. . . . The proposed budget will include some consideration for reimbursement of expenses. . . . Expect to see 'Prince Hall: The Myth and the Man' in print very soon. You will, of course, be given full credit."[20]

In September 1987 the newly elected Grand Master published his first article in *Texas Prince Hall Masonic Quarterly*. He wrote:

Beginning a new Masonic year, we must make certain resolutions and commitments if we are serious—serious about our obligations to ourselves, our families, our country, and above all, our God. . . .

Service was the mark of our first Most Worshipful Grand Master, Prince Hall, and with dedication and perseverance, he either accomplished his goal or suggested the designs on the Trestle Board.

Service will be one of the emphases for this Masonic Year, along with designing a program for Masonic Education, including ritual, history, customs, and usages.

Foremost will be the financial status of the Grand Lodge, now and in the future. Planning is absolutely necessary. Hiram Abiff thought so; so do I. We must plan where we're going and how we're going to get there. We will be limited only by our own thinking, which should be positive, not negative, progressive not regressive, building, not destroying.[21]

On February 22, 1988, two weeks before the opening of the annual convention of the Phylaxis Society in New Orleans, Routt sent a letter to the writer, stating that he would not be able to attend that year's session because of a recent surgery but assured him that his prayers would be with those in attendance.[22]

In March 1988 Routt wrote to the craft about a number of important events and organizations:

We have just witnessed the month of February, a month recently celebrated as "Black History Month"—a month-long event made necessary because of the bigotry or ignorance of the non-black historians over the years, aggravated by our own political, educational, and economic impotence. It gives us an opportunity to inform our children, as well as the community at large, of our true heritage. . . .

This issue of the *Masonic Quarterly* will cover one of the richest religious periods in the year, namely the Easter Season in its completeness, including Palm Sunday, Maundy Thursday, and Easter Day itself.

All Master Masons are expected to participate in the Palm Sunday observance services of the Eastern Stars and the Heroines of Jericho. This is *their* day; assist in every way that you can, acceptable to them, but don't try to take over. This is the one time that you will follow them in a processional. Remember that the appropriate dress is Masonic.

Those Master Masons that are also Scottish Rite Masons should encourage and participate with their Consistory in the beautiful Maundy Thursday Ritual available in that Order, and follow up with the early Easter morning activities. . . .

On March 6, 1775, Prince Hall and fourteen other "men of colour" became the first black Masons on the North American continent. The Phylaxis Society, an international organization dedicated to research and education related to Freemasonry in general and Prince Freemasonry in particular, meets on the first weekend of March each year for seminars and workshops, with this time being chosen because of that historic occasion. Any Master Mason in good standing in his jurisdiction is eligible for membership. An auxiliary, the Phyllis Chapter, examines the Adoptive Rite, Order of the Eastern Star. Any Eastern Star who is a member in good standing in his or her respective organization is eligible for membership. An excellent publication is put out by each group, with the Phylaxis being the older and more extensive. Membership in each group is rewarding and is strongly encouraged. . . .

Together and with love we can attract new members, keep the ones we have, and bring back those who have strayed. *Together and with love. So mote it be.*[23]

On June 28, 1988, Routt delivered his first Grand Master's Address, entitling it "Traveling with a Purpose." On this topic, he said:

As we end one Masonic year and begin another, it behooves us and would bode us well to examine the past, both immediate and distant. We need to know what really happened and why it happened. We can then better plot our course for the future, consider, as our Grand Chaplain describes it "The things most worth doing," and, thus, travel with a purpose. . . .

As is true in more cases than we are willing to admit, the Bible told us a long time ago, but we ignored its sage advice.

Our beloved Book of Ecclesiastes (Good News Version) tells us in the 10th Chapter, 10th Verse: "If your ax is dull, and you don't sharpen it, you have to work harder to use it. It is smarter to plan ahead."

You must know what you want to do, and what you have to work with. . . .

Our Masonic organizations . . . are attempting to meet the needs of the 20th Century and prepare for the 21st Century, using 19th Century methods. . . .

Again, Ecclesiastes 10:18 tells us: "When a man is too lazy to repair his roof, it will leak, and the house will fall." . . .

Many of us have a set of warped priorities. There are very few lodges that have home dues of less than $30 per year. Many of you have dues exceeding $50 per year. You same people don't seem to realize that the Grand Lodge must have money to operate also. Few of you give scholarship; none of you have death benefits; few of you are either buying property, or building, but you still want the Grand Lodge to be a 1988 Rolls Royce and run it off of kerosene. It won't work Brothers. Our roof is leaking. We must repair it. To consider allowing the house to fall down is unthinkable.[24]

Routt concluded his address with another quote from the Bible:

We must all remember that the Grand Master is not the final arbiter, neither is the Grand Lodge. Ecclesiastes 12:13-14 reads: "After all this, there is only one thing to say: have reverence for God, and obey His commands, because this is all that man is created for. God is going to judge everything we do, whether good or bad, even things done in secret."[25]

Distinguished visitors to the 1988 Communication included Earle Bradford, Grand Master of Louisiana; James A. Mingo, Secretary-General of the United Supreme Council of the Scottish Rite, Southern Jurisdiction; Willie Worley, Deputy for the United Supreme Council for Oklahoma; Edgar Bridges, Grand Master of Mississippi; Lewis Hall, Grand Secretary of Mississippi; Orphen Cephas, Past Master from Lawton, Oklahoma.[26]

In 1988 the Grand Lodge's Committee on State of the Country was still chaired by John H. Bullock of Buffalo, who had served in that role since the death of the writer's dear friend, A. M. Johnson of Teague, in 1981. The following are among the highlights of Bullock's 1988 report:

The Supreme Court today let New York City bar discrimination against women and minorities by private clubs with more than 400 members, giving cities and states new ammunition in a growing legal assault on such practices. The law regarding discrimination in public accommodation exempts "distinctly private organizations," but deprives non-religious groups of that *designation* if they have more than 400 members. This may affect support of the Order of Elks, Order of Moose, Order of Red Men, and Kiwanis International.[27]

A federal appellate court issued a stay temporarily blocking the back-to-nature Rainbow Family from gathering at a national forest next month.

The Forest Service had asked the 5th Circuit Court of Appeals in New Orleans to grant an emergency injunction blocking the week-long celebration of "peace, love, and justice" by the 1960s style group at an East Texas forest. . . .[28]

Elders of the Assemblies of God began considering proposed punishment for evangelist Jimmy Swaggart today in the second day of a meeting called to determine how long he should be barred from preaching.

Swaggart tearfully stepped down from his Baton Rouge, La., pulpit February 21, admitting unspecified sins. Published reports have said he paid a prostitute to pose naked.

Debra Murphree, who says she is the woman who posed, will appear in the July issue of *Penthouse* magazine.[29]

At the 1988 Communication, Grand Master Routt was reelected, as were all of the subordinate officers elected the previous year.[30] They were installed by Past Grand Master Clayborn on June 30.[31]

In September 1988, Routt wrote to the craft: "The Father has been good to each of us and our Grand Ole Order, the 'All-Seeing Eye' viewed our actions during the recent 113th Annual Grand Communication of the Most Worshipful Prince Hall Grand Lodge of Texas and Jurisdiction, smiled on us and showered us with His blessings."[32] Routt discussed events of the 1988 Communication, the payment of death benefits, a number of fund-raising projects, Grand Lodge registration fees, and the authorization of the establishment of the Knights of Pythagoras in Texas under the leadership of John H. Bullock.[33]

In his last column for 1988, Routt wrote:

In His Name and through His Love, I Greet You.
Merry Christmas and a Happy New Year.

Merry Christmas should mean that you wish for that person the very best that the Father has in His storehouse, excluding nothing. It should mean that your love for that person is so great that you feel that nothing is too good for that person. It should be an admission on your part that you are a Christian, and that you believe that, through His love and the death of His Son, you are saved. It should mean that, when you go to the altar with your supplications and praise-giving, that you should have no differences with your fellowman that you cannot resolve. . . .

My earthly Brothers and Sisters, members of the Prince Hall Family, Children of the Heavenly Father all, may you have a very Merry Christmas and a happy, prosperous New Year; and may all your efforts heavenly inspired be successful beyond your wildest dreams.[34]

On June 28, 1989, Routt delivered his second Grand Master's Address, in which he discussed the financial situation of the Grand Lodge and thanked various individuals, lodges, and appendant bodies for their contributions. He singled out with special praise for their hard work the following individuals: District Deputy Grand Master Rufus Jones, Grand Senior Warden Hubert Reece, Grand Junior Warden Robert E. Connor, Jr., Grand Legal Advisor E. Brice Cunningham, and Past Grand Master I. H. Clayborn.[35] He reported:

The month of June has been very eventful for me. I journeyed to London, England, participating in a comparative criminal law program. However, I was able to visit the usual outstanding sites, including savoring the existent Masonic flavor. One of the speakers was a barrister and member of parliament, whom I met just before the session began. As we shook hands, he noticed my square and compass pin. He said nothing, but seated me immediately on his right without comment.

On the Friday following my return, I journeyed to Boston, Mass., where on Saturday, my daughter was awarded a Master's degree in public administration from Northeastern University.

On Monday, June 19, I went to Galveston to the unveiling of a plaque dedicated to Norris Wright Cuney, and the same evening, I represented the M.W.P.H.G.L. of Tex. As it was the only organization being recognized at the Houston Juneteenth Celebration chaired by an A.F.&A.M. man.

This meant that I was able to visit the place where the Grand Lodge system was first instituted about 275 years ago; the place where the first black was raised in this country, and where the first black lodge was set aside; the entry point of the news abolishing slavery in Texas was made, and finally, the home and burial place of our first Grand Master in the same month. Now I am here again with my brothers, whom God has spared and blessed. We have been reduced numerically by 550; however, their spirit and memory propels us forward and onward.

I would like to tell you that Prince Hall Freemasonry is enjoying an era of unprecedented peace; free from attack or threats. But that would be a lie. All of Freemasonry is under attack, sometimes openly, sometimes insidiously. . . .

God loves you. I love you. God bless you, in all your worthwhile endeavors. *So mote it be*.[36]

Later that day, the writer, then Chair of the Department of Religion at Paul Quinn College in Waco, made an appeal for support for his school, which was then undergoing a major financial crisis. As a result, Routt authorized the craft to take up a special offering to aid Paul Quinn.[37]

At the 1989 Communication, Grand Master Routt and all of his subordinate officers were reelected.[38] On June 29 they were installed by Past Grand Master Clayborn.[39]

In his March 1990 column, Grand Master Routt wrote about "The Book of Holy Law," expressing the firm conviction that "The history of the Bible in the life of Masonry needs to be retold often, so that we all will know how our Masonic life began and why we should ever keep the Bible open, before the craft."[40] During this month, Routt welcomed the Phylaxis Society to Houston. He had a room at the Hilton Southwest, the site of the convention. He attended some of the sessions, including the closing night's banquet. However, for much of the week, he was confined to his room, where he received medical treatment for colon cancer. The writer visited and had prayer with him during this meeting.[41]

Among the distinguished visitors to the 1990 Grand Communication were Paul Best, Executive Secretary of the Phylaxis Society; James Mingo, Grand Secretary General of the United Supreme Council of the Southern Jurisdiction; and Rev. Howard L. Woods, Grand Master of Arkansas.[42] They were all present on June 27, when Routt gave his third and final Grand Master's Address. He was very weak at the time and required assistance from his brethren in order to stand. Nevertheless, he delivered the following inspiring charge to the craft:

The Father has been good. He continues to be good to us in spite of our misgivings, in spite of our inactions, in spite of our misdoings. He continues to shower His grace upon us. He continues to call us His own. Praise His Name forever....

Since our last Grand Communication this Grand Master has had the opportunity and privilege of setting aside three (3) U.D. lodges: One, the Nero Prince Lodge U.D., Weisbaden, Germany; two, the I. H. Clayborn U.D. Lodge, Honolulu, Hawaii; three, the U.D. Lodge, Heidelberg, Germany. Each of these lodges has already shown a real propensity for hard work and earnest endeavor ... Each of the brothers are exhibiting the very highest level of preparation and we can each be proud of their activities. We are proud to call them a part of Texas just as they are proud to be part of Texas.[43]

We can't talk about a future unless we plan for that future. I've said to you before, we have a plan and a team designed to carry out that plan. The plan is in pocket, we are continuously revising it, we are continuously looking at it to see that it will do the job we want to do. We continuously look forward to the year 2000, when we hope to have the kind of organization that each and everyone of us will be especially proud; I, frankly, am very proud of us right now. However, I do know that it is necessary for us to bring up the distasteful subject of raised dues; and brothers, let's not half step about it. $25 won't do, we need the full $30 increase....[44]

The state of the welfare of the craft is outstanding. All of the brothers are in good spirits. All is faring very well.

The loss of so many brothers of the craft leaves us somewhat saddened in spirit ... We have lost brothers that have walked the long hot roads with us, carrying and toiling, using the implements of their various offices for the betterment of the craft and in fulfillment of their duties. Our prayers go out in their behalf at this time.

The state of activity that is not witnessed often by any organization and this is good. The Most Worshipful Prince Hall Grand Lodge has had an opportunity to interact with other Masonic bodies this past year. Such include both the York Rite and Scottish Rite bodies as well as some of the bodies not particularly belonging to either of these organizations such as the Phylaxis Society, an organization dedicated to the development and growth of Masonic research and original writers.

In these instances, the jurisdiction stood out and was outstanding in its representation. Of this we can be proud.

The allocution on this year will be short because of my present state of health. However, I want you to know that my love for the organization and my prayers are by no means limited for the welfare of this organization.[45]

In 1990, for the third year in a row, the Grand Lodge reelected Grand Master Routt and his subordinate officers.[46] On June 28 they were installed by Past Grand Master Clayborn.[47]

Due to his worsening physical condition, Grand Master Routt was unable to attend the 1990 regional meetings. His very able Deputy Grand Master, Edwin B. Cash, presided in his absence.

In November 1990 the writer had his last telephone conversation with his friend and brother. He tried to explain to him his progress on writing the history of the Grand Lodge, but realized that illness made conversation difficult for the judge. He assured him that he, like others, would continue to pray for him. The writer recognizes the life-threatening nature of colon cancer but also is a great believer in miracles. Many people—black and white, Mason and non-Mason, Texan and non-Texan—

fervently prayed for the recovery of the Grand Master of the Prince Hall Grand Lodge of Texas.

In the 1990 general election, Routt was reelected as a state district judge. In his final political race, he ran unopposed. On January 1, 1991, he was sworn in for his fourth term at home, as previously reported. Two days later, the Grand Master of the Universe summoned him to the Celestial Lodge Above.

A celebration of the life of Thomas Henry Routt, Grand Master and judge, was held at Trinity United Methodist Church, 2600 Holman Avenue, Houston, at 11:00 A.M. on Tuesday, January 8, 1991. This service included a resolution by Trinity Church and tributes from the American Red Cross, the Prince Hall Grand Lodge of Texas, the Sigma Pi Phi Fraternity, and the State and County Judiciary. The eulogy was delivered by Rev. Robert E. McGee. Active pallbearers were the members of Ever Ready Lodge No. 506 of Rosenberg. Honorary pallbearers were the members of Sigma Pi Phi Fraternity and the Texas State Judiciary. Interment was in Paradise North Cemetery, 10401 West Montgomery Road, Houston. Masonic graveside services were conducted by the Prince Hall Grand Lodge of Texas, whose delegation was led by Past Grand Masters I. H. Clayborn and Reuben G. White.[48]

In attendance at Grand Master Routt's funeral were a number of prominent Prince Hall Masons from outside of Texas, including Grand Master Edgar Bridges, Sr., of Mississippi, Grand Master Howard L. Woods of Arkansas, Grand Master Deary Vaughn of Oklahoma, Grand Secretary Alvin Bradley of Oklahoma, and Phylaxis Executive Secretary Paul V. Best of North Carolina. After the burial tribute was completed, a portion of the Masonic delegation assembled at a hotel to install Deputy Grand Master Edwin B. Cash as the nineteenth Grand Master of Prince Hall Masons in Texas. At this ceremony, Past Grand Master Clayborn served as installing officer.[49]

In his first column in the *Masonic Quarterly*, Grand Master Cash paid tribute to his illustrious predecessor:

> The lives of the members of our Prince Hall Family were drastically altered by the death of our Honorable Grand Master Thomas H. Routt on January 3, 1991. Our Heavenly Father wanted him to sit in that divine lodge above and await us. The Great Architect of the Universe gives meaning to and directs our existence.
>
> Thomas H. Routt has left a legacy that those of us who follow him must observe. A quiet-spoken giant of a man who loved Freemasonry and his fellow man, Thomas H. Routt is a shining example for us all. His life was all too short but the ideas and ambitions that he espoused are footsteps for us to follow. . . .
>
> The greatest tribute that we can give to the memory of the late Thomas H. Routt is to continue to do the work that he loved. He simply is standing at the door of the unseen temple, through which each of us must pass, with his hand extended and his familiar smile.[50]

Grand Secretary C. A. Glaspie, who had taken office at the same time as Grand Master Routt, gave the following tribute to the man with whom he had worked very closely for the past three and a half years:

> Grand Master Thomas H. Routt gave so much of himself. We are most blessed, in

that God sent his many talents to us. If you were one of the vast number of fortunate individuals who had known him, you could not resist loving him....

For our works at the Temple is not completed until our G.A.O.T.U. calls us from labor... to rest... to reward. Let us work while it is day, remembering that a time shall come when no one can work. When that time does come, we will see God, all of the saints, and Brother Routt.[51]

In his column, Grand Junior Warden Robert E. Connor, Jr., reminded the craft that "The Dream Has Just Begun":

The thought of starting the new year off without our previous Grand Master Thomas Routt is frightening just to think about it. The Great Architect of the Universe saw fit to take him from our midst but, as always, the Master knows best. Grand Master Routt was a Christian man with a lot of vision who made long range goals and plans. He dreamed of the Most Worshipful Prince Hall Grand Lodge of Texas being second to no other jurisdiction. Even during the hours of illness, Prince Hall Masonry was on his mind.... The death of Grand Master Routt did not end this dream, for the dream encompassed men to carry on the torch.... Grand Master Cash has picked up the torch and with our support the dream will continue. Let's give Grand Master Cash the same support we gave Grand Master Routt and let the torch burn.[52]

Past Grand Master Clayborn reflected well on the life of one of his successors in the Grand East when he wrote:

I knew a man from a small town in Grimes County down in South Texas, north, northwest of Houston and south of Bryan-College Station; that young man was raised and nurtured in a Christian home and soon learned that there is a "God" upon whom we can cast all of our troubles and cares.

That young man carried that "God" of whom I speak with him wherever he went and that "God" became a part of his life, so he excelled in his human endeavors. He studied and made high marks in his efforts to achieve a top flight education.

The late Sherman Wilson introduced Brother Routt to Freemasonry, and showed him a ladder to climb and Brother Routt climbed it to all houses, he made a mighty good Master of Lodge No. 506 and served well the offices of Grand Senior Warden and Most Worshipful Grand Master. Prior to his Grand Mastership, he served to a high degree of acclaim in both York Rite houses.

Brother Thomas H. Routt wrote well the laws, by-laws, and constitutions for the York Rite bodies. Brother Routt devoutly served in the houses of Dougless Burrell Consistory and was elevated to the 33rd Degree in the United Supreme Council, A.A.S.R., the Southern Jurisdiction, Prince Hall Affiliation....

With these words, we say, our Brother, you have travelled well your rocky paths, you led well your Brothers to higher plateaus and we know that you served well and we look to the time when we shall all meet with *the Lord*.[53]

Letters of condolence were received from the Prince Hall Grand Lodges of New Jersey, South Carolina, Rhode Island, Ontario, Delaware, Massachusetts, Alabama, New Mexico, and Tennessee. All of these were published in the *Quarterly*.[54] A resolution was also submitted by the Phylaxis Society and signed by President Joseph A. Walkes, Jr., and Executive Secretary Paul V. Best. According to this "Resolution of Respect and Love":

Brother Thomas H. Routt was a Fellow, Life Member No. 61, and Long-term Supporter of the Phylaxis Society. Although his column is now broken, the warmth, tenderness, and affection he instilled within our hearts can never be broken, disturbed, or overshadowed....

Tom is not dead ... he is just gone home where he is resting in the arms of the Almighty Father.

Be it resolved, therefore, that he will be enshrined and memorialized at our session next upcoming in Greensboro, North Carolina in March 1991.[55]

On June 26, 1991, Edwin B. Cash delivered his first Grand Master's Address. In his opening remarks, he said: "I would ask now that our Grand Chaplain come and ask for the blessings of Heaven to now descend upon us and to express our respect for the memory of Thomas H. Routt, our late Grand Master."[56] By this time, Thomas H. Routt Lodge in Arlington, Texas, had been organized under the leadership of Grand Secretary C.A. Glaspie and was operating under dispensation."[57] Subsequently, this lodge has been chartered as Thomas H. Routt Lodge No. 639.[58] In 1999 the Thomas H. Routt Grand Council of the Order of the Knights of Pythagoras was organized.[59]

There can be no doubt that Thomas Henry Routt, Grand Master and Judge, was a high achiever. He contributed so much to the legal and judicial fields, his community, his church, his family, and the Prince Hall Masonic fraternity. He had a very positive influence on the lives of many individuals during his sixty-year earthly pilgrimage. The writer will always be grateful for his encouragement of his work as a Masonic scholar. This was well demonstrated by his creation of the office of Grand Historian and his appointment of the writer to it. The Routt legacy lives on! One day we will meet him again in the Celestial Lodge Above, when we all will receive workman's wages from the Supreme Judge and Grand Master of the Universe!

Edwin Bernard Cash

Edwin Bernard Cash (1930-) is the nineteenth Grand Master of Prince Hall Masons in Texas. He was born in Dallas on November 30, 1930. Except for time spent in school and in the military, he has resided in Dallas all of his life. He has been a member of Good Street Baptist Church since 1936 and has served this church as a deacon since 1957.[1]

Cash graduated from Lincoln High School in Dallas and received a Bachelor of Arts degree from Bishop College in Marshall, Texas, in 1952.[2] He did graduate work at Southern Methodist University in Dallas and received a Master of Education degree from North Texas State University in Denton in 1963.[3]

Cash married Maxine Lola Turner in 1957. They have one daughter, Sherrie Cash, who is now a practicing attorney with the Johnson and Johnson law firm in Dallas.[4]

From 1953 to 1994, Cash worked for Dallas Independent School District. For six years he taught Mathematics, Science, and Physical Education. He then became a visiting teacher, traveling between various schools and homes and doing more social work than traditional teaching. He retired on May 23, 1994.[5]

Cash's career in public education was disrupted by service in the United States Air Force from 1952 to 1956. He was stationed at three Texas bases (San Antonio, San Angelo, and Bryan) and at bases in Illinois and Arizona. His military travels took him to England, Germany, France, Spain, Italy, Austria, and Sweden. While in the Air Force he received some pilot's training, but most of his training was in meteorology. He spent much time as a weather observer in the various states and countries where he was stationed.[6]

Cash's father, James D. Cash, who died in 1982, was an active Prince Hall Freemason. He was a member of Dallas' Paul Drayton Lodge No. 9, Free and Accepted Masons; Dale Consistory No. 31, Ancient and Accepted Scottish Rite; and Zakat Temple No. 164, Ancient Egyptian Arabic Order of Nobles of the Mystic Shrine.

Cash's mother, who died in 1987, was active in various ladies' auxiliaries. However, he recalled, neither parent ever pressured him to join a lodge.[7]

Cash credits Past Grand Master Isadore Huddleston Clayborn, a long-time member of Good Street Baptist Church, with awakening his Masonic interests. During the early 1970s, Clayborn observed that there was no Prince Hall lodge meeting under the roof of a church anywhere in Texas. He was determined that his church would be the first to serve as home to a lodge. Thus, Clayborn conducted a campaign among the men of Good Street, giving them six months to decide whether they wished to become Masons. When a quorum of fifteen was reached, the men assembled on a Saturday morning in May 1973 and remained there until midnight. During this time, all three degrees of the Blue Lodge were conferred and officers were elected for Good Street Baptist Lodge, which was then operating "Under Dispensation." Cash was elected as this lodge's first Worshipful Master.[8]

Eventually Good Street Baptist Lodge No. 182 was chartered by the Prince Hall Grand Lodge of Texas. All of the charter members were members of Good Street Baptist Church. Today, however, the membership includes men of various denominations. Cash served as Worshipful Master from 1973 to 1991. He recalls that he knew very little about Masonry when he first joined the lodge. Nevertheless, he worked hard and learned Masonry and appreciates the help provided by older, more knowledgeable brethren in instructing him in the work of the lodge.[9]

Like his father before him, Cash received the degrees of the Scottish Rite in Dale Consistory and of the Mystic Shrine in Zakat Temple. In 1975 he received the 33° of the Scottish Rite when the United Supreme Council, Southern Jurisdiction, convened in Dallas. This degree was conferred by Sovereign Grand Commander Jno. G. Lewis, Jr.[10]

Cash was appointed to the office of Grand Junior Deacon by Grand Master Clayborn. In this capacity, he had the delightful experience of leading the 1975 Grand Lodge Centennial Parade in Fort Worth. In 1979 he was elected as Grand Senior Warden, a position he held until 1981.[11]

Cash was present at the One Hundred and Sixth Annual Grand Communication of the Most Worshipful Prince Hall Grand Lodge of Texas on June 24, 1981. At this Communication, Deputy Grand Master Reuben G. White was elected Grand Master. Cash was then promoted to Deputy Grand Master, while Judge Thomas H. Routt was elected Grand Senior Warden and Jesse L. Baines was elected Grand Junior Warden. These officers were then installed by Past Grand Master Clayborn.[12]

On June 22, 1982, I. H. Clayborn presided over the election of officers for the first time as a Past Grand Master. A. R. Jernigan, who was reported to be have been a member of the Grand Lodge longer than any of the brethren present, moved that all elected officers succeed themselves. His motion was seconded by O.W. L. Turner, T. M. Morgan, and Lee Majors. The motion passed unanimously.[13] On the following day, Deputy Grand Master Cash delivered his first report, in which he said:

> This report is presumed to be a summary of the past year and my stewardship as your Deputy Grand Master. It is all but impossible to detail the concerns that one would have as Deputy Grand Master. The past year has come and gone as a fleeting moment. It was indeed a year of learning and expansion.

Among the several events and obligations that I attended was one that will live in my memory. I allude to the leveling of a cornerstone by Grand Lodge Officers in Brenham, Texas. This was a ceremony that I enjoyed but, more than that, I observed the monument to the birthplace of Prince Hall Masons in Texas. I would venture to say that every man who calls himself a Prince Hall Mason in this jurisdiction should afford himself that opportunity. These are our roots. We dare not deny ourselves.[14]

On June 24, 1982, Past Grand Master Clayborn installed Grand Master White, who then installed Deputy Grand Master Cash and all other elected and appointed officers.[15]

On June 28, 1983, Grand Master White, Deputy Grand Master Cash, and the other officers were reelected. On the following day, Cash gave his second report, in which he stated:

There have been so many sorrows, disasters, and tragedies during the past year, that we are left astounded.

On July 9, 1982, a Pan American jet crashed in Kenner, Louisiana, killing one hundred and forty five aboard and eight on the ground.

On September 4, fire swept through the Dorothy Mae residence hotel, killing twenty-four (24) people, including nine (9) children in Los Angeles, California . . .

On November 2, near Kabul, Afghanistan, as many as one thousand two hundred (1,200) Russian soldiers and Afghan civilians died when an explosion sealed the entrances to a tunnel.

"SORROWS, DISASTERS, AND TRAGEDIES" . . .

Yet we are still here, with a reasonable amount of health and happiness. I *know* that I don't thank my God enough. I don't know about you.

This year again has been one of exploration and learning. I was happy to represent each of you at the following . . .[16]

He then described his year's itinerary and thanked the craft for the pleasure of serving them.[17] As during the previous session, brethren at the 1983 Communication agreed that all elected officers should succeed themselves.[18]

On June 27, 1984, Cash delivered his third report, stating:

God must have a place since He permitted us to see another year pass and endowed us with a reasonable amount of health and happiness. During this past year, our nation and world mourned the loss of some legendary performers: Eubie Blake, pianist; Earl (Fatha) Hines, great jazz pianist; Muddy Waters, the "Blues Man"; and Buddy Young, first black executive in the National Football League.

During the past year, the nation and free world celebrated when Harold Washington was elected as the first black Mayor of Chicago; W. Wilson Goode became Philadelphia's first black mayor; Lt. Col. Guion A. Blaford, Jr. became the first black American to fly into outer space; Louis Gossett, Jr. won an Oscar for best supporting actor in the movie An Officer and a Gentleman; Alice Walker won the Pulitzer Prize for her novel The Color Purple; Vanessa Williams, first black Miss America; and Rev. Jesse Jackson, first black candidate for the President of the United States. God didn't make no junk—God must have a plan.[19]

He then detailed his itinerary, including his attendance at the funerals of two outstanding Prince Hall Freemasons—Frank Dewberry, Sr., on September 10, 1983, and of Sam Kelley on April 1, 1984.[20] For the third year in a row, all officers were reelected.[21] During the 1985 Grand Communication, Grand Master White was reelected, defeating Grand Senior Warden Thomas H. Routt. Cash and all other officers, including Routt, were then reelected.[22]

On June 25, 1986, Cash delivered his fifth report, beginning with a review of a number of events of the past year. He reminded the craft:

> First, the tragic flight of the ill-fated space shuttle Challenger, ending the lives of eight crew members, including Dr. Ronald E. McNair, a black graduate of Massachusetts Institute of Technology. This leaves three black astronauts in our space program: Fred Gregory, Guion Bluford, and Charles Bolden, Jr.
>
> The continuing racial struggle in South Africa which has taken and is taking hundreds of lives is also a major news story. Apartheid and its evils have come under intense pressures from within Africa as well as abroad but the pattern remains the same, if not worse. President Ronald Reagan thinks that mild trade and financial sanctions are the answer to apartheid.
>
> On December 12, 1985, a chartered plane crashed and exploded in Gander, Newfoundland. It contained 248 Americans, of which 49 were black. All were killed. This is the highest number of blacks ever killed in a military disaster. Two Texans were among the dead, one from Silsbee and one from Dallas, en route home for Christmas.
>
> There were deaths of several notable persons since last we met. Do you remember any of the following?
>
> - Lincoln Theodore Perry, black motion picture comedian, better known as Stepin Fetchit,
> - Rock Hudson, Hollywood star,
> - Wayne King, bandleader known as the "Waltz King,"
> - Ricky Nelson, popular singer
> - Charles Cootie Williams, trumpet player with Duke Ellington, 1928-1940.
>
> It was a shock to learn of the passing of Brother L. W. Mathis, Grand Pursivant, on October 14, 1985. He was an outstanding peer among peers. He was an outstanding Mason and, above all, he was an outstanding man. He will be missed.
>
> On January 8, 1986, a 97-year-old Prince Hall Mason passed. I mentioned his death because he was my grandfather and my fraternal brother. Brother B. C. Cash, Sr., was a member in good standing of Good Street Baptist Lodge No. 182, of which I am Worshipful Master.
>
> May God bless the families of these and all other brothers who entered the unseen temple before us.[23]

Cash then presented his 1985-86 itinerary.[24]

In 1986, for the second year in a row, Grand Senior Warden Routt tried unsuccessfully to unseat Grand Master White. Afterward, Cash and all other officers, including Routt, were reelected.[25]

On June 24, 1987, Thomas H. Routt was elected as Grand Master, defeating Reuben G. White. Cash was reelected as Deputy Grand Master, thus obtaining the distinction of serving as Deputy to two Grand Masters.[26] On the following day, the newly elected officers were installed by Past Grand Master Clayborn.[27]

On June 28, 1988, Cash gave his seventh report, stating:

According to the news media recently, endangered species is a topic of increased interest. There is considerable attention being given to certain types of animals, fish, and birds. Now comes a different type of meaning to the term "endangered species." Black males are now being considered as a species in danger. There may be a factual basis for this hypothesis. Our white counterparts live longer than us on the average. We have a higher homicide rate than we do cancer rate. Indeed, we are likely to be killed by a member of our own race. Although we make up only 20% of the nation's total population, we make up over 45% of the nation's prison population. There are many other factors that support the claim that we are endangered. Among these are our limited education and our lack of attention to our health.

It may be true that we are an endangered species, but we are not giving up without a fight. We have come too far to turn around now. We need to love each other and keep our hand in God's hand.

> No one is beaten until he quits,
> No one is through until he stops.
> No matter how hard failure hits,
> No matter how often he drops,
> The black male is not down until he lies
> In the dirt and refuses to rise.[28]

He then described his 1987-88 itinerary.[29]

The 1988 Grand Communication was marked by the reelection of Grand Master Routt, Deputy Grand Master Cash, and all other officers.[30] The same thing occurred in 1989. At the latter session, Cash turned back a challenge from Grand Junior Warden Robert E. Connor, Jr.[31]

On June 27, 1990, Cash delivered his ninth report, in which he stated:

> The Black Male is an endangered species. The media makes it plain almost every day. You can follow accounts of crime in our communities and read about the large number of our young males who make up the populations of our nation's prisons. Yes, we are endangered and it appears that especially in danger, as our black leaders. According to our honorable brother Benjamin Hooks, in the case of Washington Mayor Marion Barry, Jr., Barry is the victim of selective law enforcement. Selective law enforcement implies that black politicians are singled out for special attention and become victims of selective prosecution. Barry has joined a list that includes Mayors Maynard Jackson, Coleman Young, Richard Arrington, Carl Stokes, Kenneth Gibson, and Charles Evers. There is so much to be said about being endangered that I would invite you to pay attention to the daily newspapers but remember that what we read is not always the complete story.
>
> Lest we forget, there is a group of evil villains among us. The group is alive and well. The group of which I speak is the KKK. Known for its vile acts, the Klan most recently has surfaced publicly on the Oprah Winfrey Television Show, espousing their wickedness openly. They are still playing on society's fear of crime and stating that whites are victims of minorities, who are trying to rob, kill, and take away their jobs. This calls for us not to be apathetic or fearful of their approach, lest we forget.[32]

Later that day, Routt delivered his third and final Grand Master's Address.[33] Afterward, the election was held, and Routt, Cash, and the other officers were re-elected.[34]

Due to complications of colon cancer, Grand Master Routt was unable to attend the 1990 regional meetings. Thus it was necessary for Cash, his very able Deputy Grand Master, to preside in his absence. Routt died on January 3, 1991. His funeral was held at Trinity United Methodist Church in Houston on January 8, 1991. Following the completion of Masonic graveside services at Paradise North Cemetery, a portion of the large Masonic delegation assembled at the Houston Hilton to install Cash as the nineteenth Grand Master of Prince Hall Masons in Texas. At this ceremony, Past Grand Master Clayborn served as installing officer.[35]

In May 1991, Cash's first "Grand Master's Column" was published in the *Texas Prince Hall Masonic Quarterly*. This column contained his Regional Address, in which he said:

> I woke up the other morning and discovered that I am the captain of a sailing ship. I never thought that I would be a captain of such a fine vessel, but here I am. I have found that this is a fine ship. It is a proven seaworthy ship that has been afloat since its first captain, Grand Master Norris Wright Cuney, was in charge. The ship of which I speak is the Most Worshipful Prince Hall Grand Lodge of Texas and Jurisdiction. In order to be a good captain, a good crew is definitely needed. I have found that I inherited a crew of exceptional ability. I have inherited a crew that has proven that they each have put aside personal grievances and have decided that the future of Prince Hall Freemasonry in Texas is in their hands. I speak, of course, of the Board of Directors and all Grand Lodge officers. I could not ask for a better working association. I am truly thankful for their help, advice, and support.
>
> I also have another more powerful crew that I can count on. In fact, this crew is really what it is all about. I am obligated to serve them, to see that their needs are met, if at all within my ability. It is a large crew, numbering in access of 12,000 dedicated men. The crew of which I speak is made up of each of you. You live the examples of our traditions, you do the work of Freemasons.
>
> As with any ship that has been sailing for a long time, this Grand Ole Order has some problems. We are not as financially sound as we would like. . . .
>
> I assure you that my attention is to solutions. With God's help, we will make progress. . . .
>
> We are proud of ourselves because of the fact that we are somebody. We believe in our Heavenly Father and our church, which comes first in our lives. Be a man and be a Mason.[36]

On June 25, 1991, the One Hundred and Sixteenth Grand Communication convened in Fort Worth. At this meeting, Grand Master Cash presided for the first time. On the first day, there were a number of reports delivered. Bros. Larry Bailey and Richard Ibarra, Worshipful Masters of two lodges in Hawaii, were presented and received a warm welcome. A collection in the amount of $527 was raised for the Texas Scottish Rite Hospital for Crippled Children in Dallas.[37] On the following day, the reports presented including that of the Committee on State of the Country, chaired by John H. Bullock of Oakwood, Texas.[38] Bro. Bullock discussed a number of national and international developments during 1990-91, then presented "A Moment of Meditation":

> A brief moment of concern and short prayer for the family of our deceased Grand Master Thomas H. Routt, Tuesday, January 8, 1991.

Persian Gulf War started, January 15, 1991. The return of American troops from Operation Desert Storm, March 1991. Grand Matron Clara Gates died May 21, 1991. To all of our fallen comrades and sisters, a moment of prayer.

On last year, our own Dr. C. A. W. Clark spoke on "Lord, Thou Hast Been Our Dwelling Place in All Generations." On last Sunday evening, Dr. Clark presented a masterpiece entitled "The Christian Marathon—You Got to Believe."

Saint John's Day Sermon delivered by Rev. L. B. George, Grand Joshua: "Art Thou the Christ, or shall we look for another—He is the One."

In closing, as we journey to Fort Worth, let us remember that Jesus stated it well what we must do—Saint John 3:4;3:25: "And he must need go through Samaria; "Behold, lift up your eyes and look on the field; for they are white already to harvest." Knights of Pythagoras and Master Masons are out there, we must go out and get them.[39]

That afternoon, Cash delivered his first Grand Master's Address, stating:

> I would ask now that our Grand Chaplain come and ask for the blessings of Heaven to now descend upon us and to express our respect for the memory of Thomas H. Routt, our late Grand Master.
>
> Needless to say, the date of January 3, 1991 will live in my memory as a day of infamy. My life changed almost completely, and so did the direction of our Grand Order. Prior to that date, I assumed the duties delegated to the office of Deputy Grand Master.[40]

Cash described a number of Masonic events he had attended in the capacities of both Deputy Grand Master and Grand Master. Included among these was the funeral of Grand Master Routt in Houston on January 8, 1991. He expressed great pride at the establishment of two new lodges in Hawaii—Aloha Military Lodge No. 635 and Pride of the Pacific Lodge, U. D. However, he described a dispute of territory with the Prince Hall Grand Lodge of California, which also has lodges in Hawaii. He stated: "I have taken the stand that any lodge established by our late Grand Master should stand on its merit."[41] As a good "team player," Cash has always been ready to acknowledge the help of those with whom he has worked:

> You have every right to be proud of the members of the Board of Directors. You elected all of them except three; these three occupy positions of advice and counsel. The program of a new Grand Master can easily be defeated by a non-cooperative board. They do not have to do anything in the form of cooperation and all will be lost. I have been most pleased to have each of the following men to help me as a new Grand Master:
>
> **Past Grand Master I. H. Clayborn** has served as counsel and advisor whenever he has been asked to do so. He is an invaluable part of our management team.
>
> **Past Grand Master Reuben G. White** has and is presently contributing to this Grand Lodge in an excellent manner. I have found that all I have to do is ask of him and it is done.
>
> **Grand Recorder A. D. Harris** is a specialist in his field of recording. He is very concerned that his recording is accurate.
>
> **Grand Legal Advisor E. Brice Cunningham** leads us in a spiritual manner as well as a legal manner. A minister, a lawyer, and a Mason is a rare combination.
>
> **Grand Treasurer Kerven Carter, Jr.,** possesses a sharp mind and contributes deep insights. An educator by career, he has been of tremendous help to this new Master.

> **Grand Secretary C. A. Glaspie** is a manager and a good leader. Most of us do not really know how many hours that our Grand Secretary spends at his tasks. He runs the Grand Lodge office in a very efficient manner and it is good that he is not paid by the hour.
>
> **Grand Senior Warden Hubert Reece and Grand Junior Warden Robert E. Connor, Jr.**, both are deserving of more time and space than I can pen. I can truly state that any time I have asked for information or asked for a task to be done by either of these men, I have been satisfied. I have stated to both that I would rather have you on board to work with, than not to have you at all.[42]

Cash described his vision for future projects, including the updating of the Grand Lodge telephone system, the housing of the entire Prince Hall Masonic Family under one roof, the consideration of Bingo as a source of revenue, the repair of the Masonic Mosque, and the upgrading of the status of the Knights of Pythagoras.[43]

Following the Grand Master's Address, the election of officers was held. Cash was elected Grand Master without opposition. Grand Junior Warden Connor defeated Grand Senior Warden Reece for the office of Deputy Grand Master. Herman L. Gabriel of Houston defeated John H. Bullock of Oakwood for the office of Grand Senior Warden. Roosevelt Tennessee of San Antonio defeated several opponents for the office of Grand Junior Warden. Joseph E. Telfair of San Antonio was elected as Grand Lecturer, while Wilbert M. Curtis of Waco was elected as Grand Tiler. Grand Secretary Glaspie, Grand Treasurer Carter, Grand Chaplain Clark, and Grand Recorder Harris were reelected without opposition.[44] On the following day, all elected and appointed officers were installed by Past Grand Master Clayborn.[45]

In his November 1991 column in the *Quarterly*, Cash addressed the issue of aging:

> It is not a secret that the majority of our craft is in the middle-age range. Middle-age to most means after fifty (50) years of age. This is a period of life when the outlook is likely to change. We tend to paternalize more than we once did. Of course, it goes without saying that these old bodies seem to slow down a bit, to say the least....
>
> Brotherly love among Prince Hall Masons is ever sustaining. We must talk with our brothers who may need some light in dealing with product selection. With a large percentage on a limited or fixed income, selection of products and determination of money spending becomes most important.
>
> As another Christmas season approaches, may God bless you and yours. Merry Christmas to all.[46]

Six months later, Cash published his 1991-92 Regional Presentation, in which he spoke on "Back to the Basics: With an Eye to the Future":

> If we consider re-living our obligations, we can not but go back to basics. For example, do we consider our widows and orphans or do we just get busy and forget that we still are obligated to protect them. I dare say that some of our number have not been taught the true meaning of what we are all about.
>
> Back to basics implies that, somehow, we have strayed from the original promise. The variation comes not from us but from that by which we are influenced. We are influenced by the dynamics around and about us. In general, we are influenced by what our immediate environment gives to us. We see and hear evidence of corruption and evil in newspapers and on television. We see it in government. We see it again and

again. In fact, we take immoral activity for granted. When we listen to gossip and untruths, it becomes hard to distinguish what is and what is not. We are victims. We bring much of this into our order. We tend to talk about what we heard and what we might think it to be. "Back to Basics" means showing that our fraternity is to be held in high esteem by ourselves and that we will not tolerate degradation by others.[47]

He then addressed the following matters: Grand Lodge Office, Grand Lodge Session of June 1991, Knights of Pythagoras, Fraternal Relations, Regional Meetings and Publicity, Boaz Industries, and Brotherly Love. He concluded by reminding the craft: "Be men and Masons. Remember that your community forms its opinion on what they see and hear about Masons."[48]

On June 23, 1992, Cash presided over his second Grand Communication. During the opening session, he ordered the craft to prepare to receive Grand Masters William Parker of North Carolina and Deary Vaughn of Oklahoma. Following their entry, he officially opened the session. The next day—the actual Feast Day of Saint John the Baptist—he delivered his second Grand Master's Address, saying:

> I bring you greetings from the Board of Directors of the Most Worshipful Prince Hall Grand Lodge of Texas and its Jurisdiction, with lodges situated in Hawaii and Germany. I pray that the Heavenly Father is blessing you and yours and that you will continue to serve and honor His presence and ask for guidance in all of your endeavors. For without Him, we are nothing. . . .
>
> A look at my stewardship and travels reveals that I was able through God's help to attend all of our eight (8) regional meetings and worship in a church in the host city the following Sunday with one (1) exception. Due to a celebration of Mother's Day, we did not worship in the northeast region. Worship in church following our meeting was accepted. We realize that many of our members have obligations in their own churches that would limit their participation. This is why it was announced that participation is strictly on a voluntary basis. We gained an insight and were highly visible during worship. God blessed us in our endeavor. . . .
>
> Relations with other Prince Hall Jurisdictions are at an all-time favorable high. There was a difference between Texas and California but the difference seems to have been resolved. All appears to be well between these two jurisdictions at this time. We have more contact with the jurisdictions of Oklahoma, Arkansas, Louisiana, and New Mexico because of the geographic locations, but contact with all Prince Hall Jurisdictions are very good. . . .
>
> An article recently appeared in the *Dallas Morning News*, entitled "Baptists To Seek Study of Masonry." Needless to say, this article caught my attention. Some persons feel that:
>
> 1. Masonry is incompatible with Christianity,
> 2. Masonry is a disruptive influence, and
> 3. The objective of the Masonic lodge is the opposite of the objective of the Christian church.
>
> The superintendent of the Masonic Home in Fort Worth, whose father was a Mason, stated that Masonry is not a religion, it is a fraternity. We agree with him. We all know what a great light means to us. We stress brotherhood. We start and end communications with prayer. We do not worship Masonry. The argument is not new. It goes back several centuries and, in all likelihood, will spring up from time to time.

It seems that someone is always unhappy with Masonry and wishes to disband it. Prince Hall Masons should know and be aware of this argument. We already know that there are people in our own communities who do not really like us just because we are who we are. We shall continue our work and stand head and shoulder above the dissenters.[49]

Following this address, Cash and his officers were reelected.[50] The only contested race was that of Grand Lecturer, in which Lawrence Anderson tried unsuccessfully to unseat Joseph Telfair. Many in attendance agreed with this writer's observation that a lot of time was wasted in the latter contest, which was quite long and drawn-out. On the following day, all elected and appointed officers were installed by Past Grand Master Reuben G. White.[51]

In November 1992, Cash sent the following message to the brethren:

I greet you in the name of the G.A.O.T.U. Pray to Him that your worthy endeavors be crowned with success.

Your Grand Master is interested in all of the important events and activities that your lodge takes part in, that reflect on the honor of our fraternity. Send a letter telling what you are doing or recently have done.

Thank you for your cooperation. I look forward to seeing you in our Regional Meeting.[52]

On December 12, 1992, Cash was involved in the 100th Anniversary Awards Banquet of Hopeful Lodge No. 78 in Marlin. The Master of Ceremonies for this occasion was Charles H. Anderson, Worshipful Master of United Brothers Lodge No. 298 in Riesel and Special Deputy for District No. 14. The program included a "History of the Texas Grand Masters" by the writer, introduction of the speaker and presentation of awards by Cash, an address by Grand Secretary Glaspie, and remarks and expressions by host Worshipful Master J. C. Williams.[53] This turned out to be a very enjoyable evening.[54]

During the 1992-93 Masonic year, Cash delivered his Regional Address, which included the following:

We offer thanks to the Grand Architect of the Universe for allowing us to see another day, this day. It is not written that this day was promised to us because we deserve it or that we have been so good that this day is our reward. Our Heavenly Father has been better to us than we have been to ourselves. If you did not thank him this morning, you may still have time. . . .

The Heavenly Father has taken from our midst many of our number this year. Death is something that we are never prepared for, accept, or look forward to. Yet we all must meet our day. So now, let us live so that when our time comes, we can face eternity like the men that we are and, most of all, like Masons. Joseph Telfair and O. E. Wilhite are among those of our number who have entered the unseen Temple before us. These two Masons were more than Masons. They each were Masons of the highest quality. There are so many others that have gone to be with them. Joseph Telfair served in many offices. He wore many hats, including that of Right Worshipful Grand Lecturer of the M.W.P.H.G.L. of Texas and its Jurisdiction. We shall miss all of our brothers and we ask that you enter their memories in your prayers.[55]

The status of our craft is affected by our national mirror of finance. This nation is in a financial crisis. Jobs are being terminated and deleted and someone is being threatened as I speak. The name of the game is debt....

It is my hope that we renew our friendship one with another. May our brotherly love arise completely new, as the phoenix in Greek mythology. May we break the chains that bind us, the chains of complacency. May we go from this place full of faith and convinced that our cause, as Masons, is just and righteous. And may we as men and Masons resolve to always, always, always, do the right thing.[56]

On June 22, 1993, Grand Master Cash presided over his third Grand Communication. At the opening session, he presented Grand Master Robert Beamon and Grand Junior Warden Clausell McCorkel of New Mexico and then proceeded with the ritualistic opening of the Grand Lodge. During this session, he presented Beamon with a plaque.[57]

On the following day, Cash delivered his third Grand Master's Address, in which he presented his 1992-93 itinerary, which he described as a "Synopsis of Stewardship." He then stated:

I paint a picture of normality for you as it relates to the current status of our jurisdiction. The conditions that exist throughout our jurisdiction are also found in other jurisdictions and in our country in general. There are some good factors as well as some not-so-good factors to be considered. Keep in mind that it is easy to view our current status from a negative side. It becomes even easier if one has a hostile attitude or mindset....

Our budget is over limits. We usually pride ourselves in our detailed outline of yearly spending. However, we are finding that it is not easy to have big plans and little money to back up those plans. Our Grand Secretary, C. A. Glaspie, has formulated, on paper, a budget that has been considered by the Grand Treasurer and the Grand Master. The Board of Directors has spent considerable hours taking the budget apart, questioning the outline and applying techniques. We are not satisfied with the finished product, but it is a true picture of what our financial status is for the near future. It is easy to move figures and give a false picture. We could not do that. The budget that you examine is as sound as possible, given the circumstances that we now face.

Our operating income is down. Our membership is not what it once was. It costs more to operate these days, as you no doubt know. Companies are feeling an economic crunch these days in one way or another. We are no different. We operate at a deficit and do not try to hide the fact. We do not like it but it is nevertheless a fact. We are trying to work with what we have and we are keeping the faith. By the way, the last I heard, the United States Government is operating at a slight deficit....

Every year before the Grand Lodge session, rumors abound. Why is it that something negative has to rear its ugly head before we convene? I wish that I had an answer but my assertion is definitely correct. It is always something spice and always negative. This year, no different. It is going to be a good one this year.

In the event I had to make a statement to our sisters about the situation that involves them. I would say to them that, whatever the situation, prayers are the answer. Money is said to be the root of all evil and, in this and many other cases, money and the lust for it has caused an embarrassing situation. Suspicion and mistrust are bound to be part of what has happened. I am truly sorry this has happened, but I know that things will work out. The entire Masonic family supports the O.E.S.; we do not ridicule or make light of their situation. We place our trust in God. This is my statement as Grand Master.

Innuendo, insinuation, and gossip have no place in our Order. These can be controlled by us, if we really want to do so. These destroy the ideals that we work hard to preserve.[58]

Following this address, the election of officers was held. The only contested office was that of Grand Lecturer. This office had been left vacant as a result of the death of Joseph Telfair. M. R. Chatham of Beaumont defeated a number of opponents for this position. Cash and the other officers were reelected without opposition.[59]

On June 24, 1993, Grand Master Cash and his elected and appointed officers were installed by Grand Master Howard L. Woods of Arkansas. After the installation, Woods gave a short but informative lecture.[60]

Cash found it necessary to write to the craft in November 1993, regarding the financial situation of the Grand Lodge:

> The Grand Master of this jurisdiction is called upon, from time to time, to make certain decisions that are in the best interest of the craft as a whole. Such decisions, while well thought out, are not always popular with the craftsmen. Recently, such a decision was made pertaining to beneficiaries. This decision is simply to delay payment until the end of June 1994. It is not the intent of this decision to imply that payment will not be made.
>
> In a letter to all Master Masons, dated September 9, 1993, the necessity for the decision was briefly addressed. Our Grand Lodge is in dire financial straits. Our present condition is such that we must consider either closing the Grand Lodge headquarters in the near future, levying an assessment, or delaying payment to beneficiaries until June 1994. I chose to delay payment to beneficiaries.
>
> The decision is an effort to help ease our current financial crisis. We, like other businesses, find that there is a shortage of money and we must take certain steps to help ourselves. When a brother passes, his beneficiary is given a remuneration, which is not a great, great sum of money. Please take due notice of this decision and govern yourselves accordingly. . . .
>
> I propose that each Mason of this jurisdiction give a contribution of five dollars ($5) to his Worshipful Master who, in turn, will forward the sum to the Grand Lodge in the form of a check or money order. . . .
>
> Thank you in advance for your efforts. This project should be considered as a donation or contribution, but not as an assessment.[61]

In his 1993-94 Regional Address, Cash again gave much attention to the financial picture of the Grand Lodge:

> The Grand Master, Grand Secretary, and Grand Treasurer met on two occasions to try to bring our budget on line. The Board met with the same intention, even calling a meeting on its own that was without the consent or permission of the Grand Master. None of these so-called meetings were of the desired results. We operate on paper at a deficit but we still operate. Next, we will start early in budget planning and hope to present something more pleasing. No one has tried to hide the facts. We operate at a *deficit*.
>
> Allow me to return to the financial condition of our order. We are in dire financial straits, repeat, dire financial straits. We are operating with a deficit and our income is very low. I have told the Grand Secretary, C. A. Glaspie, that, if necessary, he may hold

my monthly pay to help stem the tide. If you do not know it, I take home $495 per month. I sure do not try to hide anything from you. $495. The Committee on Budget met, our Board met, and still we face grave financial concerns. . . .

We agree that we shall disagree, but remember that this ancient and honorable institution of Prince Hall Freemasonry is larger than any one Mason or any group of Masons that fall within its ranks. Carefully select your leaders and align yourself with them. There will be no campaigning for offices, repeat, *no campaigning* for offices. Campaigning is forbidden by our Constitution and your Grand Master.

Let's disagree, but never let us be disagreeable.[62]

Cash delivered this address at all of the scheduled regional meetings except one. The Southeastern Regional Meeting, which he had planned to conduct at Oakwood High School in Oakwood, Texas, on Saturday, April 9, 1994, was canceled because death had invaded the ranks of the Grand Lodge.

The earthly sojourn of Past Grand Master I. H. Clayborn came to an end on Monday, April 4, 1994. Funeral services were held the following Saturday at Good Street Baptist Church in Dallas. The eulogy was delivered by Grand Chaplain Dr. C.A.W. Clark, the long-time pastor of both Clayborn and Cash.[63] Burial was in Lincoln Memorial Cemetery, with Masonic graveside services conducted by Cash.

Cash served as host Grand Master for the meeting of the 75th Conference of Grand Masters and the 46th Conference of Grand Chapters, which jointly convened at the Westin Oaks Galleria in Houston on May 11-14, 1994. Cash described this meeting as "an unqualified success." He took much pleasure in being able to meet and greet many officers from various jurisdictions who were able to enjoy a great deal of Texas-style hospitality. In addition to the formal sessions, Texans and visitors from other states enjoyed a western dance at the Post Oak Ranch, several tours, dog races, a fashion show, a queen contest, and a sumptuous banquet.[64] In many ways, this important meeting turned out to be the highlight of the Cash administration.

On May 23, 1994, Cash retired from his long-time position as a visiting teacher with the Dallas Independent School District. The writer, like many other friends and brothers, received in the mail a card announcing this retirement. Cash hoped then to be able to devote full time to the work of the Grand Master of the Prince Hall Grand Lodge of Texas. However, things did not turn out as he had hoped.

On June 28, 1994, Cash presided over his final Grand Communication.[65] The following day, he delivered his fourth and final Grand Master's Address. As usual, he presented his annual itinerary as a "Synopsis of Stewardship." He had much to say about the recent Grand Masters Conference and had much praise for members of the planning committee and others who had done their part to make this meeting a success.[66] There were many positive elements in his address, but it was necessary to turn to the negative and report on the subject of "Mosque in Trouble." He informed the craft:

The Masonic Mosque is very important to the Texas Jurisdiction. From the beginning, it was meant as a monument to glorify Texas Freemasonry. The location was never in question. The use was never questioned. The location in Fort Worth, Texas has proved to be a bad location. The Mosque is located in a high crime area and that fact causes much concern. The use of the Mosque was clear. It was built in hopes that the community of Fort Worth would patronize it regularly and, of course, defray the expenses. The truth of the matter is that the Mosque is not earning enough money to sustain itself. There are not enough bookings to pay utilities and taxes or to repay the loan. The Grand Secretary had extensive contact with a group who had expressed interest in leasing the building. However, the terms and provisions that they wanted were not in our best interest. . . .

Right now, I need the help of every Master Mason in this Jurisdiction in order to save our Mosque. We need to pull together like never before and we can do it. Each man is asked to contribute at least twenty-five dollars. Twenty-five dollars from all of us will enable us to pay off the existing loan and turn to corner of this debt.

Again, I am very serious. I need each Mason to donate twenty-five dollars to help save our Mosque. Those of us who can contribute more than twenty-five dollars, please do so. I expect 100% participation. If you do not comply with this request, please do not try to hinder your neighbor. Please help me get the request to those of our brothers who are not here. Twenty-five dollars from each brother is needed to save our Mosque.

A special roster will be prepared and sent to all local lodges by the Grand Secretary. Please comply with this request and save our Masonic Mosque.[67]

It was the opinion of many Texas Prince Hall Masons who were in attendance at the 1994 Grand Communication that the financial situation of the Grand Lodge at that time—a situation which Cash did not create but inherited—was a major factor in Cash's defeat on the following evening by Deputy Grand Master Robert E. Connor, Jr. In this election, Herman L. Gabriel was promoted to Deputy Grand Master, Roosevelt Tennessee was promoted to Grand Senior Warden, and William E. Woods of San Antonio was elected as Grand Junior Warden. All other officers were reelected. The next morning, Grand Master Connor and all elected and appointed officers were installed by Grand Master Howard L. Woods of Arkansas.[68] The installation was followed by remarks from Past Grand Master Cash.

Edwin B. Cash has served the Prince Hall Grand Lodge of Texas quite well for a quarter of a century. His record includes eighteen years as Worshipful Master of Good Street Baptist Lodge, three years as Grand Junior Deacon, two years as Grand Senior Warden, ten years as Deputy Grand Master, and three years as Grand Master.

Since his 1994 defeat, Edwin Bernard Cash has remained active in the craft and community. On December 27, 2002, he became the only living Past Grand Master upon the death of Past Grand Master Reuben G. White. On January 4, 2003, he conducted Masonic burial services for White in Texas City. On September 21, 2003, he conducted Masonic burial services for Grand Master Robert E. Connor, Jr., in Columbus, Texas. Thus he played a major role in the final tribute to two of his predecessors and one of his successors. After the burial of Connor, Cash installed Wilbert Curtis as the twenty-first Grand Master.

Edwin Bernard Cash is respected throughout Texas and beyond. The writer is proud to claim him as a friend and appreciates his support for the writer's work as Grand Historian during his administration. Let us pray that the Grand Architect of the Universe will continue to bless him with life and health so that he may inspire men and Masons for many years to come! So mote it be!

Robert Edmund Connor, Jr.

Robert Edmund Connor, Jr. (1953-2003) was the twentieth Grand Master of Prince Hall Masons in Texas. He was born in Weimar, Colorado County, Texas, on July 24, 1953, the son of Robert Edmund Connor, Sr., and Vera Miller Connor. He grew up in the Colorado County seat of Columbus, where his father was employed by the Police Department. He graduated from Columbus High School in 1971 and from Prairie View A&M University in Prairie View, Texas, where he received a bachelor's degree with a major in sociology and a minor in business administration in 1975.[1] He was a life member of Omega Psi Phi Fraternity, Inc. and of the National Association for the Advancement of Colored People. He served as an advisor to many boards connected with the enrichment of minority survival.[2] He married Deanna M. Eaton on June 5, 1993.[3]

Connor was a lifelong member of Saint Paul United Methodist Church in Columbus. He served as chair of Trustees and of the Administrative Board. His favorite prayer was "God's Will, Nothing More, Nothing Less, and Nothing Else." His favorite hymn was "Precious Lord, Take My Hand." His hobbies included Bible study, fishing, and ranching.[4]

Connor received a Master Peace Officer Certification from Texas A&M University. He was a member of the Texas Peace Officers Association and of the International Association of Police Chiefs. He began his law enforcement career with the Prairie View Police Department, then worked for four years for the Texas Alcoholic Beverage Commission and ten years for the Harris County Sheriff's Department, where he achieved the rank of sergeant.[5] While in the latter position, he founded and served as the first president of the Afro-American Sheriff's Deputy League.[6]

In 1985 he filed a lawsuit against Harris County Sheriff Johnny Klevenhagen after being fired for allegedly using profanity and discharging a weapon at a funeral. The judge ordered Connor reinstated, but an appellate court reversed the decision.

Connor insisted that he was actually fired because he addressed legislative members on a bill that would have charged arrestees a fine. Klevenhagen wanted the money to go to a fund to be used at the sheriff's discretion, while Connor wanted part of it to be earmarked for education in the black community.[7]

On November 13, 1989, Connor was sworn in as chief of police in his hometown of Columbus, becoming the first African American to hold such a position in the history of Colorado County.[8] Columbus City Councilman Martin Williams, who knew him for over forty years, said: "He wanted to come home. He loved this city. He turned down a higher paying job to come here."[9]

On June 20, 1999, Connor received a commendation from the Federal Bureau of Investigation for outstanding performance in a bank robbery investigation which led to the successful prosecution of four suspects. As a result, the Southern District of Texas handed down sentences which totaled over 143 years in prison. This commendation was presented by Allen E. Mitchell, the FBI's supervisory senior resident agent, at a ceremony at Columbus City Hall. In his acceptance of the commendation, Connor said: "I am certainly honored and proud to receive this recognition. I was simply doing my job, satisfying the citizens of the city after the criminals violated my territory."[10] He assisted the Texas Rangers in tracking down "railroad killer" Angel Maturino Resendiz, who allegedly killed one of his victims near Columbus.[11]

Connor maintained a ranch in Colorado County, and each spring he could be found astride a horse with such organizations as the Black History Trail Riders and the Southwestern Trail Riders Association. He organized many trail rides, bringing visitors to the county. He also operated a local roping arena, offering both adult and youth an opportunity to pursue roping and barrel activities. He was instrumental in bringing youth from around the state to the Prince Hall Young Boys Camp for a week of camping, fishing, and leadership education.[12]

Connor was raised to the sublime degree of Master Mason in Prince Hall Lodge No. 18 in Columbus in 1973. He was brought into Masonry by two uncles: Woodrow Connor and Clyde Toland. At the age of twenty, he served as Special District Deputy of District No. 16 under District Deputy Grand Master Sherman Wilson. He served as Worshipful Master of two lodges: John D. Paley Lodge No. 630 in Baytown and Prince Hall Lodge No. 18. In the York Rite of Freemasonry, he was a Past High Priest of Sunrise Chapter No. 7, Holy Royal Arch Masons; and a member of the Houston Commandery of Knights Templar. In the Scottish Rite he was a member of Goodwill Consistory No. 235 in Rosenberg. In 1986 he received the 33° during the annual session of the United Supreme Council, Southern Jurisdiction, in Washington, D.C. He was elected president of his 33° class, and he was a Past Potentate of Doric Temple No. 76, Ancient Egyptian Arabic Order of Nobles of the Mystic Shrine in Houston.[13]

On June 24, 1987, Connor was elected Grand Junior Warden of the Prince Hall Grand Lodge of Texas.[14] On June 28, 1988, he was reelected to this office.[15] On the following day, he gave his first report, describing his attendance at a number of regional meetings and sessions of the Grand Lodge Board of Directors. He also reported accompanying Grand Master Thomas H. Routt to the Conference of Prince Hall Grand Masters in New Mexico, where he chaired a workshop for Grand Senior and Junior Wardens. He described being elected to a Grand Lodge office as an "honor" and serving the brethren as a "privilege."[16] He concluded his report with the following quotation from Dr. Martin Luther King, Jr.:

> The ultimate measure of a man is not where he stands in moments of comfort and convenience, but where he stands at times of challenge and controversy. The true neighbor will risk his position, his prestige, and even his life for the welfare of others. In dangerous alleys and hazardous pathways, he will lift some bruised and beaten brother to a higher and more noble life. We must accept finite disappointment, but we must never lose infinite hope.[17]

Connor was reelected as Grand Junior Warden on June 28, 1989, after trying unsuccessfully to unseat Deputy Grand Master Edwin B. Cash.[18] On June 26, 1990, he gave his annual report to the Grand Lodge, describing his attendance at a number of Masonic functions and stressing the importance of lodges located in rural areas.[19] He said:

> Grand Master Routt sanctioned my involvement in the rural lodges trying to motivate and reclaim Master Masons and Masonic Lodges who had fallen by the side. Going into smaller towns talking with young adults about Masonry and encouraging them to join wasn't difficult; getting the Master Masons in those towns to meet was a problem.
>
> When meeting with rural lodges you find that most of the lodges have a lot of resources valuable to the Grand Lodge and if each lodge of the jurisdiction would put on one charitable function, just think how Prince Hall Masons throughout Texas would be respected. If you need speakers, contact your Grand Lodge officers, make them responsible to you.[20]

He was again reelected on the following day.[21]

On January 8, 1991, Connor attended the funeral of Grand Master Thomas H. Routt at Trinity United Methodist Church in Houston. Following the Masonic graveside services at Paradise North Cemetery, he joined other Grand Lodge officers at the Houston Hilton for the installation of Grand Master Edwin B. Cash.[22]

On June 26, 1991, Cash was elected Grand Master without opposition. The major contested office was Deputy Grand Master. For the latter, Grand Junior Warden Robert E. Connor, Jr., defeated Grand Senior Warden Hubert L. Reece.[23] On the previous day, Connor had given his report, expressing sorrow at the death of Routt and concern about the operations of the Grand Lodge. He said: "Grand Master Routt did an outstanding job to get us where we are today and I have no doubt that Grand Master Cash intends to do just as well. But, my brothers, our work is cut out for us and it is time for us to make some changes and one of the changes should be how we handle our finances."[24]

On June 23, 1992, Deputy Grand Master Connor gave his first report. He spoke of attending a number of important Masonic events, including the centennial celebration of the Prince Hall Grand Lodge of Oklahoma, where he represented Grand Master Cash. He stated, however, that he had to miss some meetings due to his candidacy for Colorado County sheriff. Connor quoted the following words of Dr. Martin Luther King, Jr.: "An individual has not started living until he can rise above the narrow confines of individualistic concerns to the broader concerns of all humanity." He called for more active participation in political, economic, social, and cultural affairs and declared that "the ultimate goal of education is to prepare individuals for constructive contributions to society." Insisting that, before we can be our brother's keeper, we must first be our brother's brother, he called for more active involvement of Prince Hall Masons in combating drugs and crime in the black community. He quoted the following words of Dr. Benjamin Mays: "Not failure but low aim is sin." Connor urged the brethren to set goals, accomplish them, and concentrate on peace and harmony."[25] On the following day, he was reelected.[26]

On June 22, 1993, Deputy Grand Master Connor gave his second report. He spoke of attending a number of Masonic events, including the Imperial Council of the Mystic Shrine in Kentucky and the Conference of Grand Masters in New Jersey, and he reported speaking at two Black History programs sponsored by local lodges. He expressed concern that all Masonic money be properly managed and disbursed, insisting that "We must operate this Grand Lodge like a business when we are dealing with financial matters. . . . Many organizations don't plan to fail, they fail to plan." Connor quoted the Good News Version of Ecclesiastes 10:18: "When a man is too lazy to repair his roof, it will leak, and the house will fall" and pleaded "Brothers, let's repair our roof and keep God in our daily lives." He urged everyone to be committed to making a better world for the next generation of Prince Hall Masons.[27] On the following day, he was again reelected.[28]

Deputy Grand Master Connor gave his final report on June 28, 1994. Here, he spoke of the financial problems of the Grand Lodge and revealed conflicts within the Board of Directors, in which he, on a number of occasions, had disagreed with Grand Master Cash. Connor stated:

> As an elected board member by the craft, I felt obligated to the craft to make decisions that I felt were in the best interest of the Most Worshipful Prince Hall Grand Lodge of Texas. Yes, I am the board member who informed the Grand Master that I was elected by the craft as he was and that my allegiance was to the craft. My brothers, I don't feel like this fraternity of ours should operate like a ship crew. . . . If I can prevent our ship from sinking, I will, even if I have to disagree with the captain and suggest or plot another course, being mindful that the Board of Directors must work together as a team. Brothers, we have some serious financial problems with no plans to solve them other than assessments, increase in dues, or the sale of property, which we are going to run out of some day. During our board meetings this past year, we didn't accomplish anything that would reduce our deficit. . . . As a board member, I must respond to the Grand Master's article in our last quarterly, where he stated that the board votes in a block and usually against the Grand Master. I disagree with that statement because there were times when the board voted against me also, especially when discussing the large deficit of the Mosque and I kept making motions to close the Mosque down and use it as needed. . . . My brothers, we didn't vote against the Grand Master, we voted for you.[29]

From all indications, the Grand Lodge's financial problems had a great influence on the 1994 election of officers. Thus, on June 29, Robert E. Connor, Jr., was elected Grand Master, defeating Edwin B. Cash. The following officers were elected: Herman L. Gabriel, Deputy Grand Master; Roosevelt Tennessee, Grand Senior

Warden; William E. Woods, Grand Junior Warden; C. A. Glaspie, Grand Secretary; Kerven W. Carter, Jr., Grand Treasurer; James E. Fields, Sr., Grand Lecturer; A. D. Harris, Grand Recorder; Wilbert Curtis, Grand Tiler; Rev. C. A. W. Clark, Grand Chaplain; and Howard Washington, Grand Auditor.[30] On the following day, all elected and appointed officers were installed by Grand Master Howard Woods of Arkansas.[31]

On September 17, 1994, a special Grand Lodge Session was held, with approximately 500 Master Masons in attendance. At this session, the brethren approved an increase in relief dues, sale of interest in the Masonic Mosque, permission to get bids for the completion of the Mosque, and permission to hire a management company for the Mosque.[32]

During the 1994-95 Masonic Year, the new Grand Master traveled throughout the state and delivered a Regional Address in which he covered many issues, including membership.[33] He said:

> It is a fact that our membership has decreased substantially over the years. Some Master Masons departed the Order for bigger and better things, they thought; some left to avoid assisting with the expenses of operating the Grand Lodge; some left because they felt nothing was on the trestle board; some left because of personal conflicts; and the Grand Architect of the Universe took those whom He felt were deserving. The fact is, we must replenish our membership and after we get new members we must keep them.[34]

He discussed the problems related to the management of the Prince Hall housing complexes, the indebtedness of Boaz Industries to the Grand Lodge, and the indebtedness of individual Masons to local lodges and appendant bodies. He gave a strong warning against the hazing of potential members.[35]

Connor wrote to the brethren in November 1994, reporting considerable progress since the close of the Grand Communication, including an increase in membership, the establishment of new lodges, and the reactivation of a number of lodges. He stressed the importance of local lodges paying their property taxes, lest Masonic property be lost. He requested that District Deputies create funds to help with cases of delinquent taxes, and he stated that the Grand Lodge must be informed about the existence of abandoned property and of remaining bank accounts for defunct lodges. He insisted: "We must keep Prince Hall Masonry alive in Texas."[36]

In March 1995 Connor reported further progress in regard to membership growth and community service projects. He spoke of substantial reductions in Grand Lodge operating expenses and discussed the consolidation of lodges, with District Deputies authorized to merge inactive lodges with active lodges "after exhausting all other efforts to revive them." Connor addressed the problem of long-time members being inappropriately dropped from the rolls, and expressed special concern for the older brothers who may be sick, in nursing homes, out of town living with their children, or who just forget to pay their dues. He reported progress on moving the Grand Lodge office from the old location on Evans Avenue to the Masonic Mosque and told of plans to sell the building on Evans, along with four lots across the street from it. Additionally, he discussed needed repairs on the Mosque, payments to widows, and other financial obligations.[37]

On June 28 1995, Connor delivered his first Grand Master's Address. He charged the craft: "In preparing for the 21st Century, we must place our faith in God, allow love to enter our hearts, and work together as one. We must stay focused and remain cognizant of the many forces waiting to destroy us." He reported issuing three orders for the establishment of the following lodges under dispensation: I. H. Clayborn Lodge in Beeville, Mount Pisgah Lodge in Dallas, and Joseph E. Telfair Sr. Lodge in Sumon, Korea. He recommended that each of these lodges be chartered and numbered. Also, he reported authorizing the members of West Temple Lodge No. 425 to consolidate with the Prince Hall Grand Lodge of Arizona, working out the details with Arizona Grand Master Gene Berry.[38] He had much to say about the recent meeting of the Conference of Prince Hall Grand Masters, where the issue of recognition by white Grand Lodges was discussed at length.[39] Connor reported that, during the Grand Masters Conference, the Committee on Masonic Recognition made the following recommendations:

1. That we make a strong statement that Prince Hall Grand Lodges are Sovereign and Legitimate within themselves.
2. That if a Prince Hall Grand Lodge is proposing to discuss the possibilities of mutual recognition with their counterparts, they should:
   a. Seek not to give anything up.
   b. Be sure that the benefits on both sides are equal.
3. That no Master Mason of any Jurisdiction should enter into any agreement and/or contract which could result in Masonic Recognition.
4. That it is encouraged for Prince Hall Masons to work with our counterparts on common projects for the benefit of both.[40]

He also reported that the Grand Masters Conference approved resolutions against the "Contract for America" unless it was changed to a contract for all Americans and against the repeal of Affirmative Action.[41] He spoke of the effects of the tragic Oklahoma City bombing on April 19, 1995, on the Prince Hall Masonic family in Oklahoma and stated that the Prince Hall Grand Lodge of Texas had pledged $1,000 due to the appeal of Oklahoma Grand Master Deary Vaughn.[42] He gave the following financial report:

> We ended the year in the black. We paid off our Masonic Mosque (we now own it); we paid our beneficiaries; we reduced our deficit at the Masonic Mosque by 20%, we moved into the Masonic Mosque; we reduced our Grand Lodge session's expenses by 30%; and we reduced our overall expenses by 15%. . . .
> Our previous Grand Lodge office located on Evans St. was sold for $70,000. We are anticipating using those funds to help finish the repairs on the Masonic Mosque. . . . Our Renovation Committee estimates that, to finish all repairs of the Mosque, we are looking at approximately $150,000. . . . I am recommending that a $5 building fund tax be levied against every Master Mason in the jurisdiction during the month of December. All monies collected will be used only for the repairing and operation of the Masonic Mosque. . . .
> Brothers, we are close to being debt free if we continue to work together and use our funds properly; we are close to providing larger scholarships for our youth; and we are close to providing more charity.[43]

On a less happy note, he reported suspending twelve Master Masons for "Un-Masonic conduct" or "violation of our Constitution."[44] He also spoke of the positive experiences of residents of Prince Hall apartment complexes in various Texas cities and urged the members of local lodges to visit these apartments and to remember the residents in their provision of scholarships and charitable donations.[45] Connor invited the members of all Texas Masonic bodies to participate in the Prince Hall Day Celebration in Brenham—where the Grand Lodge was organized—on September 17, 1995.[46] He concluded that "With God's help we can do anything we wish to do. We must remember that this Masonic Order is bigger than any one person and that there are no Big I's and Little You's. Everyone is on the same Level. Let us build on to what we have and not allow anyone to destroy what we have built."[47]

Later that day, Grand Master Connor was reelected, as was Deputy Grand Master Gabriel. William E. Woods unseated Roosevelt Tennessee in the race for Grand Senior Warden. Wilbert Curtis was elected Grand Junior Warden, after several opponents conceded the election to him. C. B. Cheatham was elected Grand Tiler.[48]

Two months later, in the *Texas Prince Hall Masonic Quarterly*, Connor wrote a column addressing a number of issues, including relief payments, district/regional fees, Mosque taxes, church visitation, scholarships, and voter registration. He stressed the importance of each local lodge caring for the widows and orphans of their members, suggesting that the brethren might take the widows to church and to dinner and provide for them at Thanksgiving and Christmas. He urged participation in the Prince Hall Masonic Family Pilgrimage to Brenham scheduled September 15-17, 1995.[49] In the same issue, the writer presented the historical background to this great event:

> The place was Brenham, Texas. The date was August 19, 1875. An important gathering of Texas Prince Hall Freemasons was in session. At the time, these Texas Masons were subject to the National Grand Lodge. They were meeting pursuant to the call of Norris Wright Cuney, Deputy Grand Master, and Richard Allen, District Deputy Grand Master. The purpose of the meeting was the organization of a Grand Lodge for the State of Texas....
>
> On the following day, August 10, 1875, plans for the new Grand Lodge were finalized and Cuney was elected the first Grand Master.... The place was again Brenham, Texas. The date was August 1941, exactly 66 years after Cuney's election. Another important gathering of Texas Prince Hall Freemasons was in session. These Texas Masons were meeting pursuant to the call of Grand Master William Coleman, one of Cuney's successors in the Grand East. The purpose of the meeting was the dedication of a monument to Cuney and to the organization of the Texas Grand Lodge....
>
> The place will again be Brenham, Texas. The date will be September 16, 1995—120 years since Cuney's election and 54 years since Coleman's dedication of the monument. Another important gathering will be in session. Texas Masons will meet pursuant to the call of Grand Master Robert E. Connor, Jr., one of Cuney's and Coleman's successors in the Grand East. The purpose of this meeting will be the celebration of our Masonic history. Let us all resolve to be present! Let us all resolve to do our part to make this occasion a success![50]

The Pilgrimage to Brenham began with a Friday night hospitality hour at Preference Inn. On Saturday morning, the craft assembled at Saint John AME Church, 1012 East Alamo Street for a worship service, followed by a dedication ceremony at the Masonic Monument across the street. On Saturday afternoon, there was a picnic, and in the evening, a family banquet. Another church service was held on Sunday morning at Saint John.[51]

The theme of the Pilgrimage was "A Celebration of Our Masonic History." The Saturday worship service was led by Rev. Howard Anderson, Grand Auditor, who gave the call to worship. The service included scripture by Rev. Willie J. Calvin, Deputy Grand Chaplain; prayer by Rev. Ernest L. Gates, Deputy Grand Chaplain; welcome by Wilbert M. Curtis, Grand Junior Warden; theme by the writer; sermon by Rev. C. A. W. Clark, Grand Chaplain; and recognition of special guests and remarks by Grand Master Connor.[52]

At the family banquet, the Master of Ceremonies was Rev. L. B. George, Grand Joshua of the Heroines of Jericho of Texas. The invocation was delivered by Rev. James E. Fields, Sr., Grand Lecturer. The occasion was presented by the writer. Felicitations were made by Brenham Mayor Robert Appel, Jr. Past Grand Master Cash introduced the speaker. The audience then heard an outstanding address by Judge Alexander Green, Justice of the Peace for Precinct 7, Position 2, Harris County, Texas. Remarks were made by Grand Matron Brenda A. Rorie of the Order of the Eastern Star, Most Ancient Grand Matron Margaret A. McDow of the Heroines of Jericho, and Grand Master Connor. The dinner was followed by a dance enjoyed by all in attendance, with Earl Kemp, Jr., serving as disk jockey.[53]

The November issue of the *Quarterly* contained a number of pictures made during the Pilgrimage and the following message of the Grand Master: "As we celebrate Thanksgiving, we must remain mindful of our many blessings, and those who are less fortunate. We should remember our widows and orphans in our prayers. They should be constantly reminded that we still care about them as we continue our Masonic Practices and Customs."[54]

In his March 1996 column, Connor wrote:

> The 1995-96 Masonic Year has been very productive and fruitful. . . .Masonic Lodges throughout the Jurisdiction of Texas are actively working in our local communities spreading the true spirit of Prince Hall Masonry and are more involved ritualistically. Our membership program has yielded over 700 new members, which is one of the best membership drives we have had in years. Our six months bookkeeper report indicates that we are in the black and that we have reduced our over all deficits by 30%. . . . It looks like the 1996-97 Masonic Year will be successful also.[55]

He addressed relations between the Grand Lodge and other houses of the Prince Hall Masonic Family and recommended the establishment of an Emergency Charity Fund to aid Prince Hall Masons in various states who are victims of disasters or serious misfortunes. Again he called for consolidation of inactive lodges with active ones.[56]

In the above column, for the first time, Connor alluded to the growing conflict between the Grand Lodge and the Masonic Grand Chapter of the Order of the Eastern Star. He said:

> The Order of Eastern Stars have existed in the Jurisdiction of Texas for over 100 years without being adopted by the Most Worshipful Prince Hall Grand Lodge of Texas. In the 1890s, they requested adoption and were denied. However, the Most

Worshipful Prince Hall Grand Lodge of Texas adopted the Heroines of Jericho. In the 1930s, the issue of adopting the Order of Eastern Stars was again brought before the Most Worshipful Prince Hall Grand Lodge of Texas but they were again denied.

Our records indicate that the Heroines of Jericho were started with the blessings of the Most Worshipful Prince Hall Grand Lodge at Victoria, Texas and that the Order of Eastern Stars were started by a Master Mason from the Mississippi Jurisdiction for the Jurisdiction of Louisiana. At this time we are unable to determine if the founder of the Order of Eastern Stars was a Prince Hall Mason nor are we able to determine if he acted with the permission of the Jurisdiction of Louisiana. I have contacted the Jurisdiction of Louisiana and they don't have records indicating their approval. In the 1970s, the Order of Eastern Stars amended their Incorporation with the State of Texas, changing their name from the Independent Grand Chapter, Order of Eastern Stars, to the Masonic Grand Chapter, Order of Eastern Stars, PHA of Texas and Jurisdiction. No documentation has been found yet that gave them the authority to attach PHA to their official name. . . .

In order to correct the affiliation between the Most Worshipful Prince Hall Grand Lodge of Texas and the Masonic Grand Chapter, Order of Eastern Stars, I wrote the Grand Matron a letter, requesting that the Masonic Grand Chapter, Order of Eastern Stars amend their Articles of Incorporation with the State of Texas and their Constitution to indicate their dependency upon fraternal recognition by the Most Worshipful Prince Hall Grand Lodge of Texas. The Grand Matron was given 90 days to correct this matter, beginning October 24, 1995. It was my hopes that she would contact her craft, inform them what was correct and Masonically right, and amend the above items. Instead, the Grand Matron took the position that the Order of Eastern Stars were independent, not adopted and that they didn't need Master Masons to exist. . . .

On January 18, 1996 . . . I withdrew fraternal recognition from the Masonic Grand Chapter, Order of Eastern Stars because their methods and conduct were creating a reflection on Masonry in the Jurisdiction of Texas.

After withdrawing fraternal recognition from the Masonic Grand Chapter, Order of Eastern Stars, many wives, sisters, mothers, and daughters of Prince Hall Masons contacted me. They disagreed with the Grand Matron's position and informed me that they wanted to be Prince Hall Affiliate Eastern Stars. A Certificate of Assumed Name was filed with the State of Texas for Prince Hall Grand Chapter OES of Texas and Jurisdiction, PHA and, after consultation with the Board of Directors, a new Grand Chapter was started. Shortly afterwards, the Grand Matron filed a $500,000 lawsuit against the Grand Master and the Grand Lodge, indicating that we were using their trade name and insignia, were soliciting their members, and that we were threatening their members. . . .

I will not tolerate a Grand Matron who doesn't understand Masonic Protocol and who doesn't want to learn. Once a new Grand Chapter is formed, I will assure you that harmony will exist. No more fights about the status of men in the Order of Eastern Stars and no more problems with independence. . . . I feel that if we educate our family members on from whence we came, we will have many happy days in the future.[57]

From all indications, at the time Connor wrote this column, neither he nor anyone who read it realized that it would be a long time before harmony would exist between Prince Hall Masons and members of the Order of the Eastern Star or that "happy days" for the Grand Lodge were a long way off.

Two months later, there was hope that a resolution of the conflict was imminent, as indicated by Connor's column:

> On Sunday April 28, 1996, a conference telephone call between Grand Matron Brenda Rorie, Overseer of the Orient Howard Anderson, and myself resulted in a promising resolution. Grand Matron Rorie agreed to the Masonic Grand Chapter, Order of the Eastern Star being adopted by the Most Worshipful Prince Hall Grand Lodge of Texas. This agreement now lies in the hands of the Order of Eastern Stars Board of Directors on June 1, 1996, in Austin, Texas. Those Order of Eastern Star Chapters organized by the Most Worshipful Prince Hall Grand Lodge will be warranted under the Masonic Grand Chapter, Order of Eastern Star, PHA. They will have all rights and privileges during the Grand Session in June.[58]

On June 18, 1996, Connor delivered his Grand Master's Address, in which he reported attendance at the 1995 session of the Imperial Council of the Mystic Shrine in Indianapolis, Indiana, and announced plans for the 1996 Imperial session in Houston. He expressed great pleasure in the results of the regional meetings and reported attendance at the Imperial Council's winter session, the Scottish Rite Council of Deliberation in San Antonio, and the Shriners' Gala Day in El Paso. He gave a positive report of the meeting of the Conference of Prince Hall Grand Masters in St. Louis, Missouri, where he was elected Southwest Regional Chairman. He apologized for his inability to attend a number of Masonic and other events due to back surgery in November 1995—a surgery which kept him off work until March 1996.[59] He gave the following financial report:

> As a result of hard work and dedication, our finances ended up in the black. We managed to place over $25,000 into the Rio Grand Federal Credit Union and $9,000 into the North Central Credit Union. These funds have been placed in interest bearing accounts for emergency purposes. We have now paid over half of the $150,000 loan with Unity Bank in Houston, Texas. The past year, we reduced our deficit at the Masonic Mosque another 20% and we are working hard to get it even lower.[60]

He commended the craft for the following positive developments:

> This year we brought in (1000) plus new men. Brothers, "you" have really worked. Not only did you bring in new members, you worked hard in your local communities assisting widows and orphans. You gave more scholarships, you spent more time with our youths, more voter registration drives were conducted and above all you kept us publicly exposed. I have received calls from all over the State of Texas on how good our Master Masons look in church. People are beginning to respect us again and many are making request to join our order. Brothers, we must double our prosperity because he who does not cultivate his fields will die of hunger.[61]

On the negative side, Connor reported having "to make some tough decisions that were very controversial and unpopular." Such included suspension of some brethren who borrowed money without permission (some of whom had subsequently been reinstated following repayment of the money), removal of ineffective and insubordinate Worshipful Masters, consolidation of inactive lodges, and withdrawal of fraternal recognition from the Masonic Grand Chapter, Order of the Eastern Star.[62] He reported attempting to schedule three different meetings with leaders of the latter body and coming close to reaching an agreement on April 28, only to have the Eastern Star attorney decide that the matter should be resolved by a judge.[63] He reported that, thus far, the Grand Lodge had spent $8,000 in the court battle with the Eastern Star and $12,000 in response to a lawsuit by Past Grand Secretary C. A. Glaspie.[64]

In this address, Connor spoke on the State of the Country, urging all members of the Prince Hall Masonic Family to vote in the upcoming presidential election. He warned of the dangers of efforts to abolish affirmative action, saying "If we lose affirmative action, we might as well learn how to pick cotton again."[65] He reported meeting in St. Louis with the Grand Master of California and reaching an agreement that both Grand Lodges would promote Prince Hall Masonry in Hawaii, with the anticipation that Hawaii would one day be a separate jurisdiction.[66]

Connor reported the sale of the old Grand Lodge office to the Grand High Court, Heroines of Jericho, for $50,000. He expressed satisfaction that "The building was kept in the Masonic Family and its use will be to benefit the local community." He also reported the sale of the property belonging to Blazing Star Lodge No. 363, stating that the proceeds were placed in the North Central Credit Union, with plans to give 50% of the funds to Fairfield Lodge No. 452, minus legal fees.[67]

In conclusion, Connor said:

> We have made some giant steps toward the 21st century and I feel strongly that we will make more, as a family, and as sisters and brothers. We should ever bear in mind that the Masonic Fraternity is no association of mere mystic dreamers, no aggregation of selfish individuals banded together for social amusements, but it is a great society, which under God's providence and guidance, has a duty to perform, in the generation of the human race, and that these Annual Communications should be an inspiration toward higher thoughts, nobler actions, and grander achievements, that we might attain the glorious destiny which has been marked out for us. Let's keep Prince Hall Masonry alive in Texas, and let us keep God in our lives.[68]

Later that day, Grand Master Connor and his officers were reelected.[69] On June 20, 1996, all elected and appointed officers were installed by Past Grand Master Edwin B. Cash.[70]

On October 26, 1996, Connor sent the following communication to all elected and appointed Grand Lodge officers, District Deputies, Special Deputies, Worshipful Masters, Wardens, heads of appendant bodies, Master Masons and all beholding to the Grand Lodge, with instructions to be read in four stated meetings:

> On October 25, 1996, the Injunction and Contempt of Court charges filed against the Grand Master and the Most Worshipful Prince Hall Grand Lodge of Texas and its Jurisdiction, F&AM, were dismissed and dissolved. Judge Paul Enlow of the 141st Judicial District Court of Texas in Tarrant County, ruled that the Grand Master had the authority to withdraw fraternal recognition from the Masonic Grand Chapter, Order of Eastern Stars and to organize a new Grand Chapter. This decision was favorable, but not a victory, because it will have an effect on our Masonic Family for some time.

> On October 26, 1996, I authorized the organization of a new Grand Chapter which will be beholding to the Most Worshipful Prince Hall Grand Lodge of Texas. . . .
>
> *Eastern Stars from the Masonic Grand Chapter Order of Eastern Stars (The Old Grand Chapter) are now considered Clandestine, however, their members can join the new Local Chapters regardless of age. They cannot be a member of the old Grand Chapter Order of Eastern Stars and participate in any recognized Prince Hall Masonic Body. Their membership must be unsolicited and of their own free will.*[71]

In January 1997 Grand Master Connor and his wife attended a special function for Grand Master Joseph W. Regian of the white Grand Lodge of Texas sponsored by the Masons of North Texas at Hella Shrine Temple in Garland, Texas. He observed that everyone in attendance was cordial and courteous and gave him the respect due to a Grand Master. At this event, he was able to exchange many ideas and discuss different views.[72]

On January 31, 1997, Connor attended a special Summit of Prince Hall Grand Masters in Baltimore. The focus of this summit was relations between the Grand Masters Conference and other Masonic bodies.[73] Shortly afterward, the Grand Lodge Board of Directors met and made a number of decisions. They increased educational scholarships to $20,000; discussed changing the days of the Grand Lodge Communication to Friday, Saturday, and Sunday; discussed moving the annual session around the state, returning to Fort Worth every three years; reduced honoraria; and agreed to have the Grand Lodge attorney seek the removal of the words "Prince Hall Affiliation" from the name of the Masonic Grand Chapter, Order of the Eastern Star, and restitution for all legal expenses.[74]

In March 1997 Connor urged lodges to elect officers who were able to be accessible to the craft and to consider changing their meeting times to Saturdays during the day for the benefit of older brethren and members who work at night. He also mentioned the need for consolidation, where appropriate.[75]

During the 122nd Annual Communication in June 1997, the Grand Lodge was visited by Grand Masters Howard Woods of Arkansas, Deary Vaughn of Oklahoma, and Ralph Slaughter of Louisiana.[76] Connor delivered his Grand Master's Address on June 24, expressing gratitude for being able to attend approximately seventy-five events during the 1996-97 Masonic Year.[77] He reported the following progress:

> The overall condition of the Most Worshipful Prince Hall Grand Lodge of Texas and its Jurisdictions is good. Our membership increase for the Masonic Year 1996-97 is 470 new Master Masons. As of April 30, 1997, we had 330 brothers to be called in by the Grand Master of the Universe. We continue to reduce our indebtedness. Our financial status is in the black, despite a decrease in membership and high attorney fees. The Masonic Mosque has sustained itself and the relief checks of $300 are ready to be issued by the Grand Senior Warden on tomorrow. The Most Worshipful Prince Hall Grand Lodge of Texas is now on the Internet and we have received over 600 visits since April on our Website. Our average age per member is decreasing and we have young men who are willing to keep Prince Hall Masonry alive in Texas. I have requested Masonic Recognition from the Mother Grand Lodge of England and I strongly feel that this request is a reality. . . .
>
> Our records indicate that the local Prince Hall lodges of Texas donated more than $30,000 in scholarships the past Masonic year and, brothers, that is something to be

proud of. We participated in more than 200 programs in our local communities throughout Texas this year with many of those programs geared towards voter registration and helping the unfortunate in our local communities. Master Masons, we did an outstanding job, but we have a long way to go. We need more participation in our communities, our local schools, we need to support our churches more and we need more activities that will involve our families. This will truly enhance the State of the Order.[78]

Connor reported good meetings of the Conference of Prince Hall Grand Masters and of the Southwest Region of Prince Hall Grand Masters. He also reported a number of very positive contacts with Grand Master Regian of the white Grand Lodge of Texas, who had been very respectful and cordial to our Grand Lodge. He observed that Prince Hall Masons could learn much from the programs of Regian's Grand Lodge, which is much stronger in membership and finances. However, he stressed that there had been no discussion of consolidation or recognition. He discussed plans to meet with some black non-Prince Hall Grand Masters, with the hope of one day bringing all African-American Masons together.[79]

To clear up some confusion, Connor ruled that the official emblem of the Heroines of Jericho in Texas is the Spinning Wheel rather than the Cross and the Crown, which should be regarded as the property of the Guilds, the ladies auxiliary to the Knights Templar. He said, "It was my prayer that this change would be made without a fight, separation, or court battle."[80] He reported progress being made by the new Grand Chapter of the Order of the Eastern Star which, while still in its infant stage, had already established approximately 43 chapters and obtained nearly 2,000 members.[81] He reported a successful 1996 meeting of the Imperial Council of the Mystic Shrine in Houston and looked forward to a successful 1998 meeting of the Supreme Council of the Scottish Rite in Dallas.[82]

Connor concluded his 1997 address by declaring that "Brotherly Love, Relief, and Truth are still the fundamental values of life and a civilized society. Freemasonry is just as relevant in today's world as it was in days long passed. It is only the methods and the approaches that are different! . . . With the help of God, we can accomplish and overcome anything."[83] Later that day, he and his officers were reelected.[84]

At the 122nd Annual Grand Communication, Grand Master Connor was authorized by the craft "to take all actions necessary to defend the lawsuit filed by the Masonic Grand Chapter Order of Eastern Star and to preserve the Constitution, Regulations, Statutes, Customs, Usages, and Traditions of Prince Hall Masonry."[85] A similar resolution was adopted by the Grand Lodge's Board of Directors, who authorized "the Grand Master and the Grand Legal Advisor to take all actions necessary to defend the lawsuit and to protect the existence, history, and further of the Organization and to uphold its Constitution and other laws."[86]

On June 26, 1997, Grand Master Connor and his officers were installed for the 1997-98 Masonic Year.[87]

On August 7, 1997, Justice William Brigham of the Court of the Appeals for the Second District of Texas in Fort Worth upheld the ruling of the 141st District Court of Tarrant County and "further ordered that Brenda Rorie, Grand Worthy Matron, and Masonic Grand Chapter Order of Eastern Star pay all costs of this appeal."[88]

However, subsequently, the Masonic Grand Chapter was awarded $352,000. In a special session, members of the Grand Lodge voted to appeal this decision.[89] Toward the end of the year, Connor reported:

> Each Master Mason of the Texas Jurisdiction is expected to make a donation of $100 to help in our legal battle with the Masonic Grand Chapter Order of Eastern Stars. . . .
> We were forced to put up a $396,000 cash bond to prevent the Masonic Grand Chapter from liquidating our assets—taking our land and buildings. The monies were borrowed from a bank and our monthly payments far exceeds $25,000 a month. We anticipate spending another $100,000 in legal fees fighting this case.[90]

A few months later, he wrote to the craft, reporting the recent deaths of Grand Recorder A. D. Harris, Grand Tiler C. B. Cheatham, and Scholarship Director Tommy Watson, saying, "It is my prayer that Our Heavenly Father will continue to watch over the families of those Master Masons who have traveled that last journey before us."[91] He addressed a number of matters, including merger of publications with *The Family Masonic Quarterly* succeeding *The Texas Prince Hall Masonic Quarterly* and now recognized as the only official newsletter for the Masonic family; the changing of the name of the Masonic Mosque to the Masonic Temple; and the need for more donations to the legal fund, in view of the obligation to pay $10,000 per month on a loan of $396,000 and the estimate of $60,000 for attorney fees.[92]

Connor called for changes in the Grand Lodge relief system, a system developed at a time when black men had trouble getting other types of insurance but which has much less relevance today. He called for replacing the present relief system with a Masonic Burial Association whose membership would be voluntary and which would be supported by premiums which association members would pay in addition to Grand Lodge dues.[93] He proposed the adoption of the following "Mission Statement" by the Grand Lodge:

> The Most Worshipful Prince Hall Grand Lodge of Texas, F&AM, is a non-profit organization which embodies an attractive system of morality, veiled in allegory and illustrated by symbols.
> The fraternity, founded upon Christian principles established in the Holy Bible, strives to teach a man the duty he owes to God, his neighbor, and to himself; but interferes neither with religion nor politics, as if prescribes the practice of virtues in the conduct of its business.
> The foundation is *Character*. Its purpose is *Service*. Its measure is *Giving*. Its foundation is perpetuated by making "*Good Men Better*." Its purpose is service, which is rendered to the people of Texas to improve their *social, cultural, and economic conditions. Its measure is giving, an act of unselfish sacrifice for the benefit of others.*[94]

In his May 1998 message to the craft, Connor spoke of preparations for the 1998 Communication and wrote: "I ask that each of you come to the Grand Session with a positive attitude and a vision for the future as we prepare to enter into the 21st Century. We are worthy of reaching for the greatest of accomplishments."[95]

During the 123rd Annual Grand Communication, which was held in June 1998, distinguished visitors included Grand Master Deary Vaughn of Oklahoma; Deputy Grand Master Sheldon Redden of Maryland; and both Grand Marshal Ronald James and Ways and Means Committee Chairman Fred Johnson of Arkansas. At this session, the Norris Wright Cuney Award—the highest award in Texas Prince Hall Masonry—was given to William E. Woods, Hubert L. Reece, and Willie High Coleman. The award of Lodge of the Year was given to Lyons Jr. Lodge No. 290, Master Mason of the Year to Tony Jordan, and District of the Year to District No. 19.[96] At this session, Connor asked each brother to donate $5 to the family of James Byrd, Jr., the victim of a nationally publicized hate crime in Jasper, Texas. He reported raising around $1,095 for the Byrd family.[97]

In his 1998 Grand Master's Address, Connor reported that the average age for Texas Prince Hall Masons had dropped from sixty-five to approximately fifty-eight. He spoke of a great deal of enthusiasm within the craft and addressed the need for change to keep up with a changing society, saying that "If we resist change, the world will pass us by." He reported a very busy Masonic year, with attendance at a number of banquets, initiations, elections, funerals, and functions of various concordant bodies. He described the Grand Master, Grand Secretary, and Grand Treasurer as "work horses" who are the only elected officers "who are mandated to make many sacrifices." Connor thanked the Grand Secretary and the Grand Treasurer for their hard work. He reported that the Grand Lodge was spending a lot of money on litigation with the Masonic Grand Chapter, Order of the Eastern Star, having spent more than $60,000 on litigation and over $50,000 on repayment of a $396,000 loan. He also reported selling a number of pieces of property throughout Texas, including a parking lot in downtown Fort Worth, and placing funds in excess of $20,000 in the Rio Grande Federal Credit Union for emergency purposes. He stated that each brother had been asked to donate $100 for the litigation because the loan would cost more than $40,000 per year in interest. Due to these financial demands, he said, the Board of Directors had reduced that year's relief payments to $200.[98] He reported issuing a dispensation to establish Alvin B. Amos UD Lodge in Uijonibu, Korea, on March 18, 1997. Being satisfied of the capabilities of this lodge of thirty members, he recommended that it be chartered and given a number.[99]

Connor expressed concern about inactive lodges, with more than 50% of the lodges from twelve different districts not initiating a candidate during the previous year. He also expressed concerns about lodges that are initiating candidates but not keeping them. He said: "We run them off arguing at every meeting; failing to teach and instruct them about Masonry; and we price ourselves out to the market." He also pointed out a serious problem in the deterioration of many lodge properties, with the grass left uncut, the windows knocked out and unrepaired, the buildings left unpainted, the rest rooms not properly functioning, and the neighborhood being taken over by "crackheads." He declared: "Now, Brothers, we can do better, I know we can." He called for involvement of Prince Hall Masons in the rebuilding of neighborhoods and the reestablishment of community pride.[100] Regarding possible relations with black four-letter (i. e., non-Prince Hall) Masons, he said: "I feel there is strength in unity. I don't have a problem with functioning publicly with black four-letter Masons. I don't feel we should bring them into our lodge halls unless they have been healed and a member of the Most Worshipful Prince Hall Grand Lodge of Texas." He stressed his policy of not dropping from lodge rolls any Master Mason over the age of sixty-five with forty years of membership. He urged local lodges to establish charitable programs to aid such brethren, especially those in hospitals and nursing homes who are unable to pay their dues.[101]

Connor recommended that the following "Mission Statement" be adopted:

> The Most Worshipful Prince Hall Grand Lodge of Texas, F&AM is a non-profit organization which embodies an attractive system of morality, veiled in allegory and illustrated by symbols.
>
> The fraternity, founded upon Christian principles established in the Holy Bible, strives to teach a man the duty he owes to God, his neighbor, and to himself; but interferes neither with religion nor politics as it prescribes the practice of virtues in the conduct of its business.
>
> The foundation is Character. Its purpose is Service. Its measure is Giving. Its foundation is perpetuated by making "Good Men Better." Its Purpose is service, which is rendered to the people of Texas, to improve their social, cultural, and economic conditions. Its measure is giving, an act of unselfish sacrifice for the benefit of others.
>
> The Mission statement is promulgated by the Most Worshipful Prince Hall Grand Lodge of Texas and the Subordinate Lodges owing obedience to the same, and by its Supreme Authority.[102]

Connor dealt with the continuing problem of Masons who are contributing nothing to the fraternity but always complaining and seeking to tear down rather than build up. He said:

> As of today, we are not going to accept those types of individuals and leaders. You need to lead, follow, or get out of the way. The Most Worshipful Prince Hall Grand Lodge of Texas is better off with 4,000 dedicated and sincere Master Masons rather than packing an extra 4,000 more Masons who are dead weight. If we all did what was expected of us, the burdens would be lighter and many issues would be resolved quicker and there would be more time for brotherhood. If you don't want to be a Master Mason, just get out and quit complaining because Masonry is not in your heart.[103]

In response to questions about relief payments, he put the following disclaimer on record:

> It must also be clearly understood that the Most Worshipful Prince Hall Grand Lodge of Texas, F&AM is a non-profit organization and not an insurance agency. Charity donations to beneficiaries of deceased Master Masons are voluntary and not mandatory. No donations will be given to an estate. Donations will be given to the beneficiary designated by the deceased Master Mason. In case of any controversy, the Grand Master and a committee of three will determine who the recipient will be.[104]

He reported the attendance of 250 youth at the Grand Lodge's first Annual Youth Day and described these young people as "potential Master Masons, Heroines of Jericho, and Eastern Stars." He thanked the participating Master Masons, especially Brothers Charles Dewitt and Steve Powell.[105]

Following the Grand Master's Address, the election of officers was conducted by Past Grand Master Reuben G. White. Grand Master Connor was unanimously re-elected. Herman L. Gabriel was nominated for the office of Grand Master but declined. He was later reelected as Deputy Grand Master. William E. Woods was reelected as Grand Senior Warden, turning back a challenge from Lester Williams. The following officers were also elected: Wilbert M. Curtis, Grand Junior Warden; John H. Pointer, Grand Secretary; Kerven W. Carter, Jr., Grand Treasurer; Rev. Norris Jackson, Grand Tiler; and Rev. Howard Anderson, Grand Auditor.[106]

Connor commended Tony Jordan for his excellent work with "Hope Across Texas," which raised $5,000 for each of the following organizations: American Cancer Society, American Red Cross, Make a Wish Foundation, and United Negro College Fund.[107] The Warrant Committee agreed to furnish to Mosier Valley Lodge No. 103 in Fort Worth and to True Service Lodge No. 399 in Richardson new charters at no cost. The committee recommended that Goodwill Lodge No. 313 in Ferris and St. Timothy Lodge No. 68 in Chatfield be required to purchase new charters from the Grand Lodge.[108]

At the 1998 Communication, Shaft L. Washington, Secretary of Grand Temple Lodge No. 75 in Fort Worth, was the youngest Mason in attendance; while ninety-three-year-old Soleless Glover of Madisonville was the oldest Mason in attendance.[109]

In response to concerns raised at the Grand Communication, Connor issued an edict prohibiting the wearing of earrings during Masonic functions or meetings, granting exceptions only in the case of Shriners belonging to units employing earrings as part of ritualistic dress. This edict also prohibited Master Masons from wearing any clothing with Masonic emblems or the name of a local lodge in any establishment of entertainment, such as nightclubs and bars, where alcoholic beverages are sold and consumed. This edict did not apply to Masonic rings and lapel pins. He spoke of plans for celebration of our 125th anniversary in 2000 and of the goal of 2,000 new members by 2000.[110]

On January 30, 1999, a special session of the Grand Lodge was held in Fort Worth, with over 600 Masons in attendance. At this session, the craft voted unanimously for the Grand Lodge to purchase a blanket insurance policy that would provide one million dollars of liability insurance on every Texas Prince Hall Mason when conducting business for either the local lodge or the Grand Lodge; to purchase a fidelity bond to guard against any dishonesty on the part of the financial officers of every lodge in Texas; and the payment of a premium of $40 per year by each local lodge. At this meeting, Connor explained his plans for consolidation, stating that each local lodge should have a minimum of twenty active members and that any local lodge with less than seven members on its official roll would be consolidated if it was unable to increase its membership within six months. He called upon District Deputies to monitor lodges with memberships between seven and twenty members and seek to assist them in building their memberships.[111] The craft agreed that no form of hazing should be tolerated and upheld the Grand Master's disciplinary actions against lodges charged with hazing. They unanimously voted to continue the litigation against the Masonic Grand Chapter, Order of the Eastern Star, taking the fight all the way to the U. S. Supreme Court if necessary, and to assess each Master Mason $100 to help finance the litigation.[112]

On February 1, 1999, Connor received a proposal from the Eastern Star attorneys, offering to give a $10,000 discount on the amount of the judgment, provided the Grand Lodge met certain conditions. Connor found the conditions totally unacceptable and insisted that "acceptance of this proposal would be a disgrace for all Prince Hall Masons."[113]

Three months later, Connor wrote:

> During the 1998-99 Masonic Year, we were able to accomplish many of our goals. The Knights of Pythagoras is now organized and operating. Master Masons desiring to be leaders in the Masonic Fraternity are now attending Masonic Schools of Instruction put on by District Lecturers.
>
> Our yearly calendar is now organized so that all Grand Lodge business can be completed by the last of November, thus allowing our appendant bodies to conduct their state meeting during the second half of the Masonic Year without any conflict....
>
> Our 124th Annual Grand Communication is predicted to be one of the best.... More than $1,000 in prize monies will be given out during our Youth Day Competition for the best Christian Drill Teams.
>
> We are planning on giving out approximately $20,000 in scholarship monies to graduating seniors throughout the State of Texas who participated in the J. T. Maxey Scholarship Program....
>
> The OES Litigation is still ongoing. The State Supreme Court denied our petition for review, but our attorneys are exhausting other avenues to the State Supreme Court or the United State Supreme Court.[114]

In June 1999 the 124th Annual Grand Communication was held in Houston, Texas. This marked the first session outside of Fort Worth since 1905. Distinguished visitors to this meeting included Grand Masters Ralph Slaughter of Louisiana, Howard Woods of Arkansas, and Deary Vaughn of Oklahoma. During the first day, an occasional lodge was opened by Highland Heights Lodge No. 200 of Houston. Rev. John Butler preached during the Saint John's Day and Memorial Service. Luncheon speakers were Judge Al Green and Grand Legal Advisor Willie H. Coleman. The speaker for the Masonic Family Banquet was Dr. Benjamin Hooks, Past President of the NAACP and Grand Secretary for the Prince Hall Grand Lodge of Tennessee.[115] On Sunday morning, during the Joint Family Devotion Service, the sermon was delivered by Grand Chaplain E. Brice Cunningham.[116]

On June 18, 1999, Connor delivered his Grand Master's Address, in which he reported that "we were able to accomplish many of our goals despite an ongoing litigation." Among the goals achieved was the receipt of a state charter for the Knights of Pythagoras, with four councils; and the development of Masonic Schools of Instruction by District Lecturers. He commended Grand Senior Warden William Woods for an outstanding job in supervising the Grand Lodge housing complexes, operation of conventions, and administration of the Masonic Burial Fund. He stated that Woods "saved the Grand Lodge a lot of grief and money." He commended Grand Junior Warden Wilbert Curtis for an outstanding job in performing duties related to the Knights of Pythagoras, Masonic Charitable Donations, Hope Across Texas, and Credentials/Registration during the Grand Lodge session. He commended Grand Treasurer Kerven W. Carter for an outstanding job in keeping up with our finances and supervising the J. T. Maxey Scholarship project. He commended the Grand Legal Advisor for an outstanding job in representing the Grand Lodge in the OES litigation, serving as advisor on all grievances and disciplinary actions, and assisting in the preparation of documents for the selling and leasing of various properties of the Grand Lodge.[117] Regarding Grand Secretary John Pointer, he said:

> Our Grand Secretary was assigned to manage the Grand Masonic Temple and to collect records for our archives. We survived the entire year with only one office personnel. He is currently making plans for a Prince Hall Masonic Library so that we can display our archives. The Prince Hall Library would also assist in reducing our property taxes by approximately $20,000 a year. Brother Pointer has done an outstanding job.[118]

He spoke of the establishment of the Masonic Learning Center, whose purpose is to disseminate Masonic information for use in instruction in the three degrees of the Blue Lodge and to provide a resource for Master Masons in search of more light in Masonry.[119] He reported that at the 1999 session of the Conference of Prince Hall Grand Masters, Grand Master Howard Woods of Arkansas stepped down from the office of president because of his health and was succeeded by Grand Master Deary Vaughn of Oklahoma, with Grand Master Benjamin Barksdale of Georgia elected Vice President. He stated that the Conference appointed a committee to seek to resolve existing problems between Prince Hall Masonry and the Church. He further stated that each Grand Lodge seems to be facing many of the same problems: "A drop in membership, public perception, preparation of the younger Masons for leadership roles, negative conduct by Master Masons, lack of community involvement by local lodges, and keeping up with the current times both spiritually and financially."[120] Regarding the continued legal battles, he said:

> At some point this body must make a decision about the OES Litigation. In January you voted to fight this case to the United States Supreme Court. I have carried out your orders thus far. I can not promise you we will win this litigation but we must maintain our pride and dignity and we must support and protect Norris Wright Cuney Grand Chapter. I ask the craft, for the good of the order, to seriously consider permitting the Board of Directors to pay off the Masonic Grand Chapter OES and concentrate on moving forward into the New Millennium with the Norris Wright Cuney Grand Chapter and leave the door open for any member of the Masonic Grand Chapter Order of Eastern Star to come over without any humiliation. We cannot afford to dwell and respond to a negative issue any longer. We have done what was right and I have to believe that right will prevail. Right has never wronged anybody. This Grand Body made the right decision in regards to the Masonic Grand Chapter Order of Eastern Stars. You cannot compromise what is right. If you do, you will have to make excuses from now on. The book of Jeremiah reminds me that it may be time for us to move on and not question the work of God.[121]

Connor recalled a special retreat for the Board of Directors in Port Arthur, Texas that was organized by the late Grand Master Thomas H. Routt in order to establish a plan for the future of the Grand Lodge. He cited a number of elements of Routt's vision. Such included the computerization of the Grand Lodge office, the move of the annual session from city to city, a joint *Masonic Family Quarterly*, a relief system that would maintain itself, better training of Masons for leadership roles, the payoff of the Masonic Mosque, both the Masonic Mosque and the Prince Hall apartment complexes becoming self-supportive, the activation of the Knights of Pythagoras in Texas, an efficient Grand Lodge office staff, and a balanced budget to eliminate operating at a deficit. He cited the requirement that members of every local lodge attend church once a year together as fulfillment of Routt's call to keep God in our plans.[122]

During the 1999 Communication, Grand Master Connor was reelected, turning back a challenge from Deputy Grand Master Herman Gabriel. Grand Senior Warden William Woods was promoted to Deputy Grand Master, with no opposition. Grand Junior Warden Wilbert Curtis was promoted to Grand Senior Warden, defeating Roosevelt Tennessee and Howard Anderson. Michael Anderson was elected as Grand Junior Warden, defeating Tony Jordan and George Boutee. Albert Johnson was elected Grand Tiler, with no opposition. John Pointer was reelected as Grand Secretary, defeating Albert Van Slyke. Howard Washington and Ernie Williams were elected as Grand Auditors.[123]

Two months after the 1999 session, Connor gave the following explanation of a major change adopted by the Grand Lodge:

> The Masonic Burial Association was voted on and established during a Special Grand Session. It was ratified during our Annual Grand Session.
> Letters were mailed to each local lodge explaining that every Master Mason who wanted to participate in the Masonic Burial Association received $200 each. The beneficiaries of master masons who did not participate in the Masonic Burial Association will not receive any funds.
> The operations of the Masonic Burial Association will be somewhat different for the 1999-2000 Masonic year as $10 from each Master Mason paid to the Grand Lodge will be placed into an interest-bearing account in the form of a CD.
> Upon expiration of the CD (one year), the funds will be divided equally between the beneficiaries of Master Masons who died during the 1999-2000 Masonic year. It is very important that all dues are submitted to the Grand Lodge Office in a timely manner.[124]

In the same column, Connor called for participation of Prince Hall Masons in "Operation Blood Drive" and publication of each lodge's Prince Hall Day Activities in local newspapers during September 1999.[125]

The Grand Lodge did receive publicity as a result of an event in September 1999. However, it was not the positive publicity envisioned by Connor. On September 24 it was alleged that a hazing incident occurred at Thomas H. Routt Lodge No. 639 in Arlington. The initiate who brought the charge claimed to have received injuries severe enough to require treatment in a hospital emergency room. The incident was investigated by the Arlington Police Department and the information forwarded to the Tarrant County District Attorney. Members of the lodge denied that any hazing occurred. An attorney for the plaintiff telephoned the Grand Lodge and demanded $300,000 for his client. The Grand Legal Advisor prepared for the Arlington Police Department a report which included the names, addresses, and telephone numbers of every individual who was present at the meeting where the hazing was alleged to have occurred. He reiterated the Grand Lodge rules against hazing and the position that "the Grand Lodge does not support criminal behavior and will not attempt to protect any individuals who participate in criminal activity." As a result, seventeen Masons were suspended pending hearings, and the lodge's charter was revoked. All members of this lodge who were not involved in the incident were placed in the Grand Temple Holding Lodge.[127]

Toward the end of 1999, as the Annual Communication of the white Grand Lodge of Texas in Waco approached, Connor addressed the issue of fraternal recognition:

> I have been contacted on several occasions about fraternal recognition with the Texas Grand Lodge (Caucasian Grand Lodge). I have no knowledge about any form of recognition mentioned above nor do I intend to entertain such until Prince Hall Masons are recognized as Men and Master Masons.
>
> No one should consider passing or recommending any resolutions to recognize Prince Hall Masons in Texas until the issue is first discussed. We are legitimate and not sitting around waiting on someone to recognize us.[128]

On February 26, 2000, a Special Grand Communication was held at the Grand Masonic Temple in Fort Worth. Approximately 300 Masons attended the session, which should be judged as successful and productive. The craft voted to allow brethren who had not paid the $100 assessment which was levied at the 1999 Special Grand Communication to remain on the rolls provided they pay $25 per year toward the assessment until paid in full. This action prohibited any member from holding an office in any house of Masonry until the assessment is paid in full and called for the deduction of the assessment from any beneficiary check issued to heirs of Masons who die before the assessment is paid in full. The craft voted unanimously to assess each member $20 per year for the next five years in order to remodel the Grand Masonic Temple; and to establish a Prince Hall Masonic Library and Museum to be located inside the Grand Masonic Temple. The Grand Master stated that the name change and operation would reduce our property taxes approximately 60%. The proposed budget for 2000-01 was adopted. There was also an update on litigation. Confronted by repeated setbacks in the state courts and the slim prospects of winning in the federal courts, the Grand Master and the Grand Lodge agreed to cease all litigation with the Masonic Grand Chapter, Order of the Eastern Star.[129]

On May 15, 2000, Grand Master Connor wrote a letter to Deputy Grand Master William E. Woods, informing him that he was arresting his jewels and suspending him from the Grand Lodge rolls for an indefinite period due to Un-Masonic Conduct. Such disciplinary action resulted from Woods' purchase of a 2000 Mercury Marquis for use in traveling to the Prince Hall apartment complexes owned by the Grand Lodge in various Texas cities without permission of the Grand Master or the trustees of the Prince Hall Charitable Trust. Connor informed Woods of his right to have his case heard upon its merits and stated that he would appoint a tribunal to hear the case prior to the opening of the 2000 Grand Lodge Communication, upon a written request.[130] On June 2, 2000, Woods wrote a letter to Connor, apologizing for not keeping him informed of the complete transaction and stating that it was not his intent to bring discord into the Grand Lodge and, therefore, he wished to apologize for his actions.[131]

In June 2000 the 125th Annual Grand Communication was held in Houston. During this session, the Committee on Grievance and Appeals, consisting of Howard Anderson, Wendell Smith, Charles Potter, and Malachi Dews, Jr., submitted the following report:

> Discussion: It is our opinion that Woods violated his oath of obligation; however, there was no financial loss to the Grand Lodge or to the Prince Hall Charitable Trust.... The personal gain for Woods was the use of the vehicle to conduct Trust business. Metro Property Managers recovered the vehicle from Woods and will subsequently sell the vehicle with no penalty to the Trust.
>
> Conclusion: The loose interpretation of the Trust Agreement and the manner in which the Trustees handled the business of the Trust (verbally and few written instructions) created misunderstandings. Appropriate adjustments are now in place for the Trust to move confidently into the 21st century. In our judgment, and with the concurrence of the Grand Lodge, Woods should be restored with his rights and privileges as a Master Mason.[132]

Woods was admitted to the chambers and brought before the altar. He indicated that his letter was a statement of apology to the Grand Lodge, to which he had no intention to bring discord. His apology was greeted with warm applause. He then left the room, and the craft voted to reinstate him to membership. Upon his return, Connor informed him of the vote and returned his jewels to him. This was followed by more warm applause.[133]

The speaker for the 2000 Annual Family Banquet was Rev. De'Von Jackson, a member of Highland Heights Lodge No. 200 in Houston. The speaker for the Awards Banquet was Waller County Commissioner Frank Jackson, a member of Lone Star Lodge No. 85 in Prairie View. Rev. Howard Anderson, Deputy Grand Chaplain, preached at the Annual Saint John's Day and Memorial Service.[134]

In his 2000 Grand Master's Address, Connor described an important meeting in Boston, Massachusetts:

> The Deputy Grand Master, Grand Senior Warden, Grand Junior Warden, Grand Legal Advisor, and myself went to the Conference of Grand Masters in May. We participated in the customary ten-year pilgrimage and visited the grave of Prince Hall on Copps Hill. We were afforded the opportunity of holding, in our hands, the original Prince Hall Charter. To God be the Glory. Texas was well represented. The Norris Wright Cuney Grand Chapter was well represented also.[135]

He reported that "good management of our last year's budget permitted us to end the year with $100,000 plus cash on hand." He stated that, although the Grand Lodge had been somewhat slow in making payments to the Heroines of Jericho, payments had by this time been caught up.[136] He addressed the issue of consolidation, reporting considerable success in such efforts:

> We now have lodge halls that we can be proud of. They once were eyesores in our local communities but they are now being renovated. We now have lodges meeting across Texas with more than thirty Master Masons at their regular meetings. I am expecting more consolidation throughout the Jurisdiction. Consolidation builds a

stronger lodge. It does not destroy a lodge. The name and number of a lodge does not make a lodge successful. It's the work the lodge does. . . .

We now have local lodges working in the communities and increasing their membership with good men. They are conducting lectures, studying and perfecting their ritualistic skills; they are giving more educational scholarships, visiting our widows and orphans, and visiting our sick brothers who are in the hospitals and nursing homes.[137]

Connor reported much progress with the Knights of Pythagoras and the female youth groups.[138] He reminded the craft that, despite much progress, racism is still very much alive and well.[139] He reviewed some of the problems he had faced since becoming Grand Master and concluded:

When the storms for this administration comes, the Millennium Team is going to just Stand . . . Stand . . . Stand! And do what is right, as always. . . .

Like Paul (Philippians 3:14), I will continue to "press toward the mark for the prize of the high calling of this Jurisdiction." I will get the job done! With your help, when my proceedings are written the conclusion will be: Veni, Vidi, Vici: I came I saw I conquered.[140]

During the 2000 Communication, the following items were approved:

1. To organize and sponsor a Summer Youth Camp for young men throughout the Jurisdiction of Texas. The beginning limit will be forty (40) young men.
2. To convene our 126th Annual Grand Communication in Corpus Christi, Texas.
3. To hold a Mid-Winter Session in November of each year to transact business of the Most Worshipful Prince Hall Grand Lodge of Texas when necessary, and provide training for our leaders and leaders-to-be. The Mid-Winter Session will replace our Annual Regional Meetings, except the Western Regional Meeting.
4. To change the name of Safe Council Lodge #157 to James E. Carter Lodge #157.
5. To permit Beautiful Lodge #395, located in Salt Lake City, Utah to demit into the Colorado, Wyoming, and Utah Jurisdiction.
6. Authorized life membership for Brothers Rev. C. A. W. Clark, Rev. L. B. George, T. W. Neal, J. C. Williams, Lawrence (Pap) Anderson, Charley Wadley, Rev. Ernest Gates, and Robert Brown.
7. Authorized the Honorary Past Master's Degree for Brothers James C. Jones, B. T. Washington, Elvin Alley, Solomon Mouton, and Rev. John Butler.
8. Authorized the amending of the Trust Agreement of the Prince Hall Charitable Trust.
9. Cooperating with the white Grand Lodge of Texas in eliminating property taxes on lodge halls throughout the State of Texas.
10. Establishing a Prince Hall Charitable Foundation.
11. Establishing a Prince Hall Library, Museum, and Cultural Center.[141]

At the 2000 Communication, Grand Master Connor was reelected, turning back a second challenge from Past Deputy Grand Master Herman Gabriel. Deputy Grand Master William Woods was reelected, turning back a challenge from Past Grand Senior Warden Hubert Reece. Grand Senior Warden Wilbert Curtis, Grand Junior Warden Michael Anderson, and Grand Secretary John Pointer were reelected, with no opposition. Grand Tiler Albert L. Johnson was reelected, defeating Norris Jackson and Ben Horn. Samuel Hobbs, Jr., was elected as Grand Auditor, defeating Robert Hicks.[142]

Connor issued two edicts in June 2000. The first waived the bloodline requirements for interested females over the age of twenty-one (21) to join the Grand High Court Heroines of Jericho and the Norris Wright Cuney Grand Chapter Order of the Eastern Star.[143] The second required all local lodges to provide a minimum of thirty (30) minutes of training and lectures during each monthly meeting.[144]

On July 22, 2000, a Millennium Team Meeting was held at the Grand Lodge Temple in Fort Worth. Team members received a tour of the building, in order to learn about needed repairs. There was a discussion of possible ways of paying for such repairs. Also mentioned was the need for repairs on the Masonic Monument at Brenham.[145]

At this meeting, a call was made for the establishment of a Masonic Charitable Trust operating separately and apart from the Grand Lodge. In relation to this, there was a discussion of plans for a tax-exempt Masonic Library and Museum occupying 3/4 of the Temple building. When these plans become a reality, there will be tremendous savings on taxes, as the Grand Lodge administrative offices will rent space from the Library and Museum. Grand Master Connor explained that the white Grand Lodge of Texas has for many years saved money on taxes using this method. He explained that it will be necessary for the Grand Temple to be open to the public five days per week in order to be designated as a Charitable Trust. In addition, he expressed the hopes that, eventually, we will be eligible for matching funds. Also discussed was the possibility of obtaining pictures of the graves of Past Grand Masters.[146] Connor announced plans to call a special session of the Grand Lodge in November to transact a number of items of business.[147]

On November 4, 2000, the special session was held in Fort Worth. There was much discussion about the need for repairs on the Masonic Temple. Connor explained that the problems began with the foundation of the building due to a lack of beams and improper use of brick and mortar. He also addressed problems of a leaking roof and inadequate insulation. The latter, he said, had resulted in excessively high utility bills. While there was some discussion about the possibility of selling or demolishing the building, the Grand Master observed: "We need some way, somehow, to find a way to repair this building and generate revenue." The craft was informed that the building was rented about six times each year and the rental fees were higher than most buildings in Fort Worth due to the excessive cost of utilities. No action was taken on the matter of building renovation. It was agreed that a decision would be postponed until the Grand Lodge Communication in Corpus Christi in June 2001. Connor gave assurances that an itemized estimate of repair costs would be prepared by then and that a completed survey of cost figures would be sent to each lodge prior the latter meeting.[148]

At the special session, the craft voted to change from a quarterly to a semi-annual publication. Connor described the new publication as bigger and more colorful, and he called for the solicitation of advertising in order to make it more cost-effective.[149]

The Grand Master informed the craft that the Grand Lodge currently owed $140,000 to the Heroines of Jericho. We voted to sell some property in downtown Fort Worth which is currently generating no income. It was agreed that proceeds from this sale could be used to pay the Heroines.[150]

A matter of considerable controversy at this session was the Grand Lodge relief system. Many Prince Hall Freemasons now recognize that, while the payment of death benefits by fraternal organizations was very important when few other forms of insurance were available to African Americans, this service no longer fills a great need. Connor stated and many members agreed that the money currently spent on relief could be spent of purposes more suited to the year 2000. Others argued that many widows still expected to receive a relief payment from the Grand Lodge and some complained about Masons not doing enough for their husbands while they were alive. There was motion for termination of the relief system, effective April 30, 2001, as well as another motion for limiting relief benefits to those with thirty years of service. Neither motion passed. Thus it was agreed that the present relief system would be kept in place. Nevertheless, everyone seemed to agree that this issue was not going away. Some insisted that, if and when the relief system is eliminated, it should be phased out gradually, with a grandfather clause included.[151]

The last item on the agenda of the special session was adoption of the annual budget, which was approved by the craft. The Grand Master stressed the fact that it was only a projected budget. If the projected revenue did not come in, the budget would have to be adjusted accordingly.[152]

On June 1, 2001, the Grand Lodge convened in Corpus Christi. In his Grand Master's Address, Connor reported:

> The agenda for the 2000-2001 Masonic year was full. I attended the National and State meetings of our Adopted and Concordant Bodies in and outside the Jurisdiction of Texas. I attended many functions and banquets hosted by Prince Hall Masons throughout Texas. As Grand Master, I was the invited guest speaker at twenty different public functions. I made eight trips to Austin, Texas representing the Most Worshipful Prince Hall Grand Lodge of Texas and our local lodges in promoting the passing of HB 1689 and Senate Bill 1554. I spent an average of two hours per day taking care of Grand Lodge business via telephone internet or personal contacts. I attended Board Meetings of the Most Worshipful Prince Hall Grand Lodge of Texas, the Prince Hall Charitable Trust Meetings, District Meetings and Church programs for the celebration of Prince Hall Day and Palm Sunday. I attended nine funerals and presided over three of them in rural areas. Let me just say, my plate was full. It was a good year and I thank God for it. . . .
>
> On May 25, 2001, a committee including myself met with the Trustees of the Caucasian Grand Lodge of Texas in Dallas, Texas. We had dinner and Masonic discussions at the Las Colinas Country Club. We exchanged ideas and opinions that we felt were important for Freemasonry in Texas. A journey of a thousand miles begins with the first step. We took that step and I feel that a relationship of respect and cooperation has been established. I look forward to more dialogue and joint participation in public functions in the future. . . .
>
> It is important to know where we are now and where we plan to be in a certain time period. During the last Board of Directors Meeting, I presented ten areas of concerns to the Board of Directors. I asked the Board Members to prepare a five-year-plan to implement them. The areas of concerns were increasing membership, reclaiming members, keeping members, renovation of the Grand Masonic Temple, providing leadership training, technology, community relations, preservation of our archives and history, financial stability, and increasing membership in all Masonic bodies.

> Over the years, I have observed that we are in desperate need to press on with a greater determination, renewed vigor, and rededication to the principles and precepts of this great fraternity. We must overcome all challenges, whatever they may be! We can do this if we put God first, and keep Him in all of our plans. I believe that we are at a crossroad in this jurisdiction. The things that we say and the things that we do during the next few years will determine the course of this Masonic Body for years to come. If we are to realize our full potential, we must have unity. We cannot rest. The time has come to set our sights even higher. With the foundation that we have laid in the past 126 years, this organization is ready. Are we ready?[153]

Later that day, officers were elected. Connor was reelected as Grand Master, defeating Deputy Grand Master William Woods and Past Deputy Grand Master Herman L. Gabriel. Wilbert M. Curtis was elected Deputy Grand Master, defeating Roosevelt Tennessee and Hubert L. Reese. Michael T. Anderson was elected Grand Senior Warden, defeating George Boutte. Willie High Coleman, Jr., was elected Grand Junior Warden, defeating Gary Bledsoe, Roosevelt Huggins, Donald Passmore, and Albert Johnson. John Pointer was reelected Grand Secretary, and Kervin Carter was reelected Grand Treasurer without opposition. Ernie Williams was elected Grand Auditor, defeating Robert Hicks. Norris Jackson was elected Grand Tiler, defeating Joseph Ledet, Frank Williams, Carl English, and Kenneth Portley.[154]

On June 20, 2002, the Grand Lodge convened in Fort Worth. On the second day, Connor delivered his Grand Master's Address, in which he said:

> During the 2001-02 Masonic year, I attended several banquets and functions hosted by Prince Hall Masons throughout the State of Texas. I did not attend any of the National Concordant Bodies Conferences because of the September 11 tragedy and my commitment to the Summer Youth Camp.
>
> I attended the Grand Masters Conference in Las Vegas, Nevada. I had the opportunity to attend the Shrine Desert Conference in San Antonio, Texas.
>
> As your Grand Master, I visited and telephoned Master Masons, Heroines of Jericho, and Eastern Stars who were hard struck by the rainstorm of Allison in Houston, Texas. The Prince Hall Masonic Family assisted many victims of the storm with a donation of more than $7,500 in cash to State Representative Harold Dutton, a Prince Hall Mason, who got Fiesta to match our donation dollar for dollar....
>
> I made more than 25 Master Masons, and was able to use the name and tradition of Prince Hall Masons to obtain a three-bedroom house of furniture for a family that lost everything to a fire. The furniture was donated by Gallery Furniture of Houston, Texas....
>
> I attended a number of local lodge meetings and I attended a number of funerals. The past Masonic year was a success overall....
>
> Our 2001 Youth Camp was a success. We had Master Masons who took out time to supervise more than 45 young men. This Grand Lodge provided a camp, food, and many other resources to ensure that we made a difference in their lives....
>
> Recognition of Prince Hall Masons by the Grand Lodge of Texas is some distance away. We stand ready to address the issue when the time is right. We will continue to work with the Grand Lodge of Texas in any endeavor that benefits the both of us. We will walk with them and stand side by side with them, but we will never bow down to them and beg for recognition....
>
> Our founder, Prince Hall made a commitment against some dangerous odds. His

commitment was to make the world better. This is a charitable organization. We will not get any financial rewards from her nor should we expect any. You will only achieve and receive personal satisfaction and gratification that your work in this organization, along with other Master Masons, made a difference in your local community and the world.[155]

Connor and the other officers were reelected for the 2002-03 Masonic Year.[156]

On June 20, 2003, at the Radisson Astrodome Hotel in Houston, Connor delivered his final Grand Master's Address, telling the craft:

> With much regret, I must inform you that we had approximately 122 Master Masons taken from our midst by our Grand Architect of the Universe. Many of them were personal friends of mine and good Master Masons. Again, we lost some Masonic giants and some of them were giants among giants such as Senior Past Grand Master Reuben G. White and Past Grand Mashall Charles Wadley. I ask that we as Master Masons assist the widows and orphans of those Master Masons who have gone to a better place. Let us bow our heads for a few moments of our own personal silent prayers.
>
> During the 2002-03 Masonic year, I attended a number of banquets and functions hosted by Prince Hall Masons or members of the Prince Hall Masonic Family throughout the State of Texas. . . .
>
> I had the opportunity to attend the Council of Deliberation in Dallas, Texas in March 2003 and the Shriners' Desert Conference in Dallas, Texas during the month of April. Both conferences were productive and fruitful . . . I attended a number of local lodge meetings and I attended a number of funerals.
>
> The past Masonic year was busy but successful. . . .
>
> On November 5, 2002, we saw President Bush and his Republican Party celebrate a dramatic election victory that gave him the Congressional numbers to proceed with his agenda—expanding tax breaks for wealthy Americans, winning confirmation for conservative judges, building a homeland defense agency with extraordinary powers, and pursuing a showdown with Iraqi President Saddam Hussein. . . . In Texas . . . in an election with strong racial undercurrents, the Democratic strategy to mobilize African Americans, Hispanics, and White Democrats was not enough to overcome the voter turnout of White male Texas Republicans.
>
> In 2002, George W. Bush campaigned on a pledge to appoint federal judges who fit the pattern of Supreme Court Justices Antonin Scalia and Clarence Thomas—two jurists who have consistently joined rulings that have incrementally turned back the clock on hard-won civil rights gains. . . .
>
> In December 2002, Senator Trent Lott (R-Mississippi) made remarks implying that the nation was wrong for rejecting Strom Thurmond's 1948 segregationist campaign. . . .[157]
>
> I am recommending that each local lodge continue the following programs.
>
> 1. Health Education Programs
> 2. Voter Education Programs
> 3. Renovation of our Lodge Halls
> 4. Programs for Assisting our Sick and Distressed
>
> The measure of a man's real character is what he would do if he would never be found out. Every decision we make, good or bad, has consequences. I am not bound

to win, but I am bound to be true. I am bound to succeed, but I am bound to live up to what I have. I must stand with anybody that is right and part company with him when he goes wrong.[158]

During the 2003 election, the following officers were elected unanimously: Robert E. Connor, Jr., Grand Master; Wilbert M. Curtis, Deputy Grand Master; Michael T. Anderson, Grand Senior Warden; Willie High Coleman, Jr., Grand Junior Warden; Hubert L. Reece, Grand Secretary; Kerven W. Carter, Jr., Grand Treasurer; and Samuel Hobbs, Jr., Grand Auditor. The only contested office was Grand Tiler. For this position, Norris D. Jackson defeated Charles Gray and Willie Thomas.[159]

Robert Connor died of cancer on Tuesday, September 16, 2003, at the age of fifty, at Southwest Memorial Hospital in Houston. At the time of his death, he was a candidate for Harris County Precinct Seven Constable. On receiving the news, Columbus City Manager David Stall said: "We are grief stricken and left stunned by this most unexpected loss. Our thoughts and prayers are with the family."[160]

Connor was survived by his wife Deanna, stepdaughter Stacie, three sisters, three brothers, and his mother-in-law. A wake was held from 5:00 to 8:00 P.M. at the Henneke Funeral Home in Columbus and funeral at the Knights of Columbus Hall, 3845 Interstate 10 West, Columbus. Rev. Charles Purnell, pastor of Saint Paul United Methodist Church in Columbus, officiated. The program included solos by Sis. Sophia Connor, Sis. Evelyn Smith, and Bro. George Boutte; and a Resolution by Sis. Willie Mae Williams of Saint Paul United Methodist Church. There were tributes by Columbus City Manager David Stall; Brookshire, Texas, Police Chief Joe Prejean; Dyrren Davis, Basileus of Rho Beta Beta Chapter of Omega Psi Phi Fraternity; Connor's close friend and Grand Junior Warden Willie High Coleman; Fred Gray of the Southwestern Trailriders Association; Rev. Martin Williams on behalf of ministers; Grand Master Deary Vaughn of Oklahoma, on behalf of the Prince Hall Grand Masters Conference; and Deputy Grand Master Wilbert Curtis, on behalf of Master Masons. The eulogy was delivered by Dr. Howard Anderson, pastor of Carver Park Baptist Church in San Antonio. Pallbearers were Edward Brown II, Richard Ibarra, Charles DeWitt, Gary Connor, Samuel Hobbs, Jeremiah Smith, Grady Peavy, and Charles Anderson. Willing Workers Cemetery in Columbus was selected as this Grand Master's place of final rest.[161] The Prince Hall Charitable Foundation in Fort Worth was designated for memorial contributions.[162]

Robert Edmund Connor, Jr., was the Grand Master who brought the Prince Hall Grand Lodge of Texas into the 21st Century. He was highly praised for the Prince Hall Youth Camp and other community service programs. However, his administration was quite controversial in view of a number of unpopular decisions, suspensions, and lawsuits.[163]

Wilbert Marice Curtis

Wilbert Marice Curtis (1954-) is the twenty-first Grand Master of Prince Hall Masons in Texas. He was born on November 15, 1954, in Temple, Texas. Early in life, he demonstrated considerable musical abilities. While a senior at Temple High School, he qualified for the All-State Symphony Orchestra. Upon graduation from high school in May 1973, he was undecided on what he wanted to do. He had received letters from several colleges offering him music scholarships as a percussionist, and he seriously considered joining the U. S. Air Force. He underwent the required physical examination and auditioned for the Air Force Band. Because he could not get a definite assurance that he was eligible for the band, he did not enlist.[1]

In September 1973, after receiving a music scholarship, Curtis enrolled at McLennan Community College (MCC) in Waco. For three semesters he majored in music at MCC. He qualified for the All-State Junior College Concert Band for two consecutive years. However, he soon realized that the position of music teacher was the only stable musical employment he would find, and he did not wish to pursue this avenue. Thus he changed his major to computer science while continuing to participate in the bands and percussion ensembles.[2]

Curtis spent an extra year at MCC in order to obtain an Associate of Applied Science degree in computer science. He became a member of the Data Processing Management Association and the Epsilon Chapter of Epsilon Delta Pi, a computer science honor society. In 1975 the latter organization elected him as president. He appeared in the 1975-76 edition of *Who's Who in American Junior Colleges*. During this time he worked as an intern in the MCC Computer Science Department and as a weekend night computer operator at Hillcrest Baptist Medical Center. In May 1976 he received his Associate of Applied Science degree at MCC. Nearly a decade later, he returned to MCC as an adjunct instructor in computer science. He has served on MCC's Computer Information Systems Advisory Committee since 1995.[3]

On April 1, 1976, Curtis began work as an evening-shift computer operator for the Texas Farm Bureau Insurance Companies. He then enrolled in Temple Junior College under a consortium degree plan with the University of Mary Hardin-Baylor in pursuit of a bachelor's degree in computer science. His education was temporarily interrupted in 1977, when he was promoted to computer programmer at the Texas Farm Bureau and moved to the day shift. He received another promotion in September 1984, when he was appointed supervisor of the computer services department of Texas Farm Bureau. In this position he was responsible for installing computers and communication equipment and for training the office personnel in over 200 County Farm Bureaus throughout Texas. He held this position for eight years. In April 1992 he transferred back to the application programming division. In this capacity, he was project leader for automation of the processing of claim loss notices by the county office personnel and adjusters. He was responsible for conformity to standards set by the Texas Board of Insurance. In February 1998 he was promoted to project manager of development services, the position he currently holds. In 1999 he was elected to the board of directors of the Texas Farm Bureau Federal Credit Union, where he has served in several positions, including first vice president.[4]

In November 1978 Curtis married Karen Stonum of Temple. Karen brought to the marriage two daughters, Tonia and Traci Stonum. The new Curtis family lived in Waco for the next seven years. On October 2, 1981, Karen gave birth to their daughter, Valerie Dyane Curtis. In October 1985 the family moved to the Waco suburb of Hewitt. After nearly fifteen years of marriage, the couple divorced in October 1993. After eight years of single life, he married the former LaNell Carroll Cotton of Waco on December 22, 2001.[5]

After moving to Waco, Curtis moved his church membership from Mount Zion Baptist Church in Temple to Mount Carmel Baptist Church in Waco. In May 1987 he was ordained as a deacon at Mount Carmel. For a period of time, his wife played the piano while he and their daughter both played the drums. He also served this congregation as a trustee and as financial secretary. He played a major role in computerizing the financial recordkeeping, incorporating the church, and building a new educational wing. He is now a member of Toliver Chapel Missionary Baptist Church in Waco.[6]

In November 1984 Curtis was raised to the sublime degree of Master Mason in Saint John's Lodge No. 71, in Temple. He later became a member of Ed Blair Consistory No. 286, Ancient and Accepted Scottish Rite, in Temple (1985); Cheops Temple No. 200, Ancient Egyptian Arabic Order of Nobles of the Mystic Shrine, in Austin (1986); Anchor Chapter No. 67, Holy Royal Arch Masons, in Killeen (1988); Central Texas Commandery No. 37, Knights Templar, in Killeen (1992), Carnation Chapter No. 37, Order of the Eastern Star, in Temple; and Rising Sun Court No. 150, Heroines of Jericho. In 1990 he became a life member of the Phylaxis Society, a research organization for "Prince Hall Freemasons who seek more light and who have light to impart."[7] He reported:

> This has been a major influence in my life because it is an emotional outlet and a hobby. I became active in all facets of Freemasonry. I enjoy reading the history of Prince Hall Freemasonry, and how it has contributed to the African American culture in America from its inception in 1775 to the present. In October of 1989, I received the Thirty-third Degree, which is the highest degree that can be obtained in Masonry.

In May of 1990, I was elected Master of St. James Lodge #1 of Temple, Texas. In June of 1991, I was elected to a position in the Grand Lodge of Texas, which is on the state level. I am still active in that position. In addition to that, I am on the Board of Trustees of the Grand Lodge Housing complexes which include five apartment complexes in the state of Texas. One of the most memorable experiences as a Mason was on July 16, 1994, being part of the dedication of a Texas State Historical Marker for the African Americans who partook in the Texas Revolutionary War. It was the first time that African Americans had been officially recognized for taking part in the Texas Revolutionary War. The marker is placed on the site of the original state capitol. Now, the history books for Texas will have to be re-written to include these men.[8]

Curtis returned to MCC in September 1993, taking courses transferable to Baylor University, where he hoped to pursue a bachelor's degree. However, in 1994, he transferred to the Waco campus of Paul Quinn College.[9] In May 1996 he was a member of Paul Quinn's first class to receive the Bachelor of Science in Organizational Management. He is now a member of Epsilon Epsilon Lambda Chapter of Alpha Phi Fraternity, Inc.[10]

Curtis served the Prince Hall Grand Lodge of Texas as Grand Tiler from 1991 to 1995, as Grand Junior Warden from 1995 to 1999, as Grand Senior Warden from 1999 to 2001, and as Deputy Grand Master from 2001 to 2003. Upon the completion of his first year in the second highest office in Masonry, he wrote:

> As the One Hundred and Twenty-Seventh Grand Communication of the Most Worshipful Prince Hall Grand Lodge of Texas and Jurisdiction comes to a close, I can truly say that it was one of the most memorable ones for me. For the first time, as Deputy Grand Master, I had the pleasure to receive the Most Worshipful Grand Master and present him to the craft.
>
> I also had the pleasure and honor of presiding over the craft at the will and pleasure of the Grand Master. This was the most efficient and harmonious communication that I have attended. There was entertainment to be had by all.
>
> The Grand Master, again, has placed before us an aggressive trestle board. Special emphasis has been placed on promoting our youth this year. We just concluded the Prince Hall Youth Camp 2002 at Cathedral Oaks Retreat Center in Oakland, Texas. It was the second annual Youth Camp and was again a great success. . . .
>
> Prince Hall Masonry is alive and well not only for the adults, but also for our youth. Let every Prince Hall Mason get on board and make this Masonic year a great success.[11]

During the Grand Communication of 2003, he reported:

> First, I want to thank this Grand Body for re-electing me to the office of Right Worshipful Deputy Grand Master. I enjoy serving the craft.
>
> Areas of my stewardship include participating in the Board meeting and conference calls to discuss Grand Lodge business. I attended several Masonic functions as Deputy Grand Master, including banquets, balls, and, most importantly, worked at the youth camp.
>
> Most of my time and efforts have been spent working as trustee of the 5 Prince Hall sponsored apartment complexes. We are at various stages with the apartments. Most of the resources have been concentrated on Chambre in Dallas. . . . We have been

trying to sell this complex since November of 2001 but . . . it has been a very slow process. . . .

Hopefully and prayerfully, we will be able to get this behind us so that our resources can focus on the business of the Grand Lodge. Until then, we will keep moving forward with this. I want to thank Grand Legal Advisor for his support. (Oh thank heaven for e-mail).[12]

On September 21, 2003, Curtis was elected and installed as the twenty-first Grand Master by Past Grand Master Edwin B. Cash at the Knights of Columbus Hall in Columbus, Texas, following the funeral of Past Grand Master Robert E. Connor, Jr.

On November 22, 2003, at the Masonic Temple in Fort Worth, Curtis delivered his Mid-Winter Address, in which he said:

> I greet you for the first time as Grand Master in the name of The Grand Architect of The Universe. It is my prayer that you all are experiencing a reasonable amount of health, strength, and prosperity. A lot has transpired since we last met in June of this year. Most notable is the home going of Grand Master Robert E. Connor, Jr., I must say that it was a shock to us all. I ask that you all continue to pray for Sis. Deanna Connor and the Connor family.
>
> Grand Master Connor is now in that Lodge of Perfection on High; that place that is not made by hands; that place that is beyond changes and that place that we all are traveling to be one day. He left his legacy here on earth and is now at rest. Grand Master Connor will be remembered for the youth programs he implemented as a lasting tribute to him.
>
> By the authority vested in me as Grand Master, I officially change the name of the Texas Prince Hall Youth Camp to "The Robert E. Connor, Jr., Texas Prince Hall Youth Camp."
>
> I ask that you show your approval of this change by standing. Thank you.
>
> Finally, out of the respect of the memory of Grand Master Connor, last night, sixty Fellow Crafts were raised to the Sublime Degree of Master Mason. That class was named the "Robert E. Connor, Jr. Class." Will all the Master Masons of that class please stand? Thank you!
>
> Now, I must respectfully say, I faithfully served under Grand Master Connor as Deputy Grand Master since June of 2001. He had his trestle board. I worked faithfully to promote his program. Now, as Grand Master, it is time for me to promote mine.
>
> As Grand Master I have several goals that I would like to see accomplished. Right now is not the time to implement them, but I am just making the craft aware that I do have new ideas and I plan to implement those ideas at the appropriate time.
>
> Presently, as you have heard from the various reports, this Grand Lodge is in a financial bind. Our funds are at a critical point. We are having problems meeting our monthly expense obligations. The primary reason for this is low membership. Our budget was based upon a membership of 4,000 men, but due to the low count submitted on the May Reports, late reports, and no reports, the dues did not come in.
>
> At the Grand Communication, *The Five Men For $100 Plan* was implemented and was to be in effect until April 1, 2004. Because I don't see a significant increase in the number of new members, I am terminating that plan under Edict 110303-01 effective December 1, 2003. Please take due notice thereof and govern yourselves accordingly.
>
> We have a *long-term need of finance* which is being addressed by the Board. The pur-

pose is to come up with a plan to generate funds to supplement the annual dues and sustain an even flow of income throughout the year. This can be done through various fund raisers, sale of merchandise and supplies. As they are worked out, they will be presented to the craft for approval.

More pressing is our immediate need for income. We need cash now. The proposal has been presented to you and you approved it. I ask that you support this whole heartedly. This is the only way that we are going to survive through the next few lean months.

The next item of importance is the Grand Lodge Computer System. Bro. Clary Glover is our Grand Web Master and had done a fine job on our web site. We need a complete computer system. I have met with Bro. Glover and a host of other brothers who are willing to implement a new computer system. I am thereby forming a Grand Information Technology Committee, chaired by Bro. Glover, to begin work immediately. This project will be funded by pledges from individuals, lodges, districts, concordant bodies, corporate donations, and anyone else who wants to donate. Our goal is $5,000. Work will be done based on a cash and carry basis. I ask the craft to support this initiative.

The next item of concern is Texas Prince Hall Masonic Research. I want to thank the craft for allowing us to move forward on the publishing of the History of Texas Prince Hall Grand Lodge. This is going to open up many doors by exposing others to our rich heritage.

I don't want to stop there. I want to establish a Texas Prince Hall Lodge of Research. The purpose is to capture individual lodge and concordant body history, publish it, and retain it in a single repository. At this time I am appointing Bro. Frank Jackson, Grand Historian, Bro. Robert Uzzel, and Bro. Kevin Smith as the Lodge of Research Committee. The charge to this committee is to do research and formulate a plan to establish a Texas Prince Hall Lodge of Research that will include:

- Mission Statement
- Purpose
- Constitution and By-Laws
- Membership requirements
- Financial requirements
- Officers

The charge is to report the findings at the 129th Grand Communication so that it can be adopted and have the lodge in place by September 1, 2004.

Finally, it is my goal to put this Grand Lodge on a better fraternal relationship with the Prince Hall Masonic Family within the State of Texas and throughout the *globe*. We do not need to be on an island to ourselves. The Grand Old Order's principles and precepts are based on brotherly love. We need to spread that brotherly love, extend the hand of fraternal friendship abroad and make Prince Hall Masonry and all of Freemasonry better for all.

Brothers, as you see, I have plans for the Grand Lodge to move forward. I ask that you work with me and help move the Grand Lodge into the twenty-first century, ritualistically, educationally, and, most importantly, financially. We've come too far to stop now. We have too much at stake. Even though things look dark now, know that morning will surely come after the darkness.[13]

Following this address, the annual budget was reviewed and there was an appeal for donations for the renovation of the Grand Lodge Temple in the amounts of $100

(Plumb), $200 (Compass), and $300 (Square). The Grand Lodge also voted to authorize publication of this book.

All members and friends of Prince Hall Freemasonry should give the new Grand Master their prayers and support as he seeks to lead this great order in the right direction during these troubled times when such Masonic principles as brotherly love, relief, and truth are so desperately needed.

Epilogue

The title of this book is *Prince Hall Freemasonry in the Lone Star State: From Cuney to Curtis, 1875 to 2003*. The expression "Lone Star State" owes its origin to Freemasonry. Texas was a nation before it was a state, and the Grand Lodge of the Republic of Texas was organized in 1837—the year after Texas' independence from Mexico. The overwhelming majority of leaders of early Texas were Freemasons. According to a history of Texas Masonry:

> By 1846 Masons had served in nearly every major governmental post in the Republic. All the Presidents and Vice-Presidents of the Republic of Texas were Masons. In 1844, George K. Teulon, Grand Secretary of the Grand Lodge of the Republic of Texas, addressing a gathering of Masons in Portland, ME, observed: "Texas is emphatically a Masonic Country: Our national emblem, the 'Lone Star,' was selected by Freemasonry, to illustrate the moral virtues—it is a five-pointed star, and alludes to the five points of fellowship."
>
> Freemasonry was without doubt the single most important social institution in early Texas. The first public building erected in a new community was often the familiar two-story Masonic Lodge. The first floor ordinarily served as the school classroom and town meeting hall, while the lodgeroom occupied the upper floor.[1]

Slavery existed in Texas in 1846. At that time, few Texas Masons entertained serious notions about the eligibility of persons of African descent for Masonic membership, and few Texans—Masonic or otherwise—foresaw an end to the "peculiar institution." In 1861, Texas seceded from the Union to join the Confederate States of America. Four years later, after a bloody Civil War, slavery was abolished and former slaveholders in Texas and other states had to adjust to major changes in race relations. No doubt, many Texas Masons at the time could relate to the words written by Thomas Brown, former governor of Florida, in his Report of the Committee on Foreign Correspondence for his Grand Lodge:

> The slave is now as free as his former master and, in justice, entitled with him to equal protection in his civil, religious and political rights, and in person and property.... But as to the questions of their social equality; it is a subject in which we are, as Masons, most vitally concerned.[2]

After the Civil War, few white Southerners were willing to grant social equality to former slaves. Few white Masons were willing to meet black Masons on the level of equality. Many agreed with Scottish Rite Grand Commander and former Confederate General Albert Pike, who upheld the legitimacy of Prince Hall Freemasonry, but, in 1875, wrote: "I took my obligations to white men, not to negroes. When I have to accept negroes as brothers or leave Masonry, I shall leave it."[3]

The end of slavery brought Prince Hall Freemasonry to each of the former slave states. The fraternity arrived in Texas during the early 1870s and organized into a Grand Lodge in 1875. As a result, the Prince Hall Masons of Texas, like those in other states, demonstrated the truth of the following words of Joseph A. Walkes, Jr.: "The history of Prince Hall Freemasonry is in reality the history of the Black Experience in America."[4]

The lives of the twenty-one Grand Masters who have presided over the Prince Hall Grand Lodge of Texas in the past 125 years have influenced and been influenced by many important historical events. Thus it is impossible to totally separate Masonic history from other aspects of history. Much interesting information can be gleaned by examining the lives of these twenty-one men.

Richard Allen of Houston was our second Grand Master but was sixteen years older than his predecessor Norris Wright Cuney. Allen was born in 1830—the year before a Baptist preacher named Nat Turner struck terror into the hearts of slaveholders in Southampton County, Virginia, with his fiery slave rebellion. Allen was born in slavery in Richmond, Virginia. No doubt his owners heard about Nat Turner. He was thirty years old when the Civil War broke out. He was in his mid-thirties when he obtained his freedom. As the oldest of the Grand Masters, he spent more years as a slave than his one predecessor and his many successors. He was active in politics during Reconstruction. He saw many gains by African Americans during this period, followed by many losses in the subsequent post-Reconstruction era. By the time of his death in 1909, no doubt, he had been greatly saddened by the passage of numerous "Jim Crow" laws.

Norris Wright Cuney, like Richard Allen, was born in slavery. However, he appears to have been freed by his father prior to 1861, in view of his employment on steamboats during the Civil War. The years of his life (1846-1898) were short by modern standards but, nevertheless, quite eventful. He seems to have gained power in the South when most blacks were losing theirs, and his life may be viewed as a transition between the Reconstruction and "Jim Crow" periods.

Bishop Abram Grant was born in slavery in Florida in 1848 and later was sold at auction in Georgia. When he received his freedom in 1865, he was seventeen years old. Thus he did not experience slavery as an adult.

C. C. Dean was born in Texas in 1844. L. L. James was born in North Carolina in 1850. Both J. W. Madison and W. L. Kimbrough were born in Texas in 1852. H. D. Winn was born in Texas in 1862. Bishop J. W. McKinney was born in Texas in 1864. In all probability, all were born in slavery. Dean may have experienced twenty-one years of slavery, while both Winn and McKinney knew slavery only as small children.

Two other Grand Masters were born prior to 1865. Bishop J. H. Armstrong was born in 1842 in Pennsylvania, while J. A. Kirk was born in 1860 in Ohio. Due to their

birth in free states, there can be no doubt that neither was ever a slave. Armstrong is the only Grand Master to have served in the Union Army during the Civil War.

The following Grand Masters were born in Texas: Norris Wright Cuney, C. C. Dean, J. W. Madison, W. L. Kimbrough, J. W. McKinney, H. D. Winn, L. L. Lockhart, J. T. Maxey, I. H. Clayborn, Thomas H. Routt, Edwin B. Cash, and Robert E. Connor, Jr. Of those who have died, most are to be buried in Texas. W. L. Kimbrough is buried in California. The dates of death and places of burial of L. L. James, C. C. Dean, and R. H. Bradley are unknown.

The twenty-year tenure of J. W. McKinney encompassed the eras of Populism and Progressivism and the years leading up to World War I. The administration of H. D. Winn coincided with World War I and the "Years of Normalcy"; that of J. A. Kirk with the last years of the "Roaring Twenties"; that of William Coleman with the Great Depression and World War II; that of L. L. Lockhart with post-World War II era; and that of J. T. Maxey with the early years of the civil rights movement and the Vietnam War. I. H. Clayborn's sixteen-year tenure witnessed the declining years of Civil Rights activism and the post-Vietnam era. When he stepped down in June 1981, the conservative Reagan-Bush era had begun and would continue throughout the 1980s and would coincide with the administrations of Reuben G. White and Judge Thomas H. Routt. The latter Grand Master died on January 3, 1991—just thirteen days before the first American bombs fell on Iraq and Operation Desert Storm began. Prince Hall Freemasons served in this conflict, as they have in all of America's wars. In view of the fact that Masons hold various political views, it should not be surprising that others—including Rev. Jesse Jackson—opposed this conflict, as was the case with previous wars.[5]

Prior to his death in April 1994, Clayborn, a staunch Democrat, was very pleased with the election and inauguration of President Bill Clinton. The decade of the 1990s began with the administration of Routt, who was succeeded by Edwin B. Cash, who was succeeded by Robert E. Connor, Jr., the Grand Master destined to bring the Prince Hall Masons of Texas into the 21st Century. Following Connor's death in 2003, Wilbert M. Curtis, the current Grand Master, took office.

Much has been said and written in recent years about the decline of interest in Freemasonry and other voluntary associations. Loss of Masonic membership (due largely to having more funerals than initiations) is not peculiar to Texas nor to Prince Hall lodges. The problem is real. Many contemporary people observe the trappings and parlance of Masonry and conclude that the fraternity is an anachronism. Any organization that plans to survive must be relevant to the 21st Century. Such Masonic principles as brotherhood, service, and honor will never become irrelevant. Such will always play an important role in every community, regardless of race, nationality, or creed.[6] Despite criticisms without and conflicts within, I am convinced that Freemasonry has what it takes to survive. Within the African-American communities, the Prince Hall Grand Lodge of Texas has always met the challenges. I have no doubt it will continue to do so until time shall be no more! So mote it be!

Bill McDonald in his office.

Above: McDonald building.

Left: Bill McDonald

1906 Masonic Temple in Fort Worth and Grand Lodge officers.

W. D. Cain

The 1941 Masonic monument across from Saint John Church.

Fort Worth Temple.

Grand Lodge Officers during mid-1980s. Left to right, seated: Deputy Grand Master Edwin B. Cash and Grand Master Reuben G. White. Standing: Grand Legal Advisor E. Brice Cunningham, Grand Secretary Volney B. Phillips, Past Grand Master I. H. Clayborn, Grand Senior Warden Thomas H. Routt, Grand Junior Warden Jesse L. Baines, and Grand Recorder A. D. Harris.

The author speaking at Saint John Church during 1995 Pilgrimage to Brenham.

Past Grand Master Reuben G. White presiding during Pilgrimage to Brenham.

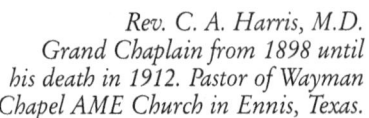
Rev. C. A. Harris, M.D. Grand Chaplain from 1898 until his death in 1912. Pastor of Wayman Chapel AME Church in Ennis, Texas.

Past Grand Master Edwin B. Cash speaking during Pilgrimage to Brenham. Standing behind him is Grand Master Robert E. Connor, Jr. Seated is Rev. L. B. George, Grand Joshua of Heroines of Jericho.

Saint John African Methodist Episcopal Church, Brenham, Texas. Site of organization of Grand Lodge in 1875 and Pilgrimage in 1995.

Endnotes

Preface
1. Joseph A. Walkes, Jr., *Jno. G. Lewis, Jr.—End of an Era: The History of the Prince Hall Grand Lodge of Louisiana, 1842-1979*. Kansas City, Missouri: Midtown Printing and Publishing Co., 1986, p. 1.

Introduction
1. Robert L. Uzzel, "Prince Hall: The Myth and the Man," *Texas Prince Hall Masonic Quarterly* 79 (December 1987): 3.
2. Ibid.
3. Ibid. For more detailed information on the life of Prince Hall, see Joseph A. Walkes, Jr., *Black Square and Compass: 200 Years of Prince Hall Freemasonry*. Richmond, Virginia: Macoy Publishing and Masonic Supply Co., Inc., 1979, and Charles H. Wesley, *Prince Hall: Life and Legacy*, Washington, D.C.: United Supreme Council, PHA, SJ, USA, Inc., 1983.
4. Charles H. Wesley, *Prince Hall Life and Legacy*, 169.
5. Joseph A. Walkes, Jr., *A Prince Hall Masonic Quiz Book*. Ames, Iowa: Research Lodge No. 2, 1981, 31-38.
6. *1875-1975 Centennial, Most Worshipful Prince Hall Grand Lodge of Texas and Jurisdiction, Free and Accepted Masons*, June 22-26, 1975 (Souvenir Journal).
7. *Proceedings of the Convention to Organize the Most Worshipful Grand Lodge, Free and Accepted Ancient York Masons of the State of Texas, held in the City of Brenham*, August 19 and 20 A.L. 5875. Galveston, Texas: McKenna and Co., 1875, 5.
8. *1875-1975 Centennial*.
9. Ibid., 13.
10. Ibid.
11. *Proceedings* (1875), 14.
12. *Proceedings of the Most Worshipful Grand Lodge, Ancient Free and Accepted Masons for the State of Texas, held in the City of Houston*, A.L. 5876, '77, '78, '79 (Galveston, Texas: McKenna and Co., 1879), 13.
13. Ibid., 20.
14. Ibid., 28.
15. *Proceedings of the Most Worshipful Grand Lodge, Ancient Free and Accepted Masons for the State of Texas, held in the Cities of Galveston, Austin and Waco A.L. 5880-81-82.* (Galveston, Texas: McKenna and Co., 1882), 12.
16. *1875-1975 Centennial*.
17. Ibid.
18. *Proceedings of the Fourteenth Annual Communication of the Most Worshipful Grand Lodge, Ancient Free and Accepted Masons for the State of Texas and Jurisdiction held in the City of Austin Commencing on the Third Tuesday in June a.d. 1889, A.L. 5889* (Houston, Texas: Smallwood, Dealy, and Baker, 1889), 7-8.
19. *1875-1975 Centennial*.

20. Ibid.
21. Ibid.
22. *Proceedings of the Forty-first Annual Communication of the Most Worshipful Grand Lodge, Free and Accepted Masons of the State of Texas and Its Jurisdiction* (Fort Worth, Texas, 1916), 21.
23. "Masonic Grand Master H. D. Winn is Dead," *Dallas Express*, March 7, 1925, 1.
24. *Proceedings of the Fifty-fifth Annual Communication of the Most Worshipful Grand Lodge, Free and Accepted Masons of Texas and Jurisdiction Belonging* (Fort Worth, Texas, 1930), 91-92.
25. *Proceedings of the Seventy-first Annual Communication of the Most Worshipful Grand Lodge of Texas, Free and Accepted Masons* (Fort Worth, Texas, 1946), 35.
26. "Hundreds Attend Rites for Grand Master Lockhart." *The Houston Informer*, October 8, 1955, 1.
27. *Proceedings of the Ninetieth Annual Grand Communication of the Most Worshipful Prince Hall Grand Lodge, Free and Accepted Masons of Texas and Jurisdiction Belonging* (Fort Worth, Texas, 1965), 43.
28. "Celebration Service," *Texas Prince Hall Masonic Quarterly* 108 (June 1994): 4.
29. *Proceedings of the One Hundred and Twelfth Annual Grand Communication of the Most Worshipful Prince Hall Grand Lodge of Texas and Jurisdiction Belonging* (Fort Worth, Texas, 1987), 21.
30. *Proceedings of the One Hundred and Sixteenth Annual Grand Communication of the Most Worshipful Prince Hall Grand Lodge of Texas and Jurisdiction* (Fort Worth, Texas, 1991), 43.

Norris Wright Cuney
1. Virginia Neal Hinze, "Norris Wright Cuney" (M.A. thesis, Rice University, 1965), abstract.
2. Paul Casdorph. *A History of the Republican Party in Texas, 1865-1965* (Austin, Texas: Pemberton Press, 1967), 46.
3. Hinze, "Norris Wright Cuney," 87. Few people in Cuney's day would have foreseen massive black involvement in the Democratic Party today. No doubt Cuney would have loudly denounced the racism exhibited in 1988—one hundred years after the "lily-white" episode—by Republican presidential nominee George Bush, who turned a tragedy involving a black man named Willie Horton into a campaign issue. Rev. Jesse Jackson, an outstanding Prince Hall Freemason, correctly exposed this type of dirty politics for the racism which it is.
4. Ibid., 89-90. Their goal was achieved during the 1930s, when many black victims of the Great Depression were helped by the social programs of the New Deal and, as a result, the majority of black voters left the party of Abraham Lincoln for the party of Franklin Delano Roosevelt. Roosevelt was a member of Holland Lodge No. 8 in New York City; see William R. Denslow, *10,000 Famous Freemasons* (Columbia, Mo.: Missouri Lodge of Research, 1961), 4:66.
5. Hinze, "Norris Wright Cuney," 124.
6. Ibid., 133.
7. Maud Cuney Hare, *Norris Wright Cuney: A Tribune to the Black People* (Austin, Texas: Steck-Vaughn Company, 1968), 162. Like one of his successors in the Grand East, I. H. Clayborn (1913-1994), Bro. Cuney regarded Texas as "God's Country."
8. Douglas Hales, *A Southern Family in White and Black: The Cuneys of Texas* (College Station, Texas: Texas A&M University Press, 2003), 4.
9. Ibid. It appears that the marriage of the widow Cuney to Caesar Archinard caused Maud Cuney Hare to mistakenly identify her grandfather's ancestors as Swiss in her biography of her father; see ibid.,143.
10. Ibid., 4-5.
11. Maud Cuney Hare, *Norris Wright Cuney: A Tribune to the Black People*, 162. Eventually, Colonel Cuney became one of the largest landowners and slaveholders in Texas. He owned 105 slaves in 1850 and 115 in 1860. However, after the end of slavery in 1865 and his death in 1866, he left his heirs with over $110,000 in debt. With no slaves and plummeting land prices after the Civil War, his debts exceeded his assets by $90,000; see Hales, *A Southern Family in White and Black*, 6-7.
12. Hinze, "Norris Wright Cuney," 3.
13. Carter G. Woodson, "The Cuney Family," *The Negro History Bulletin*, March 1948, 123.
14. Hinze, "Norris Wright Cuney," 6.
15. Hare, *Norris Wright Cuney: A Tribune to the Black People*, 7.
16. Ibid., 4.
17. Ibid. In freeing and educating his eight mulatto children, Philip Cuney has been called a "slaveholding maverick." His primary legacy was truly ironic in that his son Norris Wright Cuney became Texas' most talented and successful African-American politician during the nineteenth century, and his

granddaughter Maud Cuney Hare became a talented and important figure in the African-American community of Boston and left an important musical and literary legacy; see Hales, *A Southern Family in White and Black*, 13.
18. Ibid. Both Lewis and Pinchback were Prince Hall Freemasons.
19. Ibid., 9-10. Cuney's service in Galveston is reminiscent of the services rendered in Philadelphia in 1793 by Revs. Richard Allen and Absalom Jones, two outstanding Prince Hall Freemasons.
20. Hinze, "Norris Wright Cuney," 8.
21. Hare, *Norris Wright Cuney: A Tribune to the Black People*, 9.
22. Ibid., 80.
23. Ibid., 14.
24. Ibid., 33. Cuney died fifty-six years before *Brown v. Board of Education* declared segregated public schools unconstitutional. The attorney who argued this case before the U. S. Supreme Court was Thurgood Marshall, an outstanding Prince Hall Freemason who later would become the first African American to serve on the high court.
25. Ibid., 36-37.
26. Ibid., 32.
27. Hales, *A Southern Family in White and Black*, 37.
28. Ibid., 27.
29. Hare, *Norris Wright Cuney: A Tribune to the Black People*, 191.
30. Ibid., 14.
31. Ibid., 82.
32. Ibid., 176-77.
33. Woodson, "The Cuney Family," 125.
34. Hales, *A Southern Family in White and Black*, 108-37.
35. Hare, *Norris Wright Cuney: A Tribune to the Black People*, 80.
36. *Proceedings of the Convention to Organize the Most Worshipful Grand Lodge, Free and Accepted Ancient York Masons of the State of Texas, Held in the City of Brenham, August 19 and 20 A.L. 5875* (Galveston, Texas: McKenna and Co., 1875), 6. In Masonic time, A.L. 5875 corresponds to A.D. 1875.
37. Hare, *Norris Wright Cuney: A Tribune to the Black People*, 17-18. During Cuney's lifetime, not all white Masons shared in this racism. Galveston Masonic leader Jerome Buck favored recognition of African-American Masons; see Hales, *A Southern Family in White and Black*, 145.
38. *Proceedings* (1875), 5.
39. Ibid., 6.
40. Ibid., 9.
41. Ibid.
42. Ibid., 13.
43. Ibid., 14.
44. *Proceedings of the Most Worshipful Grand Lodge, Ancient Free and Accepted Masons for the State of Texas, held in the City of Houston, A.L. 5876, '77, '78, '79* (Galveston, Texas: McKenna and Co., 1879), 13.
45. Ibid., 20.
46. Ibid., 28.
47. *Proceedings of the Most Worshipful Grand Lodge, Ancient Free and Accepted Masons for the State of Texas, held in the Cities of Galveston, Austin and Waco A.L. 5880-81-82* (Galveston, Texas: McKenna and Co., 1882), 12.
48. Ibid., 14-18.
49. Ibid., 30-31.
50. Ibid., 49.
51. Hare, *Norris Wright Cuney: A Tribune to the Black People*, 89-90.
52. Hinze, "Norris Wright Cuney," 17-18. Anyone who compares the ritual of the Union League with that of Freemasonry will note striking parallels. In the 1870 ritual, God is addressed as "Supreme Architect and Ruler of the Universe." During the initiation, the candidate is asked the following question: "Do you pledge your honor that you will obey all rules and orders of the Union League of America which shall not conflict with your lawful rights and privileges as a loyal citizen, and keep inviolate all secrets and ceremonies of the league, when communicated to you as such?" At the conclusion of the obligation, the candidate says: "And with my hand upon the Holy Bible, Declaration of Independence and the Constitution of the United States of America, under the seal of my sacred

honor, I acknowledge myself firmly bound and pledged to the faithful performance of this my solemn obligation. So help me God." Following the obligation, the following charge is given: "The oath you have now taken of your own free will and accord, cannot now be violated without leaving the stain of perjury on your souls"; see Walter L. Fleming, ed. *Documents Relating to Reconstruction* (Morgantown, W. V.: West Virginia University Press, 1904), 18-24.
53. Hare, *Norris Wright Cuney: A Tribune to the Black People*, 42.
54. Hinze, "Norris Wright Cuney," 23-24.
55. Ibid., 25.
56. Merline Pitre, "Cuney, Norris Wright," in *The Handbook of Texas Online*, http://www.tsha.utexas.edu/handbook/online/articles/view/CC/fcu20.html, 2.
57. Ibid., 25-26.
58. Ibid., 29-31. The Knights of Labor—which owed much of its origin and ritual to Freemasonry—was noted for more liberal racial policies than most labor unions of that day. In July 1886 there were 95,000 African Americans in this union; see Robert L. Uzzel, "Freemasonry and the Knights of Labor," *The Scottish Rite Journal*, August 1999, 16-21.
59. Hinze, "Norris Wright Cuney," 33. The writer does not know if there were ritualistic features attached to Galveston's black unions. However, he suspects that, if Cuney was associated with them, there were such features, influenced by Masonry.
60. Casdorph, *A History of the Republican Party in Texas*, 46.
61. Merline Pitre, *Through Many Dangers, Toils, and Snares: The Black Leadership of Texas, 1869-1900* (Austin, Texas: Eakin Press, 1985), 189.
62. Pitre, "Cuney, Norris Wright," 1.
63. Pitre, *Through Many Dangers, Toils, and Snares*, 190. Davis was a member of Rio Grande Lodge No. 81 in Brownsville, Texas; see Normand, *The Texas Masons*, 35.
64. Pitre, *Through Many Dangers, Toils, and Snares*, 190-91.
65. Hinze, "Norris Wright Cuney," 39-40.
66. Ibid., 47-49.
67. Ibid., 53.
68. Hare, *Norris Wright Cuney: A Tribune to the Black People*, 56-58.
69. Hales, *A Southern Family in White and Black*, 66.
70. Hinze, "Norris Wright Cuney," 70.
71. Hales, *A Southern Family in White and Black*, 71. In 1861 Sul Ross joined Waco Lodge No. 92, where his father and older brother were members. During the Civil War, he became the Confederacy's youngest general, commanding the hard-riding Texas Cavalry Brigade; see Pete Normand, *The Texas Masons: The Fraternity of Ancient Free and Accepted Masons in the History of Texas* (College Station, Texas: Masonic Library and Museum Association, 1986), 27.
72. Hales, *A Southern Family in White and Black*, 71-72.
73. Ibid., 74.
74. Hare, *Norris Wright Cuney: A Tribune to the Black People*, 105.
75. Ibid., 112-13.
76. Hinze, "Norris Wright Cuney," 60.
77. Hare, *Norris Wright Cuney: A Tribune to the Black People*, 93.
78. Ibid., 108.
79. Ibid., 118-19.
80. Ibid., 120-21.
81. Ibid., 126. John H. Reagan was a member of Austin Lodge No. 12. Richard Coke, a former governor of Texas, was a member of Waco Lodge No. 92; see Normand, *The Texas Masons*, 25-26.
82. Hales, *A Southern Family in White and Black*, 16.
83. Hare, *Norris Wright Cuney: A Tribune to the Black People*, 127.
84. Ibid., 128-30.
85. Ibid., 130-31. For more on African-American participation in this event, see Robert L. Uzzel, "AMEs at the Fair: African Methodism and the World's Columbian Exposition of 1893," *The AME Church Review*, July-September 1985, 8-16.
86. Hinze, "Norris Wright Cuney," 103.
87. Ibid., 97.
88. Ibid., 106-07.
89. Ibid., 107-08.

90. Hare, *Norris Wright Cuney: A Tribune to the Black People*, 163.
91. George Clark, *A Glance Backward: Or Some Events in the Past History of My Life* (Houston, Texas: Hein and Sons, n.d.), 91. In his brief description of his unsuccessful gubernatorial race, Clark made absolutely no mention of Cuney's support. At one time, Clark and Coke had been closely associated. They occupied rooms across from each other when both were boarders at the Waco home of Dr. D. R. Wallace, the pioneer Texas psychiatrist; see ibid., 77. Clark and Wallace, like Coke, were members of Waco Lodge No. 92; see Roger N. Conger, ed., *A Century of Fraternity: Waco Lodge No. 92, A.F.&A.M., Waco, Texas, 1852-1952* (Waco, Texas, 1952). Sadly, neither Clark, Coke, nor Wallace regarded Cuney as their Masonic brother due to the claim that Prince Hall Freemasons are "clandestine." Today, Clark, Coke, and Wallace are buried in close proximity to each other in Waco's Oakwood Cemetery.
92. Hare, *Norris Wright Cuney: A Tribune to the Black People*, 163-64. Senator Richard Coke was prominent among those who lobbied for Cuney's immediate removal; see Hales, *A Southern Family in White and Black*, 87.
93. Hinze, "Norris Wright Cuney," 112.
94. Hare, *Norris Wright Cuney: A Tribune to the Black People*, 168.
95. Hinze, "Norris Wright Cuney," 116.
96. Ibid. 119-21. William B. Allison was a member of Mosaic Lodge No. 125 in Dubuque, Iowa; see Allen E. Roberts, *House Undivided: The Story of Freemasonry and the Civil War* (Richmond, Va.: Macoy Publishing and Masonic Supply Co., Inc., 1990), 333. William McKinley was a member of Canton Lodge No. 60 in Canton, Ohio; see ibid., 33.
97. Hinze, "Norris Wright Cuney," 124.
98. Ibid., 125.
99. Ibid., 125-28.
100. Casdorph, *A History of the Republican Party in Texas*, 67-68.
101. Hinze, "Norris Wright Cuney," 129.
102. Hales, *A Southern Family in White and Black*, 91.
103. Ibid., 131.
104. Woodson, "The Cuney Family," 124.
105. Hinze, "Norris Wright Cuney," 132-33.
106. Hare, *Norris Wright Cuney: A Tribune to the Black People*, 222-23.
107. Hinze, "Norris Wright Cuney," 133. The cause of Cuney's death was Phtisis Pulmonalis. He was treated by Dr. B. E. Hadra of San Antonio. He was buried by Levy Brothers Funeral Home. His place of interment is in section B, block 7, lot 1 of Lakeview Cemetery; see *Lakeview Cemetery Record* I:1887-1908 (Galveston, Texas: Galveston County Genealogical Society, 1992).
108. Hare, *Norris Wright Cuney: A Tribune to the Black People*, 223. Wilford H. Smith was Grand Master of Prince Hall Masons in New York; see Hales, *A Southern Family in White and Black*, 92.
109. Ibid., 230.
110. *Proceedings of the Sixty-sixth Annual Communication of the Most Worshipful Grand Lodge of Texas, Free and Accepted Masons* (Fort Worth, Texas, 1941), 31.
111. *Proceedings of the Eighty-ninth Annual Communication of the Most Worshipful Prince Hall Grand Lodge of Texas, Free and Accepted Masons of Texas and Jurisdiction Belonging* (Fort Worth, Texas, 1964), 70.
112. Ibid., 70-71.
113. Ibid., 39.
114. A. D. Harris. "Keep Cuney's Dream Alive," *The Masonic Family Quarterly* 110 (November 1997): 6.
115. Hinze, "Norris Wright Cuney," 140.

Richard Allen

1. There is no evidence that Grand Master Richard Allen of Texas was related to Bishop Richard Allen of Pennsylvania, the founder of the AME Church. The reader should seek to avoid confusing these two outstanding African-American leaders.
2. Alwyn Barr and Cary D. Wintz, "Allen, Richard." *The Handbook of Texas Online*. http://www.tsha.utexas.edu/handbook/online/articles/view/AA/fal24.html, 1.
3. J. Mason Brewer, *Negro Legislators of Texas and Their Descendants* (Austin, Texas: Pemberton Press, 1970), 53-54. Exactly how Allen obtained his freedom is a matter of controversy. In an interview with

Brewer, Allen's daughter, Mrs. Modestia Sharp, related that her father escaped from slavery in 1863. However, in a speech in Brenham, Texas, on August 10, 1871, Allen himself stated that he had been freed with other Texas slaves by the order of Gen. Gordon Granger on June 19, 1865; see *Brenham Semi-Weekly Banner*, August 15, 1871, as cited in ibid.

4. Barr and Wintz, "Allen, Richard," 1.
5. United States Census (Washington, D. C., 1880).
6. Brewer, *Negro Legislators of Texas and Their Descendants*, 54.
7. Barr and Wintz, "Allen, Richard," 1.
8. Merline Pitre, *Through Many Dangers, Toils, and Snares: The Black Leadership of Texas, 1869-1900* (Austin, Texas: Eakin Press, 1985), 175.
9. Barr and Wintz, "Allen, Richard," 1.
10. Brewer, *Negro Legislators of Texas and Their Descendants*, 49.
11. Prentis W. Chunn, Jr., "Education and Politics: A Study of the Negro in Reconstruction Texas" (M.A. thesis, Southwest Texas State Teachers College, 1957), 156.
12. Barr and Wintz, "Allen, Richard," 1.
13. Ibid., 1-2.
14. Ibid., 2.
15. Pitre, *Through Many Dangers, Toils, and Snares*, 177.
16. Brewer, *Negro Legislators of Texas and Their Descendants*, 54. Saint John Baptist Church is one of the larger black Baptist churches in Dallas. A number of years after the pastorate of Reverend Andrews, this church moved to its present location at 2600 South Marsalis in the South Oak Cliff section of Dallas. From 1976 to 1979, the writer was pastor of Emmanuel African Methodist Episcopal Church at 2627 South Marsalis—across the street from Saint John. According to Reverend Andrews' daughter, he also held pastorates in Houston, Fort Worth, and Indianapolis, Indiana; see Jewel Andrews Gray, letter to author, May 10, 1993.
17. *Proceedings of the Most Worshipful Grand Lodge, Ancient Free and Accepted Masons for the State of Texas, Held in the City of Houston, A.L. 5876, '77, '78, '79* (Galveston, Texas: McKenna and Co., 1879), 32.
18. *Proceedings of the Convention to Organize the Most Worshipful Grand Lodge, Free and Accepted Ancient York Masons of the State of Texas, Held in the City of Brenham, August 19 and 20 A.L. 5875* (Galveston, Texas: McKenna and Co., 1876), 5.
19. Ibid., 5-9.
20. *Proceedings* (1876), 6.
21. Ibid., 13.
22. Ibid., 20.
23. Maud Cuney Hare, *Norris Wright Cuney: A Tribune to the Black People* (Austin, Texas: Steck-Vaughn Co., 1968), 223. It appears that, despite their Masonic connections, Cuney and Allen were not close friends but political rivals. At the 1896 Republican National Convention in St. Louis, Allen supported the bolters led by John Grant who were instrumental in denying seating to Cuney and the Regular Republicans. This event helped end Cuney's political career; see Pitre, *Through Many Dangers, Toils, and Snares*, 178.
24. *Proceedings of the Most Worshipful Grand Lodge, Free and Accepted Masons, Held at Fort Worth, Texas, Commencing July 20, 1909* (Dallas, Texas: Dallas Express Print, 1909), 31.

Leroy L. James
1. United States Census (Washington, D.C., 1880).
2. Kyle was a member of Magnolia Lodge No. 3; see *Proceedings of the Most Worshipful Grand Lodge, Ancient Free and Accepted Masons for the State of Texas, held in the City of Houston, A.L. 5876, '77, '78, '79* (Galveston, Texas: McKenna and Co., 1879), 24.
3. Doris Glasser, Texas and Local History Department, Houston Public Library, personal letter, August 30, 1990.
4. *Proceedings of the Convention to Organize the Most Worshipful Grand Lodge, Free and Accepted Ancient York Masons of the State of Texas, held in the City of Brenham, August 19th and 20th, A.L. 5875* (Galveston, Texas: McKenna and Co., 1876), 5.
5. *Proceedings* (1879), 14-19.
6. Ibid., 19-20.
7. Ibid., 22.

8. Ibid., 28.
9. Ibid., 29-30.
10. *Proceedings of the Most Worshipful Grand Lodge, Ancient Free and Accepted Masons for the State of Texas and Its Jurisdiction Held in the Cities of Galveston, Austin, and Waco, A.L. 5880-81-82* (Galveston, Texas: McKenna and Co., 1882), 3.
11. Ibid., 12-13.
12. Ibid., 25.
13. Ibid., 30.
14. Ibid., 34.

Abram Grant

1. The second was Josiah Haynes Armstrong, the seventh Texas Grand Master and the twenty-fourth bishop of the African Methodist Episcopal Church. The third was John Wesley McKinney, the tenth Texas Grand Master and the sixteenth bishop of the Colored (now Christian) Methodist Episcopal Church.
2. Richard R. Wright, Jr., *The Bishops of the African Methodist Episcopal Church* (Nashville, Tenn.: AME Sunday School Union, 1963), 191.
3. *Proceedings of the Most Worshipful Grand Lodge, Ancient Free and Accepted Masons for the State of Texas and Its Jurisdiction Held in the Cities of Galveston, Austin, and Waco, A.L. 5880-81-82* (Galveston, Texas: McKenna and Co., 1882), 65.
4. Ibid., 13.
5. Ibid., 30.
6. Ibid., 31. At this session, prayer was offered by the Grand Chaplain *pro tem*—Rev. Josiah Haynes Armstrong.
7. Ibid., 34-38.
8. Ibid., 46. Paul Quinn College operates under the auspices of the AME Church and is named for William Paul Quinn, the fourth AME Bishop and a Prince Hall Freemason. It was founded in Austin in 1872, moved to Waco in 1877, and occupied the site of the old Garrison plantation in East Waco in 1881—one year before the visit by the Grand Lodge. The school relocated to the old Bishop College campus in Dallas in 1990.
9. Ibid., 47. The Grand Lodge's headquarters was later moved to Fort Worth.
10. Ibid., 49.
11. Ibid.
12. Wright, *The Bishops of the African Methodist Episcopal Church*, 192.
13. Ibid., 191.
14. Charles Spencer Smith, *A History of the African Methodist Episcopal Church* (Philadelphia, Pa.: Book Concern of the AME Church, 1922), 154-55. Bishops Wesley John Gaines and Benjamin William Arnette were elected on the first ballot. Bishop Benjamin Tucker Tanner was elected on the second ballot. No one was elected on the third ballot.
15. Wright, *The Bishops of the African Methodist Episcopal Church*, 191-92.
16. Reverdy C. Ransom, *The Pilgrimage of Harriet Ransom's Son* (Nashville, Tenn.: AME Sunday School Uion, n.d.), 76-77. Grant spelled his name "Abram" but it has often been misspelled as "Abraham."
17. Smith, *A History of the African Methodist Episcopal Church*, 190-200.
18. Ibid., 202.
19. Ibid., 202-03. During the 1896-1900 Quadrennium, Grant also had the experience of presiding over the Sierra Leone Annual Conference; see Wright, *The Bishops of the African Methodist Episcopal Church*, 192.
20. Smith, *A History of the African Methodist Episcopal Church*, 204-05.
21. Ibid., 205-06. In this sermon, Grant mentioned Richard Allen, the founder and first bishop of the AME Church. Allen served as the first treasurer for African Lodge No. 459 in Philadelphia. he was installed in the latter office by Prince Hall; see Charles H. Wesley, *Richard Allen: Apostle of Freedom* (Washington, D.C.: Associated Publishers, 1935), 94.
22. Wright, *The Bishops of the African Methodist Episcopal Church*, 191.
23. Smith, *A History of the African Methodist Episcopal Church*, 227. Roosevelt was a member of Matinecock Lodge No. 806 in Oyster Bay, New York.
24. Wright, *The Bishops of the African Methodist Episcopal Church*, 191-92.
25. *Proceedings of Texas Thirty-Sixth Annual Communication of Most Worshipful Grand Lodge Free and*

Accepted Masons held at Fort Worth, Texas Commencing July 11, 1911 (Fort Worth, Texas, 1911), 26-28.
26. Ibid., 63-64.
27. Ibid., 65.
28. Ibid., 66-70.
29. *Proceedings of the One Hundred and Fourteenth Annual Grand Communication of the Most Worshipful Prince Hall Grand Lodge of Texas and Jurisdiction Belonging* (Fort Worth, Texas, 1989), 84.
30. *The Bishops of the African Methodist Episcopal Church*, 192. In 1975 the writer was ordained to the AME ministry at the church in Austin. He later preached at the San Antonio and Palestine congregations.

Charles C. Dean
1. United States Census (Washington, D. C., 1880).
2. Doris Glasser, Texas and Local History Department, Houston Public Library, letter to author, August 30, 1990.
3. *Proceedings of the Most Worshipful Grand Lodge, Ancient Free and Accepted Masons for the State of Texas, held in the City of Houston*, A.L. 5876, '77, '78, '79 (Galveston, Texas: McKenna and Co., 1879), 15.
4. Ibid., 22.
5. *Proceedings of the Most Worshipful Grand Lodge, Ancient Free and Accepted Masons for the State of Texas and Its Jurisdiction held in the Cities of Galveston, Austin, and Waco*, A.L. 5880-'81-'82 (Galveston, Texas: McKenna and Co., 1882), 4-8.
6. Ibid., 49.
7. *Proceedings of the Twelfth Annual Communication of the Most Worshipful Grand Lodge, Ancient Free and Accepted Masons for the State of Texas held at the City of Denison, Commencing on the Third Tuesday in June* A.D. 1887, A.L. 5887 (Houston, Texas: Smallwood, Dealy, and Baker, 1887), 16.
8. *Proceedings of the Thirteenth Annual Communication of the Most Worshipful Grand Lodge, Ancient Free and Accepted Masons for the State of Texas and Jurisdiction held in the City of Austin Commencing on the Third Tuesday in June* A.D. 1888, A.L. 5888 (Houston, Texas: Smallwood, Dealy, and Baker, 1888), 10-22.
9. *Proceedings of the Fourteenth Annual Communication of the Most Worshipful Grand Lodge, Ancient Free and Accepted Masons for the State of Texas and Jurisdiction held in the City of Austin Commencing on the Third Tuesday in June* A.D. 1889, A.L. 5889 (Houston, Texas: Smallwood, Dealy, and Baker, 1889), 7-8.
10. Ibid., 27.

Rodolphus H. Bradley
1. Most of the 1890 Census records (including those from Texas) were destroyed in a tragic fire in Washington, D.C. Thus, 1890 information available to genealogical researchers is quite limited.
2. *Proceedings of the Fourteenth Annual Communication of the Most Worshipful Grand Lodge, Ancient Free and Accepted Masons for the State of Texas and Jurisdiction held in the City of Austin Commencing on the Third Tuesday in June* A.D. 1889, A.L. 5889 (Houston, Texas: Smallwood, Dealy, and Baker, 1889), 7.
3. Ibid., 27.
4. *1875-1975 Centennial, Most Worshipful Prince Hall Grand Lodge of Texas and Jurisdiction, Free and Accepted Masons, June 22-26, 1975* (Souvenir Journal).

Josiah Haynes Armstrong
1. Richard R. Wright, Jr., *The Bishops of the African Methodist Episcopal Church* (Nashville, Tenn.: AME Sunday School Union, 1963), 77.
2. Clarence E. Walker, *A Rock in a Weary Land: The African Methodist Episcopal Church During the Civil War and Reconstruction* (Baton Rouge, La.: Louisiana State University Press, 1982), 119. Armstrong was one of seven AME ministers who served in the Florida Legislature during this period. Another of this group was Reverend Bradwell, under whom Armstrong was converted. Bradwell was born in slavery in Darien, Georgia. He was a slave preacher until he obtained his freedom in 1865 and joined the AME Church the following year. He was sent to Florida to work with the freedmen and exerted considerable influence over his charges. He served in the Florida Senate from 1868 to 1870.

3. Wright, *The Bishops of the African Methodist Episcopal Church*, 77.
4. Ibid.
5. *Proceedings of the Most Worshipful Grand Lodge, Ancient Free and Accepted Masons for the State of Texas and Its Jurisdiction held in the Cities of Galveston, Austin, and Waco*, A.L. 5880-81-82 (Galveston, Texas: McKenna and Co., 1882), 66.
6. *Proceedings of the Seventeenth Annual Session of the Most Worshipful Grand Lodge, Ancient Free and Accepted Masons for the State of Texas and Jurisdiction, held in the City of Austin, Commencing Tuesday, July 12 A.D., 1892*, A.L. 5892 (Austin, Texas, 1892), 10-13. These remarks indicate that Armstrong was made a Mason in Florida in 1875 and moved his membership to Texas in 1880.
7. Wright, *The Bishops of the African Methodist Episcopal Church*, 77.
8. Charles Spencer Smith, *A History of the African Methodist Episcopal Church* (Philadelphia, Pa.: Book Concern of the AME Church, 1922), 200-02. Other bishops elected at this session were W. B. Derrick on the first ballot and J. C. Embry on the second ballot. The ordination sermon was delivered by Senior Bishop Henry McNeal Turner, a Prince Hall Freemason.
9. Ibid., 202.
10. Ibid., 203.
11. Wright, *The Bishops of the African Methodist Episcopal Church*, 77.
12. Maud Cuney Hare, *Norris Wright Cuney: A Tribune to the Black People* (Austin, Texas: Steck-Vaughn Co., 1968), 223. The cause of Armstong's death was ureamia. He was buried by Levy Brothers Funeral Home. His place of interment is in section B, block 8, lot N 1/2 of 4 of Lakeview Cemetery; see *Lakeview Cemetery Record* 1:1887-1908 (Galveston, Texas: Galveston County Genealogical Society, 1992).

John W. Madison
1. Standard Certificate of Death for Madison, John W., Texas Department of Health Bureau of Vital Statistics.
2. United States Census (Washington, D.C., 1900).
3. C. W. Abington, "The Historical and Biographical Souvenir and Program of the 25th Anniversary of Metropolitan AME Church, Austin, Texas, 1882-1907." Today, Madison's church is known as Wesley Chapel United Methodist Church. Samuel Huston College is now called Huston-Tillotson College.
4. *Proceedings of the Seventeenth Annual Session of the Most Worshipful Grand Lodge, Ancient Free and Accepted Masons for the State of Texas and Jurisdiction, held in the City of Austin, Commencing Tuesday, July 12, A.D. 1892*, A.L. 5892. (Denison, Texas: Murray's Power Printing House, 1892), 10-13.
5. Ibid., 38.
6. *Proceedings of the Nineteenth Annual Session of the Most Worshipful Grand Lodge, Ancient Free and Accepted Masons for the State of Texas and Jurisdiction, held in the City of Waco, Commencing Tuesday, July 10, A.D. 1894*, A.L. 5894. (Denison, Texas: Murray's Power Printing House, 1894), 3.
7. Ibid., 8-16. At this session, the Committee on Jurisprudence ruled: "In the case of Bro. A. K. Weathersby, of Bloomfield No. 67, we find that the actions of the Grand Master in ordering a stay of sentence consistent, and entirely within the landmarks of Masonry and the prerogatives of the Grand Master"; see ibid., 45. It is interesting that W. M. McDonald, despite his conflict with Grand Master Madison, was elected Grand Secretary in 1899—just five years later! McDonald continuously held this office until 1946. He died in Fort Worth in 1950—after a lifetime of distinguished service in business, politics, and fraternalism.
8. Ibid., 50. W. M. McDonald, who was then serving as Grand Recorder, accompanied Sutton to Chicago. The World's Columbian Exposition is also important to the history of Prince Hall Freemasonry as the alleged birthplace of Prince Hall Shrinedom; see Joseph A. Walkes, Jr., *History of the Shrine: Ancient Egyptian Arabic Order Nobles of the Mystic Shrine, Inc., Prince Hall Affiliated, A Pillar of Black Society, 1893-1993* (Detroit, Mi.: AEAONMS, Inc., 1993), 1-21.
9. *Proceedings* (1894), 57.
10. Ibid., 62.
11. "Mortuary, John W. Madison." *Austin American*, March 20, 1929.
12. *Proceedings of the Forty-fourth Annual Communication of the Most Worshipful Grand Lodge, Free and Accepted Masons of Texas Jurisdiction and Belonging* (Fort Worth, Texas: F.&A.M. Printing Department, 1929), 83.
13. Ibid. Mitchell served as Deputy Grand Master under Madison. He never served as Grand Master. The motion to pay the $50 was made by Grand Secretary McDonald.

Wiley Lawson Kimbrough

1. Standard Certificate of Death for Kimbrough, Wiley Lawson, State of California Department of Public Health.
2. *Dallas City Directory* (1890), 407.
3. *Dallas City Directory* (1891-92), 498.
4. *Dallas City Directory* (1898-99), 302. It should be pointed out that, although Kimbrough was employed by BPOE, he was not a member of this organization. From 1868 to 1973, membership was restricted to "whites only." In 1973 the Elks bowed to "changing social attitudes" and eliminated race as a condition for membership. A major factor contributing to this change was the threat that many lodges would lose their liquor licenses if they persisted in their racial discrimination. This prompted a reporter to observe: "If social change is desirable, the quickest way to get it is to threaten to cut off the booze"; see "Elks Integrate," *Chicago Tribune*, July 23, 1973, 1-20. Since 1898, the predominantly black Improved Benevolent and Protective Order of Elks of the World (IBPOEW) have had a relationship with the BPOE similar to that of Prince Hall Freemasonry with white Freemasonry; see Robert J. Wilson, Peggy J. Coplin, and Theodore D. Murray, *A Documentary History of the Improved Benevolent and Protective Order of Elks of the World: 100 Years of Benevolence and Image Building* (Philadelphia, Pa.: Imprints Unlimited, Inc., 1996). The writer does not know whether Kimbrough was ever a member of IBPOEW.
5. *Proceedings of the Nineteenth Annual Communication of the Most Worshipful Grand Lodge, Ancient Free and Accepted Masons for the State of Texas and Its Jurisdiction, held in the City of Waco, Commencing Tuesday, July 10 A.D., 1894, A.L. 5894* (Denison, Texas: Murray's Power Printing House, 1894), 5.
6. *Proceedings of the Seventeenth Annual Communication of the Most Worshipful Grand Lodge, Ancient Free and Accepted Masons for the State of Texas and Its Jurisdiction Held in the City of Austin, Commencing Tuesday, July 12 A.D., 1892, A.L. 5892* (Denison, Texas: Murray's Power Printing House, 1892, 4.
7. *Proceedings* (1894), 57.
8. Ibid., 62.
9. *Proceedings of the Twentieth Annual Communication of the Most Worshipful Grand Lodge, Free and Accepted Masons for the State of Texas and Its Jurisdiction* (Denison, Texas: Murray's Power Printing House, 1895), 8-22.
10. *Proceedings* (1895), 22. Capt. William D. Matthews of Kansas once served as Grand Master of the National "Compact" Grand Lodge. As previously stated, prior to the organization of the Texas Grand Lodge, our first Grand Master, Norris Wright Cuney, served as Matthews' Deputy Grand Master; and, on January 19, 1876, Cuney and his officers were installed by Matthews; see *Proceedings of the Convention to Organize the Most Worshipful Grand Lodge, Free and Accepted Ancient York Masons of the State of Texas held in the City of Brenham, August 19 and 20 A.L. 5875* (Galveston, Texas: McKenna, Printer, 1876), 11-13. Matthews has been well described as "without a doubt, one of the most controversial figures within Prince Hall Freemasonry"; see Joseph A. Walkes, Jr., "Captain William D. Matthews: Freemason, Leavenworth, Kansas," *The Phylaxis* 13 (Special Issue 1987-88): 3-8, 29.
11. *Proceedings* (1995), 24-25. Sadly, over one hundred years after Kimbrough's speech, some Prince Hall Masons still use the "Duncan Ritual" which is published by Ezra A. Cook Company, a Chicago firm well known for its anti-Masonic bias. The writer has long contended that no true Mason should use such materials. By doing so, we only "add fuel to the fire" of those who desire to destroy us.
12. *Proceedings* (1895), 27.
13. On July 18, 1916, McKinney delivered his twentieth and final Grand Master's Address, in which he recalled: "Twenty years ago, your humble servant was elected Grand Master of the Masons, at a session held in Austin"; see *Proceedings of the Forty-first Annual Communication of the Most Worshipful Grand Lodge, Free and Accepted Masons for the State of Texas and Its Jurisdiction* (Fort Worth, Texas, 1916), 21.
14. The writer has found no evidence that Kimbrough ever returned to Texas to visit his former Grand Lodge. However, he did, at times, send greetings by mail.
15. United States Census (Washington, D.C., 1920).
16. Certificate of Death.
17. *Proceedings of the Sixty-second Annual Communication of the Most Worshipful Sovereign Grand Lodge, Free and Accepted Masons for the State of California and Jurisdiction* (Oakland, Ca.: Bridges Print, 1916), 26.

18. Ibid., 25.
19. Certificate of Death.
20. *Proceedings of the Eighty-first Annual Communication of the Most Worshipful Prince Hall Grand Lodge, Free and Accepted Masons, Texas and Jurisdiction Belonging* (Fort Worth, Texas, 1956), 31.
21. I wish to express my appreciation to Past Grand Master Frank Boone, Grand Historian for the Prince Hall Grand Lodge of California, for providing very valuable information regarding Past Grand Master Kimbrough's involvement in California Masonry; see Frank Boone, personal letter, May 14, 1994. One of the founders of Wiley L. Kimbrough Lodge was Joseph B. Collins. When Collins was diagnosed with Alzheimer's Disease, lodge members sought to live up to their Masonic obligations by providing for this older brother in his time of need; see "Brotherly Love: Santa Ana Masons Take Their Former Leader Under Their Wing," *The Phylaxis* 21 (First Quarter 1995): 26-27.

John Wesley McKinney

1. "Rites Held for Bishop J. W. McKinney: Bishop Porter Delivers Eulogy," *Dallas Express*, September 7, 1946, 1, 8. According to a Past Grand Master of the Most Worshipful Prince Hall Grand Lodge, Free and Accepted Masons, of Colorado and Jurisdiction, Dr. McKinney and his family were members of Tyler Chapel CME Church in Denver. He was a steward in this church, frequently lifting the Sunday offering. He had three sons—John, Archie, and Wendell—who are all now deceased; see William L. Hunter, letter to author, April 11, 1991.
2. "Rites Held for Bishop J. W. McKinney," 8.
3. Ibid.
4. Nolan B. Harmon, ed., *The Encyclopedia of World Methodism*, vol. II (Nashville, Tenn.: United Methodist Publishing House, 1974), 1492.
5. Ibid., 1, 8. The date of McKinney's first marriage is unknown. His second marriage took place in 1904.
6. *Proceedings of the Nineteenth Annual Communication of the Most Worshipful Grand Lodge, Free and Accepted Masons for the State of Texas and Its Jurisdiction* (Denison, Texas: Murray's Power Printing House, 1894), 6.
7. "Rites Held for Bishop J. W. McKinney," 8. McKinney's term of twenty years is the longest of any Texas Prince Hall Grand Master.
8. *Proceedings of the Thirty-first Annual Communication of the Most Worshipful Grand Lodge, Free and Accepted Masons of the State of Texas and Its Jurisdiction* (Fort Worth, Texas: 1906), 17-18.
9. Ibid., 57-58.
10. *Proceedings of the Thirty-second Annual Communication of the Most Worshipful Grand Lodge, Free and Accepted Masons of the State of Texas and Its Jurisdiction* (Fort Worth, Texas: 1907), 8.
11. Ibid., 14.
12. *Proceedings of the Thirty-fourth Annual Communication of the Most Worshipful Grand Lodge, Free and Accepted Masons of the State of Texas and Its Jurisdiction* (Fort Worth, Texas: 1909), 30.
13. Ibid., 32-33.
14. Ibid., 35.
15. *Proceedings of the Thirty-sixth Annual Communication of the Most Worshipful Grand Lodge, Free and Accepted Masons of the State of Texas and Its Jurisdiction* (Fort Worth, Texas: 1911), 26.
16. Ibid., 27-28.
17. Ibid., 61.
18. Ibid., 87.
19. Ibid., 109.
20. *Proceedings of the Thirty-seventh Annual Communication of the Most Worshipful Grand Lodge, Free and Accepted Masons of the State of Texas and Its Jurisdiction* (Fort Worth, Texas, 1912), 58.
21. Ibid., 59.
22. Ibid., 66.
23. *Proceedings of the Thirty-ninth Annual Communication of the Most Worshipful Grand Lodge, Free and Accepted Masons of the State of Texas and Its Jurisdiction* (Fort Worth, Texas: 1914), 18.
24. Ibid., 42. In making this statement, the brethren were probably not aware of the fact that the Masonic creators of Texas selected the "Lone Star" in the Texas flag as a symbol for the Masonic five points of fellowship; see Pete Normand, *The Texas Masons: The Fraternity of Ancient Free & Accepted Masons in the History of Texas* (College Station, Texas: Masonic Library and Museum Association, 1986), 5.
25. Ibid., 47-49.

26. *Proceedings of the Forty-first Annual Communication of the Most Worshipful Grand Lodge, Free and Accepted Masons of the State of Texas and Its Jurisdiction* (Fort Worth, Texas: 1916), 21.
27. Ibid.
28. Ibid., 78.
29. *Proceedings of the Forty-second Annual Communication of the Most Worshipful Grand Lodge, Free and Accepted Masons of the State of Texas and Its Jurisdiction* (Fort Worth, Texas, 1917), 21.
30. Ibid., 52.
31. Ibid., 16.
32. Othal Hawthorne Lakey, *The History of the CME Church* (Memphis, Tenn.: CME Publishing House, 1985), 365.
33. Ibid., 365-66.
34. Ibid., 367-70.
35. Ibid., 372.
36. Ibid., 382.
37. Ibid., 671.
38. Ibid., 391.
39. *Proceedings of the Forty-sixth Annual Communication of the Most Worshipful Grand Lodge of Texas, Free and Accepted Masons* (Fort Worth, Texas, 1921), 49.
40. Lakey, *The History of the CME Church*, 391.
41. *Proceedings of the Forty-seventh Annual Communication of the Most Worshipful Grand Lodge of Texas, Free and Accepted Masons* (Fort Worth, Texas, 1922), 59-60.
42. Ibid., 63.
43. "Rites Held for Bishop J. W. McKinney," 8.
44. Harmon, *The Encyclopedia of World Methodism*, 1492.
45. "Rites Held for Bishop J. W. McKinney," 8.
46. Ibid., 1.
47. Ibid., 8.
48. Standard Certificate of Death for John W. McKinney.

Henderson D. Winn

1. The writer borrowed the term "normalcy" from President Warren G. Harding, a member of Marion Lodge No. 70 in Marion, Ohio. Harding always denied the rumors that his family line included African ancestry. During his 1920 presidential campaign, Harding misread the word "normality" in a prepared speech and called for a return to "normalcy." The media made much of this mistake and, as a result, the years following World War I are called the "years of normalcy"; see Frederick Lewis Allen, *Only Yesterday: An Informal History of the Nineteen-Twenties* (New York: Harper and Brothers, 1931), 35.
2. Standard Certificate of Death for Henderson D. Winn.
3. "Masonic Grand Master H. D. Winn is Dead," *Dallas Express*, March 7, 1925, 1.
4. Ibid.
5. Ibid.
6. *Proceedings of the Forty-first Annual Communication of the Most Worshipful Grand Lodge of Texas, Free and Accepted Masons* (Fort Worth, Texas, 1916), 21.
7. Ibid., 45.
8. Ibid., 47.
9. Ibid., 52.
10. Ibid., 78.
11. *Proceedings of the Forty-second Annual Communication of the Most Worshipful Grand Lodge of Texas, Free and Accepted Masons* (Fort Worth, Texas, 1917), 18.
12. Ibid., 20.
13. Ibid., 71-72.
14. *Proceedings of the Forty-third Annual Communication of the Most Worshipful Grand Lodge of Texas, Free and Accepted Masons* (Fort Worth, Texas, 1918), 20.
15. Ibid., 23.
16. Ibid., 57.
17. Ibid., 60.
18. Ibid., 66.

19. Ibid., 66-67. General Pershing was a Freemason and received the 33° of the Scottish Rite in Washington, D.C. in 1930; see William L. Fox, *Lodge of the Double-Headed Eagle: Two Centuries of Scottish Rite Freemasonry in America's Southern Jurisdiction* (Fayetteville, Ark.: University of Arkansas Press, 1997), 231.
20. *Proceedings of the Forty-fifth Annual Communication of the Most Worshipful Grand Lodge of Texas, Free and Accepted Masons* (Fort Worth, Texas, 1919), 15.
21. Ibid., 19.
22. Ibid., 20.
23. Ibid., 21.
24. Ibid., 41.
25. Ibid., 43.
26. Ibid., 44. The writer was a member of Eastside Lodge No. 88 while living in Waco. This lodge was later consolidated with Union Seal Lodge No. 64.
27. Ibid., 57.
28. Ibid. Samuel Gompers was raised in Dawson Lodge No. 16 in Washington, D.C., on May 9, 1904. Reportedly, he died with his hand held in a Masonic grip by James Duncan, head of the Granite Cutters' Union; see Ivan M. Tribe, "Brother John Llewellyn Lewis: American Labor Leader," *Knight Templar*, June 1998, 9.
29. *Proceedings* (1919), 99-100. In 1898, under the leadership of Past Grand Master William H. Upton, the Grand Lodge of Washington extended recognition to Prince Hall Freemasonry. A few years later, recognition was withdrawn due to pressure from other white Grand Lodges. In 1990 permanent recognition was extended. Upton had willed that no Masonic monument be erected above his grave until such could be done jointly by white and black Masons. Brethren of the two Washington Grand Lodges erected such a monument on June 8, 1991; see John D. Keliher, "Most Worshipful Grand Master William H. Upton Memorial," *The Phylaxis*, Third Quarter 1991, 3-5.
30. *Proceedings* (1919), 101.
31. *Proceedings of the Forty-fifth Annual Communication of the Most Worshipful Grand Lodge of Texas, Free and Accepted Masons* (Fort Worth, Texas, 1920), 16-17.
32. Ibid., 18.
33. Ibid., 43.
34. Ibid., 48-49. This injury temporarily knocked Coleman "out of line." However, he eventually recovered and held a number of Grand Lodge offices. He served as Grand Master from 1930 until his death in 1946.
35. Ibid., 49. The writer wonders what happened to this rule. If it is still on the books, it is obviously not enforced, as most Worshipful Masters today prefer "reading from the book" to memorization.
36. Ibid., 63.
37. *Proceedings of the Forty-sixth Annual Communication of the Most Worshipful Grand Lodge of Texas, Free and Accepted Masons* (Fort Worth, Texas, 1921), 17.
38. Ibid., 18.
39. Ibid., 19.
40. Ibid., 20.
41. Ibid., 22.
42. Ibid., 24.
43. Ibid., 25.
44. Ibid., 26.
45. Ibid., 58. In the writer's opinion, this was a very wise move on Winn's part. The "Duncan Ritual" contains printed passwords and diagrams of secret signs—in clear violation of the obligation of the Entered Apprentice Degree.
46. Ibid., 62.
47. *Proceedings of the Forty-seventh Annual Communication of the Most Worshipful Grand Lodge of Texas, Free and Accepted Masons* (Fort Worth, Texas, 1922), 22-24.
48. Ibid., 24.
49. Ibid., 25.
50. Ibid., 26.
51. Ibid., 27.
52. Ibid., 64-65.
53. Ibid., 65.

54. *Proceedings of the Forty-eighth Annual Communication of the Most Worshipful Grand Lodge of Texas, Free and Accepted Masons* (Fort Worth, Texas, 1923), 20.
55. Ibid., 21.
56. Ibid., 22.
57. Ibid., 62.
58. *Proceedings of the Forty-ninth Annual Communication of the Most Worshipful Grand Lodge of Texas, Free and Accepted Masons* (Fort Worth, Texas, 1924), 19-20.
59. Ibid., 20-21.
60. Ibid., 40.
61. Ibid., 41.
62. Ibid., 45.
63. Ibid., 67.
64. "Masonic Grand Master H. D. Winn is Dead," 1.
65. Standard Certificate of Death for Henderson D. Winn.
66. *Proceedings of the Fiftieth Annual Communication of the Most Worshipful Grand Lodge of Texas, Free and Accepted Masons* (Fort Worth, Texas, 1925), 5.
67. Ibid., 6.
68. Ibid.
69. Ibid., 7. William Decker Johnson (1869-1936) was elected to the Bishopric of the AME Church in 1920 and served as presiding prelate in Texas from 1924 to 1928. William Decker Johnson Hall proudly stands on the Waco campus of Paul Quinn College; see Richard R. Wright, Jr., *Bishops of the African Methodist Episcopal Church* (Nashville, Tennessee: AME Sunday School Union, 1963), 236-38.
70. *Proceedings* (1925), 8.
71. "Masonic Grand Master H. D. Winn is Dead," 1.
72. *Proceedings* (1925), 21-26.

John Adrian Kirk
1. The writer is a native of Waco. He did much of the research for this chapter during the summer of 1992 in connection with a Seminar in Oral History at Baylor University.
2. "Past Grand Master of Masons Laid to Rest," *Waco Messenger*, 5 October 1934, 1.
3. A. W. Jackson, *A Sure Foundation* (Houston, Tx.: A. W. Jackson, n.d.), 227.
4. "Past Grand Master of Masons Laid to Rest," 1.
5. Garry H. Radford, Sr., *African American Heritage in Waco, Texas: Life Stories of Those Who Believed They Could Overcome Impediments* (Austin, Tx.: Eakin Press, 2000), 68.
6. "The Beginning," *Waco Freedom-Press*, 26 July 1991, 7. G. L. Wiley, for whom Waco's Wiley Middle School was named, was an active Prince Hall Freemason.
7. Ibid. A. J. Moore began teaching small groups of children in his home in 1875. He served as principal from 1881 to 1905. Kirk served from 1905 to 1925. He was followed by B. T. Wilson, who served from 1925 to 1934. The latter was succeeded by his son J. J. Wilson, who served until the school was closed in 1971.
8. Ometa White, interview by author, Texas, 26 June 1992. Ms. White's father, Willis Porter, served for many years as Worshipful Master of Union Seal Lodge No. 64 in Waco and was a close friend of Kirk.
9. Henry Flowers, interview by author, 1 July 1992.
10. Gladys Reed, interview by author, 7 July 1992.
11. O. E. Wilhite, interview by author, 23 June 1992. This interview was conducted during the Annual Communication of the Prince Hall Grand Lodge of Texas.
12. John Q. Daniels, interview by author, 1 July 1992.
13. Eucolia Erby, interview by author, 20 June 1992.
14. *Proceedings of the Fiftieth Annual Communication of the Most Worshipful Grand Lodge of Texas, Jurisdiction, and Belongings* (Fort Worth, Tx., 1925), 21.
15. Ibid., 59.
16. Ibid., 60.
17. Ibid., 61.
18. Ibid., 62-87.
19. *Proceedings of the Fifty-first Annual Communication of the Most Worshipful Grand Lodge of Texas, Jurisdiction, and Belongings* (Fort Worth, Tx., 1926), 21.

20. Ibid., 24-26.
21. Ibid., 72. The aforementioned book *Life of William Madison McDonald* (Fort Worth, Tx.: Bunker Printing and Book Co., Inc., 1925) is an excellent source of information regarding Texas black history.
22. Ibid., 78.
23. Ibid., 86.
24. Ibid., 88. William D. Cain was born in Galveston and grew up in Austin. He came to Waco to attend Paul Quinn College, then spent thirty-six years as a railway mail clerk. He served as Grand Recorder from 1906 until his death in 1939 and also served for many years as Worshipful Master of Wyatt Lodge No. 21 in Waco. His home at 1106 Taylor was one block from Kirk's home at 1136 Elm. He was a member of Saint Paul AME Church. The Cain homes (once a low-income housing project which are now owned by Baylor University) were named for him; see Radford, *African American Heritage in Waco, Texas*, 186. According to John Q. Daniels: "He stood as a bulwark between white people and colored people. He was able always to maintain harmonious relationships." Daniels, interview by author.
25. *Proceedings of the Fifty-second Annual Communication of the Most Worshipful Grand Lodge of Texas, Jurisdiction, and Belongings* (Fort Worth, Tx., 1927), 32-38.
26. Ibid., 76.
27. Ibid., 91. It is customary for Prince Hall Freemasons, along with their sisters of the Order of the Eastern Star and the Heroines of Jericho, to assemble in a church for a Masonic service each Palm Sunday.
28. *Proceedings of the Fifty-third Annual Communication of the Most Worshipful Grand Lodge of Texas, Jurisdiction, and Belongings* (Fort Worth, Texas, 1928), 28-29.
29. Ibid., 29.
30. Ibid., 30.
31. Ibid., 34.
32. Ibid., 31-32.
33. Ibid., 37.
34. *Proceedings of the Fifty-fourth Annual Communication of the Most Worshipful Grand Lodge of Texas, Jurisdiction, and Belongings* (Fort Worth, Tx., 1929), 7.
35. Ibid., 16.
36. Ibid., 41.
37. Ibid., 86.
38. Ibid., 86-87.
39. Ibid., 97. At that time, Bishop College was located in Marshall, Texas. It later relocated to Dallas. In 1988 the school closed in bankruptcy. The Dallas property remained unoccupied for two years. In 1990 Paul Quinn College moved from Waco to the Bishop campus in Dallas. There, the J. J. Rhoads Educational Building continues to honor the former Bishop president.
40. *Proceedings of the Fifty-fifth Annual Communication of the Most Worshipful Grand Lodge of Texas, Jurisdiction, and Belongings* (Fort Worth, Tx., 1930), 91-92.
41. Catherine Jackson, interview by author, tape recording, Waco, Texas, 7 July 1992.
42. A number of prominent black Wacoans are buried in Greenwood Cemetery. Such include the aforementioned Past Masters William D. Cain, who died on July 26, 1939; and Willis Porter, who died on 18 October 1947.
43. Radford, *African American Heritage in Waco, Texas*, 68.
44. "Past Grand Master of Masons Laid to Rest," 1.
45. Ibid.
46. "J. A. Kirk," *Waco Messenger*, 5 October 1934, 2.
47. Radford, *African American Heritage in Waco, Texas*, 122.
48. Ibid., 122-23.
49. Catherine Jackson, interview by author, 7 July 1992.
50. "Waco Loses Most Beloved Woman: Obsequies for Mrs. N. A. Kirk," *Waco Messenger*, 11 April 1941, 1.
51. Ibid. Her death occurred on what would have been her husband's eighty-first birthday.
52. Ibid.
53. Ometa White, who has died since our 1992 interview, was a member of Nettie Kirk Court No. 472 for many years.

William Coleman

1. "William Coleman, F&AM Grand Master, Dies; Rites Held Monday," *The Dallas Express*, 25 May 1946, 1.
2. Standard Certificate of Death for Coleman, William, Texas Department of Health Vital Statistics Division.
3. John Collyns Fullmore, Jr., *The Dragon: History of Douglass School* (El Paso, Tx.: American Printing Co., 1941), 22.
4. United States Census (Washington, D. C., 1910).
5. Fullmore, *The Dragon*, 22.
6. Ibid., 23.
7. Ibid., 24.
8. Ibid.
9. Ibid., 25.
10. Ibid., 28.
11. Ibid., 29-30.
12. Ibid., 30.
13. Ibid. Due to the accident, Coleman resigned from his Masonic position as Grand Lecturer.
14. Ibid., 32.
15. Ibid., 33.
16. Ibid., 35.
17. Ibid., 36.
18. Ibid., 38.
19. Ibid.
20. Ibid., 39-40.
21. *Proceedings of the Fifty-fifth Annual Communication of the Most Worshipful Grand Lodge of Texas, Free and Accepted Masons* (Fort Worth, Tx., 1930), 92-94.
22. Ibid., 97.
23. Ibid., 91.
24. Certificate of Death.
25. *Proceedings of the Fifth-sixth Annual Communication of the Most Worshipful Grand Lodge of Texas, Free and Accepted Masons* (Fort Worth, Tx., 1931), 24. Blake was noted for his role as Imperial Potentate of the Shrine in leading the Nobles in the great victory before the U. S. Supreme Count on 3 June 1929—celebrated ever since as "Jubilee Day." Lewis served as Grand Master of Louisiana from 1902 to 1931.
26. Ibid., 27.
27. Ibid.
28. Ibid., 28.
29. Ibid., 30-31.
30. Ibid., 35.
31. Ibid., 37.
32. Ibid., 38.
33. Ibid., 39.
34. Ibid., 40.
35. Ibid., 41. In this writer's opinion, such Masters should be removed from office.
36. Ibid.
37. *Proceedings of the Fifty-seventh Annual Communication of the Most Worshipful Grand Lodge of Texas, Free and Accepted Masons* (Fort Worth, Tx., 1932), 25-26.
38. Ibid., 27.
39. Ibid., 30.
40. Ibid., 38-39.
41. Ibid., 39. Such programs were administered by Secretary of Agriculture Henry Wallace, a Freemason who influenced President Roosevelt to place the Great Seal of the United States—with the pyramid and all-seeing eye—in the dollar bill; see Robert L. Uzzel, "Brother Henry Agard Wallace: Prophet of Agrarianism," *The Philalethes*, October 1999, 102-09.
42. *Proceedings of the Sixty-first Annual Communication of the Most Worshipful Grand Worshipful Grand Lodge of Texas, Free and Accepted Masons* (Fort Worth, Tx., 1936), 27.
43. Ibid., 28.

44. Ibid., 26.
45. Ibid., 31.
46. Ibid., 35.
47. Ibid., 38.
48. Ibid., 48.
49. *Proceedings of the Sixty-second Annual Communication of the Most Worshipful Grand Lodge of Texas, Free and Accepted Masons* (Fort Worth, Tx., 1937), 25.
50. Ibid., 32-33.
51. Ibid., 35.
52. Ibid., 37.
53. Ibid., 68.
54. Ibid., 71-72.
55. *Proceedings of the Sixty-sixth Annual Communication of the Most Worshipful Grand Lodge of Texas, Free and Accepted Masons* (Fort Worth, Tx., 1941), 17. Scott A. Lewis served as Grand Master from his father's death in 1931 until his own death in 1941. He was succeeded by his younger brother Jno. G. Lewis, Jr., who served from 1941 until his death in 1979; see Joseph A. Walkes, Jr., *Jno. G. Lewis, Jr.— End of an Era: The History of the Prince Hall Grand Lodge of Louisiana, 1842-1979* (Kansas City, Mo.: Midtown Printing and Publishing Co., 1986).
56. *Proceedings* (1941), 20.
57. Ibid., 24-25. These words were spoken twenty-six years before the U. S. Supreme Court declared all state anti-miscegenation laws (including that of Texas) unconstitutional; see *Loving v. Virginia*, 388 U. S. 1 (1967).
58. Ibid., 27.
59. Ibid., 29.
60. Ibid., 31. This monument is located across from Saint John AME Church, where the organizing meeting was held. It is sacred ground to Texas Prince Hall Masons.
61. Ibid. Each year, the writer looks forward to the celebration of the Festival of Saint John the Baptist on 24 June. He has not heard of a Texas Prince Hall Lodge observing a celebration of the Festival of Saint John the Evangelist on 27 December in recent years. He feels the latter festival should be reinstated throughout the Masonic world.
62. Ibid., 32-33. Less than six months after Coleman delivered this speech alluding to the Civil War, Japan bombed Pearl Harbor and America was again at war.
63. *Proceedings of the Sixty-seventh Annual Communication of the Most Worshipful Grand Lodge of Texas, Free and Accepted Masons* (Fort Worth, Tx., 1942), 20.
64. The predominately black Grand United Order of Odd Fellows (GUOOF) was once active in Texas but has been defunct throughout the state for many years. In 1905 this order laid the cornerstone at Wayman Chapel AME Church in Ennis, where the writer currently serves as pastor. The predominately white Independent Order of Odd Fellows (IOOF) has a lodge, nursing home, and retirement center in Ennis.
65. Ibid., 21. This speech was given twelve years before the U. S. Supreme Court declared that racial segregation in public schools is unconstitutional; see *Brown v. Board of Education of Topeka*, 347 U. S. 483 (1954).
66. Ibid., 23. Coleman noted that, several years earlier, thirty Masons at Orange were dropped from the rolls because they had no jobs and, thus, no way to pay their dues. He sincerely desired that such never happen again.
67. Ibid., 24. Lockhart was then employed as a clerk with the Southern Pacific Railroad.
68. Ibid., 25.
69. Ibid., 26-27.
70. Ibid., 31.
71. Ibid., 29.
72. *Proceedings of the Sixty-eighth Annual Communication of the Most Worshipful Grand Lodge of Texas, Free and Accepted Masons* (Fort Worth, Tx., 1943), 9.
73. Ibid., 11. In the writer's opinion, this amounts to penalizing a Mason for being in the military. Prince Hall Masons have been involved in practically all American military ventures. In recent years, much has been written about the fact that many of the celebrated "Buffalo Soldiers" were Prince Hall Masons. Today, many of the finest lodges in Prince Hall Freemasonry are military lodges. The fact that, by the time of World War II, insurance benefits were a major component of membership is an

important consideration here. (NOTE: This has not always been the case. In 1892 the Grand Lodge of Arkansas became the first Prince Hall body to adopt an insurance feature. Other Grand Lodges shortly followed suit; see William A. Muraskin, *Middle-Class Blacks in a White Society: Prince Hall Freemasonry in America* [Berkeley, Ca.: University of California Press, 1975], 40.) The writer is not opposed to Masonic relief systems, but he regards such as secondary to the real purpose of membership—fraternal fellowship. He is very uncomfortable with denial of such nonmaterial benefits to Masons in the military. Such benefits include Masonic burial rites for those who make the supreme sacrifice.

74. *Proceedings* (1943), 21. At the time, the Worshipful Master of Magnolia Lodge was L. L. Lockhart, who served as Grand Master from 1946 to 1955. The Worshipful Master of Amity Lodge was J. T. Maxey, who served as Grand Master from 1955 to 1965.
75. Ibid. A number of statements made by Coleman during this period indicate that he believed that World War II was a necessary evil. He often spoke of the necessity to defeat the "powers of darkness" as embodied in the Nazis and other Axis powers. Here, he quoted from a 1938 Nazi publication which stated that "Masonic lodges are associations of men who closely bound together in a union employing symbolical usages, represent a super-national spiritual movement, the idea of humanity, a general association of mankind, without distinction of races, people, religious, social, or political convictions." Coleman remarked: "This is true as we are told to keep ourselves in due bounds with all mankind and most especially for brother Masons." It goes without saying that Masonic ideals of the Fatherhood of God and the Brotherhood of Man are totally incompatible with the principles of Nazism.
76. *Proceedings of the Sixty-ninth Annual Communication of the Most Worshipful Grand Lodge of Texas, Free and Accepted Masons* (Fort Worth, Tx., 1944), 4.
77. Ibid., 12-13. The late O. E. Wilhite, who was made a Mason in 1929, said of Coleman: "Out of the Grand Masters, he's my choice." He described him as a master of ritual, who never used a book while conducting initiations. O. E. Wilhite, interview by author, Tape recording, Fort Worth, Texas, 23 June 1992. Subsequent interviews with Masons who knew Coleman confirm his ritualistic proficiency.
78. *Proceedings* (1944), 13.
79. Ibid., 14-15.
80. Ibid., 14.
81. Ibid., 20.
82. Ibid. Grand Master Coleman probably had little knowledge of Shinto, the indigenous religion of Japan. The infamous State Shinto, which taught that the emperor was descended from the sun goddess Amaterasu and was best known for its kamikazes (suicide pilots), was disbanded at the end of World War II. Many interesting varieties of popular Shinto survive today. For a comparison of Shinto and Freemasonry, see Don G. Campbell, "Shinto: A Masonic Contrast," *The New Age*, September 1977, 47-50.
83. *Proceedings* (1944), 21.
84. *Proceedings of the Seventieth Annual Communication of the Most Worshipful Grand Lodge of Texas, Free and Accepted Masons* (Fort Worth, Tx., 1945), 7.
85. Ibid., 8. There is no indication here that any of the Masonic dead were battlefield casualties.
86. Ibid., 9.
87. Ibid., 13-14.
88. Ibid., 14.
89. Ibid., 15.
90. Ibid., 16.
91. O. E. Wilhite, interview by author, 23 June 1992.
92. DeShong Smith, interview by author, 29 June 1992.
93. Charlie Wadley, interview by author, 22 June 1993.
94. A. D. Harris, interview by author, 24 June 1993.
95. T. W. Neal, interview by author, 23 June 1993.
96. *Proceedings of the Seventy-first Annual Communication of the Most Worshipful Grand Lodge of Texas, Free and Accepted Masons* (Fort Worth, Tx., 1946), 27. Sadly, Coleman did not live to see the opening of this session. His report of the Hot Springs meeting was presented by his successor, L. L. Lockhart.
97. Certificate of Death.
98. "William Coleman, F&AM Grand Master, Dies," 1.
99. Certificate of Death.

100. O. E. Wilhite, interview by author, 23 June 1992.
101. *Proceedings* (1946), 35.
102. "William Coleman, F&AM Grand Master, Dies," 1.

Lucian L. Lockhart
1. Roosevelt (1882-1945) was a member of Holland Lodge No. 8 in New York City; see William R. Denslow, *10,000 Famous Freemasons* (Columbia, Mo.: Missouri Lodge of Research, 1961), 4:66. Truman (1884-1972) was a member of Belton Lodge No. 340 in Belton, Missouri; see Allen E. Roberts, *Brother Truman: The Masonic Life and Philosophy of Harry S. Truman* (Highland Hills, Va: Anchor Communications, 1985), 241.
2. John D. Hicks and George E. Mowry, *A Short History of American Democracy* (Cambridge, Mass.: Riverside Press, 1956), 819.
3. Standard Certificate of Death for Lockhart, Lucian L., Texas Department of Heath Bureau of Vital Statistics.
4. "William Coleman, F&AM Grand Master, Dies: Rites Held Monday." *The Dallas Express*, 25 May 1946, 1.
5. *Proceedings of the Seventy-first Annual Communication of the Most Worshipful Grand Lodge, Free and Accepted Masons, Texas and Jurisdictions Belonging,* "Prince Hall Affiliation" (Fort Worth, Tx., 1946), 25-31.
6. Ibid., 31.
7. Ibid.
8. Dr. Yancy, who died in 1995, was a former president of Paul Quinn College and was known as the "Roving Editor" of the AME Church. He was a personal friend of the writer.
9. *Proceedings* (1946), 36. Jack Roosevelt ("Jackie") Robinson was born in Cairo, Georgia, to sharecropping parents. As a child, he moved with his family to Pasadena, California, where he sold newspapers on the streets. In high school he excelled in basketball, baseball, football, and track. He attended the University of California at Los Angeles, where he received his greatest acclaim in football. At the outbreak of World War II, he was drafted into the Army. Entering as a private, he was discharged as a second lieutenant. After the war, he joined the all-black Kansas City Monarchs baseball team. On 23 October 1945, the announcement was made in Montreal, Canada, that Robinson had signed a contract to play for the Montreal Royals of the International League. The Montreal team was part of the Brooklyn Dodgers organization owned by Branch Rickey. On 8 April 1947 he was transferred from the Royals to the Dodgers. He was an outstanding player for both teams despite much racist opposition; see Phil Pepe, *Winners Never Quit* (New York: Grosset and Dunlap, Inc., 1968), 128-34. His legacy has been well described: "It is unfortunate that Jackie Robinson came to baseball too late. He was 28 years old when he joined the Brooklyn Dodgers. He played ten years and he had a lifetime batting average of .311 under the most trying conditions any athlete has ever experienced. He might have played fifteen or twenty years and set unapproachable records if he had been given the chance to play earlier. He retired after the 1956 season and, in 1961, was elected to baseball's Hall of Fame.... His contribution to baseball ... lives with Willie Mays, Frank Robinson, Hank Aaron, Maury Wills, Roberto Clemente, Tony Oliva, Richie Allen, and hundreds of others who have come and gone and are still to come. Men who might never have been given the chance had it not been for one man's courage and will to succeed"; see ibid., 138.
10. *Proceedings* (1946), 36-37. Booker T. Washington (1859-1915) was born near Hales Ford, Virginia. He graduated from Hampton Institute in Virginia and received honorary degrees from Dartmouth College and Harvard University. He founded Tuskegee Institute in 1884 and was the author of the following books: *Sowing and Reaping, Up from Slavery, The Future of the American Negro, The Negro in Business, My Larger Education,* and *Character Building: Working with Hands.* He was made a Freemason "at sight" by the Grand Lodge of Massachusetts, see Joseph Mason Andrew Cox, *Great Black Men of Masonry: Qualitative Black Achievers who were Freemasons* (Bronx, N.Y.: Blue Diamond Press, 1982), 193-94.
11. *Proceedings* (1946), 37.
12. Ibid., 59.
13. At the death of Lockhart in 1955, Maxey was elected and installed as Grand Master. He held this office until his retirement in 1965 and was known as the mentor of his successor, Isadore Huddleston Clayborn, who served from 1965 to 1981.
14. *Proceedings of the Seventy-seventh Annual Communication of the Most Worshipful Grand Lodge, Free*

and Accepted Masons, Texas and Jurisdictions Belonging, "Prince Hall Affiliation" (Fort Worth, Tx., 1947), 25. In 1946 the Republicans gained control of both houses of Congress. However, they were unsuccessful in their efforts to prevent the reelection of Democratic President Harry S. Truman in 1948. In 1994 the Republicans again gained control of both houses of Congress. Nevertheless, they were unsuccessful in their efforts to prevent the reelection of Democratic President Bill Clinton in 1996. During his teens, Clinton, like the writer, was a member of the Order of DeMolay.

15. Ibid. This institution is now known as Texas Southern University.
16. Ibid. Sadly, the "death blow" to the Hooded Order was not fatal. The Ku Klux Klan still exists. There was at one time much overlapping in membership between the Klan and the Masonic Order; see Joseph A. Walkes, Jr., "The Ku Klux Klan and Regular Freemasonry," *The Phylaxis* 18 (Fourth Quarter 1992): 4-7.
17. *Proceedings* (1947), 25-26. The writer holds B.A., M.A., and Ph.D. degrees from Baylor University. He was once a member of Waco's Karem Shrine Temple. He finds it interesting that President Truman received his honorary degree on 6 March 1947—the 172nd anniversary of the initiation of Prince Hall into Freemasonry.
18. Ibid., 26-27. In 1947 the white Grand Lodge of Massachusetts extended recognition to the Prince Hall Grand Lodge of Massachusetts but later rescinded this after a number of white Grand Lodges—including Texas—threatened to sever fraternal relations; see Joseph A. Walkes, Jr., *History of the United Supreme Council, Ancient Accepted Scottish Rite Freemasonry, Prince Hall Affiliated, Northern Jurisdiction, U.S.A., Inc.* (Philadelphia, Pa.: United Supreme Council, PHA, NJ, Inc., 1998), 111-26.
19. Ibid., 28. Leon Maddox became Grand Secretary upon the retirement of William Madison McDonald, who had held this office from 1899 to 1946.
20. Ibid., 40.
21. *Proceedings of the Seventy-third Annual Communication of the Most Worshipful GrandLodge, Free and Accepted Masons, Texas and Jurisdictions Belonging, "Prince Hall Affiliation"* (Fort Worth, Tx., 1948), 30-34. Lockhart succeeded McDonald as president of Fraternal Bank and Trust. The late O. E. Wilhite recalled that, after McDonald's death in 1950, Lockhart "just let those folks borrow a lot of money there." He stated that Lockhart was, nevertheless, a good Grand Master and functioned well despite a hearing problem. According to Wilhite: "He was straightforward." O. E. Wilhite, interview by author, tape recording, Fort Worth, Texas, 23 June 1992. Current Grand Treasurer Kerwin W. Carter, Jr., who was a customer of Fraternal Bank and Trust before he became a Mason, recalled that the bank's eventual closure resulted at least in part from unsound transactions. He was unsure what role Lockhart played in this as the closure occurred after Lockhart's death. He stated that the black community of Fort Worth was greatly affected by the bank's closure. Kervin W. Carter, Jr., interview by author, tape recording, Fort Worth, Texas, 17 September 1994.
22. Ibid., 35.
23. Ibid., 38.
24. Ibid., 42.
25. Ibid., 49-50.
26. *Proceedings of the Seventy-fourth Annual Communication of the Most Worshipful Grand Lodge, Free and Accepted Masons, Texas and Jurisdictions Belonging, "Prince Hall Affiliation"* (Fort Worth, Tx., 1949), 50. The motion that the address be referred to the committee on the Grand Master's Address was made by Reuben G. White, a future Grand Master.
27. *Proceedings of the Seventy-fifth Annual Communication of the Most Worshipful Prince Hall Grand Lodge, Free and Accepted Masons, Texas and Jurisdictions Belonging* (Fort Worth, Tx., 1950), 9. For information on Lewis, see Joseph A. Walkes, Jr., *Jno. G. Lewis, Jr.—End of an Era: The History of the Prince Hall Grand Lodge of Louisiana, 1842-1979* (Leavenworth, Ks., 1986).
28. *Proceedings* (1950), 13.
29. Ibid., 27. Such a situation is a sharp contrast from the current situation of most Masonic jurisdictions, black and white, in which the number of funerals far exceeds the number of initiations.
30. Ibid.
31. Ibid., 27-31.
32. Ibid., 42-43. The now defunct College View Court-Hotel was located on Elm Avenue near the Waco campus of Paul Quinn College and owned by Dr. Yancy.
33. Ibid., 45.
34. Ibid., 60-61.
35. Ibid., 64-66.

36. Ibid., 66-70.
37. Ibid., 73.
38. Certificate of Death for William Madison McDonald. Cause of death was listed as Chronic Degenerative Myocarditis due to Senility and Prostatic Obstruction Medium Bar. Certificate was signed by one of his successors in the office of Grand Secretary, Harold B. Baker of Baker Funeral Home. Burial was in Old Trinity Cemetery in Fort Worth; see ibid. William Madison ("Gooseneck Bill") McDonald was born on 22 June 1866 at College Mound, Kaufman County, Texas, the son of George and Elora Scott McDonald. His father was born into slavery in Nashville, Tennessee. Confederate General Nathan Bedford Forrest once owned the elder McDonald and took him from Tennessee to Alabama, where he was sold and brought to Texas, eventually becoming the property of George Martin of Kaufman County; see Mack Williams, "Negro Once Ruled Texas Republicans," *Dallas Morning News*, 18 September 1949, IV-12. As a young man, Gooseneck Bill walked to Nashville, where he received a Bachelor of Arts degree from Fisk University. After graduation, he returned to Kaufman County, where he taught in public schools until he left teaching for full-time, paid fraternal work; see Arthur H. Lewis, *The Day They Shook the Plum Tree* (New York: Harcourt, Brace, and World, Inc., 1963), 106-08. He had an outstanding career not only in fraternalism and banking but also in politics. In 1892 he was elected to the state executive committee of the Texas Republican Party. After the death of Past Grand Master and Republican leader Norris Wright Cuney in 1898, he became the leader of black Republicans in Texas. He formed a political partnership with Col. E.H.R. Green of Terrell in the leadership of the "Black and Tan" faction of Texas Republicans. This partnership continued until 1912, when former President Theodore Roosevelt's Bull Moose Party shattered Republican unity. McDonald and Green attempted to make a comeback in 1920 in support of Gen. Leonard Wood's unsuccessful efforts to challenge Warren G. Harding for the Republican Presidential nomination. McDonald supported Progressive Party candidate Robert M. "Fighting Bob" LaFollette for president in 1924. He then gave his political endorsement to Democrats Al Smith and Franklin D. Roosevelt before returning to the Republican Party in 1948 to back Thomas E. Dewey against Harry S. Truman; see Paul D. Casdorph, "McDonald, William Madison," in *The Handbook of Texas: A Supplement* (Austin, Tx.: Texas State Historical Association, 1976), 556.
39. *Proceedings* (1950), 35.
40. *Proceedings of the Seventy-fifth Annual Communication of the Most Worshipful Prince Hall Grand Lodge, Free and Accepted Masons, Texas and Jurisdictions Belonging* (Fort Worth, Tx., 1951), 10. This fund is now called the NAACP Legal Defense and Educational Fund and is administratively separate from the NAACP.
41. Ibid., 24-25.
42. Ibid., 25. Today, cosmopolitanism is called "globalism" or "multiculturalism." It appears that, in many ways, Lockhart was ahead of his time in his thinking!
43. Ibid., 26.
44. Ibid., 28. Similar prospects were faced by Grand Master Henderson D. Winn during World War I and Grand Master William Coleman during World War II. Such problems are faced in time of war by any organization providing death benefits. For such, those in military service are regarded as "high risks." In view of the fact that most white Masonic bodies provide no insurance, it has been common for such lodges to hold mass initiations of soldiers immediately prior to these newly created brethren's departure for a combat zone.
45. Ibid., 29.
46. *Proceedings of the Seventy-seventh Annual Communication of the Most Worshipful Prince Hall Grand Lodge, Free and Accepted Masons, Texas and Jurisdictions Belonging* (Fort Worth, Tx., 1952), 24-26. According to T. W. Neal, Lockhart increased the Grand Lodge membership by 33,000. T. W. Neal, interview by author, 23 June 1993.
47. *Proceedings of the Seventy-eighth Annual Communication of the Most Worshipful Prince Hall Grand Lodge, Free and Accepted Masons, Texas and Jurisdictions Belonging* (Fort Worth, Tx., 1953), 45.
48. Ibid., 46. For a study of the effects of these forces published about this time, see David Riesman, Nathan Glazer, and Reuel Denney, *The Lonely Crowd: A Study of the Changing American Character* (Hartford, Ct.: Yale University Press, 1953).
49. *Proceedings* (1953), 46-47.
50. Ibid., 47.
51. Ibid., 56-57.
52. Ibid., 58.

53. Ibid., 61. Bro. McGowen was then reelected as Grand Recorder.
54. *Proceedings of the Seventy-ninth Annual Communication of the Most Worshipful Prince Hall Grand Lodge, Free and Accepted Masons, Texas and Jurisdictions Belonging* (Fort Worth, Tx., 1954), 7.
55. Ibid., 12.
56. Ibid., 17.
57. Ibid., 47. According to Past Grand Recorder A. D. Harris, Lockhart was a good administrator but tended to be dictatorial. A. D. Harris, interview by author, 24 June 1993.
58. Ibid., 58-59.
59. Ibid., 62. The opinion of the court was written by Chief Justice Earl Warren, a Past Grand Master of Masons in California. Many southern racists felt betrayed when Justice Hugo Black of Alabama, a Freemason and former member of the Ku Klux Klan, joined in the unanimous decision. Later Black participated in another historic event when he swore in Justice Thurgood Marshall, a Prince Hall Freemason and the first African American to serve on the highest court in the land.
60. *Proceedings of the Eightieth Annual Communication of the Most Worshipful Prince Hall Grand Lodge, Free and Accepted Masons, Texas and Jurisdictions Belonging* (Fort Worth, Tx., 1995), 6-7. One of P. G. Porter's major contributions to Prince Hall Freemasonry was his founding of the International Order, Knights of Pythagoras, in Chicago in 1958. Four years earlier, he had met Frank S. Land, the founder of the Order of DeMolay. The Knights of Pythagoras is considered the Prince Hall counterpart to DeMolay. Land wrote the Pythagorean ritual; see Joseph A. Walkes, Jr., *History of the Shrine: Ancient Egyptian Arabic Order, Nobles of the Mystic Shrine, Inc., Prince Hall Affiliated, A Pillar of Black Society, 1893-1993* (Detroit, Mi.: AEAONMS, Inc., PHA, 1993), 268-69.
61. *Proceedings* (1955), 7.
62. *Proceedings* (1955), 7. Gilliam's greetings came just two months before "his great state" received international media attention as a result of the lynching of a young African American from Chicago named Emmett Till; see Stephen J. Whitfield, *A Death in the Delta: The Story of Emmett Till* (Baltimore, Md.: Johns Hopkins University Press, 1988).
63. *Proceedings* (1955), 60-62.
64. Ibid., 61.
65. Ibid., 73.
66. Certificate of Death.
67. "Hundreds Attend Rites for Grand Master Lockhart." *The Houston Informer*, 8 October 1955, 1 and 14.
68. "Dignitaries Throughout Nation Attend L. L. Lockhart Rites." *The Houston Informer*, 8 October 1955, 1. Also well represented were other branches of the Masonic family, including the Order of the Eastern Star and the Heroines of Jericho, as well as professions such as public education and mortuary science.
69. *Proceedings of the Eighty-first Annual Communication of the Most Worshipful Prince Hall Grand Lodge, Free and Accepted Masons, Texas and Jurisdictions Belonging* (Fort Worth, Tx., 1956), 84-85.
70. Ibid., 31.

John Theodore Maxey

1. *Brown v. Board of Education of Topeka*, 347 U. S. 483 (1954), at 483. This case overturned *Plessy v. Ferguson*, 163 U. S. 537 (1896), which upheld "separate but equal" in public transportation. The *Brown* case was reargued 11-14 April 1955. The Supreme Court issued its opinion and judgments on 31 May 1955, reaffirming statements made the previous year.
2. *Proceedings of the Eightieth Annual Grand Communication of the Most Worshipful Prince Hall Grand Lodge, Free and Accepted Masons, Texas and Jurisdiction Belonging* (Fort Worth, Tx., 1955), 61.
3. Kitty Kendall, "Age Can't Keep Isle Man on Sidelines," *Galveston Daily News*, 14 July 1966, 9A. From his youth, Maxey heard stories about slavery. He told a reporter: "I distinctly remember the story told to me by my paternal great-grandmother Mrs. Hagar Broughton, who was born a slave and her master was her father. She grew up in his household as a servant, and when she reached womanhood she was married or mated to Cudo, a young African slave. Later she gave birth to a daughter whom she gave the name of Rachel. When her master sold all of his slaves and his plantation, he and his family and Hagar boarded a ship and sailed around Cape Horn and landed in California, and settled in Sacramento. Grandmother Rachel married a half-breed whose name was Joe Mack. Their first child was a boy and they gave him the name of John Joseph Mack and his playmates called him Maxey and he was my father and I was named John Theodore Maxey"; see Helen Smith, "Islander, 96, Recalls

Railroad, Masonic Heydey: J. T. Maxey Remembers Mule-Drawn Trolley Cars," *Galveston Daily News*, 12 April 1970, B-12.

4. Ibid. Sam Bass—the man who put Round Rock, Texas "on the map"—was born on a farm near Mitchell, Indiana, on July 21, 1851. The son of Daniel and Elizabeth Jane Bass, he was orphaned before the age of thirteen and spent the next five years at the home of an uncle. In 1869 he ran away and spent a winter working in a Mississippi sawmill. In 1870 he arrived in Texas. He worked as a cow hand and teamster in Denton County. Riding up the trail to Nebraska with a cattle herd in 1876, he and several companions went to Deadwood, which was then in its goldmining boom. They lost their money in gambling and, during the following year, robbed seven stagecoaches without recouping their fortunes. In September 1877 they held up a Union Pacific train at Big Springs, Nebraska. They took $60,000 in gold from the baggage car and several thousand dollars from passengers. Bass returned to Texas and organized a new outlaw gang. He held up two stagecoaches and, during the spring of 1878, robbed four trains within thirty miles of Dallas. However, these robberies brought little loot. On 19 July 1878 he tried to rob a bank at Round Rock but was wounded in a gunfight with Texas Rangers. He died there two days later; see Wayne Gard, "Sam Bass," in Walter Prescott Webb, ed., *The Handbook of Texas* (Austin, Tx.: Texas State Historical Association, 1952), 1:119. Bass was buried in Round Rock, where there is today a Sam Bass Motel and Restaurant. For an interesting study of the Texas Rangers written by an admirer, see Joseph E. Bennett, *Sixguns and Masons: Profiles of Selected Texas Rangers and Prominent Westerners* (Highland Springs, Va.: Anchor Communications, 1991). For an equally interesting and much more critical study see Julian Samora, Joe Bernal, and Albert Peña, *Gunpowder Justice: A Reassessment of the Texas Rangers* (Notre Dame, In.: Notre Dame University Press, 1979). Neither the white outlaw Sam Bass nor the white lawmen (as there would be no black or brown Texas Rangers for another hundred years) who killed him knew that there was living in Round Rock at the time a black child named John Theodore Maxey who was destined for greatness.

5. Smith, "Islander, 96, Recalls Railroad, Masonic Heydey," B-12.
6. Kendall, "Age Can't Keep Isle Man on Sidelines," 9-A. Maxey's mind was given to vivid recollections even in advanced age. Thus he reported: "On Saturday morning, September 8, as I rode my bike to the office, it was raining hard with a high wind. After doing my porter's duty, I gathered the mail and rode to the shops. I went to the depot on the I&GN train and after having watered and iced the train, we were informed the train could not leave because of high water. During the storm the water in the depot and train yards was near the platform of the cars. I hurried into the station, and with several others, stayed on the baggage room platform until the storm abated. Upon leaving, we found several dead and mangled bodies on the station walk, and as I waded down 26th Street on my way home, I found plenty of wreckage and dead animals"; see Smith, "Islander, 96, Recalls Railroad, Masonic Heydey," B-12.
7. Kendall, "Age Can't Keep Isle Man on Sidelines," 9-A.
8. Smith, "Islander, 96, Recalls Railroad, Masonic Heydey," B-12.
9. Ibid.
10. Kendall, "Age Can't Keep Isle Man on Sidelines," 9-A.
11. Smith, "Islander, 96, Recalls Railroad, Masonic Heydey," B-12.
12. "Deaths, Funerals: John T. Maxey," *Galveston Daily News*, 14 February 1973, A-12.
13. *Proceedings of the Eighty-first Annual Grand Communication of the Most Worshipful Grand Lodge, Free and Accepted Masons, Texas and Jurisdiction Belonging* (Fort Worth, Tx., 1956), 31.
14. Ibid., 32.
15. Ibid., 33.
16. Ibid., 34. Thurgood Marshall, a 33° Prince Hall Mason and Shriner, was born in Baltimore, Maryland, on 2 July 1908. He graduated with honors from Lincoln University in Philadelphia, Pennsylvania. Racial discrimination resulted in his rejection by the Maryland University Law School, but he persisted and graduated from the Howard University Law School in Washington, D. C. Marshall served from 1938 to 1941 as assistant legal counsel for the NAACP and from 1941 to 1961 as chief legal counsel. In the latter capacity, he was instrumental in involving Prince Hall Shriners in the work of the NAACP Legal Defense and Education Fund; and was the lead attorney in the aforementioned *Brown v. Board of Education* case. He was appointed to the U. S. Court of Appeals for the Second Circuit (New York, Connecticut, and Vermont) in 1961 by President John F. Kennedy and as U. S. solicitor general by President Lyndon Baines Johnson in 1965. Two years later, President Johnson appointed him as the first black U. S. Supreme Court justice. Marshall held the latter position from 2 October 1967 until his retirement on 29 June 1991. He died at Bethesda Naval Medical Center in

Maryland on 24 January 1993. At the time of his death, *Pyramid* editor Fred Williams wrote: "Allah has called home this champion of civil and human rights, who always maintained that the law should not only punish, but protect the rights of all in America"; see Fred Williams, "Thurgood Marshall, 1908-1993," *The Pyramid* 52 (First Quarter 1993): ii.
17. *Proceedings* (1956), 35.
18. *Proceedings of the Eighty-second Annual Grand Communication of the Most Worshipful Prince Hall Grand Lodge, Free and Accepted Masons, Texas and Jurisdiction Belonging* (Fort Worth, Tx., 1957), 9-10.
19. In 1912 the Grand Lodge approved a resolution for the establishment of this bank, which served as the depository not only for Masons but also for Odd Fellows, Knights of Pythias, and other black organizations. Grand Secretary William Madison ("Gooseneck Bill") McDonald served as president of this bank for many years and was instrumental in keeping it solvent throughout the years of the Great Depression. Apparently, his successors did not possess the same business acumen.
20. *Proceedings* (1957), 10-11.
21. Ibid., 11.
22. Ibid., 12.
23. Ibid., 27-28.
24. Ibid., 39-40.
25. Ibid., 40.
26. Ibid., 41.
27. Ibid., 45-46.
28. *Proceedings of the Eighty-third Annual Grand Communication of the Most Worshipful Prince Hall Grand Lodge, Free and Accepted Masons, Texas and Jurisdiction Belonging* (Fort Worth, Tx., 1958), 13.
29. Ibid., 15-16.
30. Ibid., 30.
31. Ibid., 31.
32. Ibid., 31-32.
33. Ibid., 32-33. This fund—which was Maxey's brainchild—was later renamed in his honor.
34. Ibid., 33.
35. Ibid., 38-39.
36. *Proceedings of the Eighty-fourth Annual Grand Communication of the Most Worshipful Prince Hall Grand Lodge, Free and Accepted Masons of Texas and Jurisdiction Belonging* (Fort Worth, Tx., 1959), 34-38.
37. Ibid., 36.
38. Ibid., 38.
39. Ibid., 68-69.
40. *Proceedings of the Eighty-fifth Annual Grand Communication of the Most Worshipful Prince Hall Grand Lodge, Free and Accepted Masons of Texas and Jurisdiction Belonging* (Fort Worth, Tx., 1960), 25-28. When Grand Master Maxey spoke these words about "remaining young amidst aging toll of past years," he was eighty-five years old but obviously still young at heart!
41. Ibid., 28-38. No doubt, from his place in the Celestial Lodge Above, Maxey is pleased to see the recognition of Prince Hall Freemasonry by a number of white Grand Lodges since 1989.
42. Ibid., 39-40.
43. Ibid., 54-55.
44. Ibid., 55-56. The answer to Bro. Smead's question is "He can't." Forty years later, this message remains relevant indeed.
45. Ibid., 13-14.
46. *Proceedings of the Eighty-sixth Annual Grand Communication of the Most Worshipful Prince Hall Grand Lodge, Free and Accepted Masons of Texas and Jurisdiction Belonging* (Fort Worth, Tx., 1961), 13-14.
47. Ibid., 31.
48. Ibid., 34.
49. Ibid., 34-35.
50. Ibid.
51. *Proceedings of the Eighty-seventh Annual Grand Communication of the Most Worshipful Prince Hall Grand Lodge, Free and Accepted Masons of Texas and Jurisdiction Belonging* (Fort Worth, Tx., 1962), 32.
52. Ibid., 37-38.
53. Ibid., 32.

54. Ibid., 35.
55. Ibid., 38-39. In his Report of the Director of Public Relations, Dr. Yancy noted the highly significant fact that, at the Grand Masters Conference, Prince Hall Masons successfully challenged hotel segregation in Houston. He wrote: "It was the Prince Hall Masons who first went into the hotels as a group. And it was Grand Master Maxey who became the host to the first group of men to test the hotel integration system in the largest segregated city in America." Truly, Maxey was the man of the hour, the Grand Master of the Civil Rights Era! See ibid., 58-59.
56. Ibid., 39.
57. Ibid., 40.
58. Ibid., 41.
59. Ibid., 53.
60. Ibid.
61. *Proceedings of the Eighty-eighth Annual Grand Communication of the Most Worshipful Prince Hall Grand Lodge, Free and Accepted Masons of Texas and Jurisdiction Belonging* (Fort Worth, Tx., 1963), 32.
62. Ibid., 40. During the discussion of plans to purchase this property, Ernest Wisby suggested that the Grand Lodge also purchase a place of residence for the Grand Master, which would pass on to each succeeding Grand Master. At that point, Maxey reminded them that they could act officially only on the business at hand.
63. Ibid., 32-33.
64. Ibid., 38-43.
65. *Proceedings of the Eighty-ninth Annual Communication of the Most Worshipful Prince Hall Grand Lodge, Free and Accepted Masons of Texas and Jurisdiction Belonging* (Fort Worth, Tx., 1964), 33-34.
66. Ibid., 70-71.
67. Ibid., 42-43.
68. Ibid., 44-45.
69. *Proceedings of the Ninetieth Annual Grand Communication of the Most Worshipful Prince Hall Grand Lodge, Free and Accepted Masons of Texas and Jurisdiction Belonging* (Fort Worth, Tx., 1965), 7-8. The word *zeitgeist* is derived from two German words—*zeit* ("time") and *geist* ("spirit"). *Zeitgeist* refers to the spirit of the time—the general intellectual and moral state or the trend of culture and taste characteristic of an era. The *zeitgeist* of the 1960s was one of peace and freedom.
70. Ibid., 17. It is unlikely that the white Grand Master of Texas attended this 1965 meeting. However, in 1975, Prince Hall Grand Master I. H. Clayborn met with white Grand Master Robert B. O'Connor; and, in 1997, Prince Hall Grand Master Robert E. Connor, Jr., met with white Grand Master Joseph Regian.
71. Ibid., 18.
72. Ibid., 39-40.
73. Ibid., 38-39. In view of this tragedy, the Grand Lodge awarded life membership to Bro. Baker and $200 to Sis. Baker.
74. Ibid., 43. Bro. Webber had previously been employed as a clerk in the Grand Lodge office.
75. Ibid., 38, 43. There had been no living Past Grand Master of Texas since the death of W. L. Kimbrough in 1955. There would be no living Past Grand Master of Texas from the time of Maxey's death in 1973 until the time of I. H. Clayborn's stepping down in 1981.
76. Ibid., 46-47.
77. Ibid., 54-55.
78. *Proceedings of the Ninety-first Annual Grand Communication of the Most Worshipful Prince Hall Grand Lodge, Free and Accepted Masons, Texas and Jurisdiction Belonging* (Fort Worth, Tx., 1966), 31.
79. "Deaths, Funerals," A-12.
80. *Proceedings of the Ninety-eighth Annual Grand Communication of the Most Worshipful Prince Hall Grand Lodge, Free and Accepted Masons of Texas and Jurisdiction Belonging* (Fort Worth, Tx., 1973), 32-33.

Isadore Huddleston Clayborn

1. "A Celebration of Love in Memory of Isadore Huddleston Clayborn," *Texas Prince Hall Masonic Quarterly* 108 (June 1994): 3.
2. *Proceedings of the Ninety-sixth Annual Grand Communication of the Most Worshipful Prince Hall Grand Lodge of Texas and Jurisdiction Belonging* (Fort Worth, Tx., 1971), 3.

3. "A Celebration of Love in Memory of Isadore Huddleston Clayborn," 3.
4. Ibid. The latter was conferred on Wednesday, 11 April 1973, during Bishop College's Ninety-second Founder's Day Convocation. During this ceremony, honorary doctorates were also conferred upon Rev. William T. McKee, Associate General Secretary of the American Baptist Convention for Educational Ministries; and Rev. W. Sterling Cary, President of the National Council of Churches of Christ in the U.S.A.; see "Ninety-second Founder's Day Convocation." Dallas, Tx: Bishop College, April 14, 1973.
5. Roberta Clayborn, interview by author, tape recording, September 18, 1996.
6. "A Celebration of Love in Memory of Isadore Huddleston Clayborn," 3. He still held his position with Pioneer Management Company at the time of his death on April 4, 1994.
7. Joseph A. Walkes, Jr., "Remembering I. H. Clayborn," *News Quarterly* (Spring 1994): 17-18.
8. Ibid.
9. Ibid.
10. *Proceedings of the Ninetieth Annual Grand Communication of the Most Worshipful Prince Hall Grand Lodge, Free and Accepted Masons of Texas and Jurisdiction Belonging* (Fort Worth, Tx., 1965), 7-8, 11.
11. Ibid., 46.
12. "A Celebration of Love in Memory of Isadore Huddleston Clayborn," 3.
13. *Proceedings of the Ninety-first Annual Grand Communication of the Most Worshipful Prince Hall Grand Lodge of Texas and Jurisdiction Belonging* (Fort Worth, Tx., 1966), 5. The situation addressed by Grand Master Hall was rectified on December 14, 1994, when the Grand Lodge of England extended recognition to the Prince Hall Grand Lodge of Massachusetts.
14. Ibid., 42.
15. Ibid., 45.
16. Ibid., 46. On November 15, 1986 the writer was the speaker at a banquet sponsored by Key West Consistory.
17. Ibid., 47.
18. Ibid., 48.
19. Ibid., 49. Unfortunately, thirty-five years later, this remains a serious problem.
20. Ibid., 50-51.
21. Ibid., 54.
22. Ibid., 57.
23. Ibid., 60. The latter council—better known as "Vatican II"—lasted from 1962 to 1965 and brought the Roman Catholic Church into the ecumenical movement. Previously, Catholics had denounced Protestant Christians as "heretics" and Eastern Orthodox Christians as "schismatics." At Vatican II, Pope John XXIII (who died on June 3, 1963) introduced the term "separated brethren." Unfortunately, the council did nothing to alter Catholic attitudes toward Freemasonry. However, on December 11, 1962, Monsignor Méndez of Cernavaca, Mexico, called for better relations between Catholics and Masons, arguing that the Church should not continue to make Freemasons "the object of recriminations" and acknowledging "that the origins of Freemasonry were anything but anti-Christians, and that various Masonic trends were definitely in favour of a reconciliation with the Church"; see Carlo Falconi, *Pope John and the Ecumenical Council: A Diary of the Second Vatican Council, September-December 1962*, Muriel Grindrod, trans. (New York: World Publishing Co., 1964), 344.
24. *Proceedings* (1966), 61-63. The writer, along with other members of Waco Chapter, Order of DeMolay, participated in the dedication of this library and museum on September 27, 1969. During the 1970s, while active in white Masonry, he became acquainted with Robert Lee Lockwood, the man for whom this beautiful edifice was named. Lockwood was born in Waco on November 11, 1900. He graduated from Waco High School in 1918 and received a Bachelor of Business Administration degree from the University of Texas at Austin in 1922. He served as Master Councilor of DeMolay in 1921 and was raised to the sublime degree of Master Mason on January 24, 1922. He held many prominent offices in various houses of Masonry. When he was elected Grand Master of Texas in 1938, he was the youngest man ever to hold such an office. He received the 33° of the Scottish Rite in 1941, became Sovereign Grand Inspector General in Texas in 1952, and was selected as Deputy Grand Commander for the Supreme Council, Southern Jurisdiction, in 1969; see William R. White, *Texas Scottish Rite Centennial and Its Contributions to the Beginning of the Second Century* (Waco, Tx., 1973), 79-86. Lockwood died in August 1980.
25. *Proceedings* (1966), 64.

26. *Proceedings of the Ninety-second Annual Grand Communication of the Most Worshipful Prince Hall Grand Lodge of Texas and Jurisdiction Belonging* (Fort Worth, Tx., 1967), 42.
27. Ibid., 46.
28. Ibid., 51.
29. Ibid., 55. The writer was a member of the Kaufman lodge from 1981 to 1988; see Robert L. Uzzel, "History of Beehive Lodge No. 484, Kaufman, Texas," *Texas Prince Hall Masonic Quarterly* 87 (March 1988): 4-5.
30. Ibid., 56.
31. Ibid., 63.
32. Ibid., 66.
33. Ibid., 67.
34. Ibid., 67-68.
35. Ibid., 68.
36. Ibid., 72.
37. *Proceedings of the Ninety-third Annual Grand Communication of the Most Worshipful Prince Hall Grand Lodge of Texas and Jurisdiction Belonging* (Fort Worth, Tx., 1968), 3.
38. Ibid.
39. Ibid., 49-50. This committee was chaired by the writer's good friend, Harry H. Carson of Terrell. Bro. Carson died in August 1997.
40. Ibid., 53.
41. Ibid., 61.
42. *Proceedings of the Ninety-fourth Annual Grand Communication of the Most Worshipful Prince Hall Grand Lodge of Texas and Jurisdiction Belonging* (Fort Worth, Tx., 1969), 40-41.
43. Ibid., 41.
44. Ibid., 42.
45. Ibid., 45.
46. *Proceedings of the Ninety-fifth Annual Grand Communication of the Most Worshipful Prince Hall Grand Lodge of Texas and Jurisdiction Belonging* (Fort Worth, Tx., 1970), 39-40. Robert Davis, Jr., was a friend of the writer. He was serving as Deputy of the Oasis of Dallas for the Prince Hall Shriners at the time of his death in June 1985.
47. Ibid., 40.
48. Ibid.
49. Ibid., 42.
50. Ibid., 43.
51. Ibid., 44.
52. Ibid., 53.
53. *Proceedings of the Ninety-sixth Annual Grand Communication of the Most Worshipful Prince Hall Grand Lodge of Texas and Jurisdiction Belonging* (Fort Worth, Tx., 1971), 39.
54. Ibid., 40.
55. Ibid., 42.
56. Ibid., 43.
57. Ibid., 45.
58. Ibid., 68. The writer knew Bro. Flanagan and served as pastor to his wife, Sis. Minnie A. Flanagan, at Emmanuel African Methodist Episcopal Church from 1976 to 1979.
59. Ibid., 46.
60. Ibid., 47-48. The writer completed his Master of Arts degree at Baylor University in 1976. His thesis was entitled "The Nation of Islam: Belief and Practice in Light of the American Constitutional Principle of Religious Liberty." During this time, he was living in Teague, where he became a close friend of Bro. Johnson, who was very interested in his thesis. He has many fond memories of Johnson, who died in 1981. After his death, Johnson's widow gave the writer her husband's Masonic ring, which he wears proudly today.
61. Ibid., 48. Unfortunately, over thirty years later, school integration has *not* led to widespread church integration. The 11 o'clock hour on Sunday continues to be the most segregated hour of the week.
62. Ibid. In recent years, many Muslims have shown a great deal of interest in Freemasonry and some have become members of the fraternity. The writer's friend Jamal Rasheed is the first Muslim to serve as Worshipful Master of a Texas lodge. He has held a number of offices and honors, including the 33°; and has served as state director for the Knights of Pythagoras. Other Muslims, however, have been

quite hostile to Masonry. Mustafa El-Amin of Newark, New Jersey, has written three anti-Masonic books: *Al-Islam, Christianity, and Freemasonry* (Jersey City, N. J.: New Mind Productions, 1985); *Freemasonry, Ancient Egypt, and the Islamic Destiny* (Jersey City, N.J.: New Mind Productions, 1988); and *African-American Freemasons: Why They Should Accept Al-Islam* (Jersey City, N. J.: New Mind Productions, 1990). The writer held a dialogue with El-Amin at the Phylaxis Society convention in Washington, D. C. in 1987 and again in Little Rock, Arkansas, in 1989.

63. *Proceedings* (1971), 62.
64. Walkes, "Remembering I. H. Clayborn," 18.
65. *Proceedings of the Ninety-seventh Grand Communication of the Most Worshipful Prince Hall Grand Lodge of Texas and Jurisdiction Belonging* (Fort Worth, Tx., 1972), 61. In April 1991 the white and Prince Hall Grand Lodges of Minnesota established fraternal relations. The former body approved: "Full recognition . . . all the rights and privileges that accompany recognition between Regular Grand Lodges"; see Paul Bessel, "PHA Recognition," http://bessel.org/pha.htm, 2.
66. *Proceedings* (1972), 52.
67. Ibid., 53.
68. Ibid., 55-56.
69. Ibid., 56.
70. Ibid., 64.
71. Ibid., 70.
72. *Proceedings of the Ninety-eighth Annual Grand Communication of the Most Worshipful Prince Hall Grand Lodge of Texas and Jurisdiction Belonging* (Fort Worth, Tx., 1973), 32. Rev. McCormick, a 33° Mason, served as pastor of Baker Chapel AME Church in Fort Worth from 1977 until his death in 2002.
73. Ibid., 32-33.
74. Walkes, "Remembering I. H. Clayborn," 18.
75. *Proceedings* (1973), 33.
76. Ibid., 35-36. Brotherhood in Action, an inter-fraternal organization, has had a wholesome influence in Connecticut for many years. Its membership includes white Masons, Prince Hall Masons, members of the Knights of Columbus (a Roman Catholic fraternal order), and members of the B'nai B'rith (a Jewish fraternal order whose Hebrew name means "Sons of the Covenant"). No doubt involvement in this organization brought white and black Masons closer together and contributed to the mutual recognition achieved by the Caucasian and Prince Hall Grand Lodges of Connecticut on October 14, 1989; see Bessel, "PHA Recognition," 1. This recognition "broke the ice" and has been followed by similar actions in thirty-six other states. May we live to see the total collapse of the Masonic "Berlin Wall"!
77. *Proceedings* (1973), 33.
78. Ibid., 35-36.
79. Ibid., 36.
80. Ibid., 37.
81. Ibid., 44.
82. Ibid., 45-46.
83. *Proceedings of the Ninety-ninth Annual Grand Communication of the Most Worshipful Prince Hall Grand Lodge of Texas and Jurisdiction Belonging* (Fort Worth, Tx., 1974), 30. According to Nehemiah 8:1-8: "And all the people gathered themselves together as one man into the street that was before the water gate, and they spoke unto Ezra the scribe to bring the book of the law of Moses, which the Lord had commanded to Israel. And Ezra the priest brought the law before the congregation both of men and women and all that could hear with understanding . . . and the ears of all the people were attentive unto the book of the law. . . . And Ezra blessed the Lord, the great God. And all the people answered Amen, Amen, with lifting up their hands: and they bowed their heads, and worshipped the Lord with their face to the ground. . . . So they read in the book in the law of God distinctly, and gave the sense, and caused them to understand the reading." The focus of this passage of scripture is obedience to the law of God. Such is a sharp contrast with the "Watergate" of Richard Nixon, with its focus on law-breaking.
84. *Proceedings* (1974), 31.
85. Ibid., 32.
86. Ibid., 33-34.
87. Ibid., 34.

88. Ibid., 35-36.
89. Ibid., 43.
90. Ibid., 44.
91. Ibid., 45.
92. Ibid., 56.
93. *1875-1975 Centennial, Most Worshipful Prince Hall Grand Lodge of Texas and Jurisdiction, Free and Accepted Masons, June 22-26, 1975* (Souvenir Journal).
94. Ibid. Ford is numbered among the fifty-year members Doric Lodge No. 34 in Grand Rapids, Michigan. He is a 33° Scottish Rite Mason of the Northern Jurisdiction and holds the Grand Cross Court of Honour in the Southern Jurisdiction. He is also a member of Saladin Shrine Temple in Grand Rapids; see Ivan M. Tribe, "Gerald R. Ford, 33°, G:.C:. the Most Recent Masonic President," *The Scottish Rite Journal*, September 2003, http://www.srmason-sj.org/web/journal-files/Issues/sept03/tribe.htm, 3.
95. Ibid.
96. Ibid.
97. *Proceedings of the Centennial Annual Grand Communication of the Most Worshipful Prince Hall Grand Lodge of Texas and Jurisdiction Belonging* (Fort Worth, Tx., 1975), 27
98. Ibid., 28.
99. Ibid., 29.
100. Ibid., 30.
101. Ibid., 32.
102. Ibid., 33.
103. Ibid., 51.
104. Ibid., 52. This was the first Grand Lodge Communication since the Vietnam War ended with the fall of the Saigon government on 30 April 1975. According to Isaiah 8:11-14: "For the Lord spake thus to me with a strong hand, and instructed me that I should not walk in the way of this people, saying, Say ye not, a confederacy, to all them to whom this people shall say, a confederacy; neither fear ye their fear, nor be afraid. Sanctify the Lord of hosts himself; and let him be your fear, and let him be your dread. And ye shall be for a sanctuary; but for a stone of stumbling and for a rock of offence to both the houses of Israel for a gin and for a snare to the inhabitants of Jerusalem." This scripture urges people to seek the Lord!
105. *Proceedings* (1975), 52.
106. *Proceedings of the One Hundred and First Annual Grand Communication of the Most Worshipful Prince Hall Grand Lodge of Texas and Jurisdiction Belonging* (Fort Worth, Tx., 1976), 32.
107. Ibid.
108. Ibid. At the 1982 Communication, Clayborn showed the writer a pocket piece given to him by O'Connor. Regarding the 1975 meeting, he said: "Two men understood each other." On July 11, 1994, the writer wrote to O'Connor, notifying him of Clayborn's death. O'Connor sent him the following reply: "I appreciate your advising me of PGM Clayborn's passing. He was a good man and I am sure he will be sorely missed. No doubt those with whom he came in contact are better off for his passing their way. We should be grateful for his stewardship and not despair about the future because his spirit and example live on"; see Robert B. O'Connor, letter to the author, July 18, 1994.
109. *Proceedings* (1976), 41-42. According to most Bible scholars, the Arabs are descended from Ishmael, the older son of Abraham by his concubine Hagar; while the Jews are descended from Isaac, the younger son of Abraham by his wife Sarah. Thus, Jesus was of the line of Isaac, while Muhammad was of the line of Ishmael; see Genesis 16, 17, and 21.
110. *Proceedings of the One Hundred and Second Annual Grand Communication of the Most Worshipful Prince Hall Grand Lodge of Texas and Jurisdiction Belonging* (Fort Worth, Tx., 1977), 26.
111. Ibid., 28.
112. Ibid., 29.
113. Ibid., 31.
114. Ibid., 46.
115. Ibid., 47.
116. *Proceedings of the One Hundred and Third Annual Grand Communication of the Most Worshipful Prince Hall Grand Lodge of Texas and Jurisdiction Belonging* (Fort Worth, Tx., 1978), 5.
117. Ibid., 32.
118. Ibid.

119. Ibid., 33.
120. Ibid., 41.
121. Ibid., 42. The writer visited with Bro. Wesley (1892-1987) a few months before his death at Howard University Hospital in Washington, D. C.; see Robert L. Uzzel, "The Passing of a Great Masonic Historian," *Texas Prince Hall Masonic Quarterly* 91 (March 1990): 8.
122. *Proceedings* (1978), 43.
123. *Proceedings of the One Hundred and Fourth Annual Grand Communication of the Most Worshipful Prince Hall Grand Lodge of Texas and Jurisdiction Belonging* (Fort Worth, Tx., 1979), 30.
124. Ibid., 31. For more information on Lewis' life, death, and legacy, see Joseph A. Walkes, Jr., *Jno. G. Lewis, Jr.—End of an Era: The History of the Prince Hall Grand Lodge of Louisiana, 1842-1979* (Washington, D. C.: United Supreme Council, A&ASR, PHA, USA, 1979).
125. It was the sad duty of Phylaxis Society president Joseph A. Walkes, Jr., to notify Clayborn by telephone of the passing of Lewis. Three weeks later, Walkes visited Clayborn at his home in Dallas and interviewed him for publication in the next issue of the *News Quarter*, a memorial issue dedicated to Lewis. When Walkes asked Clayborn about the future of the Supreme Council, Clayborn responded: "We are not a fly-by night organization. He [Lewis] had been Commander for 18 years, so why change it? The only thing we need to do now is to take the foundation that he had laid and build on it! If you were at the memorial services in Baton Rouge, Louisiana, you heard me say to the Brethren, and I meant it, that I wanted no one to call me Sovereign Grand Commander, because during this period, from April the first until our first Executive Session, the United Supreme Council of the Southern Jurisdiction is in mourning. And as far as I am concerned our Sovereign Grand Commander is waiting to see what we are going to do"; see Walkes, "Remembering I. H. Clayborn," 18.
126. *Proceedings* (1979), 32.
127. Ibid., 52. In August 1990 the writer spoke at a meeting of this lodge. In April 1991 he returned to speak at a lodge banquet. Between the two events, he wrote letters to three members who were stationed in Saudi Arabia during Operation Desert Storm.
128. Ibid., 31.
129. Ibid., 33.
130. Ibid., 53.
131. Ibid., 36-37.
132. Ibid., 41.
133. Ibid., 40.
134. *Proceedings of the One Hundred and Fifth Annual Grand Communication of the Most Worshipful Prince Hall Grand Lodge of Texas and Jurisdiction Belonging* (Fort Worth, Tx., 1980), 24.
135. Ibid., 26-27.
136. Ibid., 27-28. President Tolbert, who served as Deputy for the Supreme Council in Liberia, was assassinated, along with twelve other government officials, in a coup led by Samuel Kenyon Doe on April 12, 1980. During the extremely violent period that followed, the Prince Hall Masonic Temple in Liberia was severely damaged and a number of Masonic leaders were put to death. After Doe became president of Liberia, he was invited to the White House by President Ronald Reagan. This invitation resulted in letters of protest from Clayborn and other leaders of Prince Hall Freemasonry; see Joseph A. Walkes, Jr., *Prince Hall's Mission: The Rise of the Phylaxis Society* (Kansas City, Mo.: Midtown Printing and Publishing Co., 1995), 139.
137. Ibid., 28.
138. Ibid., 29.
139. Ibid., 37.
140. Ibid., 39.
141. Ibid.
142. Ibid., 44.
143. Ibid. One of the distinguished visitors to the centennial celebration was Sovereign Grand Commander Stanley F. Maxwell of the white Supreme Council, Northern Jurisdiction. An historic picture of Grand Commanders Clayborn, Gideon, and Maxwell in a moment of fraternal unity was taken; see "100 Years of Unity: Northern Jurisdiction of Prince Hall Observes Anniversary," *The Phylaxis* 8 (Second Quarter): 33. Conspicuous for his absence was Sovereign Grand Commander Henry C. Clausen of the white Supreme Council, Southern Jurisdiction. Clausen could have made the circle complete. Unfortunately, he was well known for his anti-Prince Hall attitude.

144. *Proceedings of the One Hundred and Sixth Annual Grand Communication of the Most Worshipful Prince Hall Grand Lodge of Texas and Jurisdiction Belonging* (Fort Worth, Tx., 1981), 24-25. Noble Smith graduated from Paul Quinn College in Waco in 1938. The writer met him when PQC conferred upon him an honorary Doctor of Humane Letters on November 15, 1985. Prince Hall Shriners from several Texas temples were present. Immediately prior to his acceptance speech, Noble Smith was introduced by Noble Clayborn; see Harry E. Smith, "Remarks by Harry E. Smith, MPS, Past Imperial Potentate, A.E.A.O.N.M.S., Acceptance of Honorary Doctorate Degree from Paul Quinn College, Waco, Texas, November 15, 1985," *The Phylaxis* 11 (Fourth Quarter 1985): 44-45.
145. *Proceedings* (1981), 25.
146. Ibid., 25-26.
147. Ibid., 26.
148. Ibid.
149. Ibid., 32.
150. Ibid., 34.
151. Bro. Wilhite was a friend of the writer, who interviewed him during the 1992 Communication regarding the history of the Grand Lodge. In January 1993 the writer attended Bro. Wilhite's funeral at Wesley Chapel AME Church in Rockdale.
152. *Proceedings* (1981), 37-38.
153. "Ninety-Seventh Annual Session, Little Rock, Arkansas, 1983," *News Quarterly* (Summer 1984): 16. Bill Clinton, like the writer, was a DeMolay. However, he never became a Mason. While serving as governor of Arkansas, he appointed Grand Master Howard L. Woods to a position on the Arkansas State Police Commission. In 1992 and again in 1996, Clinton was elected president of the United States.
154. Ibid., 16-18. Jemison, pastor of Mount Zion First Baptist Church in Baton Rouge, Louisiana, where Jno. G. Lewis, Jr., was an active member for many years. In April 1979 Jemison preached Lewis' funeral.
155. Ibid., 20.
156. Walkes, *Prince Hall's Mission*, 132.
157. Ibid., 84.
158. The writer was present at this luncheon and has fond recollections of Clayborn's speech.
159. Walkes, *Prince Hall's Mission*, 186.
160. Ibid., 186-88.
161. I. H. Clayborn, "Sovereign Grand Commander's allocution," *News Quarterly* (Spring 1989): 4. It was quite controversial when Massachusetts Governor Michael Dukakis passed over Rev. Jesse Jackson and selected Texas Senator Lloyd Bentsen as his running mate. Unfortunately, Dukakis and Bentsen were defeated by then Vice President George Bush and Indiana Senator Dan Quayle. Bentsen is a 33° Mason. Dukakis, Bush, and Quayle are not Masons.
162. I. H. Clayborn, "A Report," *News Quarterly* (Spring 1989): 2. Liberian President Samuel Keynon Doe, whose presence at the White House had been protested by Clayborn, sent letters to Clayborn and a number of Grand Masters, informing them that he had lifted his government's ban on Freemasonry and directed the squatters occupying the Masonic Temple to immediately vacate the building. These actions appear to have resulted from the pressure placed by Prince Hall Masonic leaders on the Congressional Black Caucus; see Walkes, *Prince Hall's Mission*, 198. Eventually, Doe launched a fund-raising affair in order to repair the temple and invited Clayborn and other leaders to Liberia. Finally, Doe and Clayborn reached an agreement whereby Doe would become a Prince Hall Mason and the Grand Lodge of Liberia (which had operated underground for eight years) would be publicly reactivated; see ibid., 228. Several years later, Doe was killed in another coup, himself becoming a victim of the violence he had brought to his country; see ibid., 294.
163. I. H. Clayborn, "Sovereign Grand Commander's Allocution," *News Quarterly* (Spring 1990): 3-4.
164. I. H. Clayborn, "Sovereign Grand Commander's Allocution," *News Quarterly* (October 1990): 4. At the time Clayborn made this speech, America was in the midst of "Operation Desert Shield" which followed Iraq's invasion of Kuwait. On January 16, 1991 the first bombs were dropped on Iraq, and "Operation Desert Storm" began. Many Americans agreed with President George Bush that war against Iraq's Saddam Hussein was justified. The writer rejected this view and concurred with fellow Prince Hall Freemason Rev. Jesse Jackson that a negotiated settlement would have been possible and all bloodshed avoided.

165. I. H. Clayborn, "Sovereign Grand Commander's Allocution," *News Quarterly* (Spring 1992): 3.
166. I. H. Clayborn, "A Report," *News Quarterly* (Spring 1992): 2.
167. *Proceedings of the One Hundred and Seventeenth Annual Grand Communication of the Most Worshipful Prince Hall Grand Lodge of Texas and Jurisdiction Belonging* (Fort Worth, Tx., 1992), 29.
168. I. H. Clayborn, "Sovereign Grand Commander's Allocution," *News Quarterly* (Spring 1994): 3-4. During the last few years of Clayborn's life, there was a storm of controversy over the Washington, D. C. statue of Albert Pike, Confederate General, Masonic scholar, and Sovereign Grand Commander of the Caucasian Supreme Council, Southern Jurisdiction, from 1859 to 1891, due to the claim that Pike was a member of the Ku Klux Klan. When Joseph A. Walkes, Jr.'s article "The Ku Klux Klan and Regular Freemasonry" appeared in the Spring 1992 issue of *News Quarterly*, it came to the attention of the followers of the eccentric politician Lyndon LaRouche, who sought to use it as ammunition in their efforts to have the statue removed. The article was reprinted in the Fourth Quarter 1992 issue of *The Phylaxis*, along with several articles submitted by LaRouche's followers, who sought to persuade Prince Hall Freemasons to join their anti-Pike crusade. Their efforts were unsuccessful. Bro. Walkes finally concluded that, if the statue came down, Masonry as a whole would suffer and Prince Hall Masonry would have nothing to gain; see Joseph A. Walkes, Jr., "Letter," *The Phylaxis* 18 (Fourth Quarter 1992): 7. Grand Master Howard Woods of Arkansas agreed, recognizing that, while Pike's racial views were not "politically correct" by current standards, he was, like all men, a product of his time. Thus, Woods declared: "Let the statue stand as a reminder that the good and evil of men are in equilibrium within us, and we all should strive for perfection now and in the future, not in the past"; see Allen E. Roberts, "Let the Beauty of Freemasonry Into Your Heart," *The Phylaxis* 19 (First Quarter 1993): 10.
169. "Celebration Service," *Texas Prince Hall Masonic Quarterly* 108 (June 1994): 4.
170. Ibid.
171. "United Supreme Council Resolution," *Texas Prince Hall Masonic Quarterly* 108 (June 1994): 5.
172. "Imperial Council Resolution," *Texas Prince Hall Masonic Quarterly* 108 (June 1994): 6.
173. "Resolutions," *Texas Prince Hall Masonic Quarterly* 108 (June 1994): 4.
174. *Proceedings of the One Hundred and Twentieth Annual Grand Communication of the Most Worshipful Prince Hall Grand Lodge of Texas and Jurisdiction Belonging* (Fort Worth, Tx., 1995), 66.

Reuben Glassell White

1. Reuben G. White, interview by author, Fort Worth, Texas, 20 June 1996.
2. Ibid.
3. Ibid.
4. Ibid.
5. *Proceedings of the Ninety-first Annual Grand Communication of the Most Worshipful Prince Hall Grand Lodge of Texas and Jurisdiction Belonging* (Fort Worth, Tx., 1966), 72.
6. *Proceedings of the Ninety-second Annual Grand Communication of the Most Worshipful Prince Hall Grand Lodge of Texas and Jurisdiction Belonging* (Fort Worth, Tx., 1967), 56.
7. *Proceedings of the Ninety-third Annual Grand Communication of the Most Worshipful Prince Hall Grand Lodge of Texas and Jurisdiction Belonging* (Fort Worth, Tx., 1968), 56.
8. *Proceedings of the Ninety-fourth Annual Grand Communication of the Most Worshipful Prince Hall Grand Lodge of Texas and Jurisdiction Belonging* (Fort Worth, Tx., 1969), 54.
9. Ibid., 55.
10. *Proceedings of the Ninety-fifth Annual Grand Communication of the Most Worshipful Prince Hall Grand Lodge of Texas and Jurisdiction Belonging* (Fort Worth, Tx., 1970), 56.
11. *Proceedings of the Ninety-sixth Annual Grand Communication of the Most Worshipful Prince Hall Grand Lodge of Texas and Jurisdiction Belonging* (Fort Worth, Tx., 1971), 52-53.
12. Ibid., 53.
13. *Proceedings of the Ninety-seventh Annual Grand Communication of the Most Worshipful Prince Hall Grand Lodge of Texas and Jurisdiction Belonging* (Fort Worth, Tx., 1972), 61. The writer was also a supporter of Farenthold, a Corpus Christi attorney who was defeated in the Democratic primary by Dolph Briscoe, who was elected governor of Texas that year. The writer met Farenthold during the 1972 campaign and met her again on April 13, 1991, when they were both speakers at the Rally for Reconciliation and Hope on the steps of the Texas State Capitol in Austin. At this rally, both the writer and Farenthold made speeches in opposition to the death penalty.

14. *Proceedings of the Ninety-eighth Annual Grand Communication of the Most Worshipful Prince Hall Grand Lodge of Texas and Jurisdiction Belonging* (Fort Worth, Tx., 1973), 41.
15. Ibid.
16. *Proceedings of the Ninety-ninth Annual Grand Communication of the Most Worshipful Prince Hall Grand Lodge of Texas and Jurisdiction Belonging* (Fort Worth, Tx., 1974), 37-38.
17. *Proceedings of the Centennial Annual Grand Communication of the Most Worshipful Prince Hall Grand Lodge of Texas and Jurisdiction Belonging* (Fort Worth, Tx., 1975), 38.
18. *Proceedings of the One Hundred and First Annual Grand Communication of the Most Worshipful Prince Hall Grand Lodge of Texas and Jurisdiction Belonging* (Fort Worth, Tx., 1976), 28. At that time, the writer was a resident of Teague. He did not attend the meeting because he was not yet a member of the Prince Hall Masonic Fraternity. He joined in Kaufman five years later.
19. Ibid.
20. *Proceedings of the One Hundred and Second Annual Grand Communication of the Most Worshipful Prince Hall Grand Lodge of Texas and Jurisdiction Belonging* (Fort Worth, Tx., 1977), 34.
21. Ibid., 36.
22. *Proceedings of the One Hundred and Third Annual Grand Communication of the Most Worshipful Prince Hall Grand Lodge of Texas and Jurisdiction Belonging* (Fort Worth, Tx., 1978), 39-40.
23. *Proceedings of the One Hundred and Fourth Annual Grand Communication of the Most Worshipful Prince Hall Grand Lodge of Texas and Jurisdiction Belonging* (Fort Worth, Tx., 1979).
24. *Proceedings of the One Hundred and Fifth Annual Grand Communication of the Most Worshipful Prince Hall Grand Lodge of Texas and jurisdiction Belonging* (Fort Worth, Tx., 1981), 30-31.
25. Ibid., 33.
26. *Proceedings of the One Hundred and Sixth Annual Grand Communication of the Most Worshipful Prince Hall Grand Lodge of Texas and Jurisdiction Belonging* (Fort Worth, Tx., 1981), 30-31.
27. Ibid., 26.
28. Reuben G. White, "From the Desk of the Most Worshipful Grand Master," *Texas Prince Hall Masonic Quarterly* 74 (September 1981): 3.
29. Reuben G. White, "Masonic Tidbits," *Texas Prince Hall Masonic Quarterly* 74 (December 1981): 3.
30. Reuben G. White, "The Power and Strength of the Grand Lodge," *Texas Prince Hall Masonic Quarterly* 74 (March 1982): 3.
31. Reuben G. White, "Where Do We Go From Here?" *Texas Prince Hall Masonic Quarterly* 74 (June 1982): 5-6.
32. *Proceedings of the One Hundred and Seventh Annual Grand Communication of the Most Worshipful Prince Hall Grand Lodge of Texas and Jurisdiction Belonging* (Fort Worth, Tx., 1982), 21-22.
33. Ibid., 22.
34. Ibid., 23.
35. Ibid., 24.
36. Ibid., 42.
37. Ibid., 43.
38. Reuben G. White, "A Christmas Message from the Grand Master," *Texas Prince Hall Masonic Quarterly* 74 (December 1982): 3-4.
39. Ibid., 4.
40. Reuben G. White, "Self-Encouragement," *Texas Prince Hall Masonic Quarterly* 74 (March 1983): 3.
41. Ibid., 20-21.
42. Ibid., 21-22.
43. Ibid.
44. *Proceedings* (1983), 32. Washington was not a Mason at the time of his election as mayor. However, he was eventually initiated into Prince Hall Freemasonry and became a Noble of the Mystic Shrine just in time for the 1986 Imperial Council session in Chicago; see Joseph A. Walkes, Jr., *History of the Shrine: Ancient Egyptian Arabic Order Nobles of the Mystic Shrine, Inc., Prince Hall Affiliated, A Pillar of Black Society* (Detroit, Mi.: AEAONMS, Inc., 1993), 365.
45. *Proceedings* (1983), 32.
46. Ibid., 37.
47. Landon Y. Jones, "George Orwell: This is the Year for the Enigmatic Writer Who Devoted His Life to Speaking Unwelcome Truths," *People Weekly* (9 January 1984): 41. When Orwell published his novel in 1948, he arrived at the title by simply reversing the last two digits of that year. Since that time, "1984" has been more of a symbol than a date. Orwell's book describes a world of thought con-

trol, informers, and torture. The essential government propaganda industries, Newspeak and Doublespeak, exist to make sense out of three slogans that dominate the book: "WAR IS PEACE," "FREEDOM IS SLAVERY," "IGNORANCE IS STRENGTH"; see Robert McAfee Brown, "1984: Orwell and Barmen," *The Christian Century* (15-22 August 1984): 770. Tens of millions have read this book, which tells the story of Winston Smith, a minor bureaucrat in the totalitarian state of Oceania. War with the world's two other superpowers, Eurasia and Eastasia, is constant, although the pattern of hostilities and alliances keeps changing. Smith works at the Ministry of Truth, rewriting old newspaper stories to conform to current Party ideology. Privacy has vanished. Everyone is constantly under surveillance by telescreens. Posters everywhere proclaim BIG BROTHER IS WATCHING YOU. Smith commits a thoughtcrime by thinking "Down with Big Brother." He begins a love affair with Julia, a co-worker and fellow-malcontent. Winston and Julia are caught by the Thought Police and hauled off to the Ministry of Love. Winston is relentlessly tortured, then taken to Room 101, where a cage bearing a rat is pushed toward his face. He begs that this punishment be inflected on Julia instead. This ultimate act of betrayal eliminates his last trace of integrity. He becomes a loyal Party member and, in the end, "loves Big Brother"; see Paul Gray, "That Year Is Almost Here: But George Orwell's Message for 1984 is Bigger Than Big Brother," *Time* (28 November 1983): 46. While many insisted that Orwell's "prophecies" were off base, others felt that he made some sense. For example, Jungian analyst Dr. James Hillman observed: "If we think '1984' is about Stalinism, we are deluded into thinking that we don't have it. Stalinism isn't the danger. Political terrorism isn't the issue. It's a perversion of the psyche. That's 1984. And it's now. People can be talking about peace and making war. People can be talking about love and locking you out. People refer to a 'menu of nuclear options.' That's grotesque. And we don't react. That's Orwell. That's 1984. And that's now. That's going on"; see Jennifer Boeth, "1984: Was Orwell Right?" *Dallas Times-Herald* (23 January 1983): 1-G.
48. "From the Grand Master's Desk," *Texas Prince Hall Masonic Quarterly* 74 (March 1984): 4.
49. Ibid.
50. Reuben G. White, "It Is Later Than You Think," *Texas Prince Hall Masonic Quarterly* 74 (June 1984): 4. Vanessa Williams, the first black Miss America, had been the fourth runner-up in the 1981 Miss Prince Hall National Shrine beauty contest, held in Washington, D. C., and sponsored by the Prince Hall Shriners; see Walkes, *Prince Hall's Mission*, 167.
51. *Proceedings of the One Hundred and Ninth Annual Grand Communication of the Most Worshipful Prince Hall Grand Lodge of Texas and Jurisdiction Belonging* (Fort Worth, Tx., 1984), 8.
52. At the time, the writer was living in Kaufman, Texas, where he was serving as pastor of Macedonia African Methodist Episcopal Church. On Sunday, June 24, 1984, he drove to Fort Worth and picked up Bro. Walkes, who spoke at the morning worship service at this congregation. Walkes accompanied the writer to an afternoon Men's Day Program at Macedonia Baptist Church, where the writer was the guest speaker. Afterward, the writer drove his distinguished guest back to Fort Worth's Hyatt Regency, where they had dinner. It was a very enjoyable day.
53. *Proceedings* (1984), 23-25.
54. Ibid., 30-31.
55. Ibid., 39.
56. Reuben G. White, "Americanism Day," *Texas Prince Hall Masonic Quarterly* 74 (September 1984): 6.
57. Such myths were popularized in William H. Grimshaw, *Official History of Freemasonry among the Colored People in North America* (New York: Macoy Publishing and Masonic Supply Co., Inc., 1903). For more accurate information on the life of Prince Hall, see Joseph A. Walkes, Jr., *Black Square and Compass: 200 Years of Prince Hall Freemasonry* (Richmond, Va.: Macoy Publishing and Masonic Supply Co., Inc., 1979); and Charles H. Wesley, *Prince Hall: Life and Legacy* (Washington, D. C.: United Supreme Council, Ancient and Accepted Scottish Rite of Freemasonry, Southern Jurisdiction, Prince Hall Affiliation, 1983). After his appointment as Grand Historian, the writer sought to educate the craft regarding the correct information on the life of Prince Hall; see Robert L. Uzzel, "Prince Hall: The Myth and the Man," *Texas Prince Hall Masonic Quarterly* 79 (December 1987): 3.
58. Reuben G. White, "Operative and Speculative Masonry," *Texas Prince Hall Masonic Quarterly* 74 (December 1984): 3.
59. Reuben G. White, "Our Behaviour," *Texas Prince Hall Masonic Quarterly* 75 (March 1985): 3.
60. Walkes, *Prince Hall's Mission*, 186-88. The writer attended practically all of the convention but was not aware of the conflict at the time. During the banquet held on the last night of the convention, the writer, in recognition of his study of Masonic influences in the black Islamic tradition, was designated an actual Fellow of the Phylaxis Society and received the 1985 Certificate of Literature; see Robert L.

Uzzel, "The Moorish Science Temple: A Religion Influenced by Prince Hall Freemasonry," *The Phylaxis* 11 (First Quarter 1985): 1-9. The latter turned out to be a very popular article, with copies still being requested ten years later; see Walkes, *Prince Hall's Mission*, 186.
61. Walkes was employed for twenty years as an administrative assistant at the U.S. Penitentiary at Leavenworth, Kansas. He retired on December 31, 1993.
62. Reuben G. White, "Am I My Brother's Keeper?" *Texas Prince Hall Masonic Quarterly* 75 (June 1985): 4. Washington, DuBois, Randolph, Hooks, and Robeson were Prince Hall Freemasons.
63. *Proceedings of the One Hundred and Tenth Annual Grand Communication of the Most Worshipful Prince Hall Grand Lodge of Texas and Jurisdiction Belonging* (Fort Worth, Tx., 1985), 7.
64. Ibid., 8.
65. Ibid., 20-21.
66. Ibid.
67. Ibid., 23.
68. Ibid., 26-27.
69. Ibid., 33. For many years, the Prince Hall Grand Lodge of Texas has provided financial support to this fine Scottish Rite facility. During the 1985 Communication, there was an altar call which resulted in the raising of $601 for the hospital. In a cover letter, Grand Master White wrote: "It is our sincere desire that our contribution from the Prince Hall Grand Lodge of Texas will assist you in the fine work that the hospital has done and will continue to do in the future for all races"; see Reuben G. White, "Scottish Rite Hospital," *Texas Prince Hall Masonic Quarterly* 75 (September 1985): 5.
70. *Proceedings* (1985), 35.
71. Reuben G. White, "Think on These Things," *Texas Prince Hall Masonic Quarterly* 75 (March 1986): 4.
72. Reuben G. White, interview by author, June 20, 1996.
73. *Proceedings of the One Hundred and Eleventh Annual Grand Communication of the Most Worshipful Prince Hall Grand Lodge of Texas and Jurisdiction Belonging* (Fort Worth, Tx., 1986), 19.
74. Ibid., 20-22.
75. Ibid., 23.
76. Ibid., 31-32. Masonic historian Dr. James D. Carter counted twenty-two known Masons among the fifty-nine signers of the Texas Declaration of Independence at Washington-on-the-Brazos on 2 March 1836. Among the 188 Texans who died at the Alamo, the following have been reliably identified as Masons: James Bonham, Jim Bowie, Davy Crockett, Almaron Dickenson, and William Barret Travis; see Pete Normand, *The Texas Masons: The Fraternity of Ancient Free & Accepted Masons in the History of Texas* (College Station, Tx.: Masonic Library and Museum Association, 1986), 4.
77. *Proceedings* (1986), 37.
78. Reuben G. White, "Just a Little Talk with the Brethren," *Texas Prince Hall Masonic Quarterly* 76 (December 1986): 5.
79. *Proceedings of the One Hundred and Twelfth Annual Grand Communication of the Most Worshipful Prince Hall Grand Lodge of Texas and Jurisdiction Belonging* (Fort Worth, Tx., 1987), 21.
80. Ibid., 38.
81. Ibid., 22-23.
82. Ibid., 31.
83. Ibid.
84. Ibid., 33. When Grand Master William Coleman took office in 1930, there were three living Past Grand Masters: Wiley Lawson Kimbrough, who served from 1894 to 1896; John Wesley McKinney, who served from 1896 to 1916; and John Adrian Kirk, who served from 1925 to 1930. Kirk's death on September 29, 1934, reduced the number to two. Both Kimbrough and McKinney outlived Coleman, who died on May 16, 1946. Coleman was succeeded by Lucian L. Lockhart, who was in office when McKinney died on August 24, 1946. For the next nine years, Kimbrough (who spent the last fifty years of his life in California and died in Los Angeles on February 28, 1955) was Texas' only Past Grand Master. Lockhart died in office on October 2, 1955, and was succeeded by John Theodore Maxey, who served until his retirement in 1965.
85. *Proceedings of the One Hundred and Thirteenth Annual Grand Communication of the Most Worshipful Prince Hall Grand Lodge of Texas and Jurisdiction Belonging* (Fort Worth, Tx., 1988), 61.
86. "Installation of M. W. Grand Master Edwin B. Cash, January 8, 1991 in Houston, Texas," *Texas Prince Hall Masonic Quarterly* 95 (March 1991): 1.
87. *Proceedings of the One Hundred and Seventeenth Annual Grand Communication of the Most Worshipful Prince Hall Grand Lodge of Texas and Jurisdiction Belonging* (Fort Worth, Tx., 1992), 29.

88. "Celebration Service," *Texas Prince Hall Masonic Quarterly* 108 (June 1994): 4.
89. Funeral program for Reuben Glassell White.
90. Wilbert M. Curtis, "From the Office of the Deputy Grand Master," *Family Masonic Quarterly*, April 2003, 2.

Thomas Henry Routt
1. "Celebration of Life of Thomas Henry Routt, 1930-1991," *Texas Prince Hall Masonic Quarterly* 95 (March 1991): 4.
2. "Thomas H. Routt, One of First Black Jurists, Dies," *The Phylaxis* 16 (April 1991): 18.
3. "Vita: Thomas H. Routt." Manuscript supplied by Ritchie L. Routt.
4. "Judge Routt Dies of Cancer 2 Days after Swearing In," *Houston Post* (January 4, 1991): 21.
5. "Thomas H. Routt, One of First Black Jurists, Dies," 18.
6. "Vita: Thomas H. Routt."
7. Ibid.
8. Ibid.
9. Ibid.
10. Ibid.
11. Ibid.
12. Ibid.
13. Ibid.
14. Ibid.
15. Ibid.
16. *Proceedings of the One Hundred and Sixth Annual Grand Communication of the Most Worshipful Prince Hall Grand Lodge of Texas and Jurisdiction Belonging* (Fort Worth, Tx., 1981), 26.
17. Thomas H. Routt, "13th Annual Session Opening Speech," *The Phylaxis* 12 (Second Quarter 1986): 4-6.
18. Ibid.
19. Ibid., 33.
20. Thomas H. Routt, letter to author, 3 August 1987. The article was published, as promised; see Robert L. Uzzel, "Prince Hall: The Myth and the Man," *Texas Prince Hall Masonic Quarterly* 86 (December 1987): 3.
21. Thomas H. Routt, "From the Grand East," *Texas Prince Hall Masonic Quarterly* 86 (September 1987): 3, 8. This issue also included a copy of the speech delivered by the writer at Waridi Consistory's Sixteenth Annual Fellowship Banquet, which was held at Texas College in Tyler, Texas on March 21, 1987; see Robert L. Uzzel, "From Darkness to Light," *Texas Prince Hall Masonic Quarterly* 86 (September 1987): 6-7.
22. Thomas H. Routt, letter to author, February 22, 1988. The writer attended the New Orleans meeting, where he conducted a workshop on a newly published book by a Roman Catholic anti-Masonic writer with whom he has corresponded; see William J. Whalen, *Christianity and American Freemasonry* (Huntington, In.: Our Sunday Visitor, Inc., 1987).
23. Thomas H. Routt, "From the Grand East," *Texas Prince Hall Masonic Quarterly* 87 (March 1988): 2-3. Routt's closing paragraph echoes the motto of Prince Hall Shrinedom: "Recruit, Reclaim, Retain."
24. *Proceedings of the One Hundred and Thirteenth Annual Grand Communication of the Most Worshipful Prince Hall Grand Lodge of Texas and Jurisdiction Belonging* (Fort Worth, Tx., 1988): 37-38. Here Routt alluded to the special assessment of $90 in addition to the annual dues which was adopted by the Grand Lodge in a special session in September 1987. This assessment was paid in three consecutive installments of $30 between 1988 and 1990. Sadly, many refused to pay. As a result there were large numbers of Masons suspended for non-payment of dues throughout the state.
25. Ibid., 40.
26. *Proceedings* (1988), 48.
27. Ibid. There has been a great deal of negative publicity about racial discrimination in the "animal lodges." In July 1972 members of the Benevolent and Protective Order of Elks (B.P.O.E.) convened in Atlantic City, New Jersey, and voted down a proposal to strike the word "white" from the membership application; see Thomas Meehan, "The Other July Convention: The B.P.O.E. (Best People on Earth) in Atlantic City," *New York Times Magazine* (August 13, 1972). In July 1973 they convened in Chicago and finally voted to strike down the "whites only" provision. According to a Jesuit publication, this action was taken "only after alcoholic beverage authorities in Maine, Wisconsin, and

Massachusetts threatened to deny liquor licenses to their segregated meeting halls"; see "After a Century and a Decade," *America* (October 20, 1973). At that time, Hobson R. Reynolds of Philadelphia, Grand Exalted Ruler of the predominately black Improved Benevolent and Protective Order of Elks of the World (I.B.P.O.E.W.), voiced suspicion in view of the "loophole" which required ratification of the measure by a majority of local lodges; see "Possible 'Trick' Seen in Elks Vote to Desegregate," *Jet* (August 9, 1973): 6. Historically, the I.B.P.O.E. has had a similar relationship to the B.P.O.E. as Prince Hall Freemasonry has had to white Freemasonry. In 1973 the two Elks organizations were not even on speaking terms. Today they have a very good relationship. The reputation of the Loyal Order of Moose was even more racist at one time. From this organization's inception, its membership application had stated: "I hereby certify that I am of sound mind and body, being a member of the Caucasian, white race, and am not married to one of any other race and am a believer in a Supreme Being." In 1971 the Moose Lodge in Olympia, Washington, stirred up much controversy when a black librarian named Sylvia Finley was barred from attending a lodge luncheon in order to accept a donation for the library; see "Washington Scores Moose for Snub of Black Librarian," *Library Journal* (January 1, 1972): 11. On June 12, 1972, as a result of the refusal of the lodge in Harrisburg, Pennsylvania, to admit as a guest black state representative K. Leroy Irvis, the national organization went to the U. S. Supreme Court to win the right to discriminate as a private club; see *Moose Lodge No. 107 v. K. Leroy Irvis*, 92 S.Ct. 1965 (1972). Reportedly: "The Supreme Court considered whether the lodge's state liquor license amounted to unconstitutional governmental action in support of discrimination. The Justices concluded that it did not, and that the Moose could continue discriminating as a private club. . . . the Pennsylvania Supreme Court, considering a different claim, ruled that since the lodge allowed guests and rented its facilities to other organizations, it was a public accommodation under state law and so must stop discriminating after all"; see James Willwerth, "Of Moose and Men," *Time* (August 12, 1972): 33. In 1973 all references to race were removed from the by-laws. According to the organization's Director of Publications, at the 1999 international convention in Minneapolis, Minnesota, approximately three dozen African-American Moose—all Governors or Administrators of their lodges—were in attendance; see Kurt N. Wehrmeister, letter to author, August 19, 1999. The writer has always considered the Waco-based Red Men as a strange organization. Reportedly: "One of the chief stated purposes of the Improved Order of Red Men is 'to perpetuate the beautiful legends and traditions of a vanishing race and to keep alive its customs, ceremonies, and philosophies.' But should an American Indian seek admission to the Red Men he would be turned down. Only white men may become Red Men"; see William J. Whalen, *Handbook of Secret Organizations* (Milwaukee, Wi.: Bruce Publishing Co., 1966.), 133-34. The writer has been informed that the word "white" was struck from the membership application for tax purposes but that, nevertheless, the organization remains all-white. It appears that membership in service clubs, including Kiwanis, Rotary, Lions, Optimists, and Civitan, was once restricted to white males. However, there are increasing numbers of reports of these organizations opening their doors to minorities and women. During the 1970s, the writer was a member of the Rotary Club in Teague, Texas. At the time, the club's only black member was retired teacher A. M. Johnson, an outstanding Prince Hall Freemason and friend of Thomas H. Routt.
28. *Proceedings* (1988), 49. There appears to be no connection between the Rainbow Family and the Masonic-sponsored Order of Rainbow for Girls.
29. Ibid. The scandals of Swaggart and fellow evangelist Jim Bakker caused many Americans to become highly skeptical about televangelism. One of those hurt by the "fallout" was John Ankerberg, who made Freemasonry a special target for his venom.
30. Ibid., 40.
31. Ibid., 63.
32. Thomas H. Routt, "From the Grand East," *Texas Prince Hall Masonic Quarterly* 87 (September 1988): 3.
33. Ibid. The Knights of Pythagoras, Prince Hall Freemasonry's counterpart to the Order of DeMolay, was founded by P. G. Porter, Past Grand Master of the Prince Hall Grand Lodge of Kansas. In 1961 Porter addressed the Imperial Council of the Prince Hall Shriners in Cincinnati, Ohio, stating: "In 1954, I was fortunate to become acquainted with Frank S. Land, the founder of the DeMolays. Later I was able to arrange a conference at the Temple which included Grand Master Amos T. Hall, President of the Grand Master, President of our Grand Masters' Conference. Out of that conference came many useful suggestions given to us by Mr. Land. Some of the suggestions that came out of Mr. Land's experience of 38 years of working with the DeMolay, we used in Chicago in 1958, when the

International Order, Knights of Pythagoras was organized. Mr. Land is the author of the ritual for this organization. Land passed away in 1959. Mr. Clarence Head of Ohio was elected to succeed him. Last year, I was again fortunate to arrange a conference with Mr. Head, and our Imperial Potentate, Booker T. Alexander, at the DeMolay Temple in Kansas City"; see Joseph A. Walkes Jr., *History of the Shrine: Ancient Egyptian Arabic Order Nobles of the Mystic Shrine, Inc., Prince Hall Affiliated, A Pillar of Black Society* (Detroit, Mi.: Ancient Egyptian Arabic Order Nobles of the Mystic Shrine, Inc., 1993), 269. For further information on the Order of DeMolay, see Herbert Ewing Duncan, *Hi, Dad! A Story about Frank S. Land and the Order of DeMolay* (Kansas City, Mo.: International Supreme Council Order of DeMolay, 1970). The writer served as Master Councilor of Waco Chapter of the Order of DeMolay in 1970.

34. Thomas H. Routt, "From the Grand East," *Texas Prince Hall Masonic Quarterly* 87 (December 1988): 3.
35. *Proceedings of the One Hundred and Fourteenth Annual Grand Communication of the Most Worshipful Prince Hall Grand Lodge of Texas and Jurisdiction Belonging* (Fort Worth, Tx., 1989), 42-43.
36. Ibid., 44-45.
37. Ibid., 45.
38. Ibid.
39. Ibid., 52.
40. Thomas H. Routt, "From the Grand East," *Texas Prince Hall Masonic Quarterly* 91 (March 1990): 3. This issue also contained this writer's tribute to Dr. Charles H. Wesley (1892-1987); see Robert L. Uzzel, "The Passing of a Great Masonic Historian," *Texas Prince Hall Masonic Quarterly* 91 (March 1990): 8.
41. At this convention, the writer conducted a workshop regarding the first Grand Master of Prince Hall Freemasonry in the Lone Star State; see Robert L. Uzzel, "Norris Wright Cuney: Our First Grand Master," *The Phylaxis* 16 (March 1990): 3-9.
42. *Proceedings of the One Hundred and Fifteenth Annual Grand Communication of the Most Worshipful Prince Hall Grand Lodge of Texas and Jurisdiction Belonging* (Fort Worth, Tx., 1990), 37.
43. Ibid., 37-38. All of these lodges were eventually chartered. The first is now Nero Prince Military Lodge No. 634. It was named for the second Worshipful Master of African Lodge No. 459 in Boston. Nero Prince took office following the death of Prince Hall on December 4, 1807. He was at one time servant to a baker named Edward Tuckerman, from whom he learned the art of cookery. He made two trips to Russia, where he served as a butler to the royal family; see Charles H. Wesley, *Prince Hall: Life and Legacy* (Washington, D. C.: United Supreme Council, Ancient and Accepted Scottish Rite of Freemasonry, Southern Jurisdiction, Prince Hall Affiliation, 1983), 22. He is also mentioned in his wife's autobiography; see Nancy Prince, *A Black Woman's Odyssey Through Russia and Jamaica: The Narrative of Nancy Prince* (New York: Markus Wiener, 1990). The proposed name for the second lodge was not accepted in view of a regulation prohibiting the naming of lodges after living persons. At that time, I. H. Clayborn was still living. It was chartered as Aloha Military Lodge No. 635. The third became Right Step Lodge No. 636. Following the death of Past Grand Master Clayborn in 1994, I. H. Clayborn Lodge No. 641 in Beeville, Texas, was chartered.
44. *Proceedings* (1990), 38. It seemed inevitable to most knowledgeable Texas Prince Hall Masons that a dues increase would occur. The special assessment of $30.00 was paid in 1988, 1989, and 1990. Following the completion of this, Grand Lodge relief dues were raised from $20.80 to $30.00. The latter action faced little opposition, as compared to that of the special session of September 1987.
45. Ibid., 39.
46. Ibid.
47. Ibid., 43.
48. "Celebration of of Thomas H. Routt, 1930-1991," 4.
49. "Installation of M. W. Grand Master Edwin B. Cash, January 8, 1991 in Houston, Texas," *Texas Prince Hall Masonic Quarterly* 95 (March 1991): 1.
50. Edwin B. Cash, "Grand Master's Column," *Texas Prince Hall Masonic Quarterly* 95 (March 1991): 3.
51. C. A. Glaspie, "From the Desk of the Right Worshipful Grand Secretary," *Texas Prince Hall Masonic Quarterly* 95 (March 1991): 2.
52. Robert E. Connor, Jr., "From the Desk of the Right Worshipful Grand Junior Warden," *Texas Prince Hall Masonic Quarterly* 95 (March 1991): 3. In June 1991 Connor was elected Deputy Grand Master. In June 1994 he was elected Grand Master.
53. I. H. Clayborn, "The Late Thomas H. Routt," *Texas Prince Hall Masonic Quarterly* 95 (March 1991): 3.

54. "Letters," *Texas Prince Hall Masonic Quarterly* 95 (March 1991): 7.
55. "The Phylaxis Society Resolution of Respect and Love," *Texas Prince Hall Masonic Quarterly* 95 (March 1991): 8.
56. *Proceedings of the One Hundred and Sixteenth Annual Grand Communication of the Most Worshipful Prince Hall Grand Lodge of Texas and Jurisdiction* (Fort Worth, Tx., 1991), 43.
57. Ibid., 229.
58. *Proceedings of the One Hundred and Twentieth Annual Grand Communication of the Most Worshipful Prince Hall Grand Lodge of Texas and Jurisdiction* (Fort Worth, Tx., 1995), 231. Sadly, this lodge has not experienced "smooth sailing." In December 1999 the lodge's charter was pulled after a lawsuit was filed due to alleged hazing during an initiation; see Jason Trahan and Ben Tinsley, "Masonic Hazing Alleged: DA is Investigating Arlington Complaint," *Dallas Morning News*, 9 December 1999, 37A. Eventually, the case was settled out of court and plans made for re-chartering of the lodge. However, Judge Routt's widow requested that the lodge be re-named and that her husband's name not be given to another lodge; see *Proceedings of the One Hundred and Twenty-eighth Annual Grand Communication of the Most Worshipful Prince Hall Grand Lodge of Texas and Jurisdiction Belonging* (Fort Worth, Tx., 2003), 26.
59. "Who Was Thomas H. Routt?" http://koptexas.org/throutt.htm, 1.

Edwin Bernard Cash

1. Edwin Bernard Cash, interview by author, 9 October 1996.
2. Ibid. Bishop College later relocated from Marshall to Dallas and closed in 1988. Paul Quinn College (PQC), which had operated in Austin from 1872 to 1877 and in Waco from 1877 to 1990, occupied the Dallas campus of Bishop in 1990. The writer is a member of the PQC faculty. The interview with Cash was conducted at his PQC office.
3. Ibid. North Texas State University is now called the University of North Texas.
4. Ibid.
5. Ibid.
6. Ibid.
7. Ibid.
8. Ibid.
9. Ibid.
10. Ibid.
11. Ibid.
12. *Proceedings of the One Hundred and Sixth Annual Grand Communication of the Most Worshipful Prince Hall Grand Lodge of Texas and Jurisdiction Belonging* (Fort Worth, Tx., 1981), 26.
13. *Proceedings of the One Hundred and Seventh Annual Grand Communication of the Most Worshipful Prince Hall Grand Lodge of Texas and Jurisdiction Belonging* (Fort Worth, Tx., 1982), 24.
14. Ibid., 25. The writer had the same impression following his visit to the annual conference at Saint John African Methodist Episcopal Church in Brenham in 1987; see Robert L. Uzzel, "Visit to Sacred Ground," *Texas Prince Hall Masonic Quarterly* 88 (June 1989): 3-4.
15. Ibid., 43.
16. *Proceedings of the One Hundred and Eighth Annual Grand Communication of the Most Worshipful Prince Hall Grand Lodge of Texas and Jurisdiction Belonging* (Fort Worth, Tx., 1983), 24.
17. Ibid., 24-25.
18. Ibid., 22.
19. *Proceedings of the One Hundred and Ninth Annual Grand Communication of the Most Worshipful Prince Hall Grand Lodge of Texas and Jurisdiction Belonging* (Fort Worth, Tx., 1984), 27-28. The statement about Rev. Jackson is not correct. The distinction of being the "first black candidate for the President of the United States" belongs to Shirley Chisholm, who sought the Democratic nomination in 1972.
20. Ibid., 28. The writer also attended the funeral of Bro. Dewberry at Mount Zion Baptist Church in Forney, Texas. He has fond memories of this fine District Deputy.
21. Ibid., 25.
22. *Proceedings of the One Hundred and Tenth Annual Grand Communication of the Most Worshipful Prince Hall Grand Lodge of Texas and Jurisdiction Belonging* (Fort Worth, Tx., 1985), 23.
23. *Proceedings of the One Hundred and Eleventh Annual Grand Communication of the Most Worshipful Prince Hall Grand Lodge of Texas and Jurisdiction Belonging* (Fort Worth, Tx., 1986), 27-28.

24. Ibid., 28.
25. Ibid., 23.
26. *Proceedings of the One Hundred and Twelfth Annual Grand Communication of the Most Worshipful Prince Hall Grand Lodge of Texas and Jurisdiction Belonging* (Fort Worth, Tx., 1987), 31.
27. Ibid., 33.
28. *Proceedings of the One Hundred and Thirteenth Annual Grand Communication of the Most Worshipful Prince Hall Grand Lodge of Texas and Jurisdiction Belonging* (Fort Worth, Tx., 1988), 43.
29. Ibid., 43-44.
30. Ibid., 40.
31. *Proceedings of the One Hundred and Fourteenth Annual Grand Communication of the Most Worshipful Prince Hall Grand Lodge of Texas and Jurisdiction Belonging* (Fort Worth, Tx., 1989), 45.
32. *Proceedings of the One Hundred and Fifteenth Annual Grand Communication of the Most Worshipful Prince Hall Grand Lodge of Texas and Jurisdiction Belonging* (Fort Worth, Tx., 1990), 28-29.
33. Ibid., 39.
34. Ibid., 39-40.
35. "Installation of M. W. Grand Master Edwin B. Cash, January 8, 1991 in Houston, Texas," *Texas Prince Hall Masonic Quarterly* 95 (March 1991): 1.
36. Edwin B. Cash, "Grand Master's Column," *Texas Prince Hall Masonic Quarterly* 96 (May 1991): 3-4.
37. *Proceedings of the One Hundred and Sixteenth Annual Grand Communication of the Most Worshipful Prince Hall Grand Lodge of Texas and Jurisdiction Belonging* (Fort Worth, Tx., 1991), 23.
38. Ibid., 37-41.
39. Ibid., 41.
40. Ibid., 43-44.
41. Ibid., 45. Fortunately, the dispute between Texas and California was resolved within a year.
42. Ibid., 45-46. The latter statement seems to imply that Cash desired to keep both Reece and Connor as members of the Board of Directors. Nevertheless, in the 1991 election, Reece was removed from the Board.
43. Ibid., 46-47.
44. Ibid., 49.
45. Ibid., 50.
46. Edwin B. Cash, "Grand Master's Column," *Texas Prince Hall Masonic Quarterly* 97 (November 1991): 3.
47. Edwin B. Cash, "Grand Master's Column," *Texas Prince Hall Masonic Quarterly* 99 (May 1992): 2-3.
48. Ibid., 3.
49. *Proceedings of the One Hundred and Seventeenth Annual Grand Communication of the Most Worshipful Prince Hall Grand Lodge of Texas and Jurisdiction Belonging* (Fort Worth, Tx., 1992), 46-48. The controversies concerning Freemasonry within the Southern Baptist Convention climaxed in an anti-Masonic committee report that was adopted in Houston in 1993. The chief anti-Masonic agitator among Southern Baptists is Dr. James L. Holly of Beaumont; see the discussion of Holly as "The Physician-Fanatic" in John J. Robinson, *A Pilgrim's Path: Freemasonry and the Religious Right* (New York: M. Evans, 1993), 94-109.
50. *Proceedings* (1992), 50.
51. Ibid., 54.
52. Edwin B. Cash, "Grand Master's Column," *Texas Prince Hall Masonic Quarterly* 101 (November 1992): 3.
53. "Hopeful Lodge No. 78, F.&A.M., 100th Anniversary Award Banquet, 7:30 P.M., December 12, 1992," *Texas Prince Hall Masonic Quarterly* 103 (May 1993): 8.
54. Hopeful Lodge has a number of ministers on its roll, including Rev. W. M. Johnson, Jr., pastor of Zion Hill Baptist Church in Marlin. On February 19, 1977, Rev. Johnson performed the marriage of the writer and his wife Debra at Fairfield Baptist Church. Rev. Johnson was at this banquet, and it was great to see him again.
55. Edwin B. Cash, "Regional Address," *Texas Prince Hall Masonic Quarterly* 103 (May 1993): 3. Joseph Edward Telfair, Sr. lived from June 14, 1932, to December 23, 1992. His funeral was held on December 29, 1992, at Grace First Baptist Church in San Antonio. The writer was unable to attend but, on the day of the funeral, talked by telephone with Grand Master Cash, who agreed to convey his condolences to the Telfair family. Oscar Eugene Wilhite, Sr. lived from November 9, 1900, to January 5, 1993. He was a very good friend of the writer, who conducted a taped interview with him during the 1992 Grand Communication for a Seminar in Oral History at Baylor

University. From Bro. Wilhite, he obtained much valuable information on Past Grand Masters John Adrian Kirk, William Coleman, and Lucius L. Lockhart. On January 9, 1993, he attended his funeral at Allen Chapel African Methodist Episcopal Church in Rockdale, Texas. The eulogy was delivered by Rev. James Green, pastor of Allen Chapel and an old friend of the writer.

56. Ibid.
57. *Proceedings of the One Hundred and Eighteenth Annual Grand Communication of the Most Worshipful Prince Hall Grand Lodge of Texas and Jurisdiction Belonging* (Fort Worth, Tx., 1993), 5.
58. Ibid., 42-44.
59. Ibid., 45.
60. Ibid., 48-49.
61. Edwin B. Cash, "Grand Master's Column," *Texas Prince Hall Masonic Quarterly* 105 (November 1993): 3.
62. Edwin B. Cash, "Grand Master's Column," *Texas Prince Hall Masonic Quarterly* 107 (May 1994): 3.
63. "Celebration Service," *Texas Prince Hall Masonic Quarterly* 108 (June 1994): 4.
64. Edwin B. Cash, "Annual Address of Past Grand Master Edwin B. Cash Delivered at the 119th Grand Session," *Texas Prince Hall Masonic Quarterly* 109 (August 1994): 4.
65. At this session, the writer received a "Participation Certificate" for "Outstanding Contribution as Grand Historian."
66. Ibid.
67. Ibid., 5.
68. As far as is known, William E. Woods and Howard L. Woods are not related. However, during the installation, the Arkansas Grand Master, in his usual jovial manner, spoke of possible kinship.

Robert Edmund Connor, Jr.

1. Robert E. Connor, Jr., telephone conversation with author, September 20, 2000.
2. "Vita of Robert E. Connor, Jr.," provided to author by Connor.
3. "Columbus Loses Big-Hearted Police Chief," http://www.coloradocitizen.com/articles/2003/09/25/news/news02.prt, 3.
4. Ibid.
5. Ibid.
6. Ibid. Connor was succeeded in this position by Harris County Precinct Seven Constable Perry Wooten, whom he was seeking to succeed at the time of his death; see "Obituaries," *African-American News & Issues*, October 1-7, 2003, 2.
7. Leigh Hopper, "Police Chief of Columbus, Robert E. Connor, Jr., Dies," http://www.chron.com/cs/CDA/printstory.hts/deaths/2111749, 1.
8. "Vita of Robert E. Connor, Jr."
9. "Columbus Loses Big-Hearted Police Chief," 1.
10. Jessica Schmidt, "FBI Honors Columbus Police Chief: Connor Commended for Outstanding Performance During Operation Blowout," *The Banner Press*, July 8, 1999; reprinted in *The Family Masonic Quarterly* 112 (November 1999): 3.
11. Hopper, "Police Chief of Columbus, Robert E. Connor, Jr., Dies," 1.
12. "Columbus Loses Big-Hearted Police Chief," 1.
13. Robert E. Connor, Jr., telephone conversation.
14. *Proceedings of the One Hundred and Twelfth Annual Grand Communication of the Most Worshipful Prince Hall Grand Lodge of Texas and Jurisdiction Belonging* (Fort Worth, Tx., 1987), 31.
15. *Proceedings of the One Hundred and Thirteenth Annual Grand Communication of the Most Worshipful Prince Hall Grand Lodge of Texas and Jurisdiction Belonging* (Fort Worth, Tx., 1988), 40.
16. Ibid., 52-53.
17. Ibid., 53.
18. *Proceedings of the One Hundred and Fourteenth Annual Grand Communication of the Most Worshipful Prince Hall Grand Lodge of Texas and Jurisdiction Belonging* (Fort Worth, Tx., 1989), 45.
19. *Proceedings of the One Hundred and Fifteenth Annual Grand Communication of the Most Worshipful Prince Hall Grand Lodge of Texas and Jurisdiction Belonging* (Fort Worth, Tx., 1990), 24.
20. Ibid.
21. Ibid., 39.
22. "Installation of M. W. Grand Master Edwin B. Cash, January 8, 1991 in Houston, Texas," *Texas Prince Hall Masonic Quarterly* 95 (March 1991): 1.

23. *Proceedings of the One Hundred and Sixteenth Annual Grand Communication of the Most Worshipful Prince Hall Grand Lodge of Texas and Jurisdiction Belonging* (Fort Worth, Tx., 1991), 49.
24. Ibid., 27.
25. *Proceedings of the One Hundred and Seventeenth Annual Grand Communication of the Most Worshipful Prince Hall Grand Lodge of Texas and Jurisdiction Belonging* (Fort Worth, Tx., 1992), 30-31.
26. Ibid., 50.
27. *Proceedings of the One Hundred and Eighteenth Annual Grand Communication of the Most Worshipful Prince Hall Grand Lodge of Texas and Jurisdiction Belonging* (Fort Worth, Tx., 1993), 27-28.
28. Ibid., 45.
29. *Proceedings of the One Hundred and Nineteenth Annual Grand Communication of the Most Worshipful Prince Hall Grand Lodge of Texas and Jurisdiction Belonging* (Fort Worth, Tx., 1994), 20-21.
30. Ibid., 55.
31. Ibid., 56.
32. Robert E. Connor, Jr., "Grand Master's Regional Address," *Texas Prince Hall Masonic Quarterly* 109 (May 1995): 3.
33. Ibid.
34. Ibid.
35. Ibid., 3-4.
36. Robert E. Connor, Jr., "Grand Master's Column," *Texas Prince Hall Masonic Quarterly* 109 (November 1994): 3.
37. Robert E. Connor, Jr., "Grand Master's Column," *Texas Prince Hall Masonic Quarterly* 109 (March 1995): 1-2.
38. *Proceedings of the One Hundred and Twentieth Annual Grand Communication of the Most Worshipful Prince Hall Grand Lodge of Texas and Jurisdiction Belonging* (Fort Worth, Tx., 1995), 61-63.
39. Ibid., 63-64. The process of recognition began in October 1989, when the white and Prince Hall Grand Lodges of Connecticut established fraternal relations. At this writing, thirty-seven out of the fifty-one predominately white Grand Lodges have extended recognition to various Prince Hall Grand Lodges. On December 14, 1994, the United Grand Lodge of England extended recognition to the Prince Hall Grand Lodge of Massachusetts. Since then, England has recognized a number of other Prince Hall Grand Lodges; see Paul M. Bessel, "PHA Recognition," http://bessel.org/pha.htm, 1-15.
40. *Proceedings* (1995), 64.
41. Ibid. A better description of this so-called contract developed by the Republican Party after they gained control of both houses of Congress in November 1994 is the "Contract on America," with former House Speaker Newt Gingrich playing the role of "hit man."
42. Ibid.
43. Ibid., 64-65.
44. Ibid., 65. Among those suspended were Ray Bell, Past Grand Patron of the Masonic Grand Chapter of the Order of the Eastern Star; and C. A. Glaspie, Past Grand Secretary of the Prince Hall Grand Lodge of Texas; see ibid., 47-48. Both of these suspensions were upheld by vote of the Grand Lodge. Regarding the latter suspension, Connor wrote: "Past Grand Secretary C. A. Glaspie had problems working with the new Grand Master to the point that the problems became major problems, which would bring reproach upon the Most Worshipful Prince Hall Grand Lodge of Texas if allowed to continue. Two people can ride a horse together, but only one can ride in the front of the saddle"; see Connor, "Grand Master's Regional Address" (1995), 4.
45. Ibid., 66.
46. Ibid., 69.
47. Ibid., 70.
48. Ibid., 59-60.
49. Robert E. Connor, Jr., "Grand Master's Column," *Texas Prince Hall Masonic Quarterly* 109 (August 1995): 3.
50. Robert L. Uzzel, "Brenham, Texas—1875, 1941, and 1995—The Call of Cuney Coleman, and Connor," *Texas Prince Hall Masonic Quarterly* 109 (August 1995): 7.
51. "Local Masonic Lodge to Celebrate 120th Anniversary This Weekend," *The Banner Press*, 14 September 1995, 1.
52. Program for "Prince Hall and Americanism Day Service" hosted by Most Worshipful Prince Hall Grand Lodge of Texas, Free and Accepted Masons, Saint John AME Church, Brenham, Texas, September 16, 1995.

53. Program for "Prince Hall and Americanism Day Banquet," Fireman's Training Center, Brenham, Texas, September 16, 1995.
54. Robert E. Connor, Jr., "Grand Master's Column," *Texas Prince Hall Masonic Quarterly* 109 (November 1995): 2.
55. Robert E. Connor, Jr., "From the Grand East," *The Texas Prince Hall Masonic Quarterly* 109 (March 1996): 1.
56. Ibid.
57. Ibid., 1, 3.
58. Robert E. Connor, Jr., "From the Grand East," *The Texas Prince Hall Masonic Quarterly* 109 (May 1996): 2.
59. *Proceedings of the One Hundred and Twenty-first Annual Grand Communication of the Most Worshipful Prince Hall Grand Lodge of Texas and Jurisdiction Belonging* (Fort Worth, Tx., 1996), 25. In December 1995 the Grand Master telephoned this writer and expressed sympathy at the death of his mother and explained that his recuperation from back surgery would prevent his attendance at her funeral. He was represented there by Grand Junior Warden Wilbert M. Curtis.
60. Ibid.
61. Ibid., 26. Texas Masonic scholarships for 1995-96 amounted to over $10,000; see ibid., 31.
62. Ibid., 26.
63. Ibid., 27.
64. Ibid., 28-29.
65. Ibid., 27.
66. Ibid., 28.
67. Ibid., 31.
68. Ibid., 33-34.
69. Ibid., 35.
70. Ibid., 49.
71. Robert E. Connor, Jr., "Prince Hall Grand Chapter, O.E.S. of Texas," *The Texas Prince Hall Masonic Quarterly* 109 (November 1996): 4.
72. Robert E. Connor, Jr., "From the Grand East," *The Texas Prince Hall Masonic Quarterly* 109 (March 1997): 1. The writer had previously corresponded with Grand Master Regian and obtained from Grand Master Connor permission to provide his name, address, and phone number and suggest a meeting between the two Grand Masters; see Joseph W. Regian, letters to writer, December 17, 1996, and January 2, 1997.
73. Robert E. Connor, Jr., "From the Grand East," March 1997, 1, 12.
74. Ibid., 12.
75. Ibid.
76. *The Texas Prince Hall Masonic Quarterly* 110 (August 1997): 1.
77. *Proceedings of the One Hundred and Twenty-second Annual Grand Communication of the Most Worshipful Prince Hall Grand Lodge of Texas and Jurisdiction Belonging* (Fort Worth, Tx., 1997), 10.
78. Ibid., 13-14.
79. Ibid., 17.
80. Ibid.
81. Ibid., 19.
82. Ibid., 19-20.
83. Ibid., 23-24.
84. Ibid., 25.
85. Ibid., 26-27.
86. Ibid., 39.
87. Ibid., 65.
88. *The Texas Prince Hall Masonic Quarterly* 110 (August 1997): 3.
89. *The Texas Prince Hall Masonic Quarterly* 110 (November 1997): 1.
90. Ibid. The $100 was understood as a donation and not as an assessment.
91. Robert E. Connor, Jr., "From the Grand East," *The Family Masonic Quarterly* 110 (March 1998): 1.
92. Ibid., 1, 10.
93. Ibid., 10.
94. Ibid.
95. Robert E. Connor, Jr., "From the Grand East," *The Family Masonic Quarterly* 111 (May 1998): 1.

96. Robert E. Connor, Jr., "From the Grand East," *The Family Masonic Quarterly* 111 (August 1998): 1.
97. *Proceedings of the One Hundred and Twenty-third Annual Grand Communication of the Most Worshipful Prince Hall Grand Lodge of Texas and Jurisdiction Belonging* (Fort Worth, Tx., 1998), 23.
98. Ibid., 28.
99. Ibid., 30.
100. Ibid., 31-32.
101. Ibid., 33.
102. Ibid., 33-34.
103. Ibid., 35.
104. Ibid., 36.
105. Ibid., 39.
106. Ibid., 41.
107. Ibid., 46.
108. Ibid., 47.
109. Ibid., 51.
110. Ibid., 24.
111. Robert E. Connor, Jr., "From the Grand East," *The Family Masonic Quarterly* 111 (March 1999): 1.
112. Ibid., 20. The following exception to payment of this assessment was authorized: "A Master Mason who is destitute and is sixty-five years of age with 40 years of continuous membership." A provision was made for installment payments providing $50 was paid by May 1, 1999, and $50 by September 1, 1999, with the understanding that those who pay in installments would be placed on an inactive roll and be unable to function Masonically until the final payment was made.
113. Ibid.
114. Robert E. Connor, Jr., "From the Grand East," *The Family Masonic Quarterly* 111 (May 1999): 12.
115. Robert E. Connor, Jr., "From the Grand East," *The Family Masonic Quarterly* 111 (August 1999): 1.
116. Ibid., 24.
117. *Proceedings of the One Hundred and Twenty-fourth Annual Grand Communication of the Most Worshipful Prince Hall Grand Lodge of Texas and Jurisdiction Belonging* (Fort Worth, Tx., 1999), 7-8.
118. Ibid., 8.
119. Ibid., 10.
120. Ibid., 11-12.
121. Ibid., 14-15.
122. Ibid., 16-17.
123. Ibid., 18-19.
124. Connor, "From the Grand East," (August 1999): 1.
125. Ibid.
126. Jason Trahan and Ben Tinsley, "Masonic Hazing Alleged: DA is Investigating Arlington Complaint," *The Dallas Morning News*, December 9, 1999, 37A. White Masons in the Dallas-Fort Worth Metroplex were quick to distance themselves from this incident, saying it involved "them" and not "us."
127. Willie High Coleman, Jr., "300,000: Remember—Hazing Will Not be Tolerated by the Grand Lodge," *The Family Masonic Quarterly* 112 (November 1999): 1, 16.
128. Robert E. Connor, Jr., "From the Grand East," *The Family Masonic Quarterly* 112 (November 1999): 16. At the Waco meeting, a resolution was introduced to begin dialogue with the Prince Hall Grand Lodge of Texas, with a goal of eventual recognition. According to one Mason in attendance, approximately 100 Masons voted for the resolution while 3,800 voted against it. Those favoring the recognition of Prince Hall Freemasonry vowed to continue the struggle but acknowledged that they have a long struggle ahead of them; Warren Hardin, telephone conversation with author, December 4, 1999.
129. Robert E. Connor, Jr., "Special Grand Communication: February 26, 2000 Update," *The Family Masonic Quarterly* 112 (March 2000), 2. The Grand Lodge was forced to pay $400,000 to the Grand Chapter.
130. Robert E. Connor, Jr., letter to William E. Woods, 15 May 2000.
131. *Proceedings of the One Hundred and Twenty-fifth Annual Grand Communication of the Most Worshipful Prince Hall Grand Lodge of Texas and Jurisdiction Belonging* (Fort Worth, Tx., 2000), 10.
132. Ibid., 11.

133. Ibid., 8.
134. Robert E. Connor, Jr., "From the Grand East," *The Family Masonic Quarterly* 113 (June 2000): 1.
135. Robert E. Connor, Jr., "Annual Allocution," June 9, 2000, Radisson Astrodome Hotel, Houston, Texas, 3.
136. Ibid., 5.
137. Ibid., 5-6.
138. Ibid., 6.
139. Ibid., 7.
140. Ibid., 12.
141. Connor, "From the Grand East," June 2000, 1. The last recommendation was included in the Report of the Committee on Archives, chaired by Past Grand Master Edwin B. Cash. This report also called for Grand Lodge support for the publication of the Grand Lodge History, with the interests of the Grand Lodge protected, the Grand Legal Advisor involved in all negotiations, and the Grand Historian compensated with royalties; see *Proceedings* (2000): 19.
142. *Proceedings* (2000): 24-25.
143. Robert E. Connor, Jr., "Edict 06-27-00: Waiver of Bloodline Requirement for Females," *The Family Masonic Quarterly* 113 (June 2000): 1.
144. Robert E. Connor, Jr., "Edict 06-27-00-01: Required Training Program," *The Family Masonic Quarterly* 113 (June 2000): 1.
145. Robert L. Uzzel, "Notes from Millennium Team Meeting," Fort Worth, Texas, 22 July 2000.
146. Ibid.
147. Ibid.
148. Robert L. Uzzel, "Notes from Special Session," 4 November 2000.
149. Ibid.
150. Ibid. This property was once the site of the now defunct Fraternal Bank and Trust. It has also served as a parking lot but currently has no specific use.
151. Ibid.
152. Ibid.
153. *Proceedings of the One Hundred and Twenty-sixth Annual Grand Communication of the Most Worshipful Prince Hall Grand Lodge of Texas and Jurisdiction Belonging* (Fort Worth, Tx., 2001), 1-13.
154. Ibid., 14.
155. Robert E. Connor, Jr., "127th Annual Grand Communication Annual Allocution," *Family Masonic Quarterly*, September 2002, 1-3.
156. *Proceedings of the One Hundred and Twenty-seventh Annual Grand Communication of the Most Worshipful Prince Hall Grand Lodge of Texas and Jurisdiction Belonging* (Fort Worth, Texas, 2002), 3-5.
157. *Proceedings of the One Hundred and Twenty-eighth Annual Grand Communication of the Most Worshipful Prince Hall Grand Lodge of Texas and Jurisdiction Belonging* (Fort Worth, Tx., 2003), 21-24. U. S. Senator James Strom Thurmond (December 5, 1902–June 26, 2003) was a member of Columbia Lodge No. 50 in Edgefield, South Carolina. Since his death, there has been much controversy surrounding many aspects of his career, including his fathering of a daughter by Carrie Butler, a black woman employed by his family, in 1925. Recently, Strom Thurmond, Jr., expressed a willingness to meet his half-sister, Essie Mae Washington-Williams; see Tim Smith, "Thurmond's Daughter: 'At Last I Feel Completely Free,'" http://greenvilleonline.com/news/2003/12/17/2003121721156.htm, 1-3.
158. *Proceedings* (2003): 27-28.
159. Ibid., 5-8.
160. "Columbus Police Chief Robert Connor Jr. Passes Away in Houston Hospital," *Colorado County Citizen*, September 19, 2003, 1.
161. "Celebration for the Life of Robert Edmund Connor, Jr.," program.
162. "Columbus Loses Big-Hearted Police Chief," 3.
163. Joseph A. Walkes, Jr., letter to author, September 17, 2003.

Wilbert Marice Curtis
1. Wilbert Marice Curtis, unpublished autobiography.
2. Ibid.

3. Ibid.
4. Ibid.
5. Ibid.
6. Ibid.
7. Ibid.
8. Ibid.
9. Ibid.
10. Wilbert M. Curtis, "From the Office of the Deputy Grand Master," *Family Masonic Quarterly*, September 2002, 3.
11. Wilbert M. Curtis, "Report of Deputy Grand Master," *Proceedings of the One Hundred and Twenty-eighth Annual Grand Communication of the Most Worshipful Prince Hall Grand Lodge of Texas and Jurisdiction Belonging* (Fort Worth, Tx., 2003), 45-46.

Epilogue
1. Normand, *The Texas Masons*, 5.
2. Allen E. Roberts, *House Undivided: The Story of Freemasonry and the Civil War* (Richmond, Va.: Macoy Publishing and Masonic Supply Co., Inc., 1990), 299.
3. Joseph A. Walkes, Jr., *Black Square and Compass: 200 Years of Prince Hall Freemasonry* (Richmond, Va.: Macoy Publishing and Masonic Supply Co., 1979), 130. However, Pike is reported to have given copies of his Masonic classic *Morals and Dogma* and a number of other writings on Scottish Rite Masonry to Thornton A. Jackson, Grand Commander of the Scottish Rite, Southern Jurisdiction (Prince Hall Affiliated). If this is the case, it is obvious that he had no objection to black Masons existing as a separate organization; see ibid., 141-42.
4. Joseph A. Walkes, Jr., *Jno. G. Lewis, Jr.—End of an Era: The History of the Prince Hall Grand Lodge of Louisiana, 1842-1979* (Kansas City, Mo.: Midtown Printing and Publishing Co., 1986), 1.
5. During Operation Desert Storm, the writer wrote letters to three Prince Hall brethren in Saudi Arabia and expressed support for American troops. He, nevertheless, disagreed with the decision of President George Bush to launch the operation in the first place.
6. For a discussion of survival issues faced by white Masons in Texas, see Mark Wrolstad, "Masons Stepping Out From Behind Shroud to Woo New Members," *The Dallas Morning News* October 11, 1998, 1A, 31A.

Bibliography

Grand Lodge Proceedings (Texas)

Proceedings of the Convention to Organize the Most Worshipful Grand Lodge, Free and Accepted Ancient York Masons of the State of Texas, held in the City of Brenham, August 19 and 20 A.L. 5875. Galveston, Texas: McKenna and Co., 1875.

Proceedings of the Most Worshipful Grand Lodge, Ancient Free and Accepted Masons for the State of Texas, held in the City of Houston, A.L. 5876, '77, '78, '79. Galveston, Texas: McKenna and Co., 1879.

Proceedings of the Most Worshipful Grand Lodge, Ancient Free and Accepted Masons for the State of Texas, held in the Cities of Galveston, Austin and Waco A.L. 5880-81-82. Galveston, Texas: McKenna and Co., 1882.

Proceedings of the Twelfth Annual Communication of the Most Worshipful Grand Lodge, Ancient Free and Accepted Masons for the State of Texas and Jurisdiction held at the City of Denison, Commencing on the Third Tuesday in June A.D. 1887, A.L. 5887. Houston, Texas: Smallwood, Dealy, and Baker, 1887.

Proceedings of the Thirteenth Annual Communication of the Most Worshipful Grand Lodge, Ancient Free and Accepted Masons for the State of Texas and Jurisdiction held in the City of Austin Commencing on the Third Tuesday in June A.D. 1888, A.L. 5888. Houston, Texas: Smallwood, Dealy, and Baker, 1888.

Proceedings of the Thirteenth Annual Communication of the Most Worshipful Grand Lodge, Ancient Free and Accepted Masons for the State of Texas and Jurisdiction held in the City of Austin Commencing on the Third Tuesday in June A.D. 1889, A.L. 5889. Houston, Texas: Smallwood, Dealy, and Baker, 1889.

Proceedings of the Seventeenth Annual Communication of the Most Worshipful Grand Lodge, Ancient Free and Accepted Masons for the State of Texas and Jurisdiction, held in the City of Austin, Commencing Tuesday, July 12 A.D., 1892, A.L. 5892. Denison, Texas: Murray's Power Printing House, 1892.

Proceedings of the Nineteenth Annual Communication of the Most Worshipful Grand Lodge, Ancient Free and Accepted Masons for the State of Texas and Jurisdiction held in the City of Waco, Commencing Tuesday, July 10 A.D. 1894, A.L. 5894. Denison, Texas: Murray's Power Printing House, 1894.

Proceedings of the Twentieth Annual Communication of the Most Worshipful Grand Lodge, Free and Accepted Masons for the State of Texas and Its Jurisdiction. Denison, Texas: Murray's Power Printing House, 1895.

Proceedings of the Thirty-first Annual Communication of the Most Worshipful Grand Lodge, Free and Accepted Masons of the State of Texas and Its Jurisdiction. Fort Worth, Texas, 1906.

Proceedings of the Thirty-second Annual Communication of the Most Worshipful Grand Lodge, Free and Accepted Masons of the State of Texas and Its Jurisdiction. Fort Worth, Texas, 1907.

Proceedings of the Thirty-fourth Annual Communication of the Most Worshipful Grand Lodge, Free and Accepted Masons of the State of Texas and Its Jurisdiction. Fort Worth, Texas, 1909.

Proceedings of the Thirty-sixth Annual Communication of the Most Worshipful Grand Lodge, Free and Accepted Masons of the State of Texas and Its Jurisdiction. Fort Worth, Texas, 1911.

Proceedings of the Thirty-seventh Annual Communication of the Most Worshipful Grand Lodge, Free and Accepted Masons of the State of Texas and Its Jurisdiction. Fort Worth, Texas, 1912.

Proceedings of the Thirty-ninth Annual Communication of the Most Worshipful Grand Lodge, Free and Accepted Masons of the State of Texas and Its Jurisdiction. Fort Worth, Texas, 1914.

Proceedings of the Forty-first Annual Communication of the Most Worshipful Grand Lodge, Free and Accepted Masons of the State of Texas and Its Jurisdiction. Fort Worth, Texas, 1916.

Proceedings of the Forty-second Annual Communication of the Most Worshipful Grand Lodge, Free and Accepted Masons of the State of Texas and Its Jurisdiction. Fort Worth, Texas, 1917.

Proceedings of the Forty-third Annual Communication of the Most Worshipful Grand Lodge, Free and Accepted Masons of the State of Texas and Its Jurisdiction. Fort Worth, Texas, 1918.

Proceedings of the Forty-fourth Annual Communication of the Most Worshipful Grand Lodge, Free and Accepted Masons of the State of Texas and Its Jurisdiction. Fort Worth, Texas, 1919.

Proceedings of the Forty-fifth Annual Communication of the Most Worshipful Grand Lodge, Free and Accepted Masons of the State of Texas and Its Jurisdiction. Fort Worth, Texas, 1920.

Proceedings of the Forty-sixth Annual Communication of the Most Worshipful Grand Lodge, Free and Accepted Masons of the State of Texas and Its Jurisdiction. Fort Worth, Texas, 1921.

Proceedings of the Forty-seventh Annual Communication of the Most Worshipful Grand Lodge, Free and Accepted Masons of the State of Texas and Its Jurisdiction. Fort Worth, Texas, 1922.

Proceedings of the Forty-eighth Annual Communication of the Most Worshipful Grand Lodge, Free and Accepted Masons of the State of Texas and Its Jurisdiction. Fort Worth, Texas, 1923.

Proceedings of the Forty-ninth Annual Communication of the Most Worshipful Grand Lodge, Free and Accepted Masons of the State of Texas and Its Jurisdiction. Fort Worth, Texas, 1924.

Proceedings of the Fiftieth Annual Communication of the Most Worshipful Grand Lodge, Free and Accepted Masons of the State of Texas and Its Jurisdiction. Fort Worth, Texas, 1925.

Proceedings of the Fifty-first Annual Communication of the Most Worshipful Grand Lodge, Free and Accepted Masons of Texas Jurisdiction and Belonging. Fort Worth, Texas, 1926.

Proceedings of the Fifty-second Annual Communication of the Most Worshipful Grand Lodge, Free and Accepted Masons of Texas Jurisdiction and Belonging. Fort Worth, Texas, 1927.

Proceedings of the Fifty-third Annual Communication of the Most Worshipful Grand Lodge, Free and Accepted Masons of Texas Jurisdiction and Belonging. Fort Worth, Texas, 1928.

Proceedings of the Fifty-fourth Annual Communication of the Most Worshipful Grand Lodge, Free and Accepted Masons of Texas Jurisdiction and Belonging. Fort Worth, Texas, 1929.

Proceedings of the Fifty-fifth Annual Communication of the Most Worshipful Grand Lodge, Free and Accepted Masons of Texas Jurisdiction and Belonging. Fort Worth, Texas, 1930.

Proceedings of the Fifty-sixth Annual Communication of the Most Worshipful Grand Lodge, Free and Accepted Masons of Texas Jurisdiction and Belonging. Fort Worth, Texas, 1931.

Proceedings of the Fifty-seventh Annual Communication of the Most Worshipful Grand Lodge, Free and Accepted Masons of Texas Jurisdiction and Belonging. Fort Worth, Texas, 1932.

Proceedings of the Sixty-first Annual Communication of the Most Worshipful Grand Lodge, Free and Accepted Masons of Texas Jurisdiction and Belonging. Fort Worth, Texas, 1936.

Proceedings of the Sixty-second Annual Communication of the Most Worshipful Grand Lodge, Free and Accepted Masons of Texas Jurisdiction and Belonging. Fort Worth, Texas, 1937.

Proceedings of the Sixty-sixth Annual Communication of the Most Worshipful Grand Lodge, Free and Accepted Masons of Texas Jurisdiction and Belonging. Fort Worth, Texas, 1941.

Proceedings of the Sixty-seventh Annual Communication of the Most Worshipful Grand Lodge, Free and Accepted Masons of Texas Jurisdiction and Belonging. Fort Worth, Texas, 1942.

Proceedings of the Sixty-eighth Annual Communication of the Most Worshipful Grand Lodge, Free and Accepted Masons of Texas Jurisdiction and Belonging. Fort Worth, Texas, 1943.

Proceedings of the Sixty-ninth Annual Communication of the Most Worshipful Grand Lodge, Free and Accepted Masons of Texas Jurisdiction and Belonging. Fort Worth, Texas, 1944.

Proceedings of the Seventieth Annual Communication of the Most Worshipful Grand Lodge, Free and Accepted Masons of Texas Jurisdiction and Belonging. Fort Worth, Texas, 1945.

Proceedings of the Seventy-first Annual Communication of the Most Worshipful Grand Lodge, Free and Accepted Masons of Texas Jurisdiction Belonging, "Prince Hall Affiliation." Fort Worth, Texas, 1946.

Proceedings of the Seventy-second Annual Communication of the Most Worshipful Grand Lodge, Free and Accepted Masons of Texas Jurisdiction Belonging, "Prince Hall Affiliation." Fort Worth, Texas, 1947.

Proceedings of the Seventy-third Annual Communication of the Most Worshipful Grand Lodge, Free and Accepted Masons of Texas Jurisdiction Belonging, "Prince Hall Affiliation." Fort Worth, Texas, 1948.

Proceedings of the Seventy-fourth Annual Communication of the Most Worshipful Grand Lodge, Free and Accepted Masons of Texas Jurisdiction Belonging, "Prince Hall Affiliation." Fort Worth, Texas, 1949.

Proceedings of the Seventy-fifth Annual Grand Communication of the Most Worshipful Prince Hall Grand Lodge, Free and Accepted Masons of Texas and Jurisdiction Belonging. Fort Worth, Texas, 1950.

Proceedings of the Seventy-sixth Annual Grand Communication of the Most Worshipful Prince Hall Grand Lodge, Free and Accepted Masons of Texas and Jurisdiction Belonging. Fort Worth, Texas, 1951.

Proceedings of the Seventy-seventh Annual Communication of the Most Worshipful Prince Hall Grand Lodge, Free and Accepted Masons of Texas and Jurisdiction Belonging. Fort Worth, Texas, 1952.

Proceedings of the Seventy-eighth Annual Communication of the Most Worshipful Prince Hall Grand Lodge, Free and Accepted Masons of Texas and Jurisdiction Belonging. Fort Worth, Texas, 1953.

Proceedings of the Seventy-ninth Annual Communication of the Most Worshipful Prince Hall Grand Lodge, Free and Accepted Masons of Texas and Jurisdiction Belonging. Fort Worth, Texas, 1954.

Proceedings of the Eightieth Grand Annual Communication of the Most Worshipful Prince Hall Grand Lodge, Free and Accepted Masons of Texas and Jurisdiction Belonging. Fort Worth, Texas, 1955.

Proceedings of the Eighty-first Annual Grand Communication of the Most Worshipful Prince Hall Grand Lodge, Free and Accepted Masons of Texas and Jurisdiction Belonging. Fort Worth, Texas, 1956.

Proceedings of the Eighty-second Annual Grand Communication of the Most Worshipful Prince Hall Grand Lodge, Free and Accepted Masons of Texas and Jurisdiction Belonging. Fort Worth, Texas, 1957.

Proceedings of the Eighty-third Annual Grand Communication of the Most Worshipful Prince Hall Grand Lodge, Free and Accepted Masons of Texas and Jurisdiction Belonging. Fort Worth, Texas, 1958.

Proceedings of the Eighty-fourth Annual Grand Communication of the Most Worshipful Prince Hall Grand Lodge, Free and Accepted Masons of Texas and Jurisdiction Belonging. Fort Worth, Texas, 1959.

Proceedings of the Eighty-fifth Annual Grand Communication of the Most Worshipful Prince Hall Grand Lodge, Free and Accepted Masons of Texas and Jurisdiction Belonging. Fort Worth, Texas, 1960.

Proceedings of the Eighty-sixth Annual Grand Communication of the Most Worshipful Prince Hall Grand Lodge, Free and Accepted Masons of Texas and Jurisdiction Belonging. Fort Worth, Texas, 1961.

Proceedings of the Eighty-seventh Annual Grand Communication of the Most Worshipful Prince Hall Grand Lodge, Free and Accepted Masons of Texas and Jurisdiction Belonging. Fort Worth, Texas, 1962.

Proceedings of the Eighty-eighth Annual Grand Communication of the Most Worshipful Prince Hall Grand Lodge, Free and Accepted Masons of Texas and Jurisdiction Belonging. Fort Worth, Texas, 1963.

Proceedings of the Eighty-ninth Annual Grand Communication of the Most Worshipful Prince Hall Grand Lodge, Free and Accepted Masons of Texas and Jurisdiction Belonging. Fort Worth, Texas, 1964.

Proceedings of the Ninetieth Annual Grand Communication of the Most Worshipful Prince Hall Grand Lodge, Free and Accepted Masons of Texas and Jurisdiction Belonging. Fort Worth, Texas, 1965.

Proceedings of the Ninety-first Annual Grand Communication of the Most Worshipful Prince Hall Grand Lodge, Free and Accepted Masons of Texas and Jurisdiction Belonging. Fort Worth, Texas, 1966.

Proceedings of the Ninety-second Annual Grand Communication of the Most Worshipful Prince Hall Grand Lodge, Free and Accepted Masons of Texas and Jurisdiction Belonging. Fort Worth, Texas, 1967.

Proceedings of the Ninety-third Annual Grand Communication of the Most Worshipful Prince Hall Grand Lodge, Free and Accepted Masons of Texas and Jurisdiction Belonging. Fort Worth, Texas, 1968.

Proceedings of the Ninety-fourth Annual Grand Communication of the Most Worshipful Prince Hall Grand Lodge, Free and Accepted Masons of Texas and Jurisdiction Belonging. Fort Worth, Texas, 1969.

Proceedings of the Ninety-fifth Annual Grand Communication of the Most Worshipful Prince Hall Grand Lodge, Free and Accepted Masons of Texas and Jurisdiction Belonging. Fort Worth, Texas, 1970.

Proceedings of the Ninety-sixth Annual Grand Communication of the Most Worshipful Prince Hall Grand Lodge, Free and Accepted Masons of Texas and Jurisdiction Belonging. Fort Worth, Texas, 1971.

Proceedings of the Ninety-seventh Annual Grand Communication of the Most Worshipful Prince Hall Grand Lodge, Free and Accepted Masons of Texas and Jurisdiction Belonging. Fort Worth, Texas, 1972.

Proceedings of the Ninety-eighth Annual Grand Communication of the Most Worshipful Prince Hall Grand Lodge, Free and Accepted Masons of Texas and Jurisdiction Belonging. Fort Worth, Texas, 1973.

Proceedings of the Ninety-ninth Annual Grand Communication of the Most Worshipful Prince Hall Grand Lodge, Free and Accepted Masons of Texas and Jurisdiction Belonging. Fort Worth, Texas, 1974.

Proceedings of the Centennial Annual Grand Communication of the Most Worshipful Prince Hall Grand Lodge of Texas and Jurisdiction Belonging. Fort Worth, Texas, 1975.

Proceedings of the One Hundred and First Annual Grand Communication of the Most Worshipful Prince Hall Grand Lodge of Texas and Jurisdiction Belonging. Fort Worth, Texas, 1976.

Proceedings of the One Hundred and Second Annual Grand Communication of the Most Worshipful Prince Hall Grand Lodge of Texas and Jurisdiction Belonging. Fort Worth, Texas, 1977.

Proceedings of the One Hundred and Third Annual Grand Communication of the Most Worshipful Prince Hall Grand Lodge of Texas and Jurisdiction Belonging. Fort Worth, Texas, 1978.
Proceedings of the One Hundred and Fourth Annual Grand Communication of the Most Worshipful Prince Hall Grand Lodge of Texas and Jurisdiction Belonging. Fort Worth, Texas, 1979.
Proceedings of the One Hundred and Fifth Annual Grand Communication of the Most Worshipful Prince Hall Grand Lodge of Texas and Jurisdiction Belonging. Fort Worth, Texas, 1980.
Proceedings of the One Hundred and Sixth Annual Grand Communication of the Most Worshipful Prince Hall Grand Lodge of Texas and Jurisdiction Belonging. Fort Worth, Texas, 1981.
Proceedings of the One Hundred and Seventh Annual Grand Communication of the Most Worshipful Prince Hall Grand Lodge of Texas and Jurisdiction Belonging. Fort Worth, Texas, 1982.
Proceedings of the One Hundred and Eighth Annual Grand Communication of the Most Worshipful Prince Hall Grand Lodge of Texas and Jurisdiction Belonging. Fort Worth, Texas, 1983.
Proceedings of the One Hundred and Ninth Annual Grand Communication of the Most Worshipful Prince Hall Grand Lodge of Texas and Jurisdiction Belonging. Fort Worth, Texas, 1984.
Proceedings of the One Hundred and Tenth Annual Grand Communication of the Most Worshipful Prince Hall Grand Lodge of Texas and Jurisdiction Belonging. Fort Worth, Texas, 1985.
Proceedings of the One Hundred and Eleventh Annual Grand Communication of the Most Worshipful Prince Hall Grand Lodge of Texas and Jurisdiction Belonging. Fort Worth, Texas, 1986.
Proceedings of the One Hundred and Twelfth Annual Grand Communication of the Most Worshipful Prince Hall Grand Lodge of Texas and Jurisdiction Belonging. Fort Worth, Texas, 1987.
Proceedings of the One Hundred and Thirteenth Annual Grand Communication of the Most Worshipful Prince Hall Grand Lodge of Texas and Jurisdiction Belonging. Fort Worth, Texas, 1988.
Proceedings of the One Hundred and Fourteenth Annual Grand Communication of the Most Worshipful Prince Hall Grand Lodge of Texas and Jurisdiction Belonging. Fort Worth, Texas, 1989.
Proceedings of the One Hundred and Fifteenth Annual Grand Communication of the Most Worshipful Prince Hall Grand Lodge of Texas and Jurisdiction Belonging. Fort Worth, Texas, 1990.
Proceedings of the One Hundred and Sixteenth Annual Grand Communication of the Most Worshipful Prince Hall Grand Lodge of Texas and Jurisdiction Belonging. Fort Worth, Texas, 1991.
Proceedings of the One Hundred and Seventeenth Annual Grand Communication of the Most Worshipful Prince Hall Grand Lodge of Texas and Jurisdiction Belonging. Fort Worth, Texas, 1992.
Proceedings of the One Hundred and Eighteenth Annual Grand Communication of the Most Worshipful Prince Hall Grand Lodge of Texas and Jurisdiction Belonging. Fort Worth, Texas, 1993.
Proceedings of the One Hundred and Nineteenth Annual Grand Communication of the Most Worshipful Prince Hall Grand Lodge of Texas and Jurisdiction Belonging. Fort Worth, Texas, 1994.
Proceedings of the One Hundred and Twentieth Annual Grand Communication of the Most Worshipful Prince Hall Grand Lodge of Texas and Jurisdiction Belonging. Fort Worth, Texas, 1995.
Proceedings of the One Hundred and Twenty-first Annual Grand Communication of the Most Worshipful Prince Hall Grand Lodge of Texas and Jurisdiction Belonging. Fort Worth, Texas, 1996.
Proceedings of the One Hundred and Twenty-second Annual Grand Communication of the Most Worshipful Prince Hall Grand Lodge of Texas and Jurisdiction Belonging. Fort Worth, Texas, 1997.
Proceedings of the One Hundred and Twenty-third Annual Grand Communication of the Most Worshipful Prince Hall Grand Lodge of Texas and Jurisdiction Belonging. Fort Worth, Texas, 1998.
Proceedings of the One Hundred and Twenty-fourth Annual Grand Communication of the Most Worshipful Prince Hall Grand Lodge of Texas and Jurisdiction Belonging. Fort Worth, Texas, 1999.
Proceedings of the One Hundred and Twenty-fifth Annual Grand Communication of the Most Worshipful Prince Hall Grand Lodge of Texas and Jurisdiction Belonging. Fort Worth, Texas, 2000.
Proceedings of the One Hundred and Twenty-sixth Annual Grand Communication of the Most Worshipful Prince Hall Grand Lodge of Texas and Jurisdiction Belonging. Fort Worth, Texas, 2001.
Proceedings of the One Hundred and Twenty-seventh Annual Grand Communication of the Most Worshipful Prince Hall Grand Lodge of Texas and Jurisdiction Belonging. Fort Worth, Texas, 2002.
Proceedings of the One Hundred and Twenty-eighth Annual Grand Communication of the Most Worshipful Prince Hall Grand Lodge of Texas and Jurisdiction Belonging. Fort Worth, Texas, 2003.

Grand Lodge Proceedings (California)
Proceedings of the Sixty-second Annual Communication of the Most Worshipful Sovereign Grand Lodge, Free and Accepted Masons for the State of California and Jurisdiction. Oakland, Ca.: Bridges Print, 1916.

Documents

Standard Certificate of Death for Coleman, William. Texas Department of Health Bureau of Vital Statistics.
Standard Certificate of Death for Kimbrough, Wiley Lawson. California Department of Public Health.
Standard Certificate of Death for Lockhart, Lucian L. Texas Department of Health Bureau of Vital Statistics.
Standard Certificate of Death for Madison, John W. Texas Department of Health Bureau of Vital Statistics.
United States Census. Washington, D. C., 1880.
United States Census. Washington, D. C., 1910.

Court Cases

Brown v. Board of Education of Topeka, 347 U. S. 483 (1954).
Loving v. Virginia, 388 U. S. 1 (1967).
Moose Lodge v. K. Leroy Irvis, 92 S. Ct. 1965 (1972).
Plessy v. Ferguson, 163 U. S. 537 (1896).

Books

Allen, Frederick Lewis. *Only Yesterday: An Informal History of the Nineteen-Twenties*. New York: Harper and Brothers, 1931.
Bennett, Joseph E. *Sixguns and Masons: Profiles of Selected Texas Rangers and Prominent Westerners*. Highland Springs, Va.: Anchor Communications, 1991.
Brewer, J. Mason, *Negro Legislators of Texas and Their Descendants*. Austin, Texas: Pemberton Press, 1970.
Brown, Harvey Newton. *Freemasonry among Negroes and Whites in America: A Study in Masonic Legitimacy and Regularity*. Nottingham, Md., 1965.
Bundy, W. O. *Life of William Madison McDonald*. Fort Worth, Texas: Bunker Printing and Book Co., Inc., 1925.
Casdorph, Paul. *A History of the Republican Party in Texas, 1865-1965*. Austin, Texas: Pemberton Press, 1967.
Clark, George. *A Glance Backward: Or Some Events in the Past History of My Life*. Houston, Texas: Hein and Sons, n.d.
Conger, Roger N., ed. *A Century of Fraternity: Waco Lodge No. 92, A.F.&A.M., Waco, Texas, 1852-1952*. Waco, Texas, 1952.
Cox, Joseph Mason Andrew. *Great Black Men of Masonry: Qualitative Black Achievers who were Freemasons*. Bronx, N. Y.: Blue Diamond Press, 1982.
Duncan, Herbert Ewing. *Hi, Dad! A Story about Frank S. Land and the Order of DeMolay*. Kansas City, Mo.: International Supreme Council Order of DeMolay, 1970.
El-Amin, Mustafa. *African-American Freemasons: Why They Should Accept Al-Islam*. Jersey City, N. J.: New Mind Productions, 1990.
———. *Al-Islam, Christianity, and Freemasonry*. Jersey City, N. J.: New Mind Productions, 1985.
———. *Freemasonry, Ancient Egypt, and the Islamic Destiny*. Jersey City, N. J.: New Mind Productions, 1988.
Falconi, Carlo. *Pope John and the Ecumenical Council: A Diary of the Second Vatican Council, September-December 1962*. Muriel Grindod, trans. New York: Word Publishing Co., 1964.
Fleming, Walter, ed. *Documents Relating to Reconstruction*. Morgantown, W. V.: West Virginia University Press, 1904.
Fox, William L. *Lodge of the Double-Headed Eagle: Two Centuries of Scottish Rite Freemasonry in America's Southern Jurisdiction*. Fayetteville, Ark.: University of Arkansas Press, 1997.
Fullmore, Jr., John Collyns. *The Dragon: History of Douglass School*. El Paso, Texas: American Printing Co., 1941.
Grimshaw, William H. *Official History of Freemasonry among the Colored People of North America*. New York: Macoy Publishing and Masonic Supply Co., Inc., 1903.
Hales, Douglas. *A Southern Family in White and Black: The Cuneys of Texas*. College Station, Texas: Texas A&M University Press, 2003.
The Handbook of Texas: A Supplement. Austin, Texas: Texas State Historical Association, 1976.
Hare, Maud Cuney. *Norris Wright Cuney: A Tribune to the Black People*. Austin, Texas: Steck-Vaughn Co., 1968.

Harmon, Nolan B., ed. *The Encyclopedia of World Methodism*, vol. II. Nashville, Tenn.: United Methodist Publishing House, 1974.

Hicks, John D., and George E. Mowry. *A Short History of American Democracy*. Cambridge, Mass.: Riverside Press, 1956.

Jackson, A. W. *A Sure Foundation*. Houston, Texas: A. W. Jackson, n.d.

Lakey, Othal Hawthorne. *The History of the CME Church*. Memphis, Tenn.: CME Publishing House, 1985.

Lewis, Arthur H. *The Day They Shook the Plum Tree*. New York: Harcourt, Brace, and World, Inc., 1963.

Muraskin, William A. *Middle-Class Blacks in a White Society: Prince Hall Freemasonry in America*. Berkeley, Ca.: University of California Press, 1975.

Normand, Pete. *The Texas Masons: The Fraternity of Ancient Free and Accepted Masons in the History of Texas*. College Station, Texas: Masonic Library and Museum Association, 1986.

Pepe, Phil. *Winners Never Quit*. New York: Grosset and Dunlap, Inc., 1968.

Pitre, Merline. *Through Many Dangers, Toils, and Snares: The Black Leadership of Texas, 1869-1900*. Austin, Texas: Eakin Press, 1985.

Prince, Nancy. *A Black Woman's Odyssey Through Russia and Jamaica: The Narrative of Nancy Prince*. New York: Markus Wiener, 1990.

Radford, Sr., Garry H. *African American Heritage in Waco, Texas: Life Stories of Those Who Believed They Could Overcome Impediments*. Austin, Texas: Eakin Press, 2000.

Ransom, Reverdy C. *The Pilgrimage of Harriet Ransom's Son*. Nashville, Tenn.: AME Sunday School Union, n.d.

Riesman, David, Nathan Glazer, and Reuel Denny. *The Lonely Crowd: A Study of the Changing American Character*. Hartford, Ct.: Yale University Press, 1953.

Roberts, Allen E. *House Undivided: The Story of Freemasonry and the Civil War*. Richmond, Va.: Macoy Publishing and Masonic Supply Co, Inc., 1990.

Robinson, John J. *A Pilgrim's Path: Freemasonry and the Religious Right*. New York: M. Evans, 1993.

Samora, Julian, Joe Bernal, and Albert Peña. *Gunpowder Justice: A Reassessment of the Texas Rangers*. Notre Dame, In.: Notre Dame University Press, 1979.

Smith, Charles Spencer. *A History of the African Methodist Episcopal Church*. Philadelphia, Pa.: Book Concern of the AME Church, 1922.

Walker, Clarence E. *A Rock in a Weary Land: The African Methodist Episcopal Church During the Civil War and Reconstruction*. Baton Rouge, La.: Louisiana State University Press, 1982.

Walkes, Jr., Joseph A. *Black Square and Compass: 200 Years of Prince Hall Freemasonry*. Richmond, Va.: Macoy Publishing and Masonic Supply Co., Inc., 1979.

———. *History of the Shrine: Ancient Egyptian Arabic Order Nobles of the Mystic Shrine, Inc., Prince Hall Affiliated, A Pillar of Black Society, 1893-1993*. Detroit, Mi.: AEAONMS, Inc., 1993.

———. *History of the United Supreme Council, Ancient Accepted Scottish Rite Freemasonry, Prince Hall Affiliated, Northern Jurisdiction, U.S.A., Inc*. Philadelphia, Pa.: United Supreme Council, PHA, NJ, USA, Inc., 1998.

———. *Jno. G. Lewis, Jr.—End of an Era: The History of the Prince Hall Grand Lodge of Louisiana, 1842-1979*. Kansas City, Mo.: Midtown Printing and Publishing Co., 1986.

———. *A Prince Hall Masonic Quiz Book*. Ames, Ia.: Research Lodge No. 2, 1981.

———. *Prince Hall's Mission: The Rise of the Phylaxis Society*. Kansas City, Mo.: Midtown Printing and Publishing Co., 1995.

Webb, Walter Prescott, ed. *The Handbook of Texas*. Austin, Texas: Texas State Historical Association, 1952.

Wesley, Charles H. *Prince Hall: Life and Legacy*. Washington, D. C.: United Supreme Council, PHA, SJ, USA, Inc., 1983.

———. *Richard Allen: Apostle of Freedom*. Washington, D. C.: Associated Publishers, 1935.

Whalen, William J. *Christianity and American Freemasonry*. Huntington, In.: Our Sunday Visitor, Inc., 1987.

———. *Handbook of Secret Organizations*. Milwaukee, Wi.: Bruce Publishing Co., 1966.

White, William R. *Texas Scottish Rite Centennial and Its Contributions to the Beginning of the Second Century*. Waco, Texas, 1973.

Whitfield, Stephen J. *A Death in the Delta: The Story of Emmett Till*. Baltimore, Md.: Johns Hopkins University Press, 1988.

Wilson, Robert J., Peggy J. Coplin, and Theodore Murray. *A Documentary History of the Improved*

Benevolent and Protective Order of Elks of the World: 100 Years of Benevolence and Image Building. Philadelphia, Pa.: Imprints Unlimited, Inc., 1996.

Wright, Jr., Richard R. *The Bishops of the African Methodist Episcopal Church.* Nashville, Tenn.: AME Sunday School Union, 1963.

Articles

"After a Century and a Decade." *America*, October 20, 1973, 280.

Barr, Alwyn, and Cary D. Wintz. "ALLEN, RICHARD." *The Handbook of Texas Online.* http://www.tsha.utexas.edu/handbook/online/articles/view/AA/fal24.html,1.

"The Beginning." *Waco Freedom-Press,* July 26, 1991, 7.

Boeth, Jennifer. "1984: Was Orwell Right?" *Dallas Times-Herald*, January 23, 1983, 1-G.

"Brotherly Love: Santa Ana Masons Take Their Former Leader Under Their Wing." *The Phylaxis* 21 (First Quarter 1995): 26-27.

Brown, Robert McAfee. "1984: Orwell and Barmen." *The Christian Century*, August 15-22, 1984, 770.

Campbell, Don G. "Shinto: A Masonic Contrast." *The New Age*, September 1977, 47-50.

Cash, Edwin B. "Annual Address of Past Grand Master Edwin B. Cash Delivered at the 119th Grand Session." *Texas Prince Hall Masonic Quarterly* 109 (August 1994): 4.

———. "Grand Master's Column." *Texas Prince Hall Masonic Quarterly* 95 (March 1991): 3.

———. "Grand Master's Column." *Texas Prince Hall Masonic Quarterly* 96 (May 1991): 3-4.

———. "Grand Master's Column." *Texas Prince Hall Masonic Quarterly* 97 (November 1991): 3.

———. "Grand Master's Column." *Texas Prince Hall Masonic Quarterly* 99 (May 1992): 2-3.

———. "Grand Master's Column." *Texas Prince Hall Masonic Quarterly* 101 (November 1992): 3.

———. "Regional Address." *Texas Prince Hall Masonic Quarterly* 103 (May 1993): 3.

———. "Grand Master's Column." *Texas Prince Hall Masonic Quarterly* 105 (November 1993): 3.

———. "Grand Master's Column." *Texas Prince Hall Masonic Quarterly* 107 (May 1994): 3.

"Celebration of Life of Thomas Henry Routt, 1930-1991." *Texas Prince Hall Masonic Quarterly* 95 (March 1991): 4.

"A Celebration of Love in Memory of Isadore Huddleston Clayborn." *Texas Prince Hall Masonic Quarterly* 108 (June 1994): 3.

"Celebration Service." *Texas Prince Hall Masonic Quarterly* 108 (June 1994): 4.

Clayborn, I. H. "A Report." *News Quarterly* (Spring 1989): 2.

———. "A Report." *News Quarterly* (Spring 1992): 2.

———. "The Late Thomas H. Routt." *Texas Prince Hall Masonic Quarterly* 95 (March 1991): 3.

———. "Sovereign Grand Commander's Allocution." *News Quarterly* (October 1990): 4.

———. "Sovereign Grand Commander's Allocution." *News Quarterly* (Spring 1992): 3.

———. "Sovereign Grand Commander's Allocution." *News Quarterly* (Spring 1994): 3-4.

Coleman, Jr., Willie High. "$300,000: Remember—Hazing Will Not be Tolerated by the Grand Lodge." *The Family Masonic Quarterly* 112 (November 1999): 1, 16.

"Columbus Loses Big-Hearted Police Chief." http://www/coloradocitizen.com/articles/2003/09/25/news02.prt, 3.

"Columbus Police Chief Robert Connor, Jr., Passes Away in Houston Hospital." *Colorado County Citizen*, 19 September 2003, 1.

Connor, Jr., Robert E. "Edict #1-98/99," *The Family Masonic Quarterly* 111 (August 1998): 6.

———. "Edict 06-27-00: Waiver of Bloodline Requirement for Females." *The Family Masonic Quarterly* 113 (June 2000): 4.

———. "Edict 06-27-00-01: Required Training Program." *The Family Masonic Quarterly* 113 (June 2000): 4.

———. "From the Desk of the Right Worshipful Grand Junior Warden." *Texas Prince Hall Masonic Quarterly* 95 (March 1991): 3.

———. "From the Grand East." *Texas Prince Hall Masonic Quarterly* 109 (March 1996): 1.

———. "From the Grand East." *Texas Prince Hall Masonic Quarterly* 109 (May 1996): 2.

———. "From the Grand East." *Texas Prince Hall Masonic Quarterly* 109 (May 1997): 1.

———. "From the Grand East." *Texas Prince Hall Masonic Quarterly* 110 (November 1997): 1.

———. "From the Grand East." *The Family Masonic Quarterly* 110 (March 1998): 1.

———. "From the Grand East." *The Family Masonic Quarterly* 111 (May 1998): 1.

———. "From the Grand East." *The Family Masonic Quarterly* 111 (August 1998): 1.

———. "From the Grand East." *The Family Masonic Quarterly* 111 (March 1999): 1.

———. "From the Grand East." *The Family Masonic Quarterly* 111 (May 1999): 1.
———. "From the Grand East." *The Family Masonic Quarterly* 111 (August 1999): 1.
———. "From the Grand East." *The Family Masonic Quarterly* 112 (November 1999): 1, 16.
———. "From the Grand East." *The Family Masonic Quarterly* 112 (March 2000): 2.
———. "From the Grand East." *The Family Masonic Quarterly* 113 (June 2000): 1.
———. "Grand Master's Column." *Texas Prince Hall Masonic Quarterly* 109 (November 1994): 3.
———. "Grand Master's Column." *Texas Prince Hall Masonic Quarterly* 109 (March 1995): 1-2.
———. "Grand Master's Column." *Texas Prince Hall Masonic Quarterly* 109 (August 1995): 3.
———. "Grand Master's Regional Address." *Texas Prince Hall Masonic Quarterly* 109 (November 1995): 2.
———. "127th Annual Grand Communication Annual Allocution." *Family Masonic Quarterly* 115 (September 2002): 1-3.
———. "Prince Hall Grand Chapter, O.E.S. of Texas." *Texas Prince Hall Masonic Quarterly* 109 (November 1996): 4.
———. "Proclamation." September 17, 2000.
———. "Special Grand Communication: February 26, 2000, Update." *The Family Masonic Quarterly* 112 (March 2000): 2.
Curtis, Wilbert M. "From the Office of the Deputy Grand Master." *Family Masonic Quarterly*, April 2003, 2.
———. "From the Office of the Deputy Grand Master." *Family Masonic Quarterly*, September 2002, 3.
———. "Mid-Winter 2004 Address."
———. Unpublished autobiography.
"Deaths, Funerals: John T. Maxey." *Galveston Daily News*, February 14, 1973, A-12.
"Dignitaries Throughout Nation Attend L. L. Lockhart Rites." *The Houston Informer*, October 8, 1955, 1.
"Elks Integrate." *Chicago Tribune*, July 23, 1973, I-20.
Glaspie, C. A. "From the Desk of the Right Worshipful Grand Secretary." *Texas Prince Hall Masonic Quarterly* 95 (March 1991): 2.
"Grand Lodge Officers: 2000-2001." *The Family Masonic Quarterly* 112 (June 2000): 2.
"Grand Lodge Resolution." *Texas Prince Hall Masonic Quarterly* 108 (June 1994): 5.
Harris, A. D. "Keep Cuney's Dream Alive." *The Family Masonic Quarterly* 110 (November 1997): 6.
"Hopeful Lodge No. 78, F.&A.M., 100th Anniversary Award Banquet, 7:30 p.m., December 12, 1992." *Texas Prince Hall Masonic Quarterly* 103 (May 1993): 8.
Hopper, Lee. "Police Chief of Columbus, Robert E. Connor, Jr., Dies." http://www.chron.com/cs/CDA/printstory.hts/deaths/211749, 1.
"Hundreds Attend Rites for Grand Master Lockhart." *The Houston Informer*, October 8, 1955, 1 and 14.
"Imperial Council Resolution." *Texas Prince Hall Masonic Quarterly* 108 (June 1994): 6.
"Installation of M. W. Grand Master Edwin B. Cash, January 8, 1991, in Houston, Texas." *Texas Prince Hall Masonic Quarterly* 95 (March 1991): 1.
"J. A. Kirk." *Waco Messenger*, October 5, 1934, 2.
Jones, Landon Y. "George Orwell: This is the Year for the Enigmatic Writer Who Devoted His Life to Speaking Unwelcome Truths." *People Weekly*, January 9, 1984, 41.
"Judge Routt Dies of Cancer 2 Days after Swearing In." *Houston Post*, January 4, 1991, 21.
Keliher, John D. "Most Worshipful Grand Master William H. Upton Memorial." *The Phylaxis*, Third Quarter 1991, 3-5.
Kendall, Kitty. "Age Can't Keep Isle Man on Sidelines." *Galveston Daily News*, July 14, 1966, 9A.
"Letters." Texas Prince Hall Masonic Quarterly 95 (March 1991): 7.
"Local Masonic Lodge to Celebrate 120th Anniversary This Weekend." *The Banner Press*, September 14, 1995, 1.
"Masonic Grand Master H. D. Winn is Dead." *Dallas Express*, March 7, 1925, 1.
Meehan, Thomas. "The Other July Convention: The B.P.O.E. (Best People on Earth) in Atlantic City." *New York Times Magazine*, August 13, 1972, 64-71.
"Mortuary, John W. Madison." *Austin American*, March 20, 1929.
"Ninety-Seventh Annual Session, Little Rock, Arkansas, 1983." *News Quarterly* (Summer 1984): 16.
"Obituaries." *African-American News & Issues*, October 1-7, 2003, 2.
"100 Year of Unity: Northern Jurisdiction of Prince Hall Masons Observes Anniversary." *The Phylaxis* 8 (Second Quarter 1982): 33.

"Past Grand Master of Masons Laid to Rest." *Waco Messenger*, October 5, 1934, 1.

"The Phylaxis Society Resolution of Respect and Love." *Texas Prince Hall Masonic Quarterly* 95 (March 1991): 8.

Pitre, Merline, "Cuney, Norris Wright." *The Handbook of Texas Online*, http://www.tsha.utexas.edu/handbook/online/articles/view/CC/fcu20.html, 2.

"Possible 'Trick' Seen in Elks Vote to Desegregate." *Jet*, August 9, 1973, 6.

"Resolutions." *Texas Prince Hall Masonic Quarterly* 108 (June 1994): 4.

"Rites Held for Bishop J. W. McKinney: Bishop Porter Delivers Eulogy." *Dallas Express*. September 7, 1946, 1, 8.

Roberts, Allen E. "Let the Beauty of Freemasonry Into Your Heart." *The Phylaxis* 19 (First Quarter 1993): 10.

Routt, Thomas H. "From the Grand East." *Texas Prince Hall Masonic Quarterly* 86 (September 1987): 3, 8.

———. "From the Grand East." *Texas Prince Hall Masonic Quarterly* 87 (March 1988): 2-3.

———. "From the Grand East." *Texas Prince Hall Masonic Quarterly* 87 (September 1988): 3.

———. "From the Grand East." *Texas Prince Hall Masonic Quarterly* 87 (December 1988): 3.

———. "From the Grand East." *Texas Prince Hall Masonic Quarterly* 91 (March 1990): 3.

———. "13th Annual Session Opening Speech." *The Phylaxis* 12 (Second Quarter 1986): 4-6.

Schmidt, Jessica. "FBI Honors Columbus Police Chief: Connor Commended for Outstanding Performance During Operation Blowout." *Banner Press*, July 8, 1999.

Smith, Harry E. "Remarks by Harry E. Smith, MPS, Past Imperial Potentate, A.E.A.O.N.M.S., Acceptance of Honorary Doctorate from Paul Quinn College, Waco, Texas, November 15, 1985." *The Phylaxis* 11 (Fourth Quarter 1985): 44-45.

Smith, Helen. "Islander, 96, Recalls Railroad, Masonic Heydey: J. T. Maxey Remembers Mule-Drawn Trolley Cars." *Galveston Daily News*, April 12, 1970, B-12.

"Thomas H. Routt, One of First Black Jurists, Dies." *The Phylaxis* 16 (April 1991): 18.

Trahan, Jason, and Ben Tinsley. "Masonic Hazing Alleged: DA is Investigating Arlington Complaint." *The Dallas Morning News*, December 9, 1999, 37A.

Tribe, Ivan M. "Brother John Llewellyn Lewis: American Labor Leader." *Knight Templar*, June 1998, 9.

———. "Gerald R. Ford, 33° G:.C:. The Most Recent Masonic President." The Scottish Rite Journal, September 2003, http://www.srmason-sj.org/web/journal-files/issues/sept03/tribe.htm.3.

"United Supreme Council Resolution." *Texas Prince Hall Masonic Quarterly* 108 (June 1994): 4.

Uzzel, Robert L. "AMEs at the Fair: African Methodism and the World's Columbian Exposition of 1893." *The AME Church Review*, July-September 1985, 8-16.

———. "Brenham, Texas—1875, 1941, and 1995—The Call of Cuney, Coleman, and Connor." *Texas Prince Hall Masonic Quarterly* 109 (August 1995): 7.

———. "Brother Henry Agard Wallace: Prophet of Agrarianism." *The Philalethes*, October 1999, 102-09.

———. "Freemasonry and the Knights of Labor." *The Scottish Rite Journal*, August 1999, 16-21.

———. "From Darkness to Light." *Texas Prince Hall Masonic Quarterly* 86 (September 1987): 6-7.

———. "History of Beehive Lodge No. 484, Kaufman, Texas." *Texas Prince Hall Masonic Quarterly* 87 (March 1988): 4-5.

———. "The Moorish Science Temple: A Religion Influenced by Prince Hall Freemasonry." *The Phylaxis* 11 (First Quarter 1985): 1-9; 29 (Fall 2003): 7-18.

———. "Norris Wright Cuney: Our First Grand Master." *The Phylaxis* 16 (March 1990): 3-9.

———. "The Passing of a Great Masonic Historian." *Texas Prince Hall Masonic Quarterly* 91 (March 1990): 8.

———. "Prince Hall: The Myth and the Man." *Texas Prince Hall Masonic Quarterly* 79 (December 1987): 3.

———. "Visit to Sacred Ground." *Texas Prince Hall Masonic Quarterly* 88 (June 1989): 3.

"Waco Loses Most Beloved Woman: Obsequies for Mrs. N. A. Kirk." *Waco Messenger*, April 11, 1941, 1.

Walkes, Jr., Joseph A. "Captain William D. Matthews: Freemason, Leavenworth, Kansas." *The Phylaxis* 13 (Special Issue 1987-88): 3-8, 29.

———. "The Ku Klux Klan and Regular Freemasonry." *The Phylaxis* 18 (Fourth Quarter 1992): 4-7.

———. "Letter." *The Phylaxis* 18 (Fourth Quarter 1992): 7.

———. "Remembering I. H. Clayborn." *News Quarterly* (Spring 1994): 17-18.

"Washington Scores Moose for Snub of Black Librarian." *Library Journal*, January 1, 1972, 11.

White, Reuben G. "Am I My Brother's Keeper?" *Texas Prince Hall Masonic Quarterly* 75 (June 1985): 4.

———. "Americanism Day." *Texas Prince Hall Masonic Quarterly* 74 (September 1984): 6.
———. "A Christmas Message from the Grand Master." *Texas Prince Hall Masonic Quarterly* 74 (December 1982): 3-4.
———. "From the Desk of the Most Worshipful Grand Master." *Texas Prince Hall Masonic Quarterly* 74 (September 1981): 3.
———. "From the Grand Master's Death." *Texas Prince Hall Masonic Quarterly* 74 (March 1984): 4.
———. "It Is Later Than You Think." *Texas Prince Hall Masonic Quarterly* 74 (June 1984): 4.
———. "Just a Little Talk with the Brethren." *Texas Prince Hall Masonic Quarterly* 76 (December 1986): 5.
———. "Masonic Tidbits." *Texas Prince Hall Masonic Quarterly* 74 (March 1982): 3.
———. "Operative and Speculative Masonry." *Texas Prince Hall Masonic Quarterly* 74 (December 1984): 3.
———. "Our Behaviour." *Texas Prince Hall Masonic Quarterly* 75 (March 1985): 3.
———. "Scottish Rite Hospital." *Texas Prince Hall Masonic Quarterly* 75 (September 1985): 5.
———. "Think on These Things." *Texas Prince Hall Masonic Quarterly* 75 (March 1986): 4.
———. "Self-Encouragement." *Texas Prince Hall Masonic Quarterly* 74 (March 1983): 3.
———. "Where Do We Go From Here?" *Texas Prince Hall Masonic Quarterly* 74 (June 1982): 5-6.
"Who Was Thomas H. Routt?" http://koptexas.org/throutt.htm, 1-2.
"William Coleman, F&AM Grand Master, Dies; Rites Held Monday." *Dallas Express*, May 25, 1946, 1.
Williams, Fred. "Thurgood Marshall, 1908-1993." *The Pyramid* 52 (First Quarter 1993): ii.
Willwerth, James. "Of Moose and Men." *Time*, August 12, 1972, 33.
Woodson, Carter G. "The Cuney Family." *The Negro History Bulletin*, March 1948, 123.
Wrolstad, Mark. "Masons Stepping Out From Behind Shroud to Woo New Members." *The Dallas Morning News*, October 11, 1998, 1A, 31A.

Correspondence and Interviews

Boone, Frank. Letter to author, May 14, 1994.
Carter, Jr., Kervin W. Interview by author, tape recording, Fort Worth, Texas, September 17, 1994.
Cash, Edwin B. Interview by author, tape recording, Dallas, Texas, October 9, 1996.
Clayborn, Roberta Cathcart. Interview by author, tape recording, Dallas, Texas, September 18, 1996.
Connor, Jr., Robert E. Telephone conversation with author, September 20, 2000.
Daniels, John Q. Interview by author, tape recording, Waco, Texas, July 1, 1992.
Erby, Eucolia. Interview by author, tape recording, Waco, Texas, June 20, 1992.
Flowers, Henry. Interview by author, tape recording, Waco, Texas, July 1, 1992.
Glasser, Doris. Letter to author, August 30, 1990.
Gray, Jewel Andrews. Letter to author, May 10, 1993.
Hardin, Warren. Telephone conversation with author, December 4, 1999.
Harris, A. D. Interview by author, tape recording, Waco, Texas, June 24, 1993.
Hunter, William L. Letter to author, April 11, 1991.
Jackson, Catherine. Interview by author, tape recording, Waco, Texas, July 7, 1992.
Neal, T. W. Interview by author, tape recording, Fort Worth, Texas, June 24, 1993.
O'Connor, Robert B. Letter to author, July 18, 1994.
Reed, Gladys. Interview by author, tape recording, Waco, Texas, July 7, 1992.
Regian, Joseph W. Letter to author, December 17, 1996, and January 2, 1997.
Routt, Thomas H. Letter to author, August 3, 1987.
Smith, DeShong. Interview by author, tape recording, Waco, Texas, June 29, 1992.
Wadley, Charlie. Interview by author, tape recording, Fort Worth, Texas, June 24, 1993.
Wehrmeister, Kurt N. Letter to author, August 19, 1999.
White, Ometa. Interview by author, tape recording, Waco, Texas, June 26, 1992.
White, Reuben G. Interview by author, Fort Worth, Texas, June 20, 1996.
Wilhite, O. E. Interview by author, tape recording, Fort Worth, Texas, June 23, 1992.

Miscellaneous

1875-1975 Centennial, Most Worshipful Prince Hall Grand Lodge of Texas and Jurisdiction, Free and Accepted Masons, June 22-26, 1975 (Souvenir Journal).
Abingdon, C. W. "The Historical and Biographical Souvenir Program of the 25th Anniversary of Metropolitan AME Church, Austin, Texas, 1882-1907."
"Celebration for the Life of Robert Edmund Connor, Jr." program.

Chunn, Jr., Prentis W. "Education and Politics: A Study of the Negro in Reconstruction Texas." M.A. thesis, Southwest Texas State Teachers College, 1957.

Curtis, Wilbert M. Unpublished autobiography.

Dallas City Directory. Dallas, Texas, 1885-92.

Funeral program of Reuben Glassell White.

Hinze, Virginia Neal. "Norris Wright Cuney." M.A. thesis, Rice University, 1965.

Lakeview Cemetery Record I: 1887-1908. Galveston, Texas: Galveston County Genealogical Society, 1992.

"Ninety-Second Founder's Day Convocation." Dallas, Texas: Bishop College, April 14, 1973.

"Prince Hall and Americanism Day Banquet." Most Worshipful Prince Hall Grand Lodge of Texas. Brenham, Texas: Fireman's Training Center, September 16, 1995.

"Prince Hall and Americanism Day Service." Most Worshipful Prince Hall Grand Lodge of Texas, Free and Accepted Masons. Brenham, Texas: Saint John AME Church, September 16, 1995.

Uzzel, Robert L. "Notes from Millennium Team Meeting." Fort Worth, Texas, July 22, 2000.

———. "Notes from Special Session." Fort Worth, Texas, November 4, 2000.

"Vita of Robert E. Connor, Jr." Manuscript supplied by Robert E. Connor, Jr.

"Vita of Thomas H. Routt." Manuscript supplied by Ritchie L. Routt.

Index

A. J. Moore High School, 64
Abbington, C. W., 94
Abif Lodge No. 61, 118
Abner, David, Jr., 6
"Administratives," 48-49
Afghanistan, 167
AFL-CIO, 56, 132
African Lodge No. 459, xi, 140
African Methodist Episcopal (AME) Church, 23-30, 35-36, 50-51, 52, 61, 62, 64, 87
Afro-American Sheriff's Deputy League, 179
AIDS, 149
Alexander and Martin, 105
Alexander, Austin, 57
Alexander, Booker T., 125, 131, 132
Alexander, J. L., 70
Allen, Albert, 16
Allen, Annie, 16
Allen Chapel Methodist Church, 116
Allen, Frank G., 132
Allen, Julia, 16
Allen, Modestia, 16
Allen, Nancy, 16
Allen, Richard, xii-xiii, 6, 13, 16-18, 19, 20, 24, 57, 121, 185, 121, 214
Allen, Venora, 16
Alley, Elvin, 201
Allison, William B., 11
Aloha Military Lodge No. 635, 171
Alvin B. Amos UD Lodge, 193
AME Church Review, 94
American Airlines Admiral Club, 112

American Baptist Missionary Association, 17
American Oil Company, 136
Amity Lodge No. 4, xii, 5, 13, 35, 80, 97
Amity, Louisiana, 14, 30
Anchor Chapter No. 67, 208
Anderson, Charles, 174, 206
Anderson, Howard, 186, 188, 195, 198, 200, 206
Anderson, I. P., 98-99, 100
Anderson, J. E., 89
Anderson, Lawrence (Pap), 150, 174, 201
Anderson, Michael, 198, 201, 204, 206
Andrews, R. T., 17
Andrews, Robert N., 135
Antioch Baptist Church, 17
Appel, Robert, Jr., 186
Archinard, Caesar, 2
Arkansas Baptist College, 111
Arlington Police Department, 198
Arlington, Texas, 164, 198
Armstrong, Josiah Haynes, xiii, 13, 17, 24, 34, 35-36, 37, 51, 57, 214
Arnall, Governor, 86
Arnette, B. W., 23
Arrington, Richard, 169
Athens, Texas, 115
Augusta, Georgia, 48
Austin, Leon J., 135
Austin, Texas, xii, xiii, , 20, 21, 23, 30, 32, 37, 39, 42, 47, 90, 208

Bailey, Larry, 170
Bailey's Boarding House, 96
Baines, Jesse L., 125, 128, 129, 145, 155, 166, 219
Baker Funeral Home, 83
Baker, Harold B., 102, 105, 106, 109
Baker, Newton D., 55
Bakers Hill community, 152
Bakker, Jim, 149
Baldwin Lodge No. 16, xii
Ball, J. P., Jr., xii
Ballard, Aubrey E., 134
Banks, N. A., 66
Barksdale, Benjamin, 197
Barnett, Ross, 143
Barnsville, Ohio, 64
Barry, Marion, Jr., 169
Bass, Sam, 96
Bates, Daisy, 130
Bates, Garth, 153
Batt, John, xi
Battle Creek, Michigan, 62
Baylor University, 88
Baytown, 180
Beacon Light No. 50, 61
Beall School, 73
Beamon, Robert, 175
Beaumont, Texas, 30, 81, 115
Beautiful Lodge #395, 201
Bee County, Texas, 135
Bee Hive Investment Fund, 77
Beeville, Texas, 135, 184
Bellaire High School, 64
Bellaire, Ohio, 64, 69
Bendall, Oliver, 73
Benedict College, 71
Bennett, S. J., 118, 132, 135

Bentsen, Lloyd, 122
Berry, Gene, 184
Best, Paul, 127, 160, 162, 163
Bethel AME Church, 62
Binford, H. C., 46
Birch, Bro., 61
Bishop College, 78, 111, 137, 165
Bishop Grant Lodge No. 72, 30, 81
Black History Month, 157, 182
Black History Trail Riders, 180
Black Square and Compass, 126
Blacks in Criminal Justice, 145
Blaford, Guion A., Jr., 167, 168
Blaine, James G., 8
Blake, Caesar R., 74
Blake, Eubie, 167
Blazing Star Lodge No. 363, 189
Bledsoe, Gary, 204
Bledsoe, W. F., Jr., 129
Bloomfield Lodge, 38, 41, 91
Bluitt, B. R., 45
Boaz Industries, 183
Bolden, James W., 93
Bolton, Patrick, 93, 102, 120
Bon Weir, Texas, 152
Bond, Cecil W., 140
Bonner, A. H., 24
Boston, Massachusetts, 30, 117, 118, 140
Boutte, George, 198, 204, 206
Brackettville, Texas, 75
Bradford, Earle, 126, 131, 132, 146, 158
Bradley, Alvin, 162
Bradley, Rodolphus H., xiii, 33, 34, 215
Bradwell, C. L., 35
Branch, E. H., 94, 109, 116, 126, 139
Brenham, Texas, xii, 5, 13, 17, 19, 53, 65, 78, 79-80, 123, 167, 185, 186, 202
Brewer, Harry A., 140
Brezhnev, Leonid, 126
Bridges, Edgar, 125, 131, 132, 146, 158, 162
Brigham, William, 191
Briscoe, Dolph, 122, 153
Brooks, I. B., 50
Brown, Edward, II, 206
Brown, Robert Turner, 48-49, 50
Brown, Robert W., 132, 132, 201
Brown, Thomas, 213
Brown University, 71
Brown v. Board of Education, 93, 96

Brown, Willis, 132
Brumskine, J. L., 131
Bryan, Texas, xiii
Bryant, William Cullen, 63
Buffalo Bayou, 16
Bullock, John H., 50, 143, 144, 146, 147, 149, 158, 159, 170, 172
Bunche, Ralph, 90
Bundy, W. O., 65, 66
Burgan, J. M., 47, 49
Burnett, William H., 27, 53, 77
Burns, Michael, 7
Bush, George, 131, 132
Bush, George W., 205
Butler, Harold, 126, 128
Butler, John, 196, 201
Bynum, Charles, 115

Cain, J. J., 16
Cain, McDonald, 67
Cain, W. D., 27, 47, 49, 62, 66, 218
Calhoun, M. L., 26
Calvin, Willie, Jr., 186
Carnation Chapter No. 37, 208
Carnation Court No. 44, Order of Calanthe, 70
Carson, W. R., 57
Carter, Jimmy, 125, 126
Carter, Kerven W., Jr., 100, 150, 171, 172, 183, 195, 196, 204, 206
Cash, B. C., Sr., 168
Cash, Edwin B., xiv, 120, 125, 128, 129, 130, 134, 145, 148, 149, 150, 151, 155, 161, 162, 163, 164, 165-178, 181, 182, 186, 189, 210, 215, 219, 221
Cash, James D., 165
Cash, Maxine Lola Turner, 165, 166
Cash, Sherrie, 165
Cathcart, Samuel, 121
Centennial Souvenir Journal, 122
Central High School, 97
Central Republican Club of Houston, 9
Central Texas Commandery No. 37, 208
Cephas, Orphen, 158
Challenger, 146, 168
Chapel Hill, Texas, xii, 52, 55, 85
Chapman, C. E., 50
Chatfield, 195
Chatham, M. R., 176

Cheatham, C. B., 185, 192
Cheatham, Marion, 135
Cheops Temple No. 200, 208
Chernobyl, 146
Chicago, Illinois, 30, 32, 38, 143
Christianity, 119, 125, 128, 173, 194
Cirri, Father, 97
civil rights movement, 114, 115, 117, 143, 144, 158, 205
Civil Rights Act of 1975, 9
Clark, C.A.W., 118, 119, 130, 134, 145, 150, 171, 172, 177, 183, 186, 201
Clark, George, 10
Clark, Joshua, 134
Clark, M. W., 32
Clark, Samuel W., 22, 32
Clarkson, James S., 9
Clayborn, Gregory Lynn, 134
Clayborn, I. H., xiii-xiv, 107, 108, 109, 110, 111-135, 136, 137, 139, 141, 142, 143, 144, 145, 146, 148, 150, 155, 156, 159, 160, 161, 162, 163, 166, 168, 170, 171, 172, 177, 215, 219
Clayborn, Kasheeda, 134
Clayborn Lodge, 184
Clayborn, Roberta Cathcart, 111, 134
Clement, Bishop, 87
Clement, Emma Clarissa, 87
Clements, William P., 149
Clemons, H. C., 122
Cleveland, Grover, 8, 9, 11
Clinton, Bill, 130, 133
Cocke Rifles, 13
Coffee, D. E., 50
Coke, Richard, 9, 10
Coleman, Bertha Jackson, 71
Coleman, Emma, 71
Coleman, Luke, 71
Coleman, P. A., 57
Coleman, William, xiii, 13, 57, 60, 62, 68, 69, 71-83, 84, 88, 89, 121, 185, 215
Coleman, Willie High, 193, 196, 204, 206
Collin County, Texas, 111
Collins, D. C., 106, 107, 109, 113, 114, 117, 120
Colorado County, Texas, 180
Colored (now Christian) Methodist Episcopal (CME) Church, xiii, 44, 47, 48, 49-51
Columbus, Georgia, 21

Columbus High School, 179
Columbus, Ohio, 24
Columbus, Texas, 179, 180, 206
Combs, Elroy, 107
Community Chest, 70
Conference of Prince Hall Grand Masters, 94, 97, 102, 103, 105, 106, 113, 115, 116, 117, 118, 119, 120, 121, 123, 126, 129, 139, 140, 141, 144, 145, 177, 180, 182, 184, 188, 191, 197, 200
Connor Building, 82
Connor, Deanna M. Eaton, 179, 206, 210
Connor, Gary, 206
Connor, Robert E., Jr., xiv, 14, 135, 149, 150, 159, 163, 169, 172, 178, 179-206, 210, 215, 221
Connor, Robert Edmund, Sr., 179
Connor, Sophia, 206
Connor, Vera Miller, 179
Connor, Woodrow, 180
Constitution of the Grand Lodge, 41, 53
Continental National Bank, 98, 99
Copperas Cove, Texas, 126
Copps Hill Burying Ground, xi, 105, 118, 126, 140, 200
Corbin, J. C., 32
Corpus Christi, Texas, xii, xiv, 79, 201, 203
Corsicana, Texas, 79
Cotton Screwmen, 7, 13, 15
Cottonwood School, 70
Cowan Lodge No. 421, 150
Crockett, Texas, 118
Cullen, Mr., 87
Cumberland Presbyterian Church, 82
Cuney, Adeline Supurlock, 2, 4
Cuney, Charlotte Scott, 2
Cuney, Col. Philip, 2, 3
Cuney, Eliza Ware, 2
Cuney, Joseph, 12
Cuney, Lloyd, 4, 12
Cuney, Louise, 2
Cuney, Maud, *see* Hare, Maud
Cuney, Norris Wright, xii-xiii, 1-15, 17, 19, 20, 23, 35, 36, 57, 65, 80, 101, 108, 114, 170, 185, 214, 215
Cuney, Norris Wright, monument to, 13-14, 108, 160, 185
Cuney, Richmond Edmond, 2
Cuney, Tabitha Wells, 2
Cunningham, E. Brice, 150, 159, 171, 196, 219
Curtis, Karen Stonum, 208
Curtis, LaNell Carroll Cotton, 208
Curtis, Valerie Dyane, 208
Curtis, Wilbert M., 151, 172, 178, 183, 185, 186, 195, 196, 198, 204, 206, 207-212, 215
Cutrer, Louis, 106

Dale Consistory No. 31, 112, 134, 165, 166
Dallas Black Chamber of Commerce, 112
Dallas County Commissioners Court, 112
Dallas County Democratic Party, 112
Dallas Express, 47
Dallas Independent School District, 165, 177
Dallas Lodge of the Benevolent and Protective Order of Elks (BPOE), 40
Dallas Planning and Zoning Committee, City of, 112
Dallas, Texas, xii, xiii, 21, 34, 37, 40, 52, 62, 106, 111, 112, 114, 115, 118, 132, 145, 165, 184
Dallas United Methodist Church, 149
Dallas Urban League, 112
Daniels, John Q., 65
Daniels, Samuel T., 129
Daughters of Isis, 105
Daughters of the American Revolution, 86
Davis, D. B., 50
Davis, Dyrren, 206
Davis, Edmund Jackson, 7, 8, 16
Davis, James D., 8
Davis, L. L., 102, 106
Davis, Mrs. P. E., 70
Davis, Robert, Jr., 117
Dawson, Clanton N., 135
Day, Joel, 132
Deaf, Dumb, and Blind Institute in Austin, 4
Dean, Charles C., xii, 23, 31-33, 34, 57, 214, 215
Dean, Hattie, 31
Delhi School, 23
Democratic Party, 1, 84, 205

Denison, Texas, xii, 31, 41, 91
Denton, Arvell W., 139
Denver, Colorado, 44
Depression, 75-76
Derrick, W. B., 24
Dewberry, Frank, Sr., 168
Dewitt, Charles, 194, 206
Dews, Malachi, Jr., 200
Dickerson, Eugene, Jr., 126
District No. 14, 174
District No. 19, 193
Dixon Orphans Home, 53
Dobbs, John Wesley, 82, 102, 119
Dogan, M. W., 87
Donahue, Phil, 126
Doric Temple No. 76, 154, 180
Dorothy Mae Hotel, 167
Douglass Burrell Consistory, 163
Douglass, Frederick, 145
Douglass High and Grammar School, 72-73
Dowdie, Adelina, 4
Downsville, xii
DuBois, W.E.B., 145
Dukakis, Michael, 131
Duke, David, 149
"Duncan ritual," 41-42, 58
Dutton, Harold, 204
Duval County, Texas, 21
Duwane, Roberto, 126
Dyer Anti-Lynch Law, 60

Eagle Lake, Texas, 79
Eastern Star, *see* Order of the Eastern Star
Eastman Kodak Corporation, 111
Eastside Lodge No. 88, 56
Ebony magazine, 130
Ed Blair Consistory No. 286, 208
Edwards, George, 93
El Katif Temple No. 85, 97, 136
El Paso High School, 72
El Paso, Texas, 71-73, 74
Ellaville, Georgia, 30
Ellington, Duke, 168
Ellis Funeral Home, 70
Ellis, Matthew, Jr., 135
Embry, J. C., 24
Emergency Charity Fund, 186
English, Carl, 204
Enlow, Paul, 189
Ephraim S. Alphonse Lodge No. 621, 126
Erby, Eucolia, 65

Euless, Texas, 115
Ever Ready Lodge No. 506, 154, 162
Evers, Charles, 143, 169
Evers, Medgar, 143
Excelsior Guards, 13
Exodus Movement, 17

Fair Employment Practice Committee, 86
Fair, Louis, Jr., 139
Fairfield Lodge No. 452, 189
Family Masonic Quarterly, 192
Farenthold, Frances "Sissy," 138
Favorite Saloon, 40
Federal Bureau of Investigation, 180
Federal Housing Administration, 145
Felton, James F., 100, 103
Ferguson, Charles M., 6, 8-9
Ferris, Texas, 195
Fields Funeral Home, 110
Fields, James E., Sr., 183, 186
Fiesta, 204
Fitch, Leroy, 120
Flanagan, Lee, 118
Fleming, Charles, 150
Florida Legislature, 35
Flowers, Henry, 65
Ford, Gerald R., 122
Forney, Texas, 38, 91
Fort Bend County, Texas, 6, 8-9, 154
Fort Bliss, Texas, 72
Fort Grant, Arizona, xii
Fort Worth National Bank, 99, 100, 101
Fort Worth, Texas, xiii, xiv, 33, 45, 55, 71, 74, 81, 108, 110, 115, 116, 118, 125, 146, 147, 177, 195
Fountain, J. M., 50
Four Minute Men, 97
Fourteenth Amendment, 96, 105
Fraternal Bank and Trust Company, 47, 88, 98, 99-101, 102, 105, 106, 110, 124, 142, 144, 145
Fred Douglass High School, 44
Freedmen's Bureau, 16
"Freedom Day," 96
"Freedom Riders," 105
Freeman, Bessie, 42
Freeman, Flora, 42

G. I. Bill, 86
Gabriel, Herman L., 172, 178, 182, 185, 195, 198, 201, 204
Gaines, W. J., 23
Gainesville, Texas, xiii
Gallery Furniture, 204
Galveston City Council, 8
Galveston Cotton Exchange, 7
Galveston County, Texas, 136
Galveston County Union League, 7
Galveston Lodge No. 25, xii, 5
Galveston Memorial Cemetery, 110
Galveston, Texas, xii, xiii, 3-4, 5, 6, 7, 8, 11, 13, 15, 35-36, 41, 80, 82, 97, 108, 136, 160
Gander, Newfoundland, 168
Garland, Texas, 190
Garrison, William Lloyd, 4
Gates, Clara, 171
Gates, Ernest L., 186, 201
George, L. B., 171, 186, 201, 221
GH&H Railroad Company, 97
Gibson, E. L., 88
Gibson, Kenneth, 169
Gideon, Russell S., 125, 130
Gilead Baptist Church, 83
Gilliam, James C., 90, 93, 113
Givens, Joseph W., 139
Givens, T. G., 100, 106, 107, 109, 121
Glaspie, C. A., 134, 141, 149, 150, 162, 164, 172, 174, 175, 176, 183, 189
Glover, Clary, 211
Glover, Soleless, 195
Gold Democrats, 10
Gomez, Joseph, 94
Gompers, Samuel, 56
Gonzales, Texas, 65
Good Street Baptist Church in Dallas, 111, 118, 134, 143, 165, 166, 177
Good Street Baptist Lodge No. 182, 120, 166, 168, 178
Goode, W. Wilson, 167
Goodwill Consistory No. 235, 154, 180
Goodwill Lodge No. 313, 195
Gossett, Louis, Jr., 167
Grand Commission, 156
Grand Lodge of England, xi
Grand Lodge of Knights of Pythias, 47
Grand Lodge of Texas, A.F.&A.M., 107

Grand Lodge of the Republic of Texas, 2
Grand Masters Conference, *see* Conference of Grand Masters
Grand Matrons, 115
Grand Temple Lodge No. 75, 195
Grand United Order of Odd Fellows, 6, 47
Grant, Abraham, 23
Grant, Abram, xiii, 6, 20, 21-30, 31, 35, 36, 51, 57, 214
Grant AME Churches, 30
Grant Elementary School, 30
Grant Hall, 30
Grant, John T., 11
Gray, Charles, 206
Gray, Claude W., Sr., 135
Gray, Earl, 131
Gray, Fred, 206
Gray, P. L., 50
Green, Alexander, 186, 196
Green, S. L., 110
Greene, James E., 139
Greenville, Kentucky, 70
Greenwood Cemetery, 68, 70
Gregg, E. J., 23
Gregory, Fred, 168
Gregory Institute, 17, 97
Grey Eagle, 3
Grimes County, Texas, 152
Grimshaw myths, 144
Guadalupe College, 68
Guaranty Bank, 111
Guess, Richard, 85
Gulf Lodge No. 13, xii
Guthrie, William A., 115
Guyana, 126

Haley, Alex, 125
Hall, Amos T., 97, 102, 106, 113, 119
Hall, Lewis, 158
Hall, Prince, xi, 2, 41, 105, 118, 121-122, 140, 156, 157, 200
Hamlett, J. A., 49
Hardeman, Jimmy, 120
Hare, Maud Cuney, 3, 4, 12
Hare, William P., 5
Harmony Hall, 13
Harris, A. D., 14-15, 82, 102, 109, 115, 121, 146, 149, 150, 171, 172, 183, 192, 219
Harris, C. A., 26
Harris County Criminal Court at Law No. 6, 153

Harris County Sheriff's Department, 179
Harris County, Texas, 153
Harris, T. A., 42
Harrison, Benjamin, 9, 11
Harrison Switch, Texas, 111
Harte, Bret, 45
Hastie, William, 87
Hawley, R. B., 65
hazing, 195, 198-199
Health Education, 205
Heights Lodge No. 280, 85
Hella Shrine Temple, 190
HemisFair, 116
Henderson, J. B., 132
Henderson, Joseph, 125
Henderson, W. M., 57
Henneke Funeral Home, 206
Henries, Richard A., 103
"Henry the Fiddler," 3
Herman Park, 55
Heroines of Jericho, 29, 65, 66, 67, 70, 74, 78, 79, 99, 106, 109, 116, 157, 186, 187, 189, 191, 200, 201, 202, 208
Hewitt, Texas, 208
Hi 12 Lodge No. 559, 150
Hicks, Frederick T., 140
Hicks, Robert, 201, 204
Higgins, Roosevelt, 204
Highland Heights Lodge No. 200, 196, 200
Hill, J. H., 97
Hines, Earl (Fatha), 167
Hinze, Virginia Neal, 1, 15
History of Texas Prince Hall Grand Lodge, 211
"History of the Texas Grand Masters," 174
Hobbs, Samuel, Jr., 201, 206
Hogan, B. T., 106
Hogg, James S., 10-11
Hollie, A. H., 102, 109
Holloway Lodge No. 7, xii
Holly Springs, Mississippi, 50
Holsey, C. W., 49
Home for Aged Masons, 98, 99, 101, 120
Hooks, Benjamin, 126, 131, 134, 139, 145, 169, 196
"Hope Across Texas," 195, 196
Hopeful Lodge No. 78, 174
Hopkins, W. L., 106, 109, 114, 117, 120
Horn, Ben, 201
Hot Springs, Arkansas, 82

Houston and Texas Central Railroad, 19
Houston College for Negroes, 87
Houston Legal Foundation, 153
Houston National Cemetery, 151
Houston Seminary, 19
Houston, Texas, xii, xiii, xiv, 3, 6, 16, 17, 19, 31, 79, 80, 81, 85, 87, 96, 97, 115, 117, 118, 152, 153, 154, 160, 162, 196
Howard, J. A., 68
Howard University, 4, 54, 71, 77
Hudson, Rock, 168
Hughes, Roger, 99, 101, 107, 108, 119, 121
Hughes Tool Co., 85
Hunter, William L, 125
Hurricane Allison, 204
Hurst, John, 64
Hussein, Saddam, 205

I. H. Clayborn Lodge No. 641, 135
I. H. Clayborn U. D. Lodge, 161
Ibarra, Richard, 170, 206
Imperial Council of the Mystic Shrine, 118, 117, 121, 123, 124, 126, 128, 129, 135, 182, 188, 191
Impulse Lodge No. 631, 146
Indemnity Bonding Company of Kansas City, 67
International Conference of Grand Masters, 82
International Masonic Congress, 60
"Invincibles," 48-49
Iranian Hostage Crisis, 128
Iron Creek, 2
Isaacs, Clement F., 139
Islam, 119, 125, 128

J. T. Maxey Lodge No. 630, 146
J. T. Maxey Scholarship Program, 140, 143, 147, 196, 197
Jackson, A. F., xiii, 33, 34
Jackson, B. T., 146, 150
Jackson, Catherine, 68, 70
Jackson, De'Von, 200
Jackson, Frank, 200, 211
Jackson, Jesse, 131, 144, 167, 215
Jackson Lodge No. 15, xii
Jackson, Maynard, 119, 169

Jackson, Mrs. M. D., 64
Jackson, Norris, 195, 201, 204, 206
Jackson, W. W., 150
Jacksonville, Florida, 21, 30, 35
James E. Carter Lodge #157, 201
James, Leroy, xiii, 6, 17, 19-20, 34, 214, 215
James, Ronald, 193
James, Susan, 19
Jamison, M. F., 49
Jarvis Christian College, 111
Jasper, Florida, 35
Jasper, Texas, 193
"Jaybirds," 8-9
Jefferson United Methodist Church, 121
Jemison, T.J., 130
Jernigan, A. R., 141, 166
"Jim Crow" laws, 1, 10, 58, 214
Jno. G. Lewis Lodge No. 622, 126
John D. Paley Lodge No. 630, 180
John XXIII, 114
Johnson, A. C., 116
Johnson, A. J., 41
Johnson, A. M., 119, 124, 126, 128, 129, 158
Johnson, Albert, 198, 201, 204
Johnson and Johnson, 165
Johnson, Candy, 62
Johnson, Eddie Bernice, 122
Johnson, Fred, 193
Johnson, J. Hugo, 32
Johnson, Lyndon Baines, 113, 115
Johnson, S. J., 26, 52, 53, 61, 62
Johnson, W. J., 50
Johnson, William Decker, 62
Jones, A., 27
Jones, James C., 201
Jones, Jesse, 134
Jones, Joshua H., 53
Jones, Mrs. A. V., 64
Jones, Rufus, 159
Jordan, Barbara, 121, 122
Jordan, Grand Master, 103
Jordan, Tony, 193, 195, 198
Jose Justo Lindo land grant, 2
Joseph E. Telfair Sr. Lodge, 184
Joyce Stamps Day Nursery, 70

Katy Flyer, 97
Kaufman, Texas, 138
Keeland, F.C.H., 19

Kelley, Sam, 144, 168
Kemp, Earl, Jr., 186
Kendleton, xii
Kenner, Louisiana, 167
Key West Consistory No. 307, 113
Killeen, Texas, 151, 208
Kimbrough, Molly, 42
Kimbrough, Richard, 40
Kimbrough, Susan, 40
Kimbrough, Wiley Lawson, xiii, 39, 40-43, 57, 88, 214, 215
King, Martin Luther, Jr., 104, 112, 145, 181
King, Wayne, 168
Kirk, Adrian, 64
Kirk, Mrs. Adrian, 64
Kirk, John Adrian, xiii, 53, 62, 63, 64-70, 74, 214, 215
Kirk, Nettie, 64, 68, 69-70
Kiwanis International, 158
Klevenhagen, Johnny, 179-180
Knights of Labor, 7
Knights of Pythagoras, 159, 164, 172, 196, 198, 201
Knights of Pythias, 6, 13, 47, 65, 70
Knights Templar, 180, 191
Knowles, H. K., 27
Knoxson, Jane, 52
Korean War, 92
Ku Klux Klan, 86, 87-88, 130, 149, 169
Kyle, James, 19

La Marque, Texas, 136, 138
La Marque Lodge No. 373, 136, 150
labor unions, 85, 86, 92, 125
LaGrange Lodge No. 112, 14
Lake City, Florida, 21
Lakeview Cemetery, 5, 13, 17, 36, 108
Lakey, Othal Hawthorne, 49
Lamarr, Zeno, 132
Lampton, E. V., 45
Lancaster County, Pennsylvania, 35
Lands, John, xii
Lanier, Dean O'Hara, 87
Lawrence, 13
Lawrence, E., 41
Leavenworth, Kansas, 6
Ledet, Joseph, 204
Lee Lockwood Scottish Rite Library and Museum, 114

Leonard, G. W., 60, 65
Lewis, James, 3
Lewis, Jno. G., Jr., 90, 102, 115, 119, 123, 126, 130, 131, 166
Lewis, Jno. G., Sr., 74, 78
Lewis, Scott A., 78
Liberia, 115, 118, 119, 120, 128, 131, 138, 139, 140
Lincoln Guards, 13
Lincoln High School, 165
Lincoln Memorial Cemetery, 177
Little Rock, Arkansas, 104, 130
Lockhart, James H., 94, 98-99, 102, 109
Lockhart, Lucian L., xiii, 79, 83, 84-95, 96, 113, 215
Lockhart, Mrs., 99
Lodge No. 41, Irish Constitutions, xi
Lodge of Research, 81
Logan, ——, 146
Logan, H. C., 62
Lone Star Grand Commandery of Knights Templar, 112
Lone Star Lodge No. 85, 200
Long Beach, California, 30
Longshoreman's Aid Association, 13
Longshoremen, 7, 15
Los Angeles, California, 30, 42
Los Angeles Elks Lodge, 42
Lott, Trent, 205
Louis, Joe, 90
Lovelady, Bracy, 147
Luling, Texas, xii
lynchings, 55, 60, 88
Lyons Jr. Lodge No. 290, 193
Lyons, L. D., 69

M.W.G. Lodge of Massachusetts, 41
MacGregor, H. F., 12
Mackey, D. L., 62
Macon, Georgia, 49
Maddox, Leon, 88, 94, 102, 106
Madison County, Texas, 79
Madison, Elizabeth, 37
Madison, Emmanuel, 37
Madison, John W., xiii, 26, 27, 37-39, 40, 57, 62, 214, 215
Madison, Letitia, 37
Madisonville, Texas, 195
Magnolia Lodge No. 24, xii
Magnolia Lodge No. 3, xii, 13, 14, 17, 19, 31, 80, 85
Majors, Lee, 141, 166

Marlin, Texas, 174
Marshall, Texas, xii, 78
Marshall, Thurgood, 97, 102, 103, 105, 106, 121, 134
Martin, J. C., 49
Martin, Richard L., 105, 106
Mashack, B. J., 62
Masonic agricultural cooperatives, 76, 78, 79, 86
Masonic Bank and Trust Company, 74; *also see* Fraternal Bank and Trust
Masonic Burial Association, 192, 196, 198
Masonic Cemetery, San Antonio, 25
Masonic Charitable Trust, 202
Masonic Credit Union, 124, 126
Masonic death benefits, 38, 75, 92, 117, 158, 159, 172, 176, 192, 194, 198, 203
Masonic education, 97, 105, 157, 196
Masonic emblems, 195
Masonic employment bureaus, 76, 78, 79, 81, 82
Masonic Family Quarterly, 198
Masonic history, 106, 121-122, 123, 156, 157, 158, 161, 174, 186, 211, 213-215
Masonic Hospital, 120
Masonic Learning Center, 197
Masonic Library and Museum, 202
Masonic rings, 195
Masonic ritualism, 41, 42, 57, 58, 77, 81, 86, 106, 156, 157
Masonic scholarships, 103, 109, 113, 140, 143, 147, 185, 190, 196, 197
Masonic secrecy, 42, 46, 75
Mathis, L. W., 168
Matthews, William D., 6, 14, 41, 57, 123
Maxey, John Theodore, xiii, 13-14, 43, 87, 88, 90, 93, 94, 95, 96-110, 113, 114, 116, 120, 127, 130, 136, 215
Maxey, John Joseph, 96
Maxey, Mrs. John Joseph, 96
Maxey, Lucille E. Garrett, 97
Maxey, Sallie A. Harris, 97
Mays, Benjamin, 182
McCorkell, Clausell, 175
McCormick, B. L., 120
McCowan, ——, 146
McDonald, Joe M., 59

McDonald memorial, 77
McDonald, William Madison "Gooseneck Bill," 11, 38, 41, 47, 53, 54, 65, 68, 69, 74, 77, 80, 83, 88, 89, 91, 99, 147
McDow, Margaret A., 186
McGee, Robert E., 162
McGowen, J. H., 93, 94, 101, 102, 104, 105, 106
McKinley, William, 11-12
McKinney, Alice Warner, 44
McKinney, Archie, 44
McKinney Chapel CME Church, 50
McKinney Hall, 50
McKinney, Jane, 44
McKinney, John Wesley, xiii, 13, 17-18, 25, 27, 36, 39, 42, 44-51, 52, 57, 62, 66, 67, 74, 106, 147, 214, 215
McKinney, M. T., 44
McKinney, Ruby E. Cochran, 44, 66
McKinney, Texas, 111
McKinney, T. T., 44
McKinney, William, 44
McLennan Community College, 207
McLennan County, Texas, 111
McNair, Ronald E., 168
Meloy, Francis E., Jr., 124
Melton, Laddie L., 123, 124, 125, 126
Memphis, Tennessee, 120
Mendenhall, 100
Metropolitan AME Church in Austin, 23
Metropolitan Lodge No. 146, 106
Midway, Texas, 79
Milford, Dale, 122
Millben, Lawrence A., 140
Millennium Team Meeting, 202
Mingo, James, 134, 146, 158, 160
Mississippi Industrial College, 50
Mississippi River, 3
Mitchell, Allen E., 180
Mitchell, Clarence, 145
Mitchell, Grand Master, 60
Mitchell, H. J., 62
Mitchell, Rachel, 96
Mitchell, W. H., 39
Moberly, Missouri, 30
Moody, M. R., 13
Moody, William, xi, 7
Moore, A. J., 64
Moore, J. H., 49

Moore, Mrs. Mary E., 64
Moore High School, 69
Moorland Branch YMCA, 111
Morgan, T. M., 141, 166
Morris Brown College, 23, 30
Morris, J. H., xii
Morris, Joseph R., 16
Mosier Valley Lodge No. 103, 115, 195
Moss, Quintus, 150
Most Worshipful Prince Hall Grand Lodge of Texas, see Prince Hall Grand Lodge of Texas
Moten, D. S., 26
Moultrie, Georgia, 30
Mount Bonnell Lodge No. 2, xii, 21, 32, 37
Mount Bonnell Lodge No. 23, xii
Mount Carmel Baptist Church, 208
Mount Lebanon Lodge No. 26, xii
Mount Moriah Lodge No. 6, xii, 22, 37, 65
Mount Moriah Lodge No. 234, 57
Mount Olive Baptist Church, 116, 125
Mount Paran Baptist Church, 150
Mount Pisgah Lodge, 184
Mouton, Solomon, 201
Murphree, Debra, 159

NAACP, 86, 91, 97, 103, 132, 134, 196
NAACP Legal Defense Fund, 91, 93, 105, 124
Nassau, 140
National Colored Men's Convention, 17
National Federal Credit Union, 139
National Grand Lodge, 5, 6, 17, 57
Navasota, Texas, 50, 116, 118, 152
Neal, T. W., 82, 201
Neal, X. L., 118, 123
Negro Business League, 45
Nelson, O. E., 103
Nelson, Ricky, 168
Nero Prince Lodge, 161
Nettie Kirk Court No. 472, 70
Neustadter, Marcus, 134

New Deal, 76, 84
New Light Lodge #242, 151
New Orleans, Louisiana, 3
Newcomb, J. P., 7, 8
Newton, Joseph Fort, 106
Nichols, Wilson, xii
Nixon, Richard, 132, 139
Norfolk, Virginia, 25
Norris, A. R., 20
Norris Wright Cuney Award, 193
Norris Wright Cuney Grand Chapter, 197, 200, 202
North Central Credit Union, 188, 189
North Texas State University, 165
Northcutt, R. R., 50

O'Connor, Robert B., 124
Oak Cliff Chamber of Commerce, 112
Oak Forest Cemetery, 94
Oakland, Texas, 209
Oakwood Cemetery, 39
Oakwood, Texas, 177
Oberlin College, 69
Odd Fellows, 6, 13, 47
Ohio Wesleyan College, 69
Oklahoma City bombing, 184
Olive Leaf Lodge, 65
Operation Desert Storm, 171, 215
Orange, Texas, 79
Order of Moose, 158
Order of Red Men, 158
Order of the Eastern Star, 65, 67, 70, 78, 79, 87, 106, 109, 116, 136, 157, 186-190, 191-192, 193, 195-196, 197, 199, 208
Orlando, Florida, 30
Orwell, George, 143
Owens, J. Garfield, 121
Oyoma Lodge No. 222, 154

Paine, Thos., 28
Palestine, Texas, 30
Paley, J. D., 126, 139
Panama, 126
Paradise North Cemetery, 162, 170, 181
Paris, Texas, 33, 64, 70
Parker, William, 173
Parmer, Hugh, 125
Passmore, Donald, 204

Patrick, James, 120
Patterson, W. E., 50
Paul Drayton Lodge No. 9, xii, 34, 40, 43, 62, 112, 114, 115, 134, 165
Paul, Francis H., 134
Paul Quinn College, 4, 21, 23, 30, 47, 48, 52, 64, 65, 66, 68, 70, 160, 209
Paul VI, 114
Payne Theological Seminary, 23
Peavy, Grady, 206
People's Burial Park, 83
People's Temple, 126
People's Undertaking Company, 63
Perry, Lincoln Theodore, 168
Perry, W. J., 62
Pershing, John J., 55
Philalethes Society, 131
Phillips, C. H., 48
Phillips, Volney B., 117, 124, 145, 149, 219
Phoole, J. A., 27
Phylaxis Society, 128, 131, 144, 145, 154, 155, 157, 160, 161, 163-164, 208
Phyllis Chapter, 157
Phyllis Wheatley Library, 70
Pike, Albert, 134, 214
Pilgrim Lodge No. 10, xii, 31, 91
Pinchback, Pinckney B. S., 3
Pioneer Management, 111, 129
Plummer, Howard Z., 128
Plymouth Lodge, 78
Pointer, John, 195, 197, 198, 201, 204
Polar Star Lodge No. 33, 44
Port Arthur, Texas, 115, 197
Porter, H. P., 50
Porter, P. G., 93
Portley, Kenneth, 204
Post Oak Ranch, 177
Potter, Charles, 200
Powell, Adam Clayton, 86
Powell, Albert Lee, Sr., 115
Powell, Steve, 194
Prairie View A&M, 4, 152, 179, 200
Prairie View Normal School, 4-5, 44, 55
Prairie View Police Department, 179
Prairie View, Texas, 44
Pratt, T. W., 106
Prejean, Joe, 206

President's Minority Resources Committee, 102
Price, H. L., 81
Pride of the Pacific Lodge, U. D., 171
Pride of Waco Court No. 238, 70
"Prince Hall Affiliation," 81, 90
Prince Hall Centennial Celebration, 5
Prince Hall Chambre, 117
Prince Hall Charitable Trust, 201, 206
Prince Hall Day, 115, 144, 185
Prince Hall Freemasonry, bicentennial, 121-122, 139
Prince Hall Freemasonry, origins of, xi-xii, 65, 167, 185
Prince Hall Garden, 116
Prince Hall Grand Lodge Days, 119
Prince Hall Grand Lodge of Arizona, 184
Prince Hall Grand Lodge of California, 171, 173
Prince Hall Grand Lodge of Oklahoma, 181
Prince Hall Grand Lodge of Tennessee, 196
Prince Hall Grand Lodge of Texas: 50th anniversary, 62; 75th anniversary, 90; 100th anniversary, 139; building committee, 99-100; Communication, xiii, xiv, 14, 17, 19, 20, 21, 31, 33, 34, 35, 37, 39, 40, 42, 43, 44-45, 47, 53, 62, 65, 74, 75, 83, 86, 87, 88, 90, 91, 93, 97, 99, 103, 105, 106, 108, 109, 110, 113, 120, 123, 133, 140, 142, 144, 145, 146, 150, 155, 158, 159, 160, 166, 167, 168, 169, 170, 173, 175, 177, 178, 190, 191, 192, 196, 198, 199, 200, 201; dues and fees, 54, 67, 76, 80, 158, 159, 161, 183, 185, 192, 194, 199; Educational Program, 93; finances, 175-177, 178, 182-183, 184, 186, 188, 190, 200, 210-211; headquarters, 45, 46, 47, 74, 76, 98, 107-108, 146, 147, 172, 183, 189; housing, 113, 115, 117, 118, 130, 145, 153, 185, 196, 198, 209; litigation, 67, 187-190, 191-192, 193, 195-196, 197, 199; monument, 77, 78, 79, 106, 108, 118, 146, 147,

148, 172, 177-178, 183, 184, 192, 198, 202, 218; Mosque, 46, 50, 76, 109, 141, 143, 182, 192, 199, 202; origins, xii-xiv, 5, 65, 78, 80, 185; recognition by Grand Lodge of Texas, 199, 203, 204; relief system, 67, 107, 128, 192, 198, 203; Temple, 45, 47, 53, 211; Trustee Board, 98, 99
Prince Hall Grand Masters Conference, see Conference of Prince Hall Grand Masters
Prince Hall Library and Museum, 197, 199, 201
Prince Hall: Life and Legacy, 126
Prince Hall Lodge No. 18, 180
Prince Hall Masonic Family Pilgrimage, 117, 185-186
Prince Hall Plaza, 116
Prince Hall Terrace, 117
Prince Hall Villa, 116
Prince, Paul H., 50
Purnell, Charles, 206

racial equality, 86-87, 89, 96, 104, 112-113, 119, 120, 121, 129-130, 133, 214
racism, 1, 3-4, 7, 8-9, 10, 11, 12, 15, 17, 53, 54, 55, 56, 57, 58, 60, 75, 82, 86, 87-88, 105, 155, 169, 201
Railey, Walker, 149
Rainbow Coalition, 144
Rainbow Family, 158
Randolph, A. Philip, 145
Ransom, Reverdy Cassius, 64
Reagan, John H., 9
Reagan, Ronald, 130-131, 132, 143, 147, 168
Redd, J. C., 53
Redden, Sheldon, 193
Reece, Hubert L., 131, 132, 149, 150, 159, 172, 181, 193, 201, 204, 206
Reed, Gladys, 65
Reed, L. R., 65
Reed, Thomas B., 11
Reed Lodge No. 14, xii
Reedy Chapel AME Church, 13, 14, 108, 110
Rega, Prince K. Kaba, 56
Regian, Joseph W., 190, 191
Regular Democrats, 10
religious equality, 88, 92, 155

Republican National Convention, 8, 9, 11, 16
Republican Party, 1, 7, 8, 9-10, 11, 16, 17, 142, 205
Republican State Convention, 8, 10, 11, 16
Rescue Lodge No. 20, 33
Resendiz, Angel Maturino, 180
Reynolds, L. H., 13
Rhoads, J. J., 68, 78
Rhyne, Curtis, 123
Richardson, Texas, 195
Riesel, Texas, 174
Riklin, Ed Jay, 153
Rio Grande Federal Credit Union, 188, 193
Rising Star Baptist Church, 136, 150
Rising Sun Court No. 150, 208
Robert E. Connor, Jr., Texas Prince Hall Youth Camp, 210
Roberts, A. J., 43
Roberts Sons, 43
Robeson, Paul, 145
Robinson, I. A., Sr., 140
Robinson, Jackie, 87
Rockdale, Texas, 82
Roosevelt, Franklin D., 84, 101
Roosevelt Lodge No. 8, xii
Roosevelt, Mrs. F. D., 86
Roosevelt, Theodore, 25
Roots, 125
Rorie, Brenda, 186, 188, 191
Rosedale Cemetery, 43
Rosenberg, Texas, 154, 162, 180
Ross, Mrs., 68
Ross, O. P., 24
Ross, Sul, 9
Round Rock, Texas, 96
Routt, Lora Dean, 152
Routt, Ritchie L. Wilson, 152
Routt, Thomas H., xiv, 125, 129, 130, 145, 147, 149, 150, 152-164, 166, 168, 169, 170, 171, 180, 181, 197, 215, 219
Routt, Thomas, Jr., 152
Rowe, John, xi
Ruby, George T., 7-8
Rusk State Hospital, 109
Russel, Dinah, 64
Russell, D. L., 23

Safe Council Lodge #157, 201
Saint Elizabeth Hospital, 94
St. James Lodge #1, 208
St. James Lodge #71, 151

Saint John African Methodist Episcopal Church, xii, 5, 13, 185, 221
Saint John Baptist Church, 17
Saint John CME Church, 50
St. John's Day, 116
Saint John Lodge No. 5, 42
Saint John Lodge No. 12, xii
Saint John Lodge No. 71, 208
Saint Joseph Hospital, 83
Saint Mary's Hospital, 110
Saint Paul AME Church, 37, 65, 68, 70, 120
Saint Paul Methodist Episcopal Church, 12-13
St. Paul, Minnesota, 119
Saint Paul United Methodist Church, 179, 206
St. Timothy Lodge No. 68, 195
SALT II, 126
Samuel Huston College, 37
San Angelo, Texas, xii
San Antonio, Texas, xii, xiii, 21, 25, 45, 81, 116
San Antonio Lodge No. 1, xii, 14, 21
San Antonio Lodge No. 22, xii
San Francisco, California, 45
Sanderson Commandery No. 2, 154
Santa Ana, California, 43
Santa Fe Railroad, 15, 97
Santa-Anna, 65
Santanna Mound, 65
Scalia, Antonin, 205
Scott, H. O., 102
Scott, Hazel, 86
Scott, J. W., 50
Scottish Rite Hospital for Crippled Children, 118, 120, 121, 124, 146, 170
Scottish Rite of Freemasonry, South Jurisdiction, 111, 180
Screwmen's Benevolent Association, 7
Second District Negro School, 64
segregated schools, 3, 8, 79, 87, 90, 93, 96, 105, 119, 126
segregation, 10, 54, 55, 58, 90, 93, 120, 126, 158
Seguin, Texas, 10
Separate Coach Law, 10
September 11 tragedy, 204
Shack, Arthur T., 135
Shamblin, J. M., 8
Sherman, John, 8

Sherman, Texas, xiii, 44, 48, 50
Shields, G. B., 8
Shivers, D. A., 27
shock probation, 153
Shreveport, Louisiana, 136
Shriners, 55, 105, 188
Sigma Pi Phi, 162
Silsbee, Texas, 116, 118
Silver Circle Chapter No. 101, 136
Silver Trowell Lodge No. 47, 13
Simmons, Roscoe Conkling, 77
Singleton, George A., 94
Slaughter, Ralph, 190, 196
slavery, 213-215
Sloan, R., 53
Smalls, Benjamin, 114
Smead, S. P. 104
Smith Chapel AME Church, 114
Smith, DeShong, 82
Smith, Evelyn, 206
Smith, G. D., 62
Smith, Harry E., 129
Smith, Jeremiah, 206
Smith, Kevin, 211
Smith, Lonnie, 104
Smith, W. S., 62
Smith, Wendell, 200
Smith, Wilford H., 13
Smotherson, Melvin, 131
South Africa, 124, 168
South Gate Lodge No. 32, 13
Southern Baptist Convention, 146
Southern Methodist University, 149, 165
Southern Pacific railway, 15
Southwestern Trail Riders Association, 180, 206
Stall, David, 206
Star East Lodge No. 276, 106
Sterns, Governor, 21
Stewart, G. W., 48-49
Stewart, T. McCants, 24
Stokes, Carl, 169
Stokes, D. R., 39
Stonum, Tonia, 208
Stonum, Traci, 208
Stout, R. S., 49
Stovall, R. M., 119, 122
Stringer Grand Lodge, 113
Stuart, Adeline, 2-3
Stuart, Hester Neale, 2-3
Sullivan, Leon, 120
Summer Youth Camp, 201, 204, 206, 209
Summit of Prince Hall Grand Masters, 190

Sumon, Korea, 184
"Sunnyside," 2, 3, 14
Sunrise Chapter No. 7, Holy Royal Arch Masons, 180
Sunrise Chapter No. 77, 154
Sunset Lodge No. 76, 74
Supreme Camp of the American Woodmen, 44
Supreme Council of Germany, 134
Supreme Council of Italy, 134
Supreme Council of the Scottish Rite, 90, 112, 113, 115, 116, 117, 119, 120, 123, 125, 126, 127, 128, 129, 130, 131, 132, 133, 135, 137, 141, 154, 160, 163, 166, 180, 191
Sutton, S. J., 38
Swaggart, Jimmy, 159
Sweatt, Herman, 87, 104

Tabernacle Lodge No. 1195, 107
Talton, Mrs. P. A., 64
Tarrant County, Texas, 198
Taylor, J. R., xii
Taylor, Roswell A., 130
Teague, Texas, 119, 139
Telfair, J. W., 23
Telfair, Joseph, 134, 172, 174, 176
Temple High School, 207
Temple, Texas, 151, 207, 208, 209
Tenaha, Texas, 75
Tennessee, Roosevelt, 172, 178, 182, 185, 198, 204
Terrell, Texas, 77
Teulon, George K., 213
Texas A&M University, 4, 179
Texas Alcoholic Beverage Commission, 179
Texas City, Texas, 136, 137
Texas College, 50, 68
Texas Farm Bureau Federal Credit Union, 208
Texas Farm Bureau Insurance Companies, 208
Texas Grand Lodge, 199
Texas Grand Theatre, 72
Texas Legislature, 9
Texas Militia, 17
Texas Prince Hall Lodge of Research, 211
Texas Prince Hall Masonic Quarterly, 192
Texas Rangers, 96, 180
Texas Revolution, 16
Texas Southern University, 152

Texas Union League, 7
38th Regiment of Foot, British Army, xi
Thomas, Clarence, 132, 205
Thomas H. Routt Grand Council, 164
Thomas H. Routt Lodge No. 639, 164, 198
Thomas, Mrs. A. B., 64
Thomas, Willie, 206
Thompson, H. M., 123, 125, 127, 144
Thurgood Marshall Award, 97
Thurmond, Strom, 205
Tichenor, George, 9
Tillotson College, 4
Toland, Clyde, 180
Tolbert, William R., 120, 128
Toliver Chapel Missionary Baptist Church, 208
Trade Assembly, 7
Trial Commission, 150
Trinidad, West Indies, 50
Trinity CME Church, 48
Trinity, Texas, 96
Trinity United Methodist Church, 153, 162, 170, 181
True Service Lodge No. 399, 195
Truman, Harry S., 84, 87, 88, 148
Tubman, William V. S., 119
Turf Exchange and Pool Room, 40
Turner, H. M., 23
Turner, Nat, 214
Turner, O.W.L., 102, 107, 120, 141, 146, 166
208th District Court of Texas, 153
Tyler, Texas, 50

Uijonibu, Korea, 193
Unford, Africa, 56
Union League, 6-7, 17
United Brothers Lodge No. 298, 174
United Grand Lodge of England, 113
United Nations, 84, 86, 125
United Supreme Council, Ancient and Accepted Scottish Rite, Southern Jurisdiction, *see* Supreme Council
United Way, 65, 111
Unity Bank, 188
University for Negroes in Texas, 87

University of Houston, 111
University of Oklahoma, 90
University of Texas, 90, 104
Uzzel, Robert, 211, 220

Van Alstyne, Texas, 44
Van Cott, Charles, 104
Van Slyke, Albert, 198
Vashon, George B., 3
Vaughn, Deary, 162, 173, 184, 190, 193, 196, 197, 206
Victoria, Texas, xii, xiii, 187
Vietnam War, 114, 115, 118, 119, 124, 137, 138
Virgin Islands, 87
voter education, 205
voter registration, 61, 113, 133, 185, 191
Voting Rights Act, 130

Waco, Texas, xii, xiii, 6, 20, 31, 37, 45, 56, 64, 68, 70, 82, 86
Waco Shrine Temple, 88
Waco's Interracial Commission, 70
Wadley, Charles, 82, 201, 205
Walker, A. W., 27
Walker, Alice, 167
Walker, Carl, Jr., 153
Walkes, Joseph A., Jr., 126, 131, 144, 145, 163, 214
Wallace, W. M., 27
Waller County, Texas, 2, 200
"War Clause," 115
Warning, Robert, 124
Warren, Earl, 96
Washington, B. T., 201
Washington, Booker T., 87, 145
Washington County, Texas, 85
Washington, George, 45, 132, 134
Washington, Harold, 143, 167
Washington, Howard, 183, 198
Washington, J. H., 8
Washington Lodge No. 22, 87
Washington, Shaft L., 195
Wasson, James L., 140
Watergate, 121, 138
Waters, Muddy, 167
Watkins, Ulysses W., Jr., 133
Watson, B. F., 32
Watson, Tommy, 192
Weathersby, A. K., 38, 41
Webber, Bobby G., 109, 114, 117, 120

Weimar, Texas, 179
Wesley Chapel AME Church, 37, 85, 94
Wesley, Charles H., 126
West Hill Cemetery, 50
West Palm Beach, Florida, 30
West, Royce, 134
West Temple Lodge No. 425, 184
Western Star Lodge No. 11, xii
White, Ometa, 64-65
White, Reuben G., xiv, 103, 107, 109, 114, 117, 120, 125, 128, 129, 130, 131, 136-151, 155, 162, 166, 167, 168, 171, 174, 178, 195, 205, 215, 219, 220
White Rose Court No. 33, 70
White, Walter, 145
Whitehead, Clinton, 103
Wichita Falls, Texas, 113
Widow Son Lodge No. 5, xii
widows and orphans, 82, 172, 185, 203, 205
Wilberforce University, 64
Wiley College, 87
Wiley, G. L., 64
Wiley L. Kimbrough Lodge No. 91, 43
Wilhite, O. E., 65, 82, 83, 129, 174
Wilkins, Roy, 145
Wilkinson, Edward, xii
Williams, Charles, 126, 168
Williams, David A., 134
Williams, Mrs. David A., 134
Williams, Ernie, 198, 204
Williams, F. B., 27
Williams, Frank, 204
Williams, J. C., 174, 201
Williams, J. K., 37
Williams, Lester, 195
Williams, Martin, 180, 206
Williams, R. L., 53
Williams, R. S., 48
Williams, Vanessa, 167
Williams, W. D., 94
Williams, Willie Mae, 206
Willing Workers Cemetery, 206
Willis, W. S., 64, 65
Wilmington, North Carolina, 36
Wilson, Carl, 131
Wilson, Sherman, 146, 163, 180
Wilson, Woodrow, 55, 79, 97
Winfrey, Oprah, 169
Winn Consistory No. 243, 136, 150
Winn, Henderson D., xiii, 48, 49, 52-63, 65, 214, 215
Winn, Roberta Hall, 52
Wisby, Ernest, 107, 137
Womack, P. E., 90
Woodland Cemetery, 63
Woodlawn School, 73
"Woodpeckers," 8-9
Woods, Howard L., 132, 160, 162, 176, 178, 183, 190, 196, 197
Woods, William E., 178, 183, 185, 193, 195, 196, 198, 199-200, 201, 204
Woodson, Carter G., 12
Woodville, Mississippi, 4
World War I, 53, 54, 55, 56, 57
World War II, 79, 80-81, 84, 85
World's Columbian Exposition, 38
World's Fair, 10
Worley, Willie, 134, 158
Wyle Street School, 3

Xenia, Ohio, 64

Yancy, J. W., II, 86, 87, 90, 102, 108, 114
York Rite Masonry, 67
Young, Andrew, 125
Young, Buddy, 167
Young, Coleman, 169
Young, G. B., 70
Young, Joseph D., 140
Young Men's Democratic Club, 8
Young Women's Christian Association, 70
Youth Camp, 201, 204, 206, 209
Youth Day, 194, 196

Zakat Temple No. 164, 112, 134, 165, 166

About the Author

Dr. Robert L. Uzzel was born on May 22, 1951, in Waco, Texas. He graduated from Waco High School in 1969. He received an Associate in Arts degree from McLennan Community College in 1971, a Bachelor of Arts degree from Baylor University in 1973, a Master of Arts degree from Baylor in 1976, and a Doctor of Philosophy degree from Baylor in 1995.

Uzzel has been a minister in the African Methodist Episcopal Church since 1975. He served as pastor of Emmanuel AME Church in Dallas from 1976 to 1979, of Macedonia AME Church in Kaufman from 1979 to 1987, of the Blooming Grove-Maypearl Circuit from 1996 to 1999, and of Forest Hill AME Church in Fort Worth from 1999 to 2002. He currently serves as pastor of Wayman Chapel AME Church in Ennis, Texas.

Uzzel worked as a social worker for the State of Texas from 1974 to 1986. He served as chairman of the Religion Department at Paul Quinn College from 1987 to 1997 and as associate director of Adult and Continuing Education at the same institution since 2002. He also has served as an adjunct instructor in Religion and History at Mountain View College, Cedar Valley College, Temple College, Navarro College, and Tarrant County College.

Uzzel served as Master Councilor of Waco Chapter, Order of DeMolay, in 1970. He became a Freemason in 1972. Currently, he is a member of Goodwill Lodge No. 313, Free and Accepted Masons in Ferris, Texas; Dale Consistory No. 31, Ancient and Accepted Scottish Rite in Dallas, Texas; and Zakat Temple No. 164, Ancient Egyptian

Arabic Order of Nobles of the Mystic Shrine in Dallas. In 1987 he was appointed as Grand Historian for the Prince Hall Grand Lodge of Texas by Grand Master Thomas H. Routt. He holds the 1985 Certificate of Literature from Phylaxis Society and the 1999 Certificate of Literature from the Philalethes Society. He is a member of the DeMolay Alumni Association, the Scottish Rite Research Society, the Prince Hall Scottish Rite Research Institute, and the Lux e Tenebris Research Chapter. In February 2003, at the Washington Hotel in Washington, D. C., he was inducted into the Society of Blue Friars, an invitation-only organization of Masonic authors and editors. He was designated as Blue Friar No. 92 and delivered the Blue Friars Lecture entitled "Thomas Riley Marshall: Country Lawyer, Hoosier Statesman, and Freemason."

Uzzel's articles on theological, historical, and Masonic subjects have appeared in a number of publications. His biography of a famous blues artist, *Blind Lemon Jefferson: His Life, His Death, and His Legacy*, was published by Eakin Press in 2002.

Uzzel is married to the former Debra Bass, a native of Fairfield, Texas. They have four children and seven grandchildren.

www.ingramcontent.com/pod-product-compliance
Lightning Source LLC
Chambersburg PA
CBHW080911170426
43201CB00017B/2287